KODOCHA
SANA'S STAGE

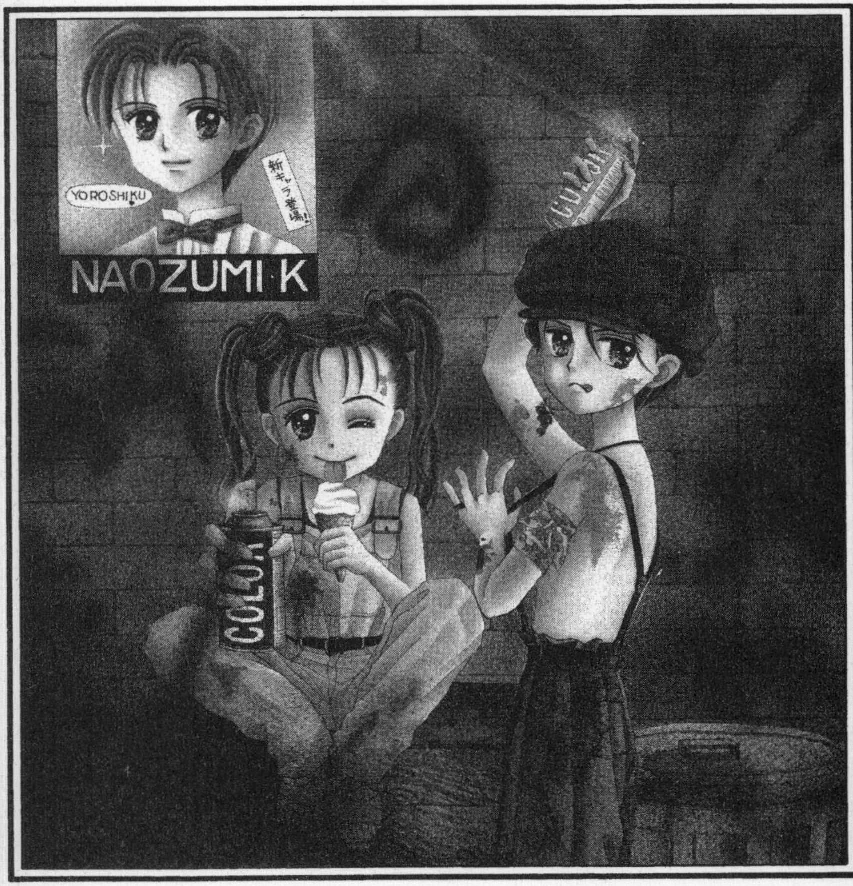
COLOR
新キャラ登場!
YOROSHIKU
NAOZUMI K
COLOR

KODOCHA
SANA'S STAGE

Vol. 3

Written and Illustrated by Miho Obana
English Adaptation by Sarah Dyer

TOKYOPOP®

Los Angeles - Tokyo

Story and Art - Miho Obana
Translator - Yukio Ichimura
Reprint Editor - Mark Paniccia
Retouch and Lettering - Justin Renard
Graphic Designer - Anna Kernbaum
Editorial Consultant - Kelly Soucie

Senior Editor - Julie Taylor
Production Manager - Jennifer Miller
Art Director - Matthew Alford
VP of Production & Manufacturing - Ron Klamert
President & C.O.O. - John Parker
Publisher - Stuart Levy

Email: editor@TOKYOPOP.com
Come visit us online at www.TOKYOPOP.com

A TOKYOPOP® Manga

TOKYOPOP® is an imprint of Mixx Entertainment, Inc.
5900 Wilshire Blvd. Ste 2000, Los Angeles, CA 90036

ISBN: 1-931514-52-6

First TOKYOPOP® printing: September 2002

10 9 8 7 6 5 4 3 2

Printed in Canada

KODOCHA
SANA'S STAGE

Vol. 3

CONTENTS

OUR CHARACTERS

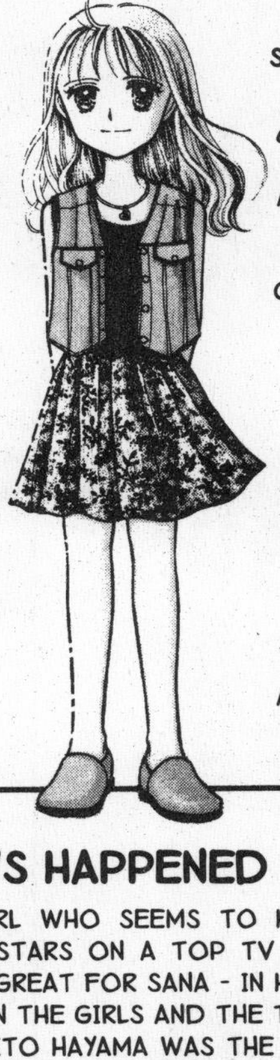

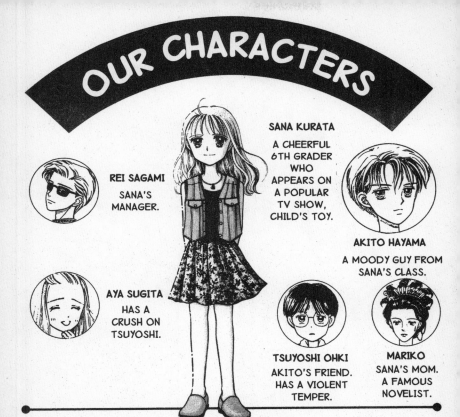

SANA KURATA

A CHEERFUL 6TH GRADER WHO APPEARS ON A POPULAR TV SHOW, CHILD'S TOY.

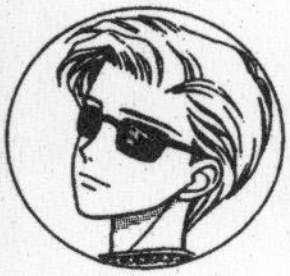

REI SAGAMI

SANA'S MANAGER.

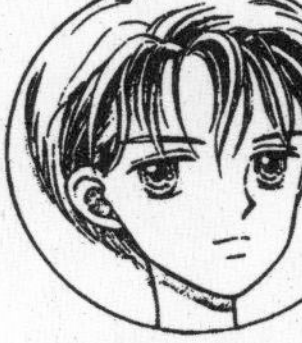

AKITO HAYAMA

A MOODY GUY FROM SANA'S CLASS.

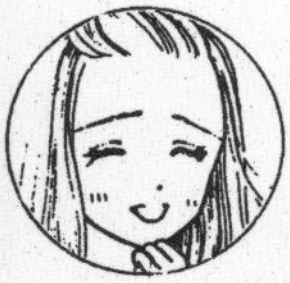

AYA SUGITA

HAS A CRUSH ON TSUYOSHI.

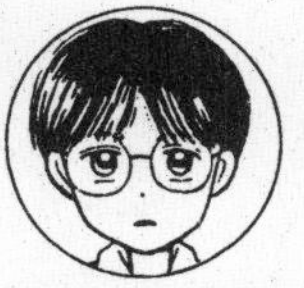

TSUYOSHI OHKI

AKITO'S FRIEND. HAS A VIOLENT TEMPER.

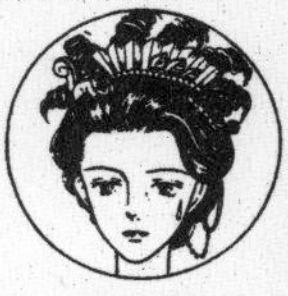

MARIKO

SANA'S MOM. A FAMOUS NOVELIST.

WHAT'S HAPPENED SO FAR:

SANA KURATA IS A GIRL WHO SEEMS TO HAVE EVERYTHING - SHE'S POPULAR, HAPPY, AND STARS ON A TOP TV SHOW, CHILD'S TOY. BUT THINGS AREN'T ALWAYS GREAT FOR SANA - IN HER 6TH GRADE CLASS, THE BOYS DECLARED WAR ON THE GIRLS AND THE TEACHER, AND NO ONE WAS LEARNING ANYTHING! AKITO HAYAMA WAS THE RINGLEADER OF THE GANG OF MONKEYS (AS SANA CALLS THEM), AND WHEN SANA FINALLY CHALLENGED HIM, SHE WAS ABLE TO PUT A STOP TO THE BOYS' BEHAVIOR AND GET THE CLASS SETTLED DOWN. SHE HATED AKITO AT FIRST, BUT WHEN SHE GOT TO KNOW HIM SHE REALIZED HE ONLY ACTED THE WAY HE DID BECAUSE HIS FAMILY MADE HIM FEEL SO AWFUL. SANA DID HER BEST TO MAKE HIS FAMILY REALIZE THAT THE WAY THEY TREATED AKITO WAS WRONG. AS THINGS GOT BETTER FOR HIM AT HOME, HE BEGAN TO OPEN UP TO SANA AND EVEN SURPRISED HER WITH A KISS! SANA AND AKITO BEGAN TO GROW CLOSER, HELPING EACH OTHER THROUGH SOME TOUGH TIMES. EVERYTHING SEEMED TO BE GOING WELL AT LAST...UNTIL SUDDENLY TSUYOSHI DISAPPEARED FROM SCHOOL!

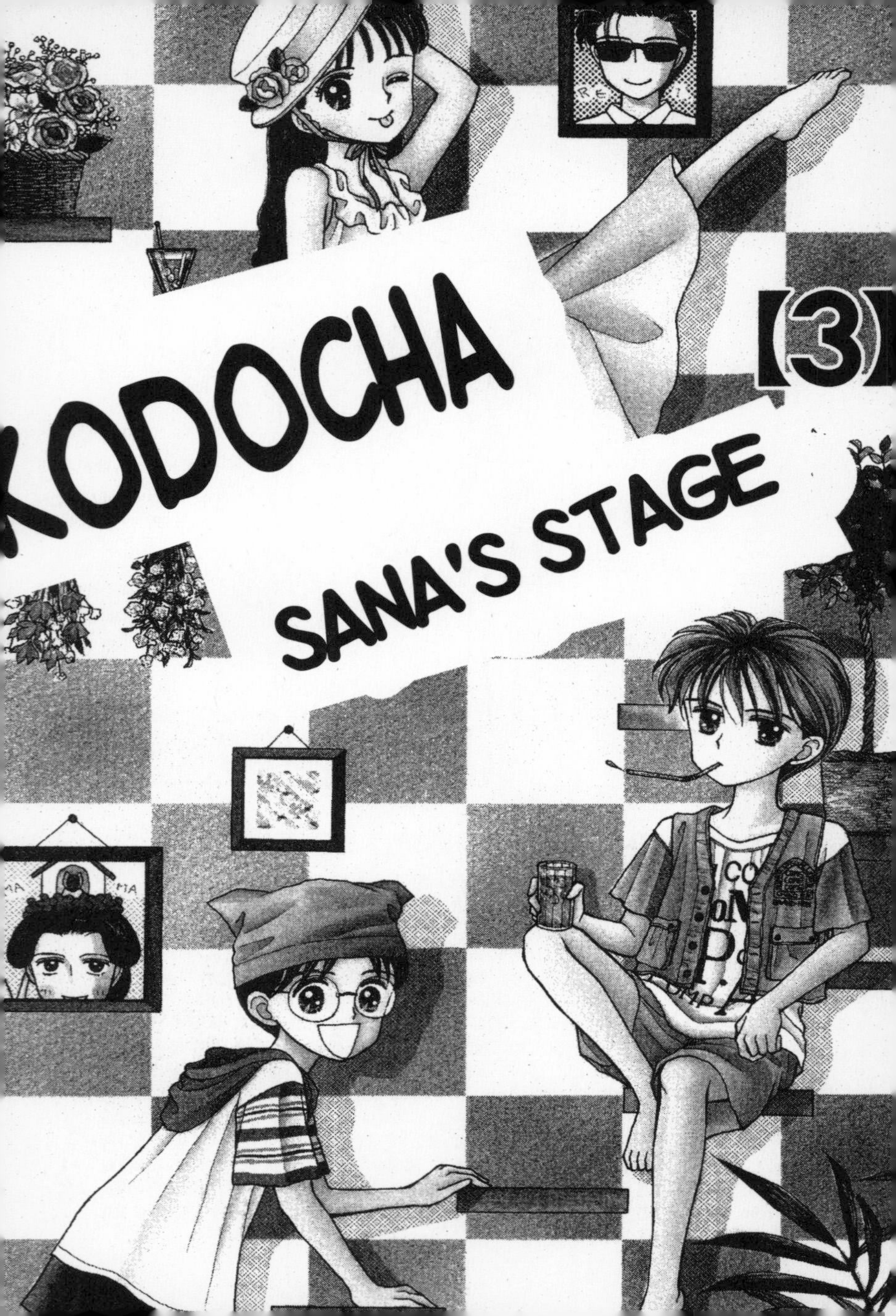
KODOCHA
[3]
SANA'S STAGE

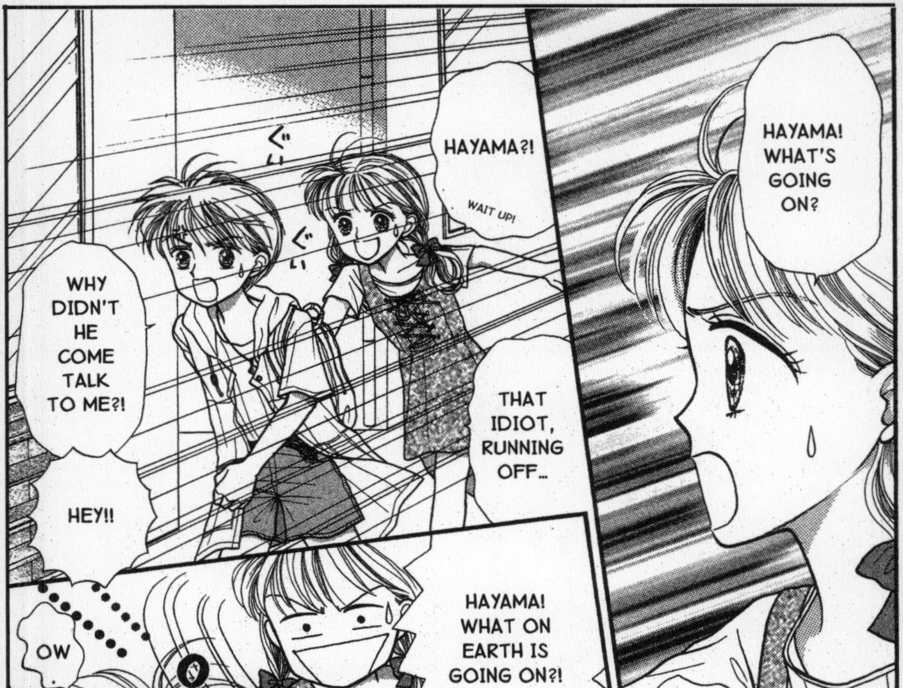
HAYAMA! WHAT'S GOING ON?
WHAT HAPPENED TO TSUYOSHI?!
HAYAMA?!
WAIT UP!
ぐい
ぐい
THAT IDIOT, RUNNING OFF...
WHY DIDN'T HE COME TALK TO ME?!
HEY!!
HAYAMA! WHAT ON EARTH IS GOING ON?!
PONK
OW

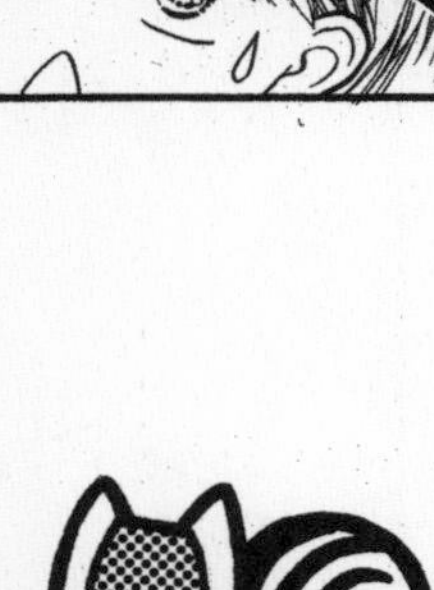

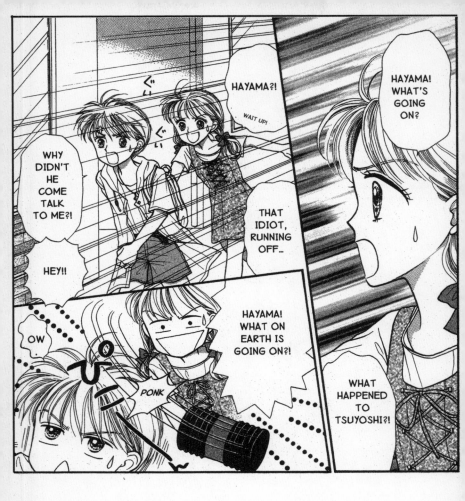

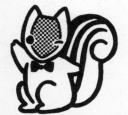

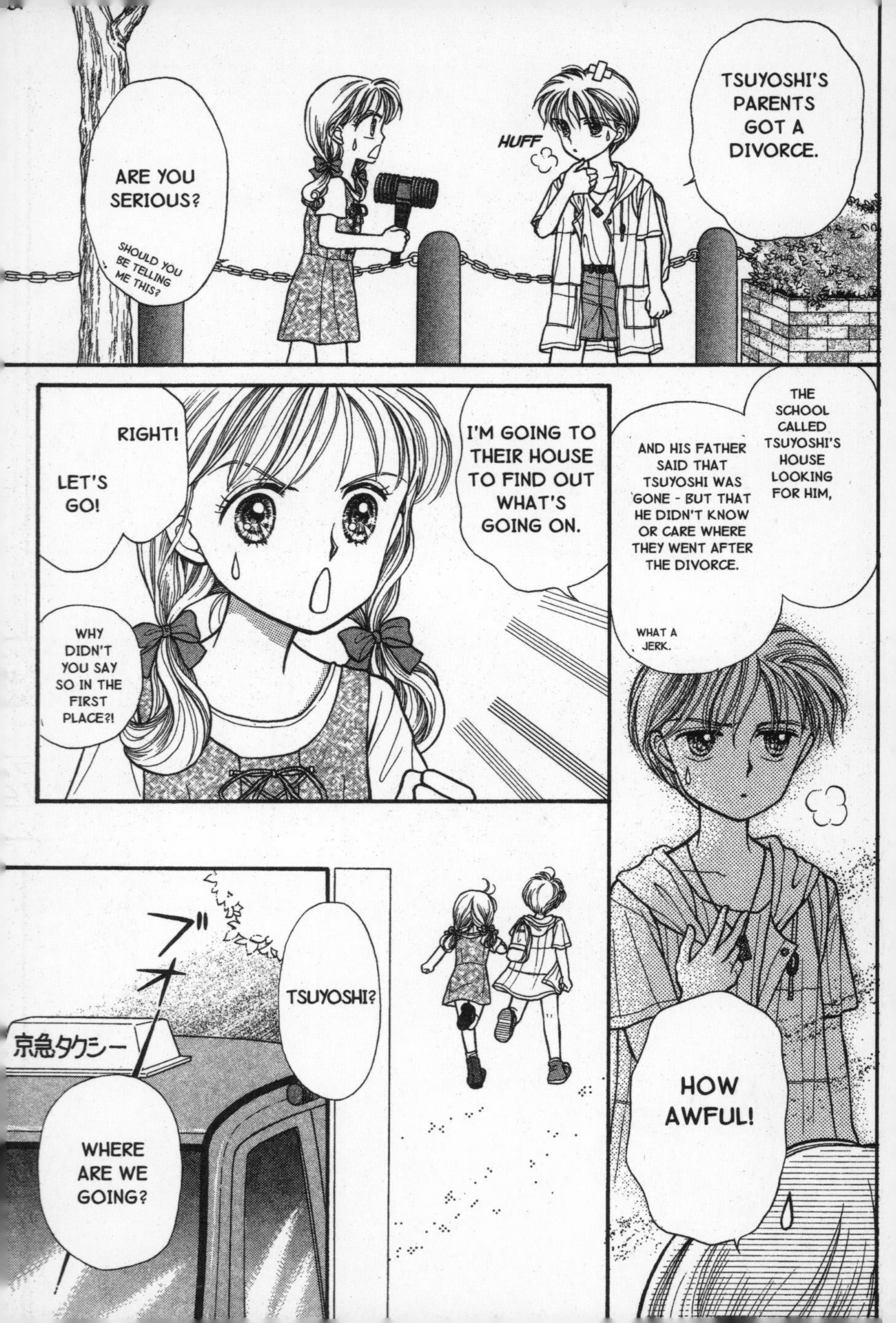
TSUYOSHI'S PARENTS GOT A DIVORCE.
HUFF
ARE YOU SERIOUS?
SHOULD YOU BE TELLING ME THIS?
THE SCHOOL CALLED TSUYOSHI'S HOUSE LOOKING FOR HIM,
AND HIS FATHER SAID THAT TSUYOSHI WAS GONE - BUT THAT HE DIDN'T KNOW OR CARE WHERE THEY WENT AFTER THE DIVORCE.
WHAT A JERK.
HOW AWFUL!
I'M GOING TO THEIR HOUSE TO FIND OUT WHAT'S GOING ON.
RIGHT!
LET'S GO!
WHY DIDN'T YOU SAY SO IN THE FIRST PLACE?!
TSUYOSHI?
京急タクシー
WHERE ARE WE GOING?

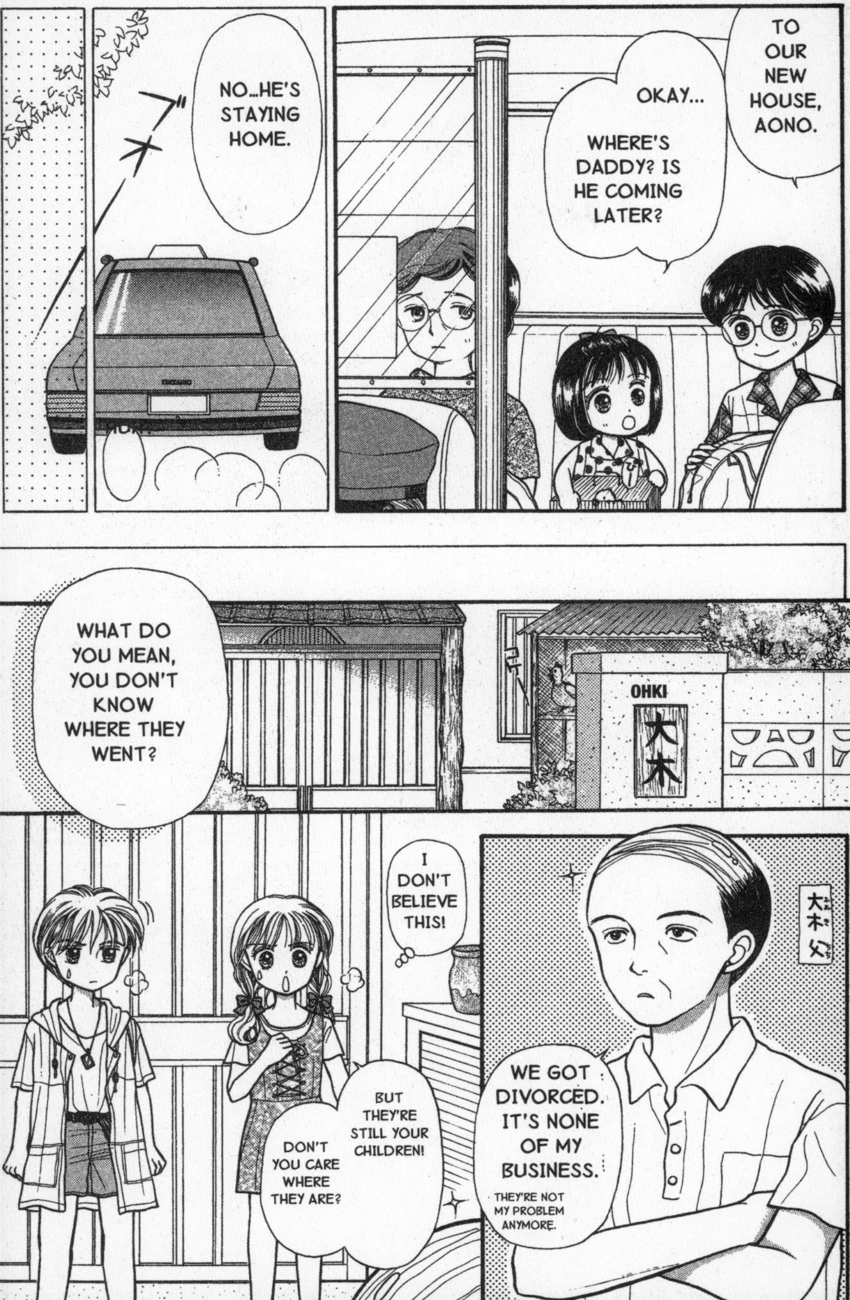
TO OUR NEW HOUSE, AONO.
OKAY...
WHERE'S DADDY? IS HE COMING LATER?
NO...HE'S STAYING HOME.
WHAT DO YOU MEAN, YOU DON'T KNOW WHERE THEY WENT?
OHKI
大木
大木父
WE GOT DIVORCED. IT'S NONE OF MY BUSINESS.
THEY'RE NOT MY PROBLEM ANYMORE.
I DON'T BELIEVE THIS!
BUT THEY'RE STILL YOUR CHILDREN!
DON'T YOU CARE WHERE THEY ARE?

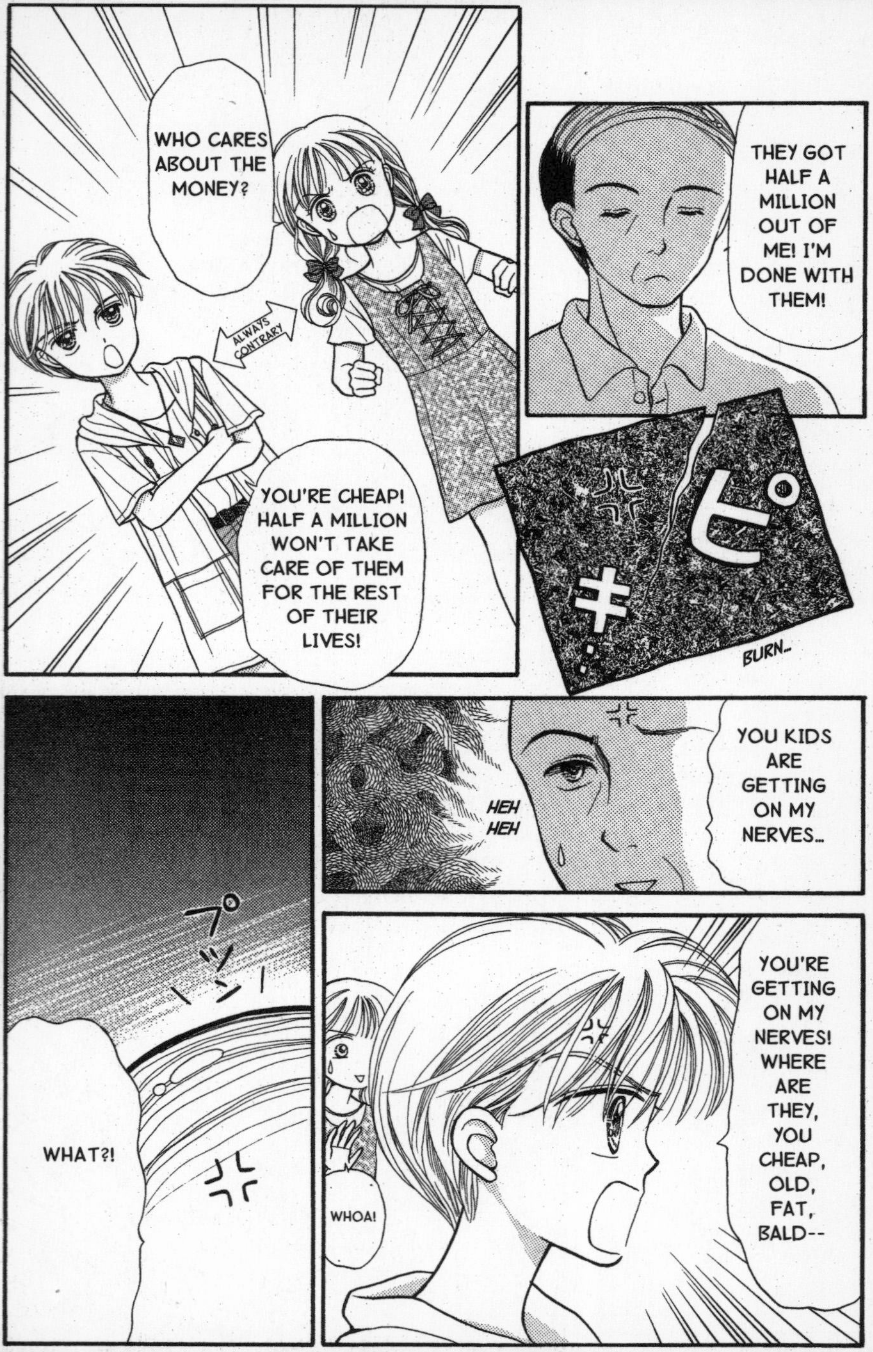
THEY GOT HALF A MILLION OUT OF ME! I'M DONE WITH THEM!
ピキ…
BURN…
WHO CARES ABOUT THE MONEY?
ALWAYS CONTRARY
YOU'RE CHEAP! HALF A MILLION WON'T TAKE CARE OF THEM FOR THE REST OF THEIR LIVES!
YOU KIDS ARE GETTING ON MY NERVES…
HEH HEH
YOU'RE GETTING ON MY NERVES! WHERE ARE THEY, YOU CHEAP, OLD, FAT, BALD--
WHOA!
プツン
WHAT?!

Obana's Incoherent Babbling

Hello! It's me, Obana! How are you doing?

So, I made it to a third book thanks to all your support! I can't believe I've kept the series going for over a year. It isn't easy, but I'm having fun doing it. I can tell from all the great fan mail you send that you all love the series — but I think I love it even more than you! Hee-hee.

When these books are put together from the original comics, I try to fix things.

But I confess, sometimes I just leave them because it's too much work! (Sorry!) So just enjoy them the way they are. Hee-hee.

For example: I drew Mariko's book backwards. Things like that. I check the pages over and over...but still I keep missing things. Man...

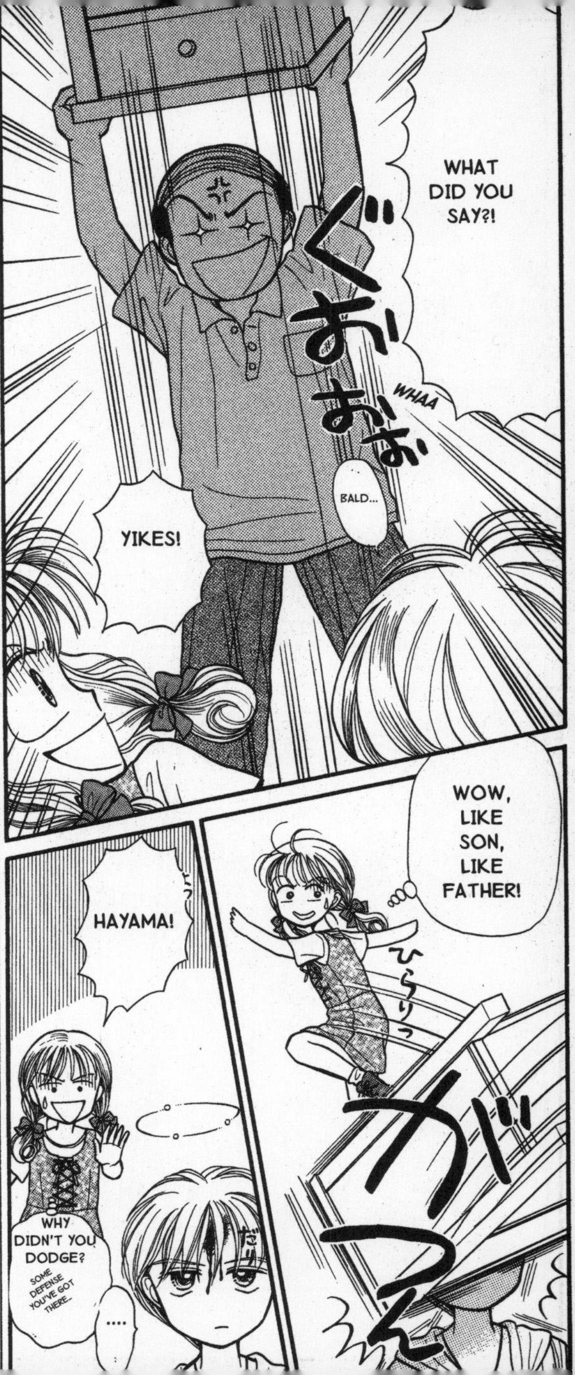
WHAT DID YOU SAY?!
WHAA
BALD...
YIKES!
WOW, LIKE SON, LIKE FATHER!
HAYAMA!
WHY DIDN'T YOU DODGE?
SOME DEFENSE YOU'VE GOT THERE.
....

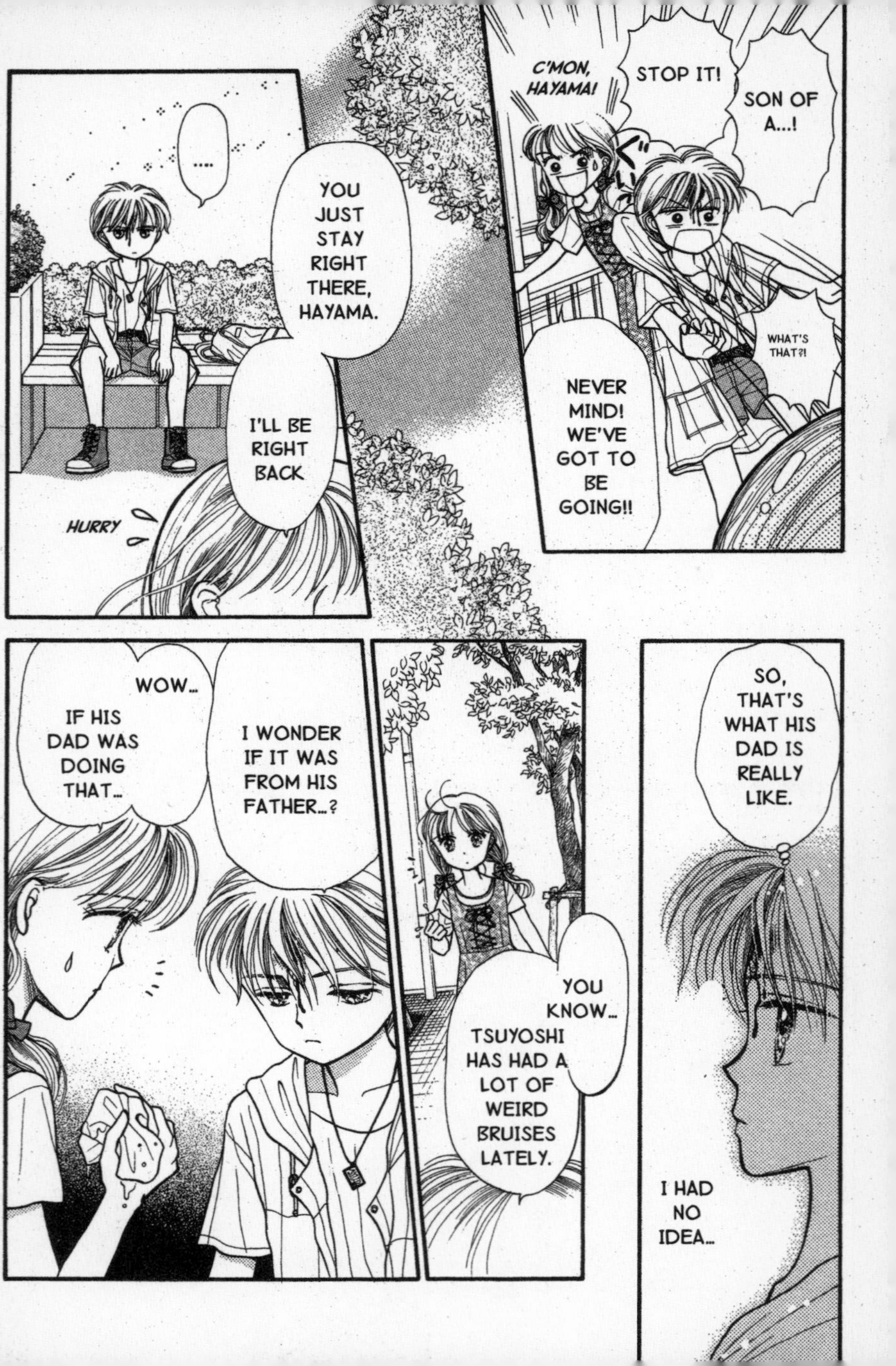
SON OF A...!
STOP IT!
C'MON, HAYAMA!
WHAT'S THAT?!
NEVER MIND! WE'VE GOT TO BE GOING!!
....
YOU JUST STAY RIGHT THERE, HAYAMA.
I'LL BE RIGHT BACK
HURRY
SO, THAT'S WHAT HIS DAD IS REALLY LIKE.
I HAD NO IDEA...
YOU KNOW... TSUYOSHI HAS HAD A LOT OF WEIRD BRUISES LATELY.
I WONDER IF IT WAS FROM HIS FATHER...?
WOW...
IF HIS DAD WAS DOING THAT...

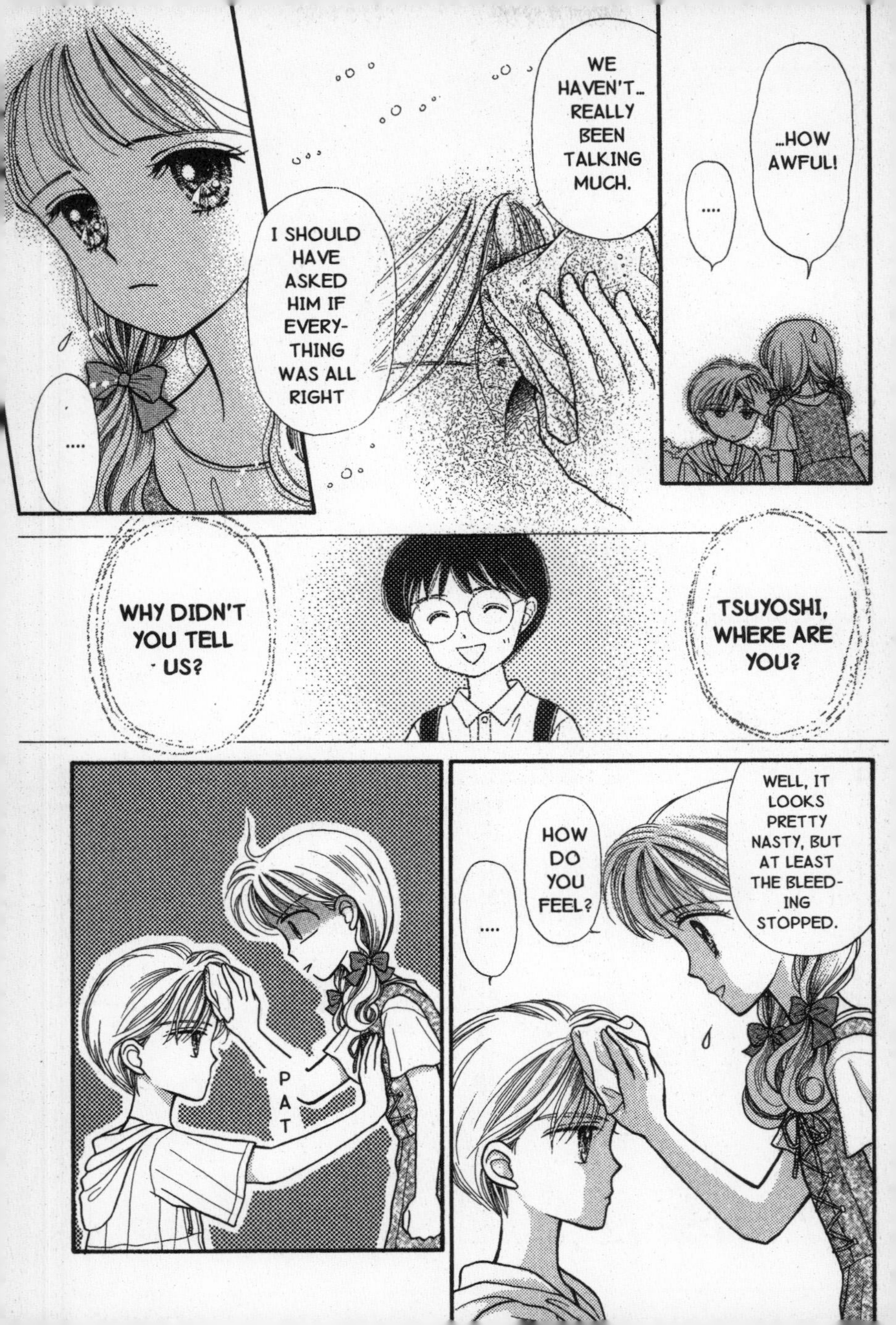
...HOW AWFUL!
....
WE HAVEN'T... REALLY BEEN TALKING MUCH.
I SHOULD HAVE ASKED HIM IF EVERY-THING WAS ALL RIGHT
....
TSUYOSHI, WHERE ARE YOU?
WHY DIDN'T YOU TELL US?
WELL, IT LOOKS PRETTY NASTY, BUT AT LEAST THE BLEED-ING STOPPED.
HOW DO YOU FEEL?
....
PAT

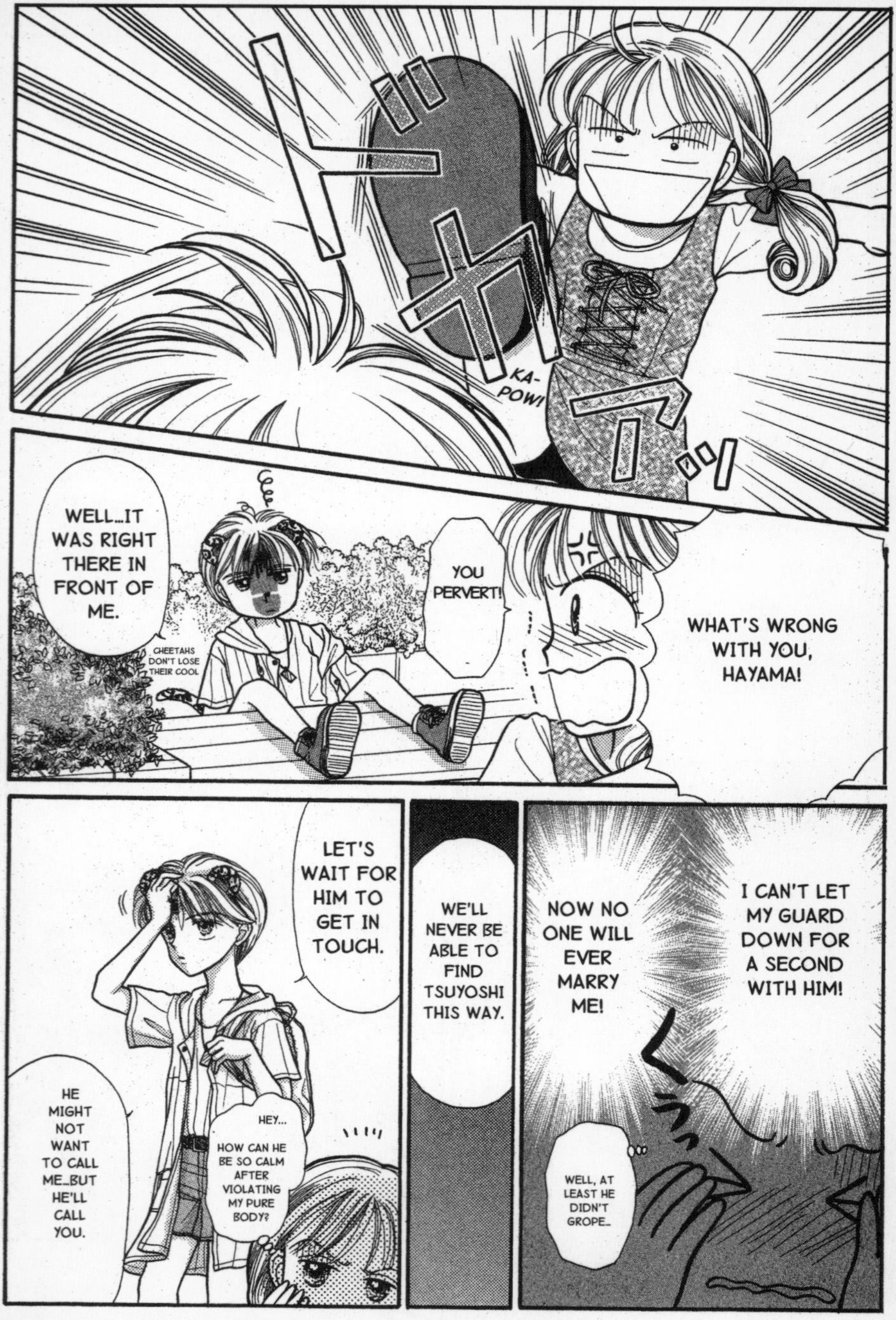
KA-POW!
WHAT'S WRONG WITH YOU, HAYAMA!
YOU PERVERT!
WELL...IT WAS RIGHT THERE IN FRONT OF ME.
CHEETAHS DON'T LOSE THEIR COOL
I CAN'T LET MY GUARD DOWN FOR A SECOND WITH HIM!
NOW NO ONE WILL EVER MARRY ME!
WELL, AT LEAST HE DIDN'T GROPE...
WE'LL NEVER BE ABLE TO FIND TSUYOSHI THIS WAY.
LET'S WAIT FOR HIM TO GET IN TOUCH.
HEY... HOW CAN HE BE SO CALM AFTER VIOLATING MY PURE BODY?
HE MIGHT NOT WANT TO CALL ME...BUT HE'LL CALL YOU.

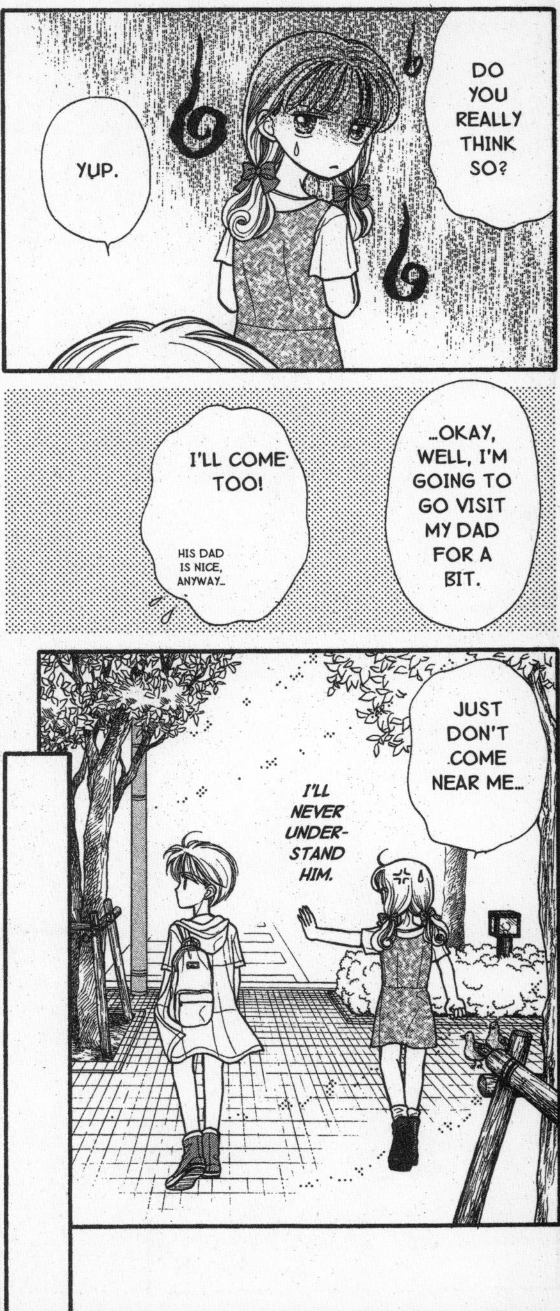
DO YOU REALLY THINK SO?
YUP.
...OKAY, WELL, I'M GOING TO GO VISIT MY DAD FOR A BIT.
I'LL COME TOO!
HIS DAD IS NICE, ANYWAY...
JUST DON'T COME NEAR ME...
I'LL NEVER UNDERSTAND HIM.

What's Up With Me

I've been working so hard lately, I'm constantly spacing out while I draw. I just don't think about anything. It's like I become a drawing robot or something. Am I ok? I don't know if I'm going forward or backward, but I kinda like it. It's a good thing, I think.

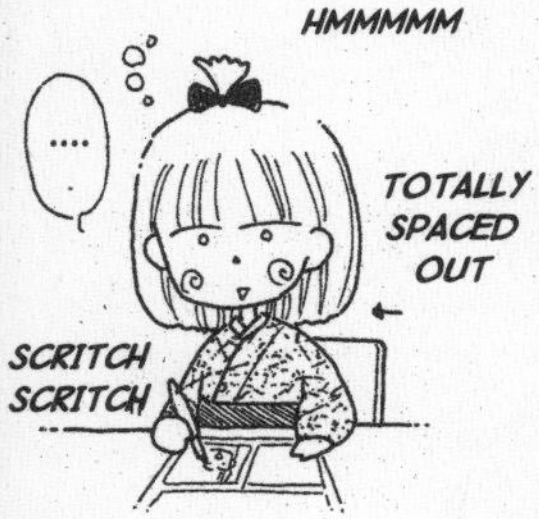
HMMMMM
....
TOTALLY SPACED OUT
SCRITCH SCRITCH

Sometimes, I suddenly snap out of it.

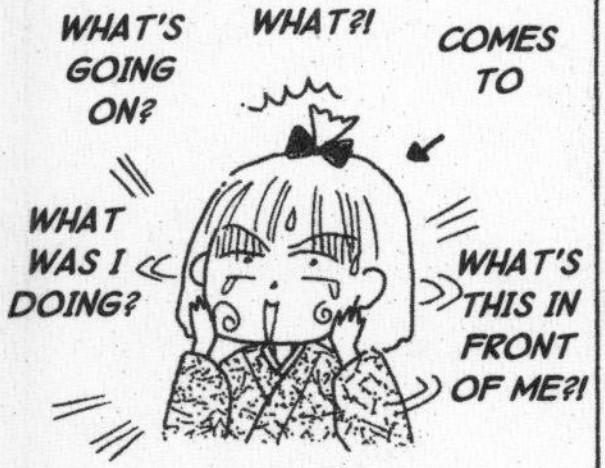
WHAT'S GOING ON?
WHAT?!
COMES TO
WHAT WAS I DOING?
WHAT'S THIS IN FRONT OF ME?!

I guess I'm only human. When I have nothing on my mind, it's hard for me to come up with things to say in these extra spaces. I have to try and write things down when I'm focused!

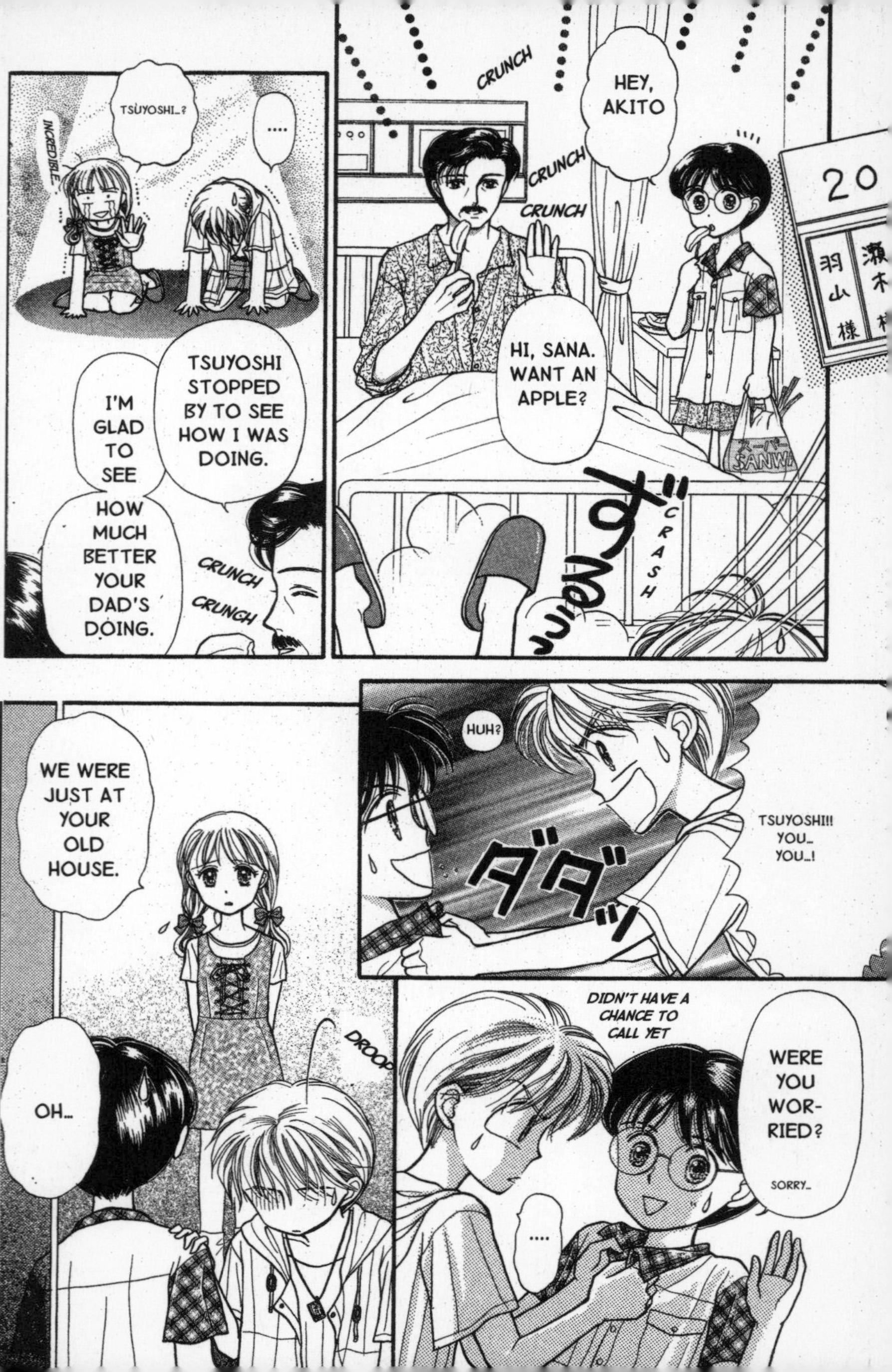
HEY, AKITO
CRUNCH
CRUNCH
CRUNCH
20
瀬木様
羽山様
HI, SANA. WANT AN APPLE?
スーパー SANWA
CRASH
TSUYOSHI...?
INCREDIBLE
....
TSUYOSHI STOPPED BY TO SEE HOW I WAS DOING.
I'M GLAD TO SEE HOW MUCH BETTER YOUR DAD'S DOING.
CRUNCH
CRUNCH
HUH?
ダダッ
TSUYOSHI!!! YOU... YOU...!
DIDN'T HAVE A CHANCE TO CALL YET
WERE YOU WOR-RIED?
SORRY...
....
WE WERE JUST AT YOUR OLD HOUSE.
DROOP
OH...

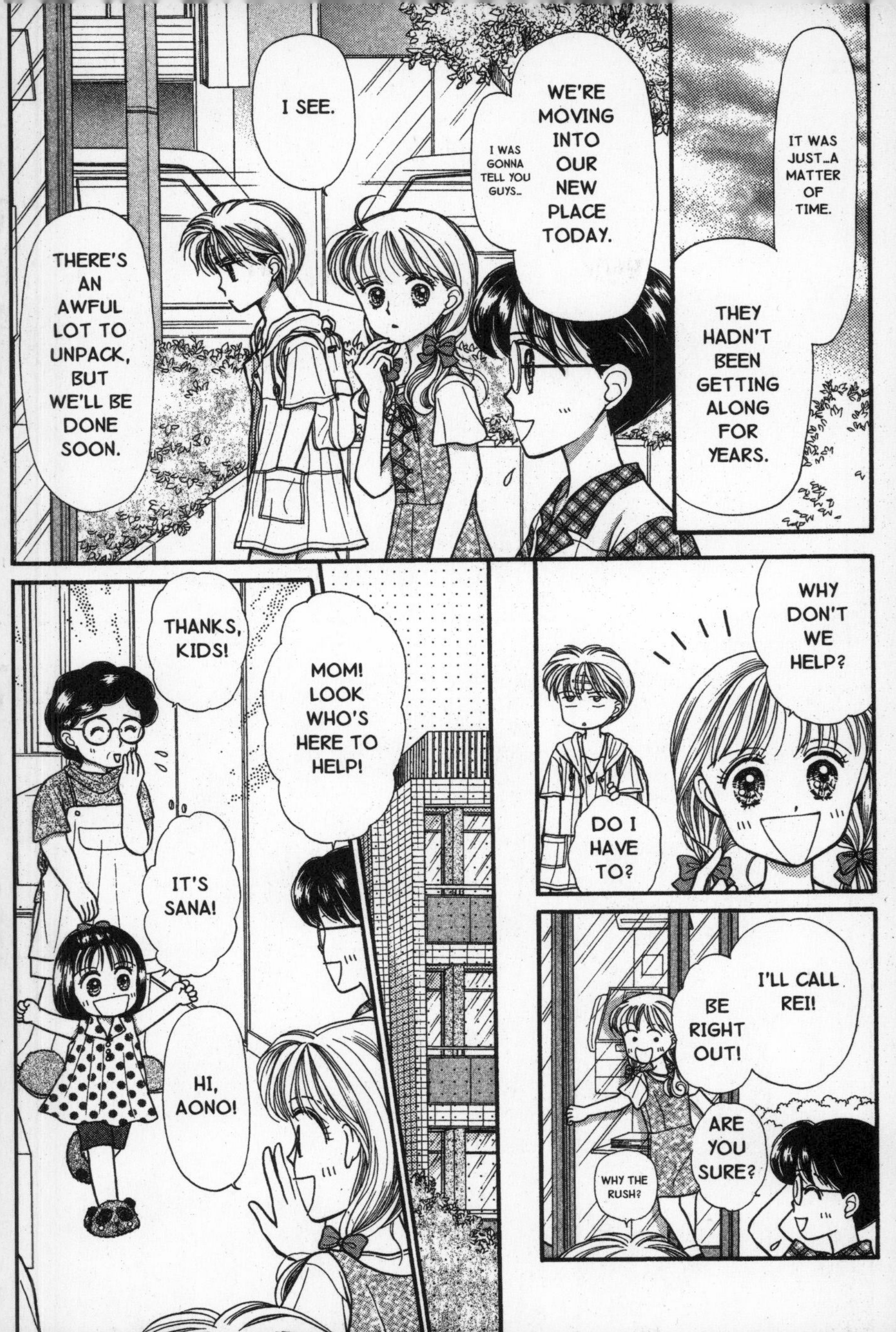
IT WAS JUST...A MATTER OF TIME.
THEY HADN'T BEEN GETTING ALONG FOR YEARS.
WE'RE MOVING INTO OUR NEW PLACE TODAY.
I WAS GONNA TELL YOU GUYS...
I SEE.
THERE'S AN AWFUL LOT TO UNPACK, BUT WE'LL BE DONE SOON.
WHY DON'T WE HELP?
DO I HAVE TO?
I'LL CALL REI!
BE RIGHT OUT!
ARE YOU SURE?
WHY THE RUSH?
MOM! LOOK WHO'S HERE TO HELP!
THANKS, KIDS!
IT'S SANA!
HI, AONO!

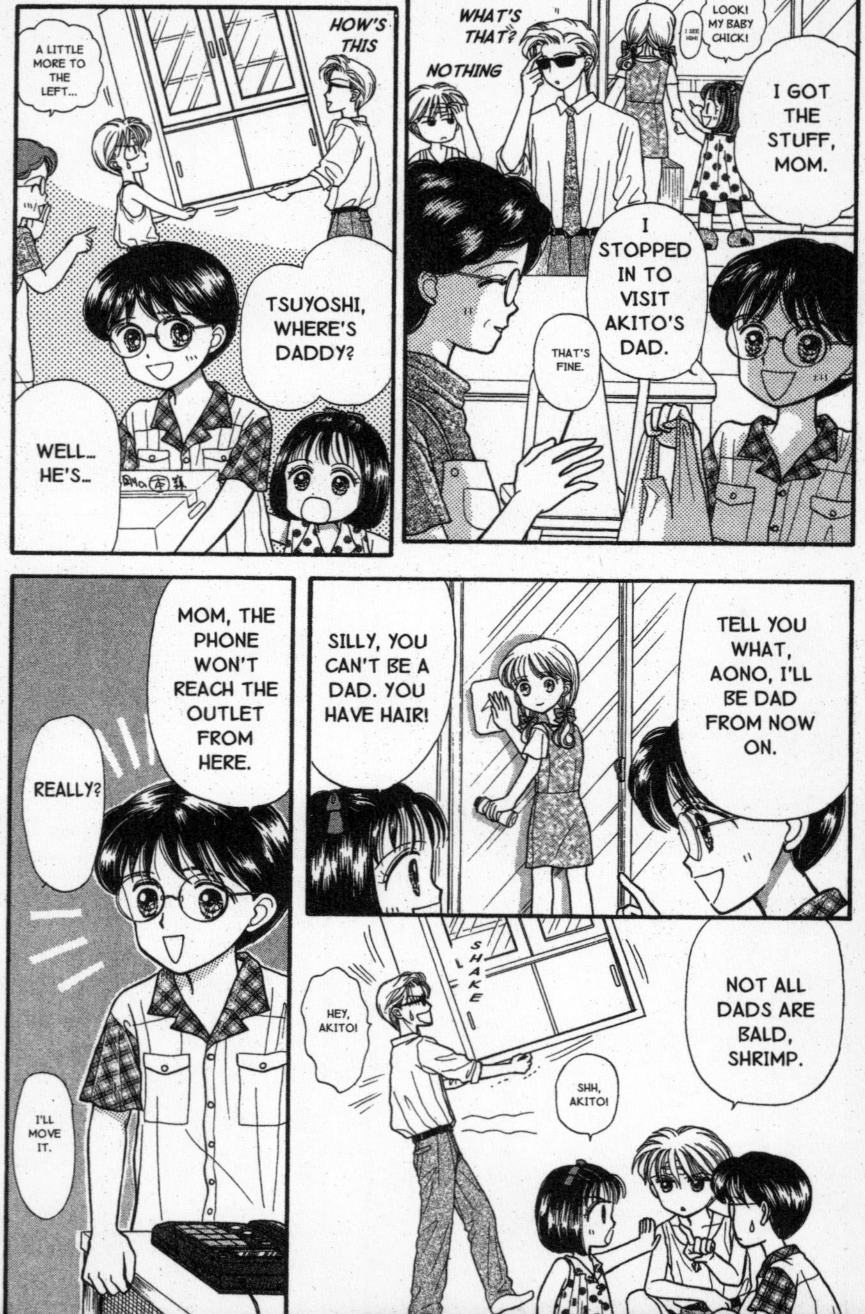
LOOK! MY BABY CHICK!
I SEE HIM!
WHAT'S THAT?
NOTHING
I GOT THE STUFF, MOM.
I STOPPED IN TO VISIT AKITO'S DAD.
THAT'S FINE.
HOW'S THIS
A LITTLE MORE TO THE LEFT...
TSUYOSHI, WHERE'S DADDY?
WELL... HE'S...
TELL YOU WHAT, AONO, I'LL BE DAD FROM NOW ON.
SILLY, YOU CAN'T BE A DAD. YOU HAVE HAIR!
NOT ALL DADS ARE BALD, SHRIMP.
SHAKE
HEY, AKITO!
SHH, AKITO!
MOM, THE PHONE WON'T REACH THE OUTLET FROM HERE.
REALLY?
I'LL MOVE IT.

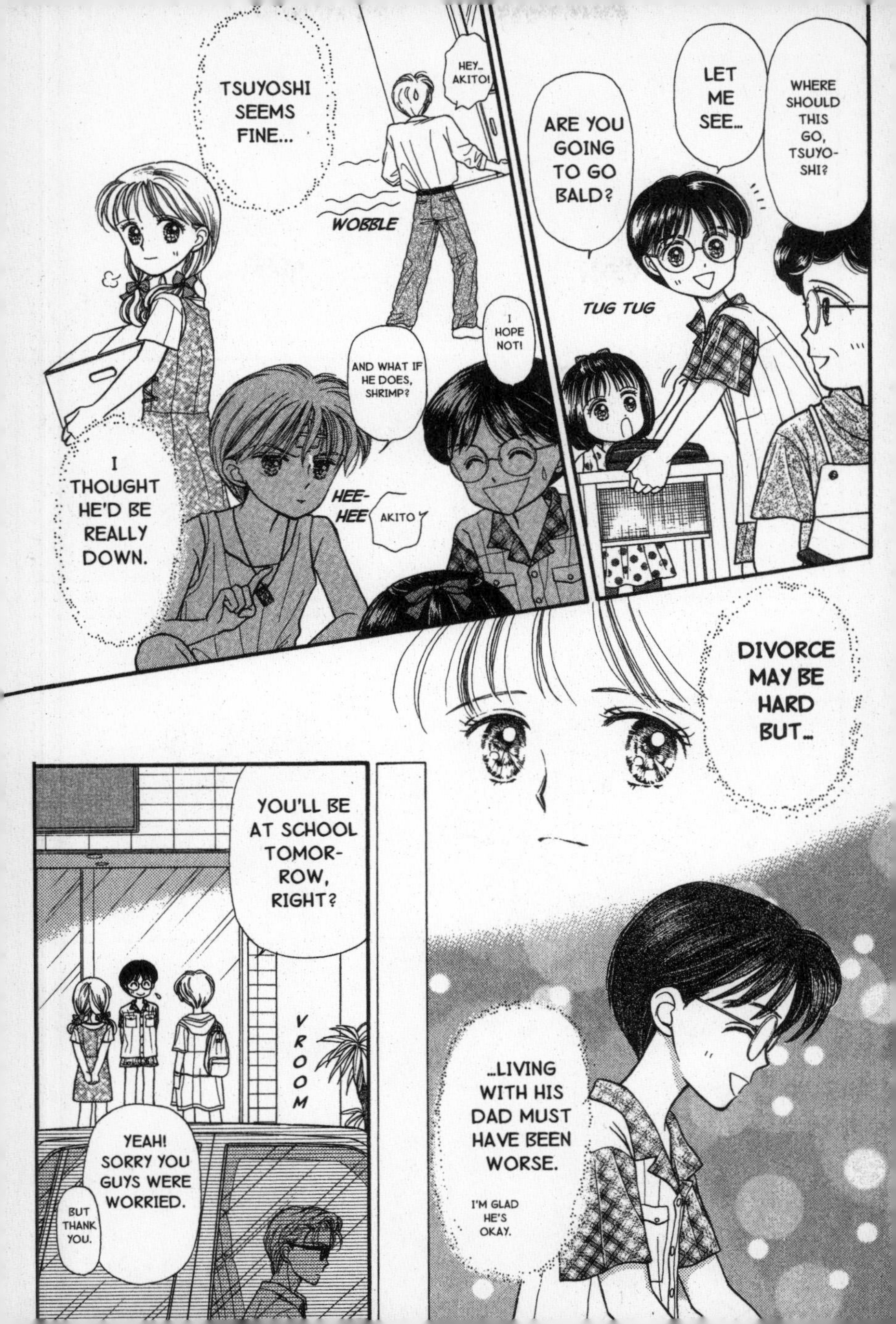
WHERE SHOULD THIS GO, TSUYOSHI?
LET ME SEE...
ARE YOU GOING TO GO BALD?
TUG TUG
HEY... AKITO!
TSUYOSHI SEEMS FINE...
WOBBLE
I HOPE NOT!
AND WHAT IF HE DOES, SHRIMP?
HEE-HEE
AKITO
I THOUGHT HE'D BE REALLY DOWN.
DIVORCE MAY BE HARD BUT...
...LIVING WITH HIS DAD MUST HAVE BEEN WORSE.
I'M GLAD HE'S OKAY.
YOU'LL BE AT SCHOOL TOMORROW, RIGHT?
VROOM
YEAH! SORRY YOU GUYS WERE WORRIED.
BUT THANK YOU.

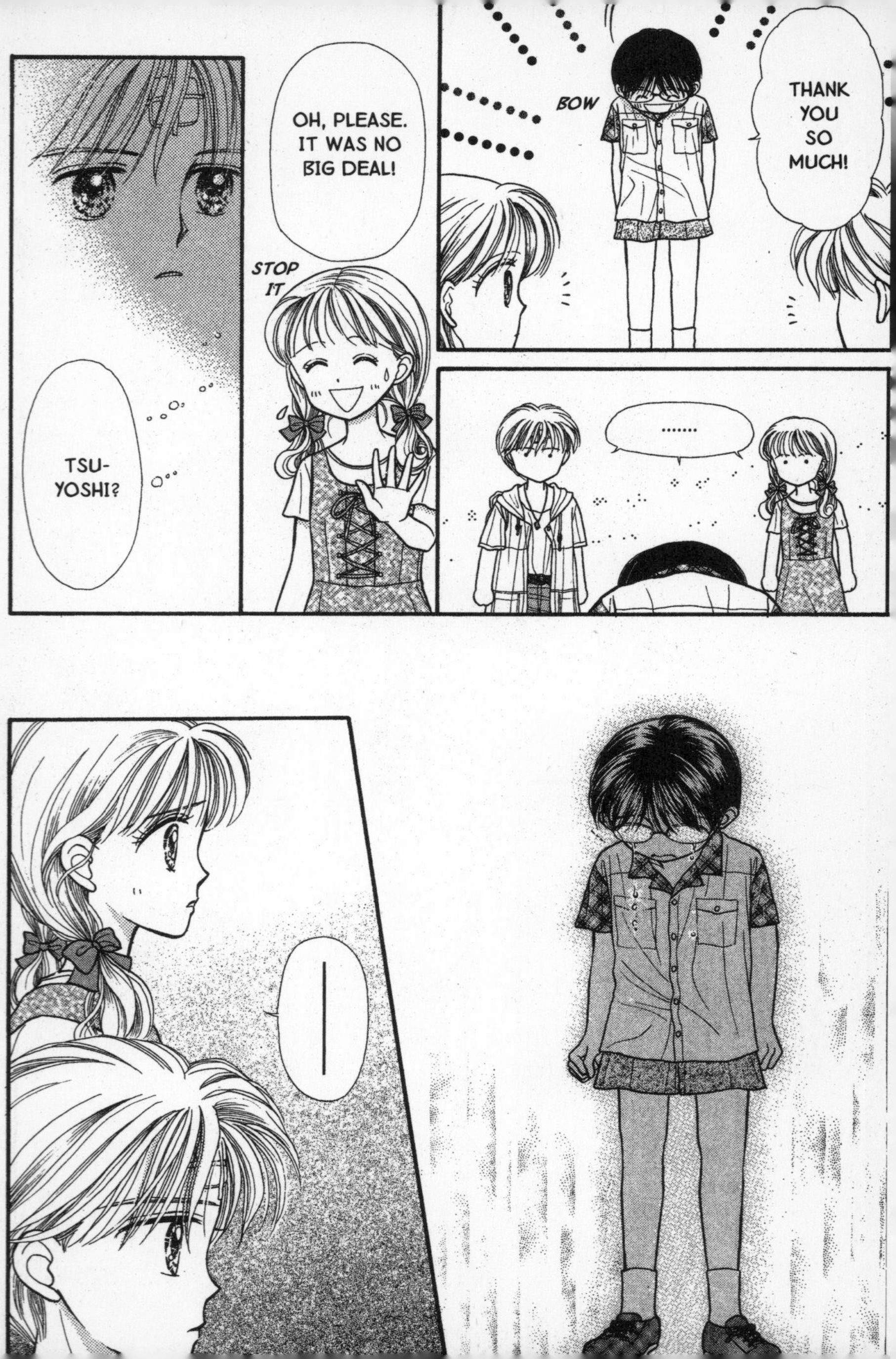
THANK YOU SO MUCH!
BOW
......
OH, PLEASE. IT WAS NO BIG DEAL!
STOP IT
TSU-YOSHI?
—

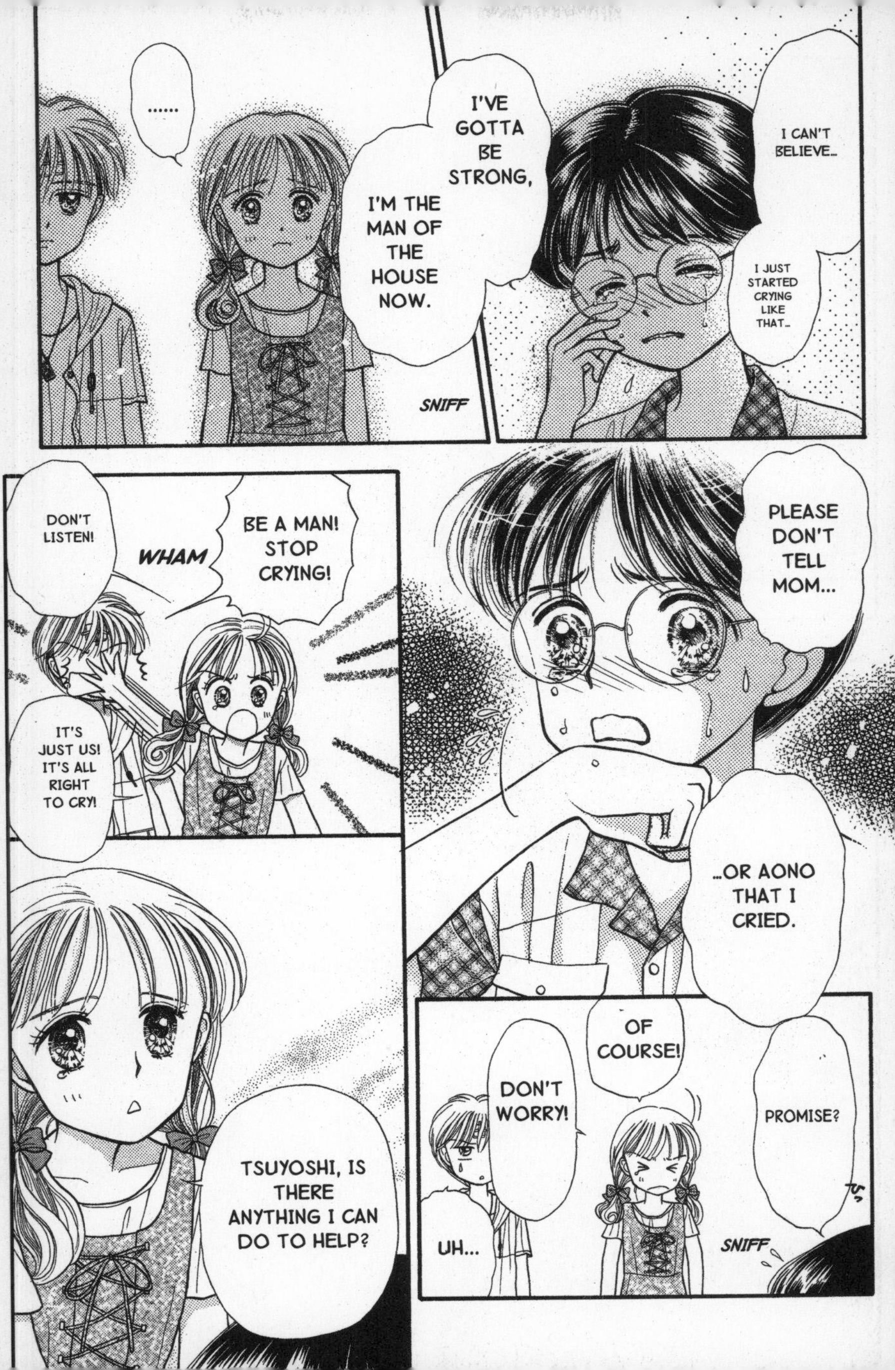

I CAN'T BELIEVE...
I JUST STARTED CRYING LIKE THAT...
I'VE GOTTA BE STRONG,
I'M THE MAN OF THE HOUSE NOW.
SNIFF
......
PLEASE DON'T TELL MOM...
...OR AONO THAT I CRIED.
PROMISE?
SNIFF
OF COURSE!
DON'T WORRY!
UH...
BE A MAN! STOP CRYING!
WHAM
DON'T LISTEN!
IT'S JUST US! IT'S ALL RIGHT TO CRY!
TSUYOSHI, IS THERE ANYTHING I CAN DO TO HELP?

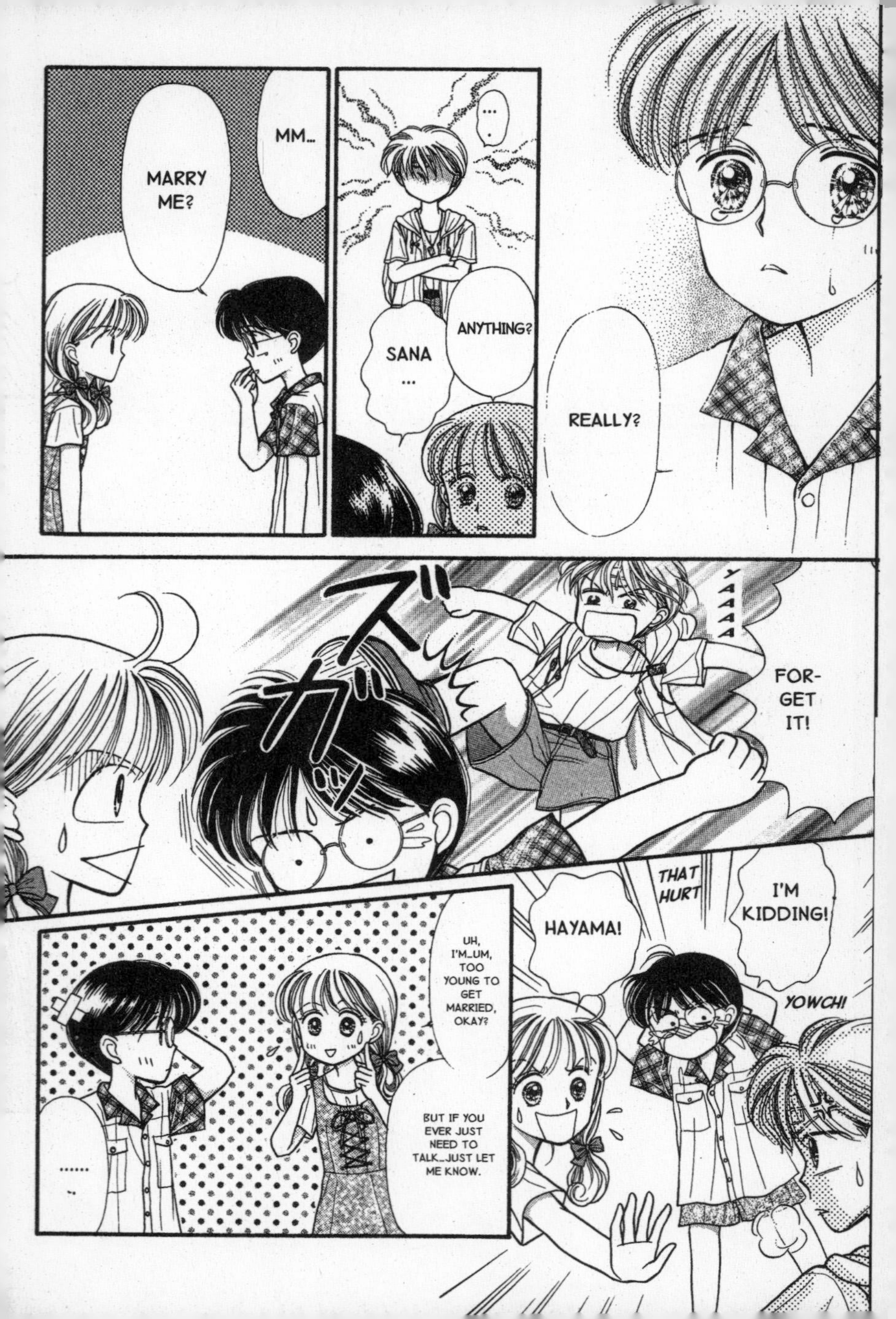
REALLY?
....
ANYTHING?
SANA ...
MM...
MARRY ME?
YAAAA
FOR-GET IT!
ズガッ
I'M KIDDING!
THAT HURT
HAYAMA!
YOWCH!
UH, I'M...UM, TOO YOUNG TO GET MARRIED, OKAY?
BUT IF YOU EVER JUST NEED TO TALK...JUST LET ME KNOW.
....

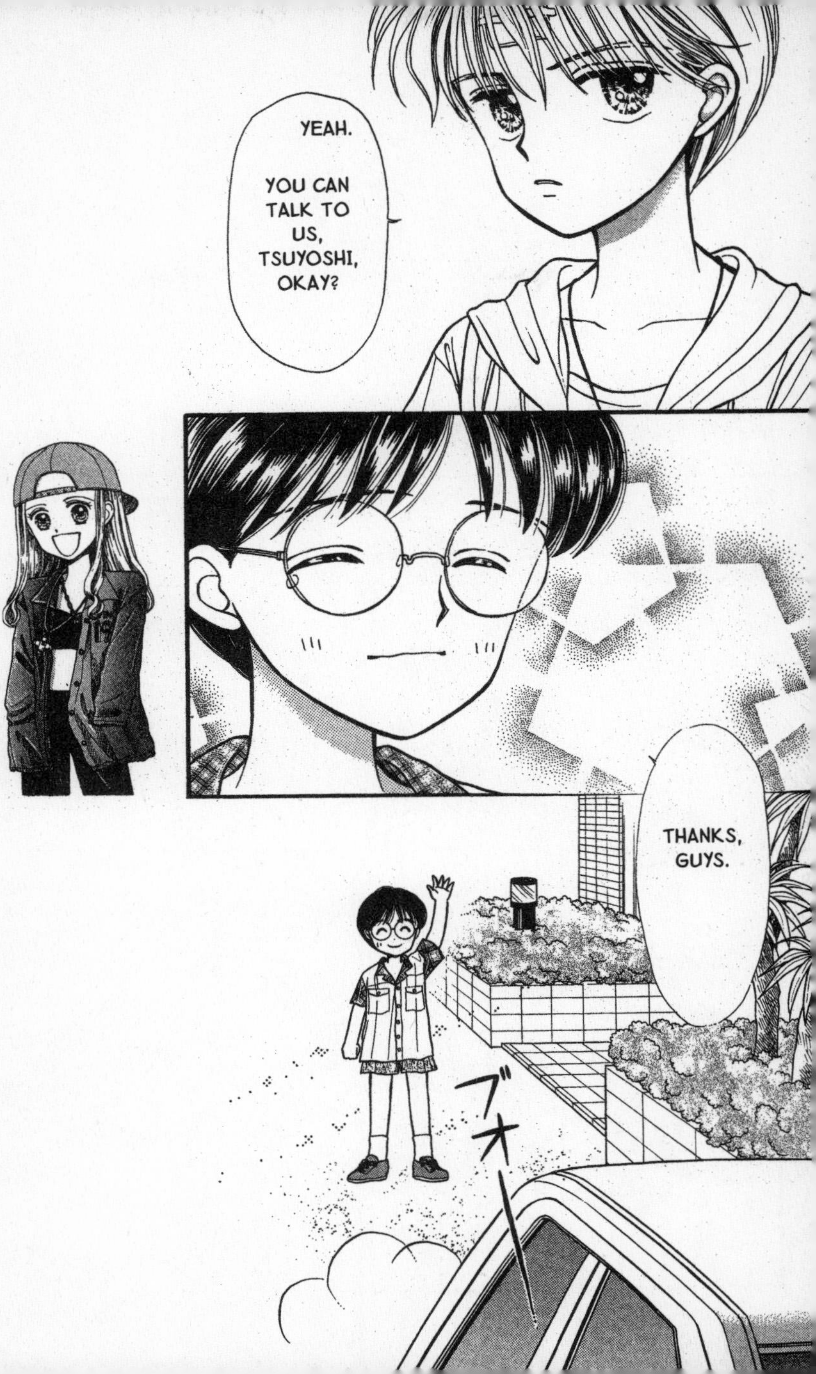
YEAH.
YOU CAN TALK TO US, TSUYOSHI, OKAY?
THANKS, GUYS.
ブオー

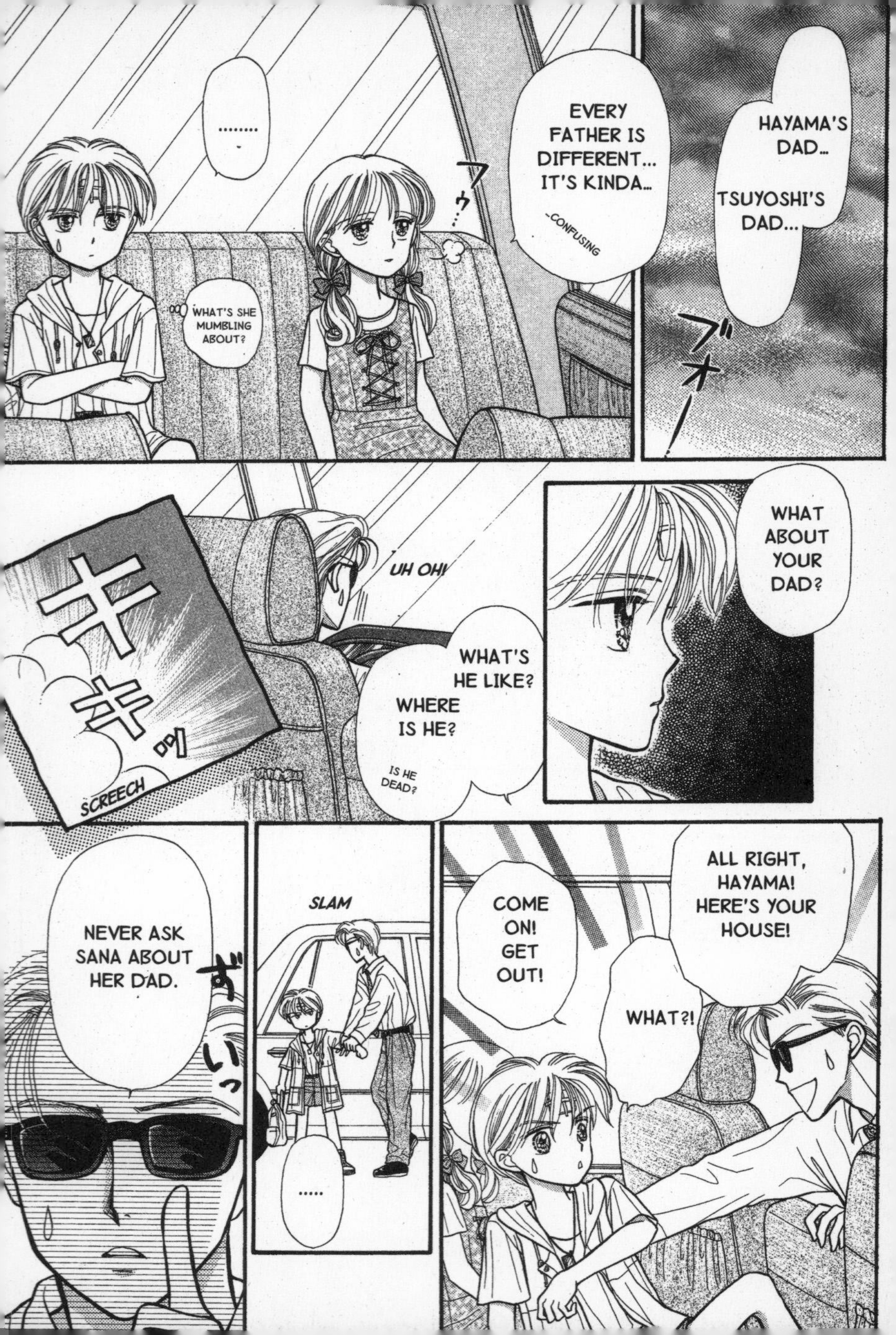
HAYAMA'S DAD...
TSUYOSHI'S DAD...
ブォー
EVERY FATHER IS DIFFERENT... IT'S KINDA...
-CONFUSING
フゥ…
....
WHAT'S SHE MUMBLING ABOUT?
WHAT ABOUT YOUR DAD?
WHAT'S HE LIKE? WHERE IS HE?
IS HE DEAD?
UH OH!
キキッ
SCREECH
ALL RIGHT, HAYAMA! HERE'S YOUR HOUSE!
WHAT?!
COME ON! GET OUT!
SLAM
......
NEVER ASK SANA ABOUT HER DAD.
ずいっ

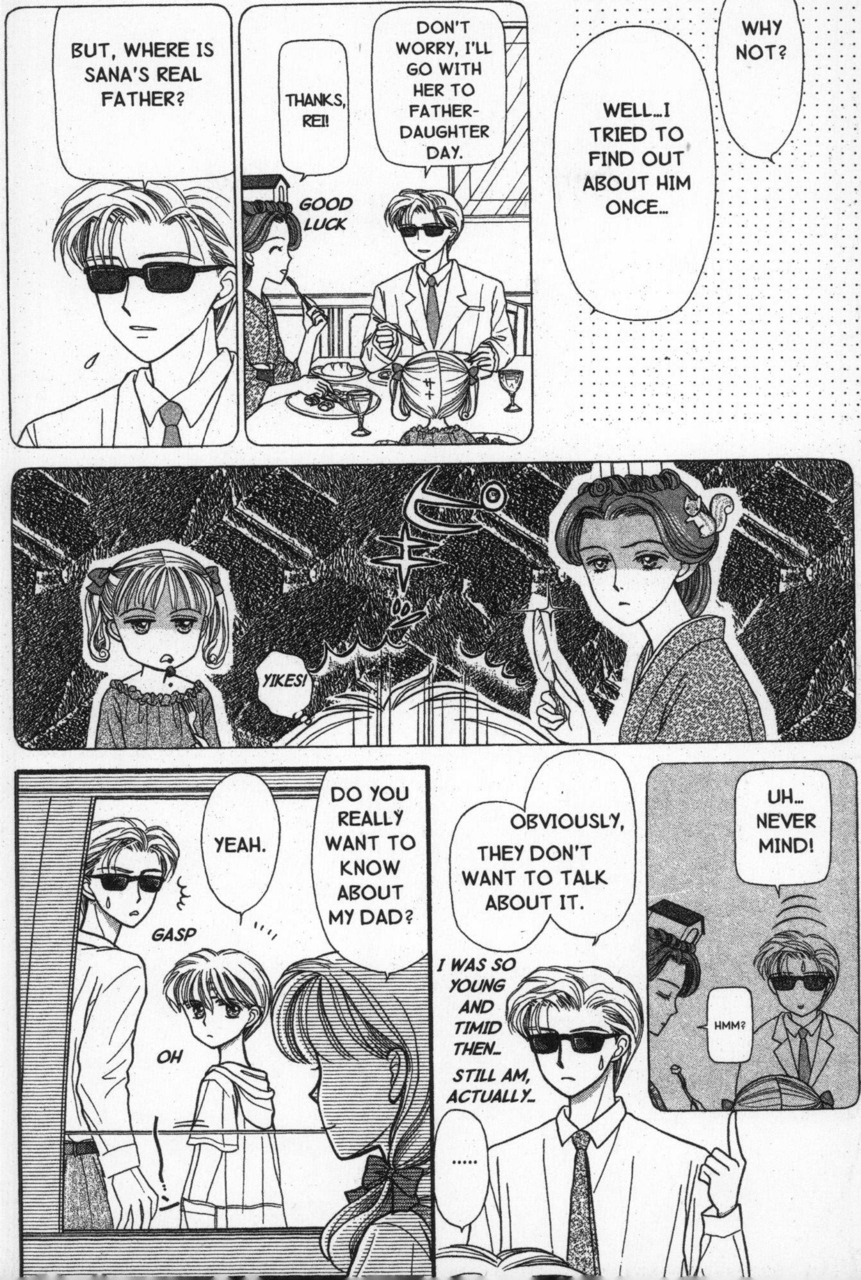
WHY NOT?
WELL...I TRIED TO FIND OUT ABOUT HIM ONCE...
DON'T WORRY, I'LL GO WITH HER TO FATHER-DAUGHTER DAY.
THANKS, REI!
GOOD LUCK
BUT, WHERE IS SANA'S REAL FATHER?
YIKES!
UH... NEVER MIND!
HMM?
OBVIOUSLY, THEY DON'T WANT TO TALK ABOUT IT.
I WAS SO YOUNG AND TIMID THEN...
STILL AM, ACTUALLY...
.....
DO YOU REALLY WANT TO KNOW ABOUT MY DAD?
YEAH.
GASP
OH

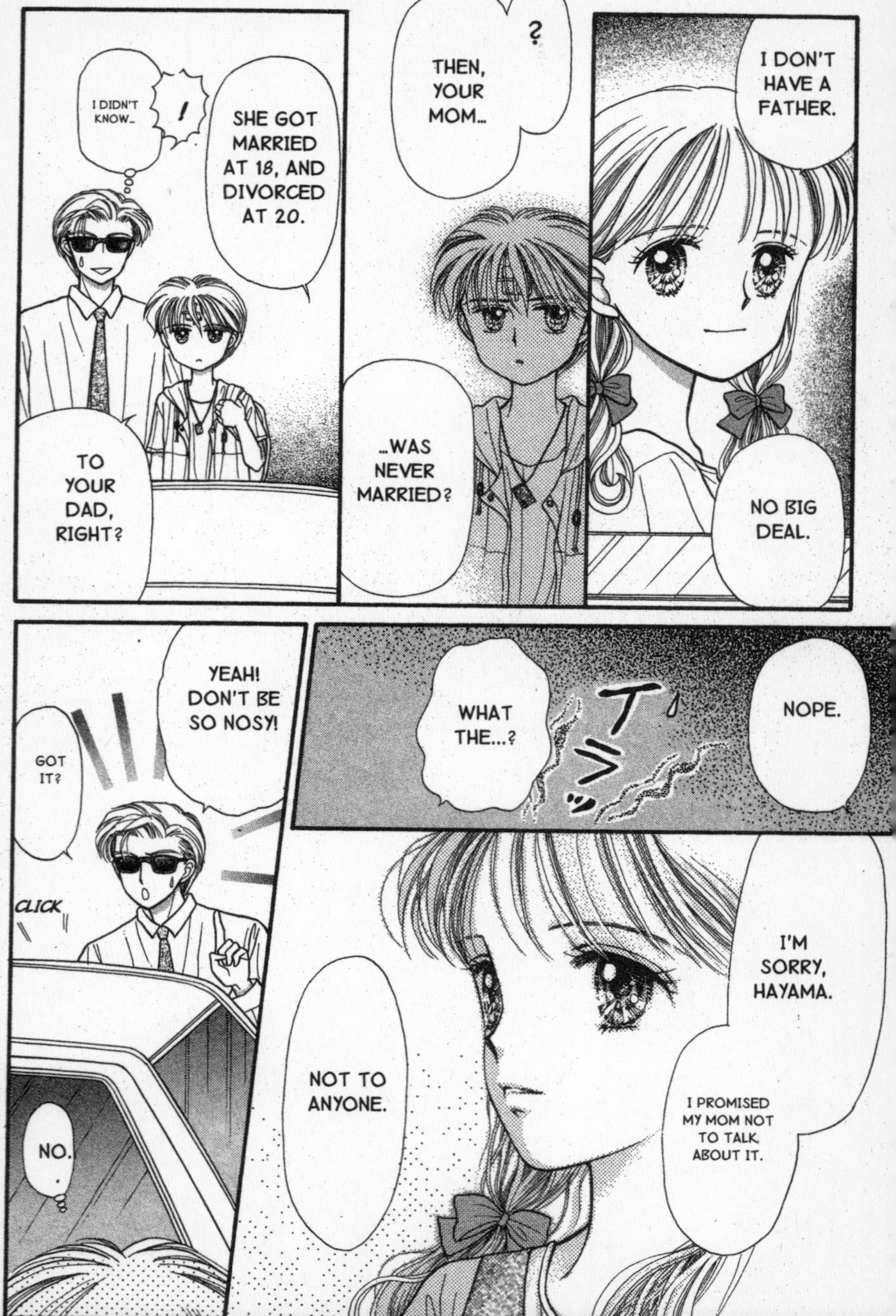
I DON'T HAVE A FATHER.
NO BIG DEAL.
?
THEN, YOUR MOM...
...WAS NEVER MARRIED?
SHE GOT MARRIED AT 18, AND DIVORCED AT 20.
!
I DIDN'T KNOW...
TO YOUR DAD, RIGHT?
NOPE.
イラッ
WHAT THE...?
I'M SORRY, HAYAMA.
I PROMISED MY MOM NOT TO TALK ABOUT IT.
NOT TO ANYONE.
YEAH! DON'T BE SO NOSY!
GOT IT?
CLICK
NO.

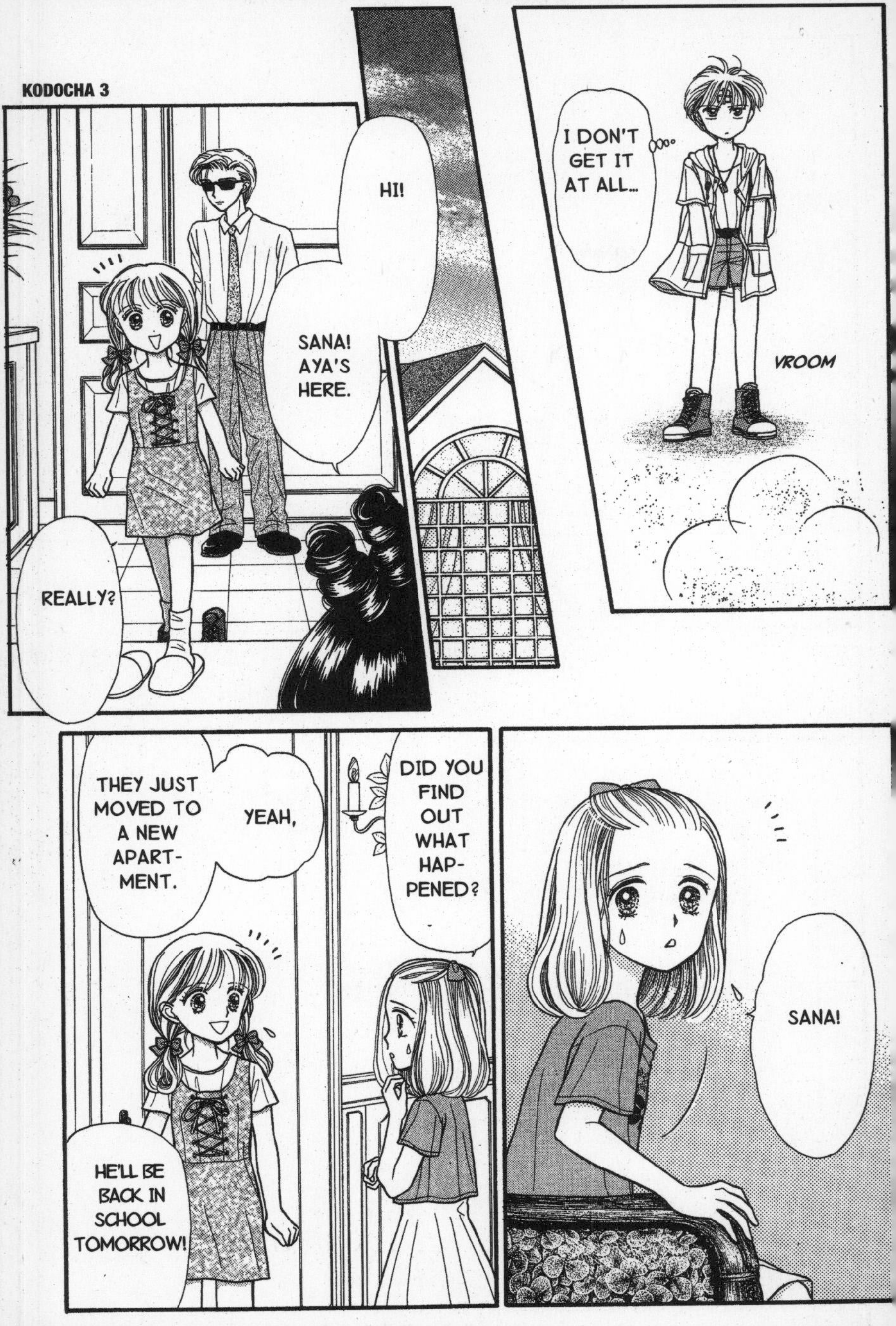
I DON'T GET IT AT ALL...
VROOM
HI!
SANA! AYA'S HERE.
REALLY?
SANA!
DID YOU FIND OUT WHAT HAP-PENED?
YEAH,
THEY JUST MOVED TO A NEW APART-MENT.
HE'LL BE BACK IN SCHOOL TOMORROW!

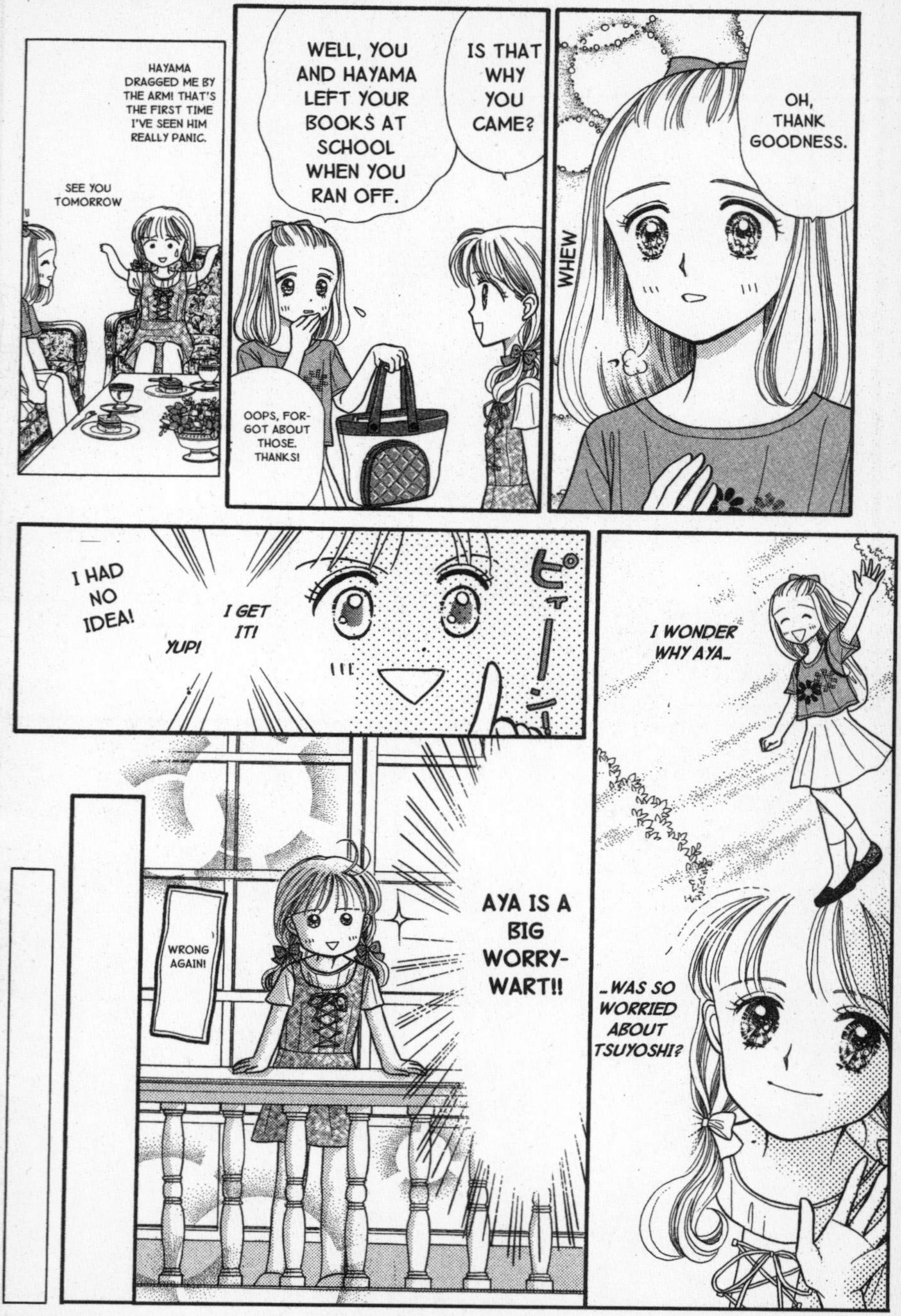
OH, THANK GOODNESS.
WHEW
IS THAT WHY YOU CAME?
WELL, YOU AND HAYAMA LEFT YOUR BOOKS AT SCHOOL WHEN YOU RAN OFF.
OOPS, FORGOT ABOUT THOSE. THANKS!
HAYAMA DRAGGED ME BY THE ARM! THAT'S THE FIRST TIME I'VE SEEN HIM REALLY PANIC.
SEE YOU TOMORROW
I WONDER WHY AYA...
...WAS SO WORRIED ABOUT TSUYOSHI?
ピィーン
I GET IT!
YUP!
I HAD NO IDEA!
AYA IS A BIG WORRY-WART!!
WRONG AGAIN!

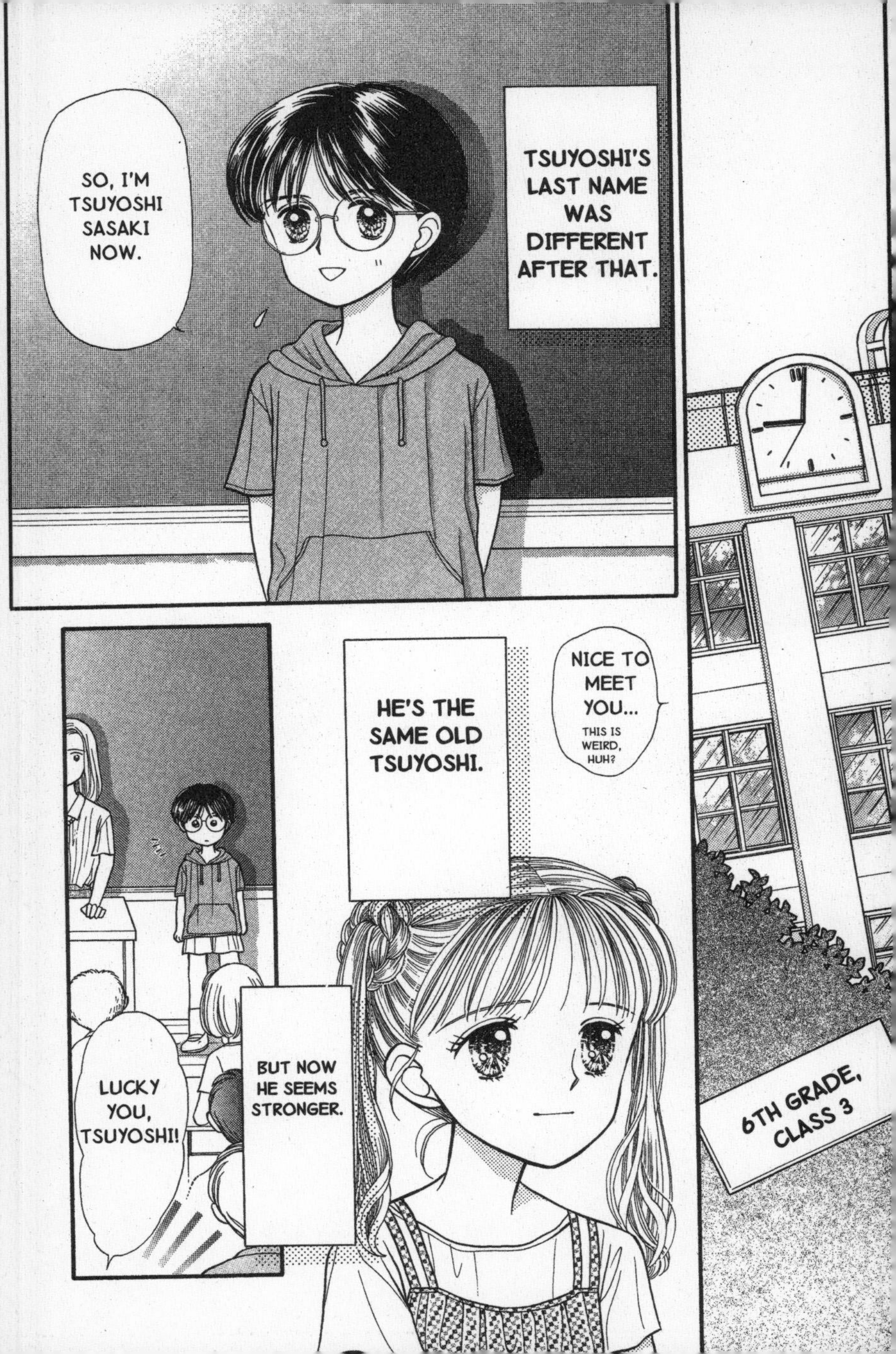
6TH GRADE, CLASS 3
TSUYOSHI'S LAST NAME WAS DIFFERENT AFTER THAT.
SO, I'M TSUYOSHI SASAKI NOW.
NICE TO MEET YOU... THIS IS WEIRD, HUH?
HE'S THE SAME OLD TSUYOSHI.
BUT NOW HE SEEMS STRONGER.
LUCKY YOU, TSUYOSHI!

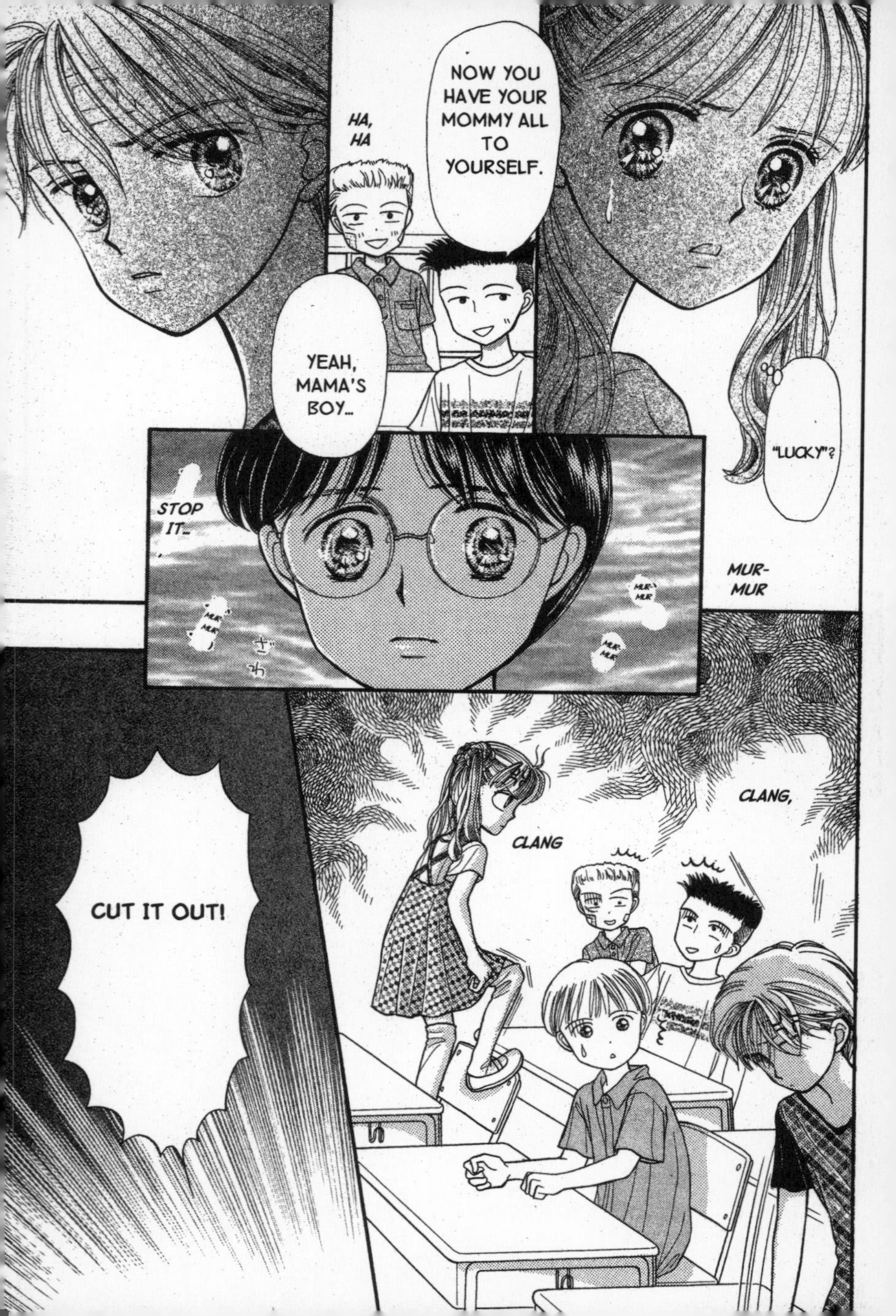
"LUCKY"?
NOW YOU HAVE YOUR MOMMY ALL TO YOURSELF.
HA, HA
YEAH, MAMA'S BOY...
MUR-MUR
STOP IT...
CLANG,
CLANG
CUT IT OUT!

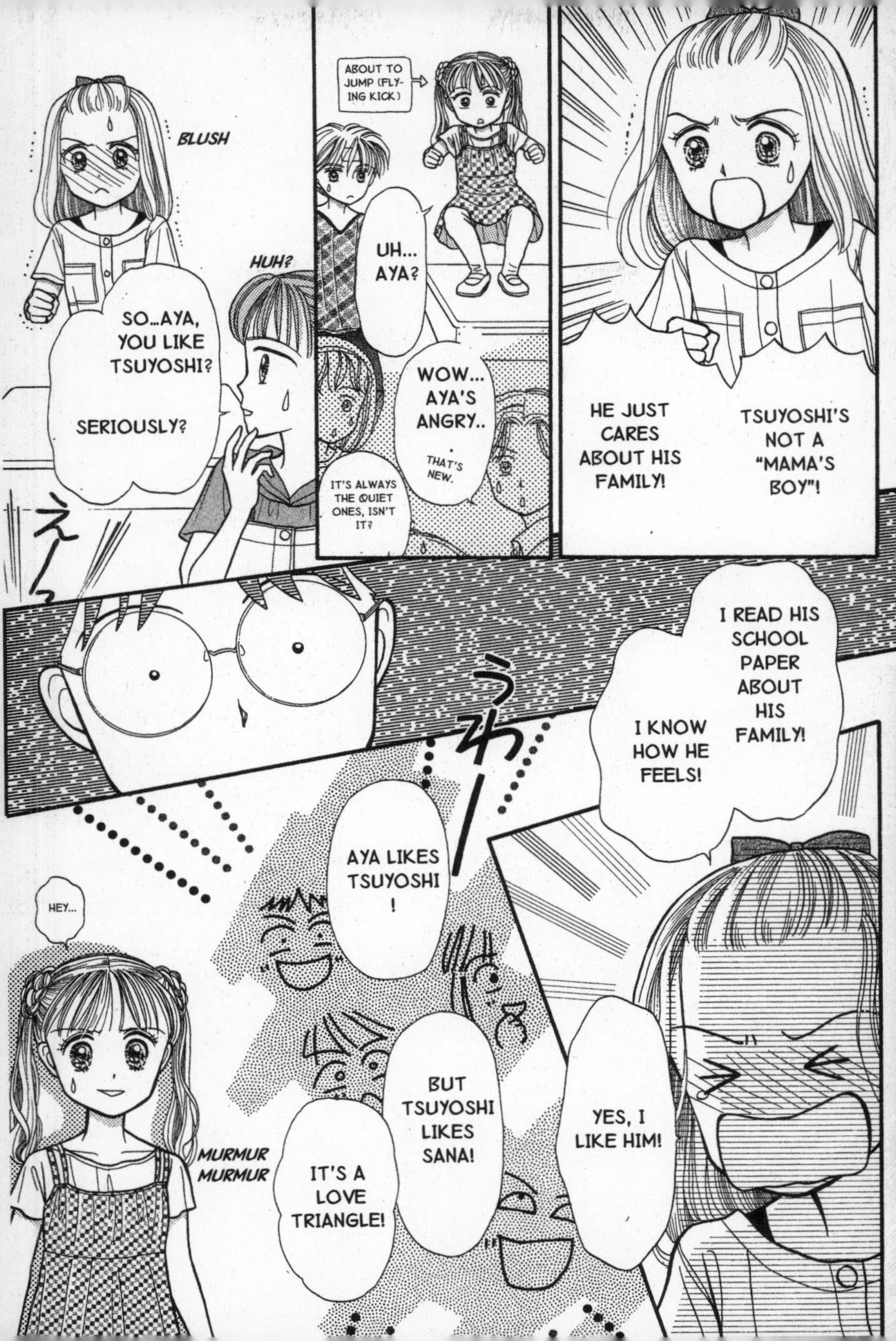
TSUYOSHI'S NOT A "MAMA'S BOY"!
HE JUST CARES ABOUT HIS FAMILY!
ABOUT TO JUMP (FLYING KICK)
UH... AYA?
WOW... AYA'S ANGRY..
THAT'S NEW.
IT'S ALWAYS THE QUIET ONES, ISN'T IT?
BLUSH
HUH?
SO...AYA, YOU LIKE TSUYOSHI?
SERIOUSLY?
I READ HIS SCHOOL PAPER ABOUT HIS FAMILY!
I KNOW HOW HE FEELS!
YES, I LIKE HIM!
AYA LIKES TSUYOSHI!
BUT TSUYOSHI LIKES SANA!
IT'S A LOVE TRIANGLE!
HEY...
MURMUR MURMUR

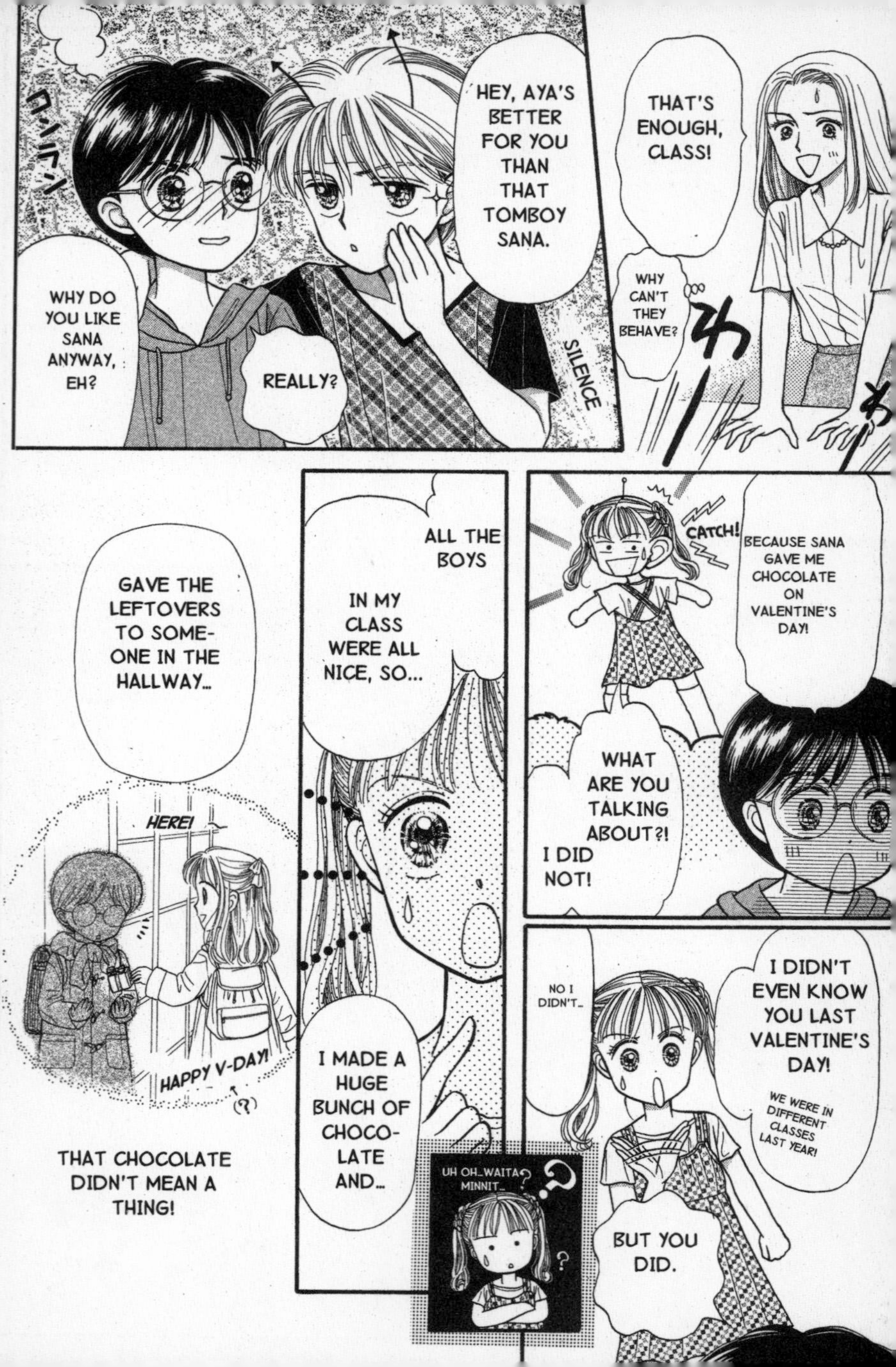
THAT'S ENOUGH, CLASS!
WHY CAN'T THEY BEHAVE?
HEY, AYA'S BETTER FOR YOU THAN THAT TOMBOY SANA.
SILENCE
REALLY?
WHY DO YOU LIKE SANA ANYWAY, EH?
CATCH!
BECAUSE SANA GAVE ME CHOCOLATE ON VALENTINE'S DAY!
WHAT ARE YOU TALKING ABOUT?!
I DID NOT!
I DIDN'T EVEN KNOW YOU LAST VALENTINE'S DAY!
WE WERE IN DIFFERENT CLASSES LAST YEAR!
NO I DIDN'T...
BUT YOU DID.
UH OH...WAITA MINNIT...
ALL THE BOYS
IN MY CLASS WERE ALL NICE, SO...
I MADE A HUGE BUNCH OF CHOCO-LATE AND...
GAVE THE LEFTOVERS TO SOME-ONE IN THE HALLWAY...
HERE!
HAPPY V-DAY!
(?)
THAT CHOCOLATE DIDN'T MEAN A THING!

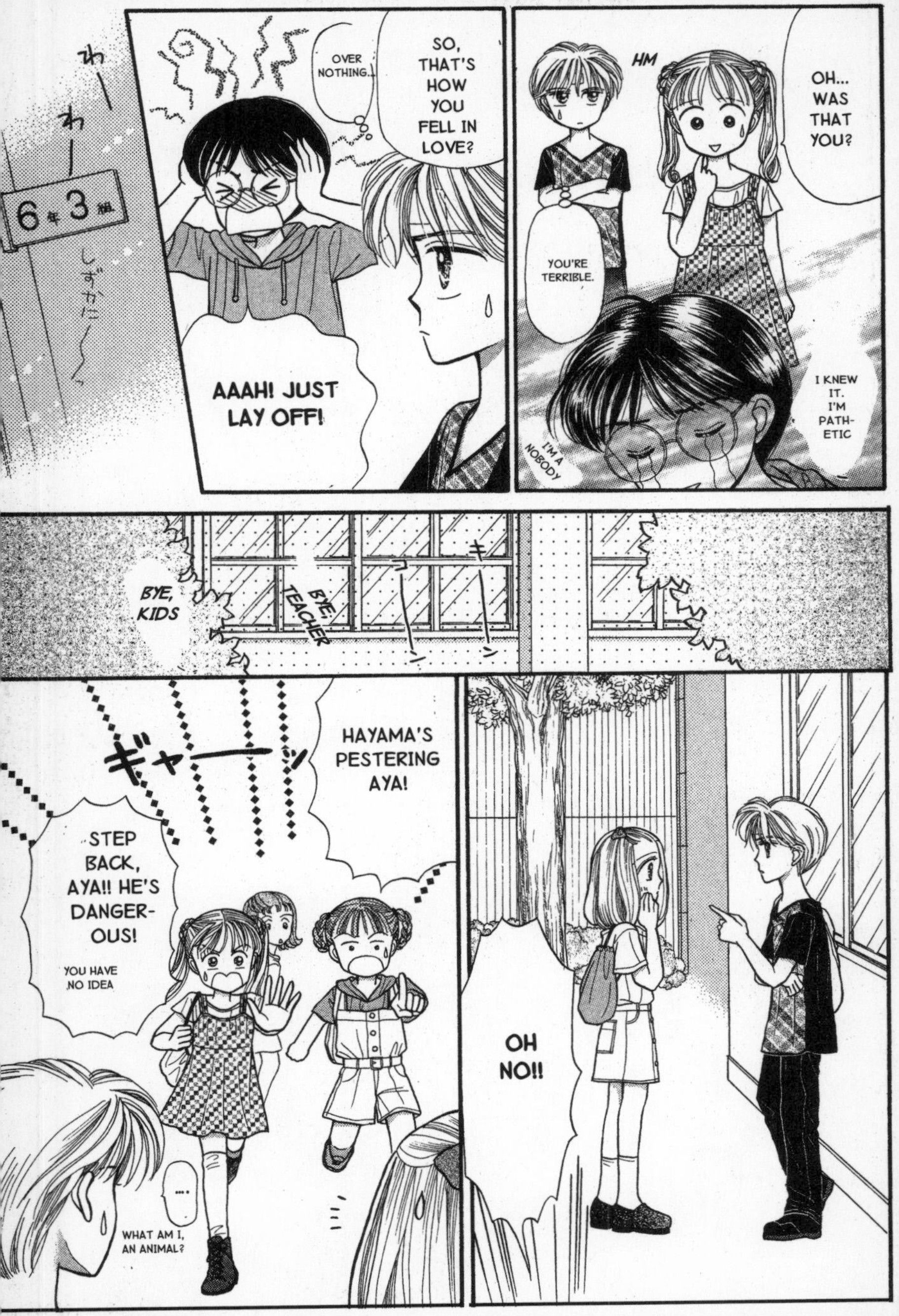

OH... WAS THAT YOU?
HM
YOU'RE TERRIBLE.
I KNEW IT. I'M PATHETIC
I'M A NOBODY
SO, THAT'S HOW YOU FELL IN LOVE?
OVER NOTHING...
AAAH! JUST LAY OFF!
わーわー
6年3組
しずかに～～
キーン
コーン
BYE, TEACHER
BYE, KIDS
OH NO!!
HAYAMA'S PESTERING AYA!
ギャーッ
STEP BACK, AYA!! HE'S DANGER-OUS!
YOU HAVE NO IDEA
...
WHAT AM I, AN ANIMAL?

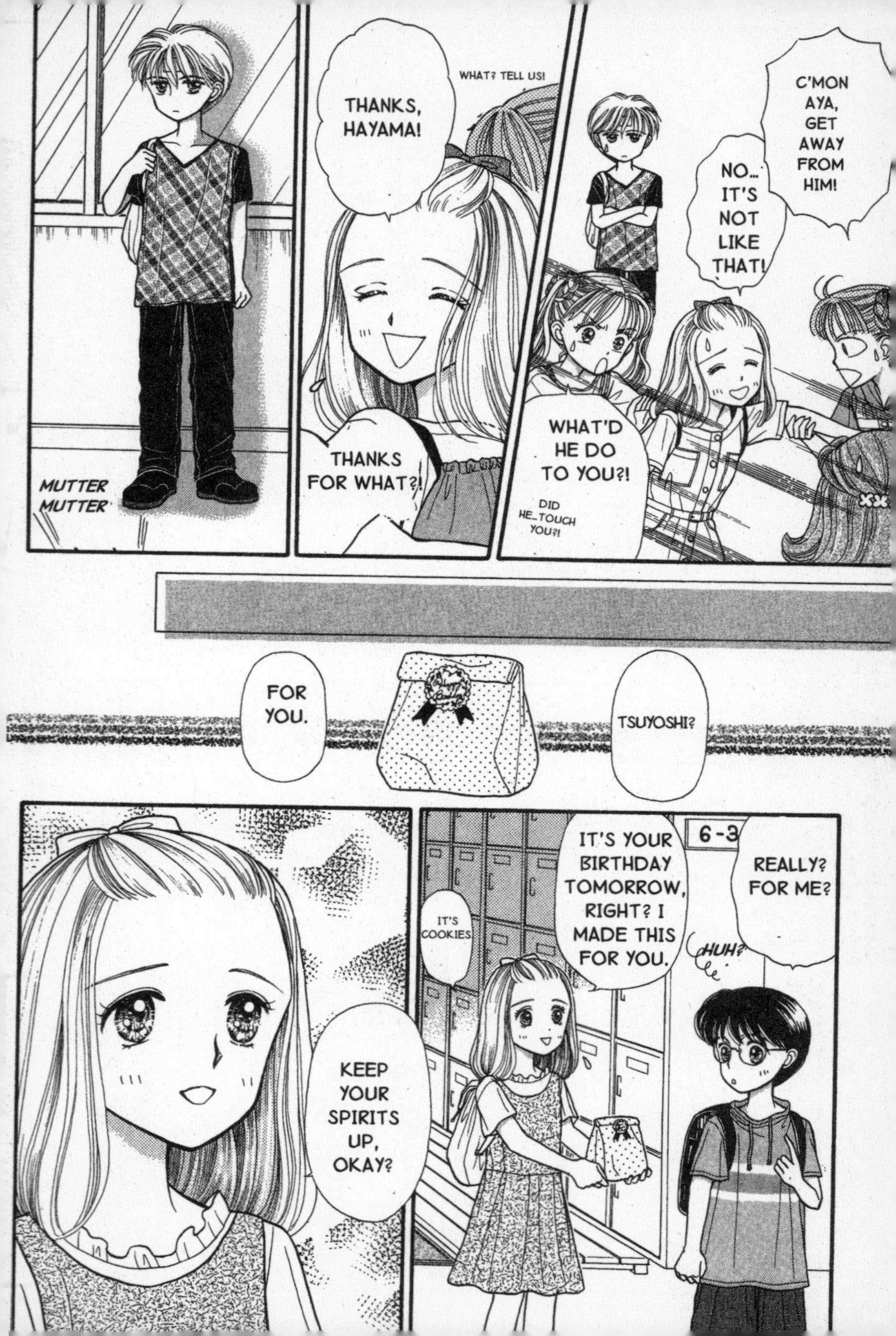
C'MON AYA, GET AWAY FROM HIM!
NO... IT'S NOT LIKE THAT!
WHAT'D HE DO TO YOU?!
DID HE...TOUCH YOU?!
THANKS, HAYAMA!
WHAT? TELL US!
THANKS FOR WHAT?!
MUTTER MUTTER
TSUYOSHI?
FOR YOU.
REALLY? FOR ME?
HUH?
IT'S YOUR BIRTHDAY TOMORROW, RIGHT? I MADE THIS FOR YOU.
IT'S COOKIES
6-3
KEEP YOUR SPIRITS UP, OKAY?

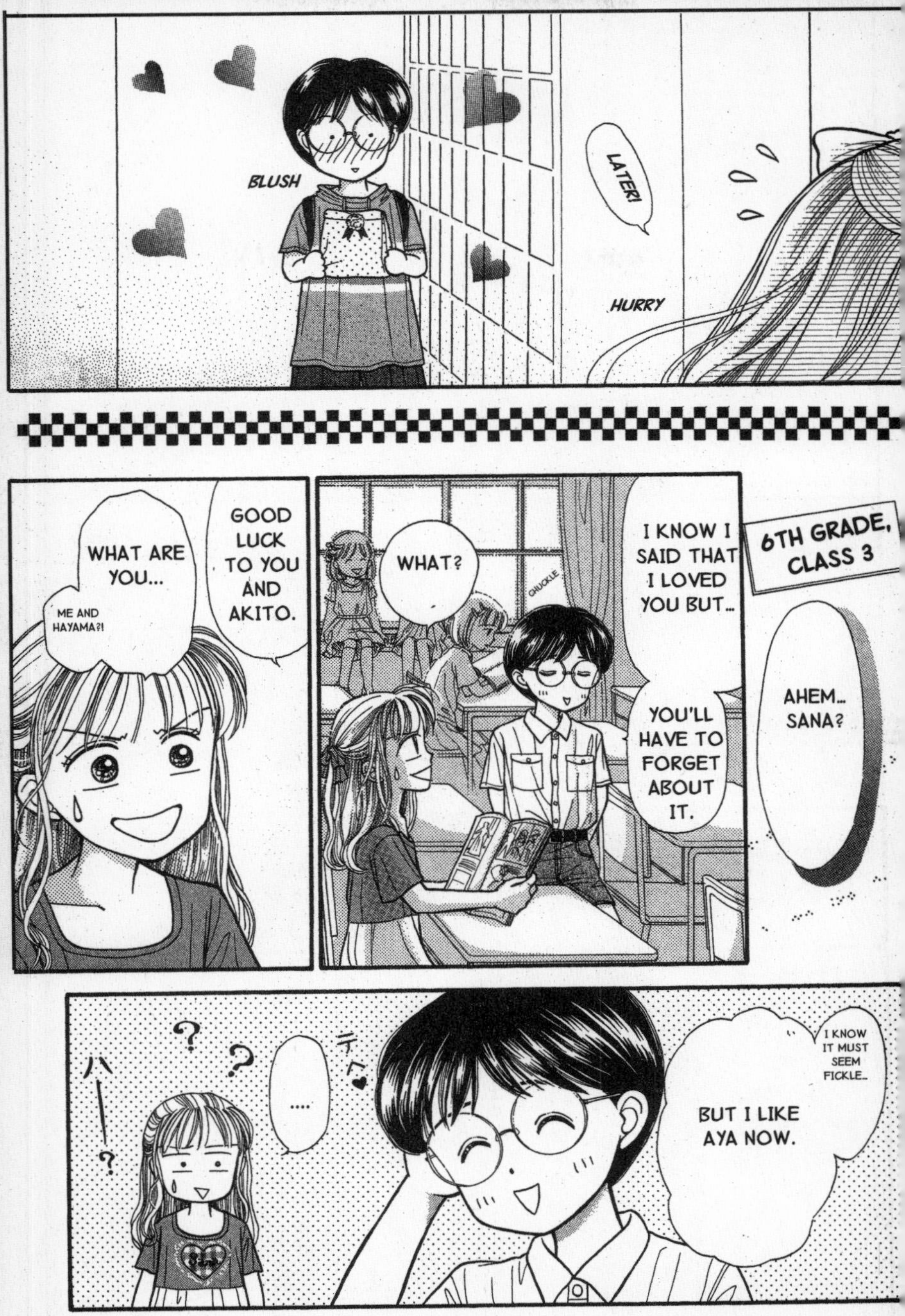
LATER!
HURRY
BLUSH
6TH GRADE, CLASS 3
AHEM... SANA?
I KNOW I SAID THAT I LOVED YOU BUT...
YOU'LL HAVE TO FORGET ABOUT IT.
CHUCKLE
WHAT?
GOOD LUCK TO YOU AND AKITO.
WHAT ARE YOU...
ME AND HAYAMA?!
I KNOW IT MUST SEEM FICKLE...
BUT I LIKE AYA NOW.
....

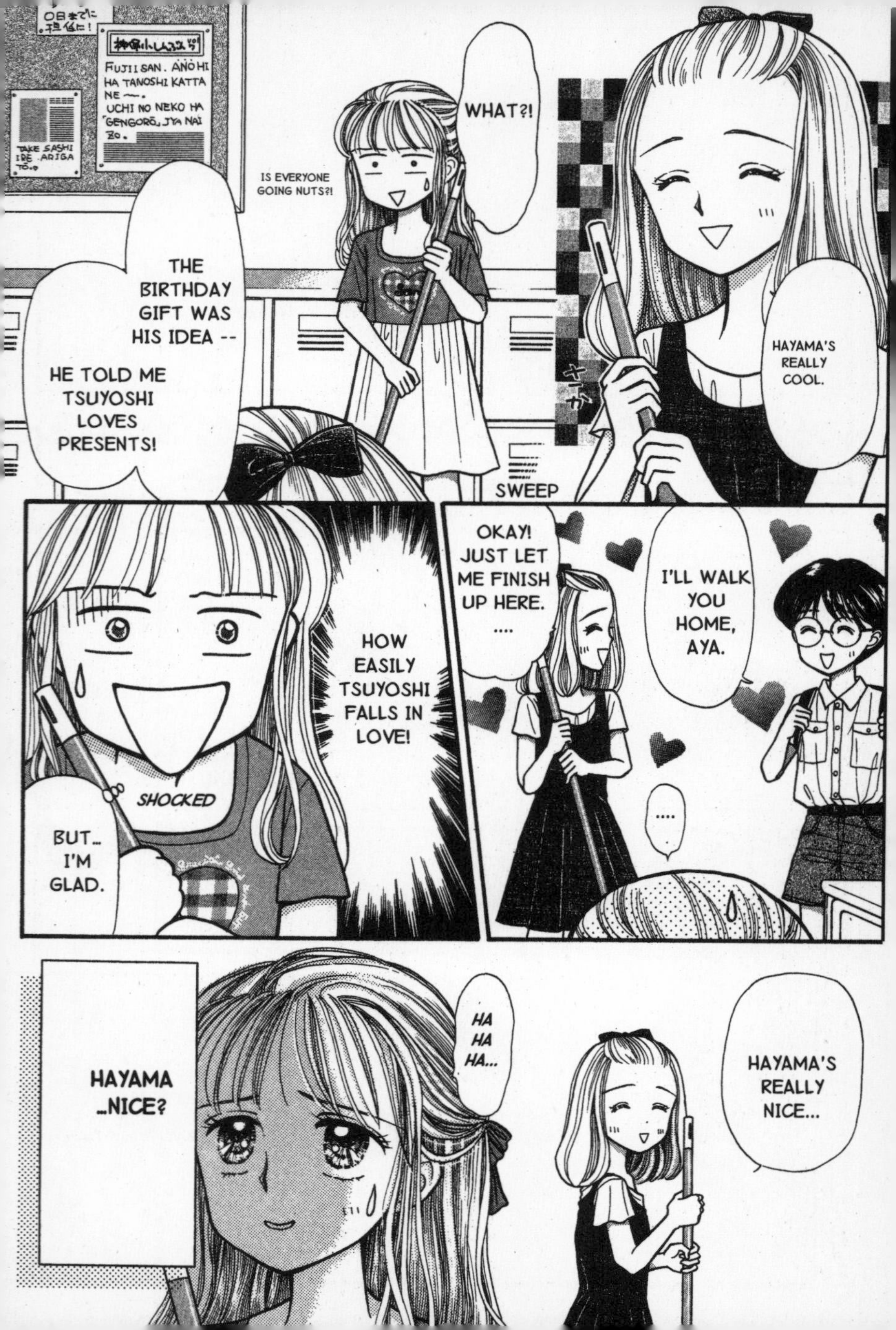
HAYAMA'S REALLY COOL.
SWEEP
WHAT?!
IS EVERYONE GOING NUTS?!
FUJII SAN. ANO HI HA TANOSHI KATTA NE—. UCHI NO NEKO HA "GENGORŌ" JYA NAI ZO.
TAKE SASHI IRE ARIGA TŌ.
THE BIRTHDAY GIFT WAS HIS IDEA --
HE TOLD ME TSUYOSHI LOVES PRESENTS!
I'LL WALK YOU HOME, AYA.
OKAY! JUST LET ME FINISH UP HERE. ....
....
HOW EASILY TSUYOSHI FALLS IN LOVE!
SHOCKED
BUT... I'M GLAD.
HAYAMA'S REALLY NICE...
HA HA HA...
HAYAMA ...NICE?

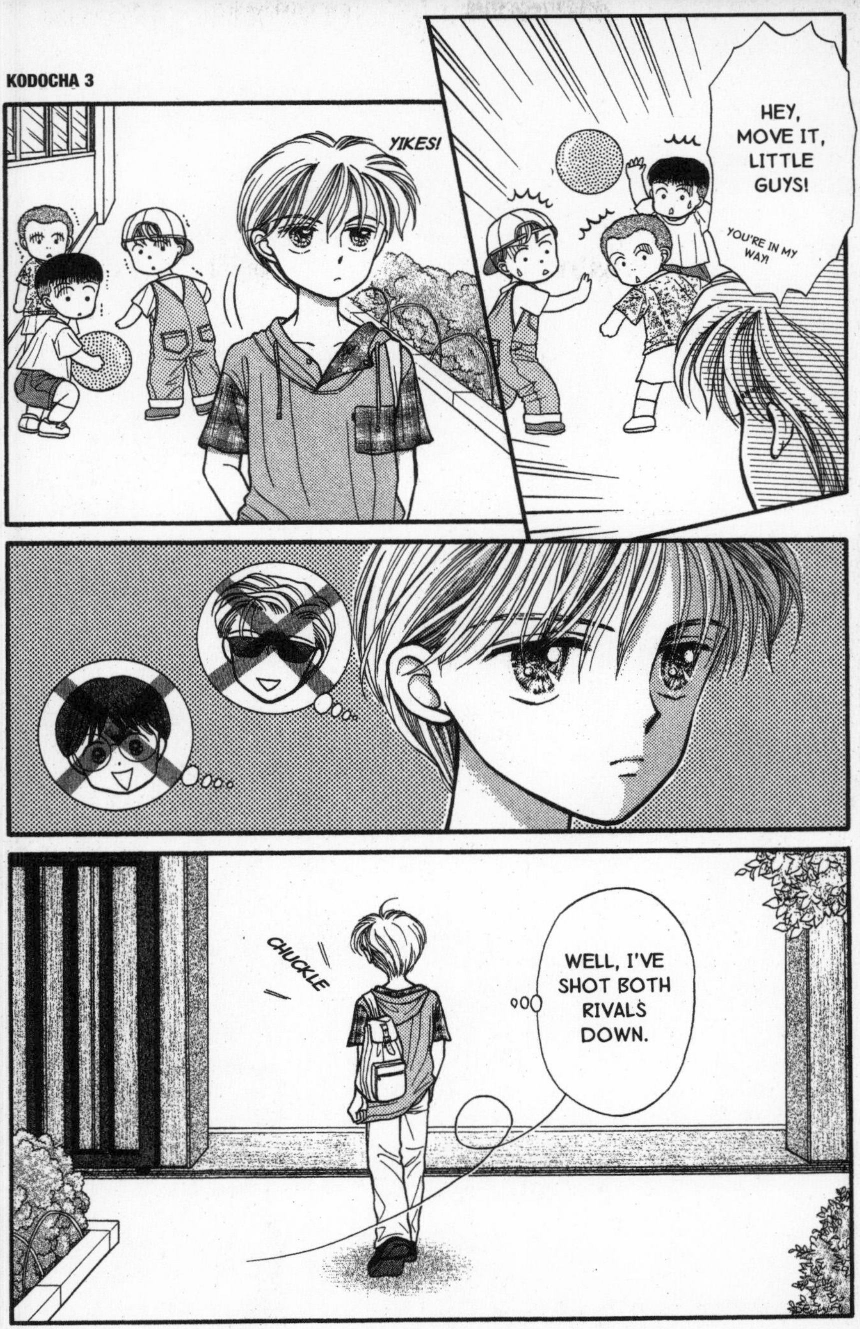
HEY, MOVE IT, LITTLE GUYS!
YOU'RE IN MY WAY!
YIKES!
WELL, I'VE SHOT BOTH RIVALS DOWN.
CHUCKLE

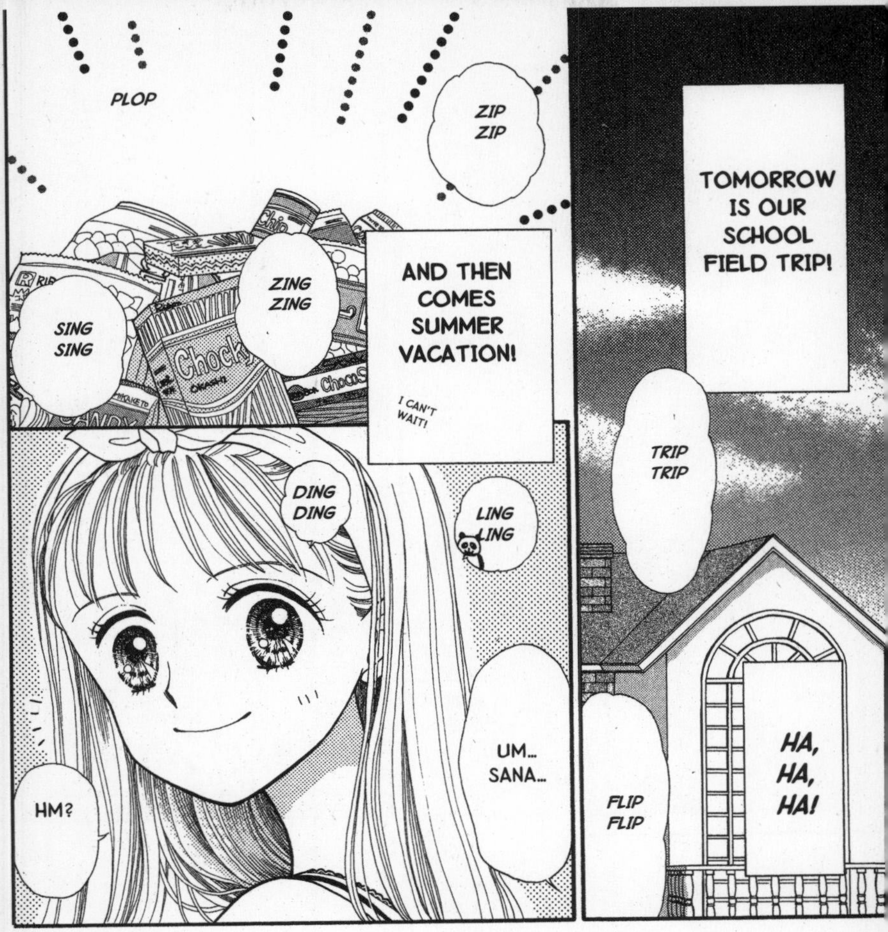
TOMORROW IS OUR SCHOOL FIELD TRIP!
TRIP TRIP
HA, HA, HA!
FLIP FLIP
AND THEN COMES SUMMER VACATION!
I CAN'T WAIT!
ZIP ZIP
ZING ZING
PLOP
SING SING
UM... SANA...
LING LING
DING DING
HM?

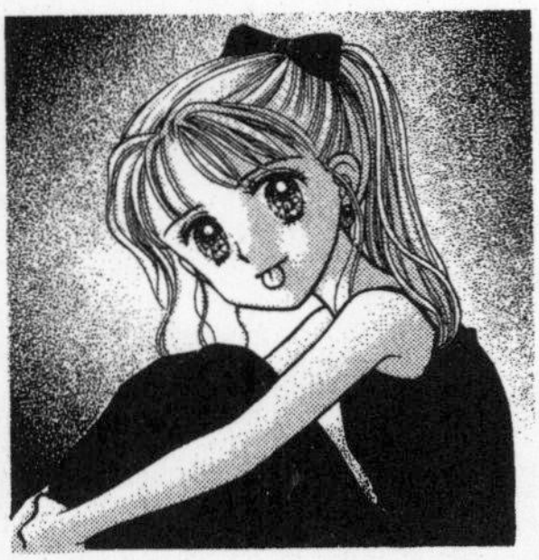

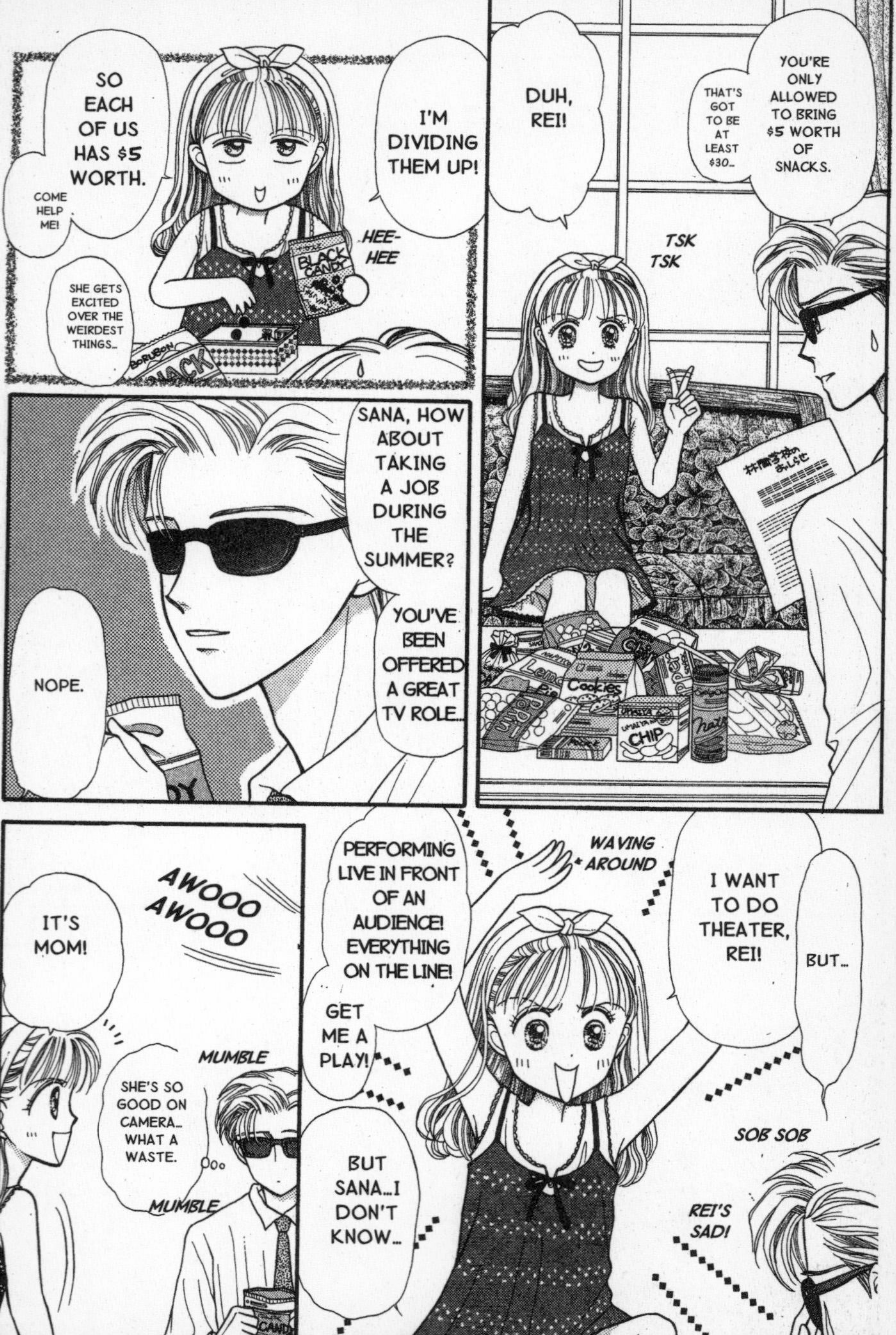
YOU'RE ONLY ALLOWED TO BRING $5 WORTH OF SNACKS.
THAT'S GOT TO BE AT LEAST $30...
DUH, REI!
TSK TSK
Cookies
CHIP
I'M DIVIDING THEM UP!
SO EACH OF US HAS $5 WORTH.
COME HELP ME!
HEE-HEE
BLACK CANDY
SHE GETS EXCITED OVER THE WEIRDEST THINGS...
SNACK
SANA, HOW ABOUT TAKING A JOB DURING THE SUMMER?
YOU'VE BEEN OFFERED A GREAT TV ROLE...
NOPE.
I WANT TO DO THEATER, REI!
BUT...
WAVING AROUND
PERFORMING LIVE IN FRONT OF AN AUDIENCE! EVERYTHING ON THE LINE!
GET ME A PLAY!
SOB SOB
REI'S SAD!
BUT SANA...I DON'T KNOW...
AWOOO AWOOO
IT'S MOM!
MUMBLE
SHE'S SO GOOD ON CAMERA... WHAT A WASTE.
MUMBLE

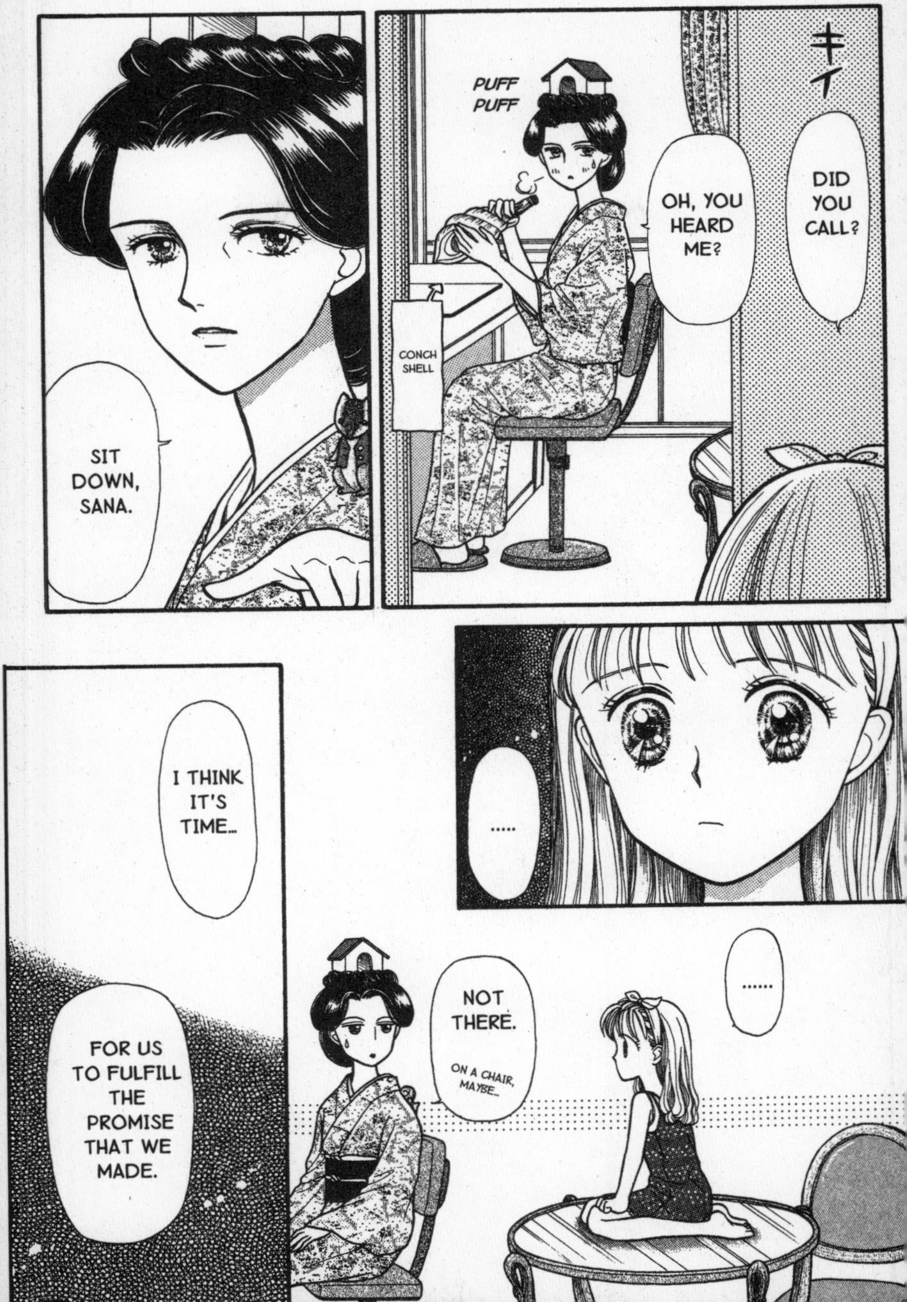

キイ
DID YOU CALL?
OH, YOU HEARD ME?
PUFF PUFF
CONCH SHELL
SIT DOWN, SANA.
.....
......
NOT THERE.
ON A CHAIR, MAYBE...
I THINK IT'S TIME...
FOR US TO FULFILL THE PROMISE THAT WE MADE.

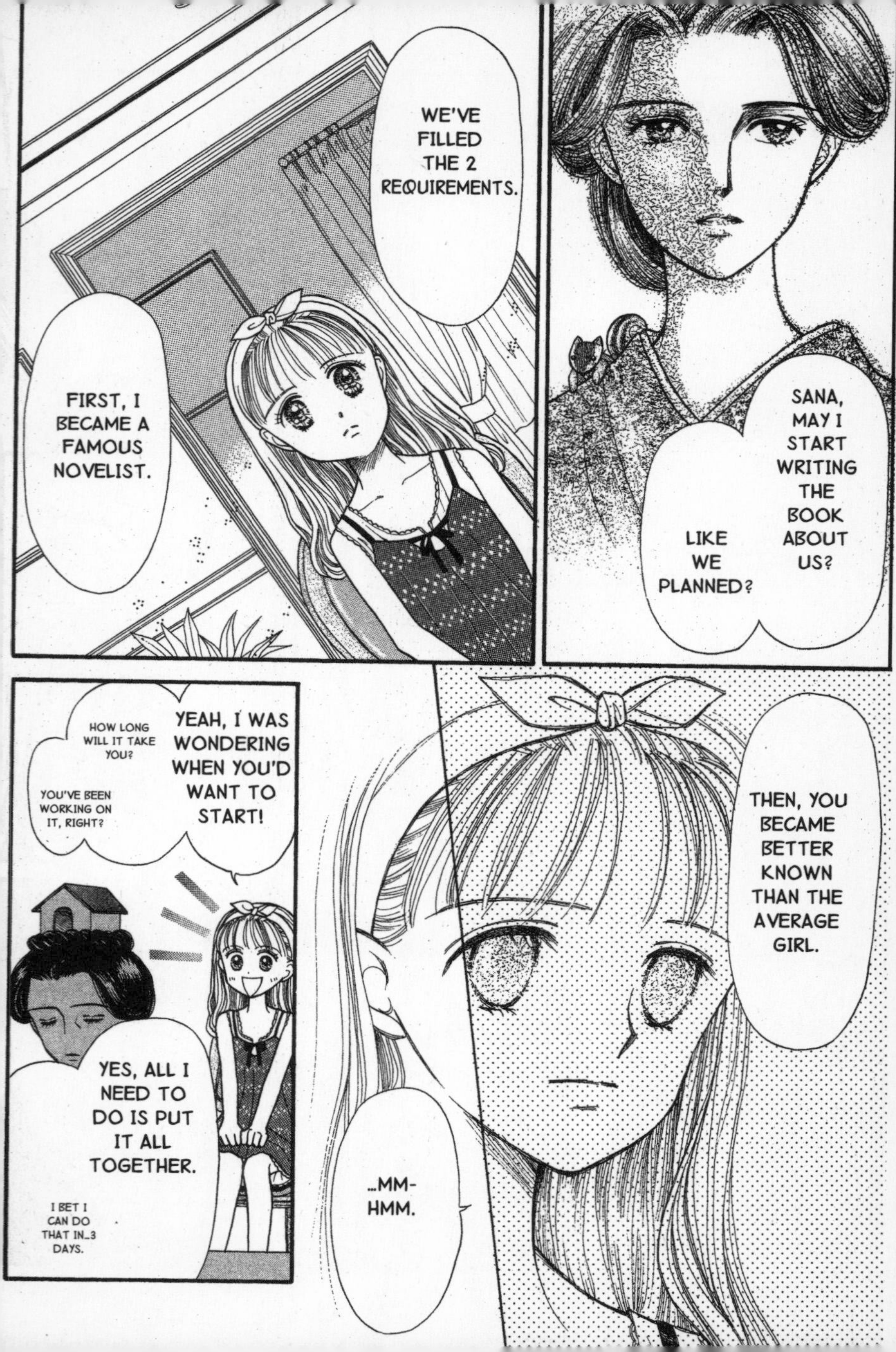
SANA, MAY I START WRITING THE BOOK ABOUT US?
LIKE WE PLANNED?
WE'VE FILLED THE 2 REQUIREMENTS.
FIRST, I BECAME A FAMOUS NOVELIST.
THEN, YOU BECAME BETTER KNOWN THAN THE AVERAGE GIRL.
...MM-HMM.
YEAH, I WAS WONDERING WHEN YOU'D WANT TO START!
HOW LONG WILL IT TAKE YOU?
YOU'VE BEEN WORKING ON IT, RIGHT?
YES, ALL I NEED TO DO IS PUT IT ALL TOGETHER.
I BET I CAN DO THAT IN...3 DAYS.

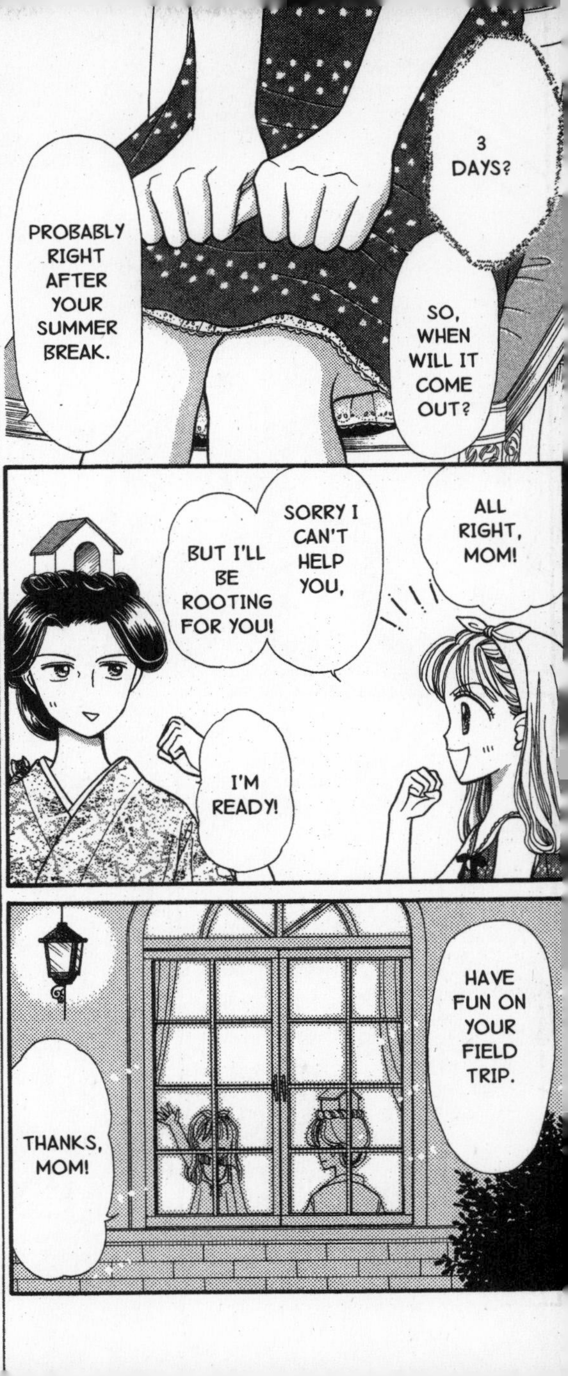
3 DAYS?
SO, WHEN WILL IT COME OUT?
PROBABLY RIGHT AFTER YOUR SUMMER BREAK.
ALL RIGHT, MOM!
SORRY I CAN'T HELP YOU,
BUT I'LL BE ROOTING FOR YOU!
I'M READY!
HAVE FUN ON YOUR FIELD TRIP.
THANKS, MOM!

All About Chipmunks

I have a chipmunk, just like Mariko. I don't keep him in my hair though! (hee hee) In the comic, Maro sits calmly on Mariko's head (most of the time) — but in real life, chipmunks are never calm! He's always moving around.

If I drew it realistically, it would look like this.

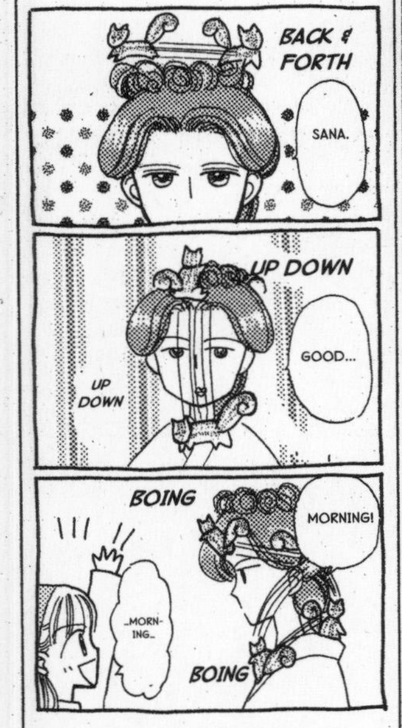
BACK & FORTH
SANA.
UP DOWN
GOOD...
UP DOWN
MORNING!
BOING
...MORNING...
BOING

It's too much! That's why I don't portray Maro like a real chipmunk. *To be continued.*

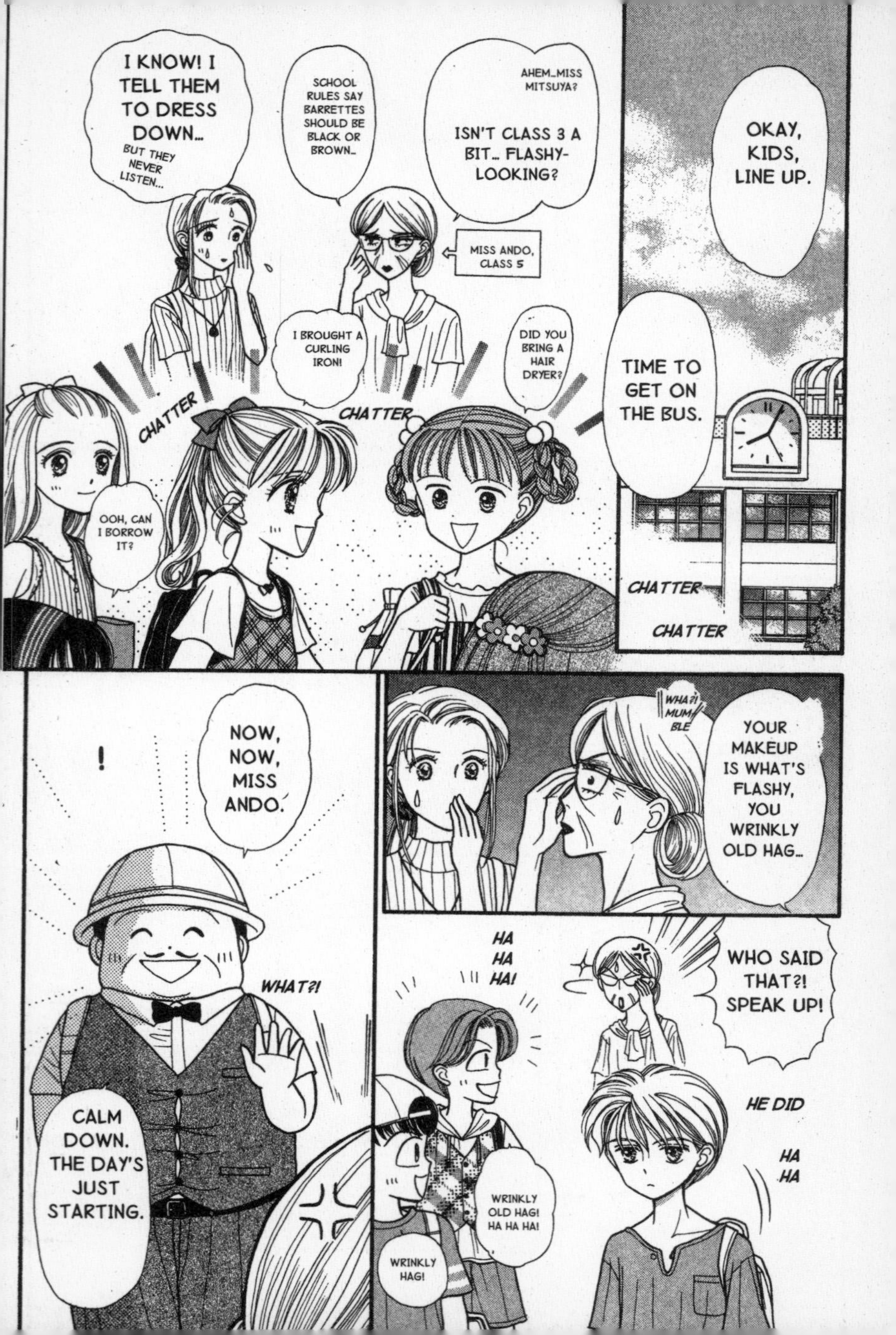

OKAY, KIDS, LINE UP.
TIME TO GET ON THE BUS.
CHATTER
CHATTER
AHEM...MISS MITSUYA?
ISN'T CLASS 3 A BIT... FLASHY-LOOKING?
MISS ANDO, CLASS 5
SCHOOL RULES SAY BARRETTES SHOULD BE BLACK OR BROWN...
I KNOW! I TELL THEM TO DRESS DOWN...
BUT THEY NEVER LISTEN...
DID YOU BRING A HAIR DRYER?
I BROUGHT A CURLING IRON!
CHATTER
CHATTER
OOH, CAN I BORROW IT?
WHA?! MUMBLE
YOUR MAKEUP IS WHAT'S FLASHY, YOU WRINKLY OLD HAG...
WHO SAID THAT?! SPEAK UP!
HE DID
HA HA
HA HA HA!
WRINKLY OLD HAG! HA HA HA!
WRINKLY HAG!
NOW, NOW, MISS ANDO.
!
WHAT?!
CALM DOWN. THE DAY'S JUST STARTING.

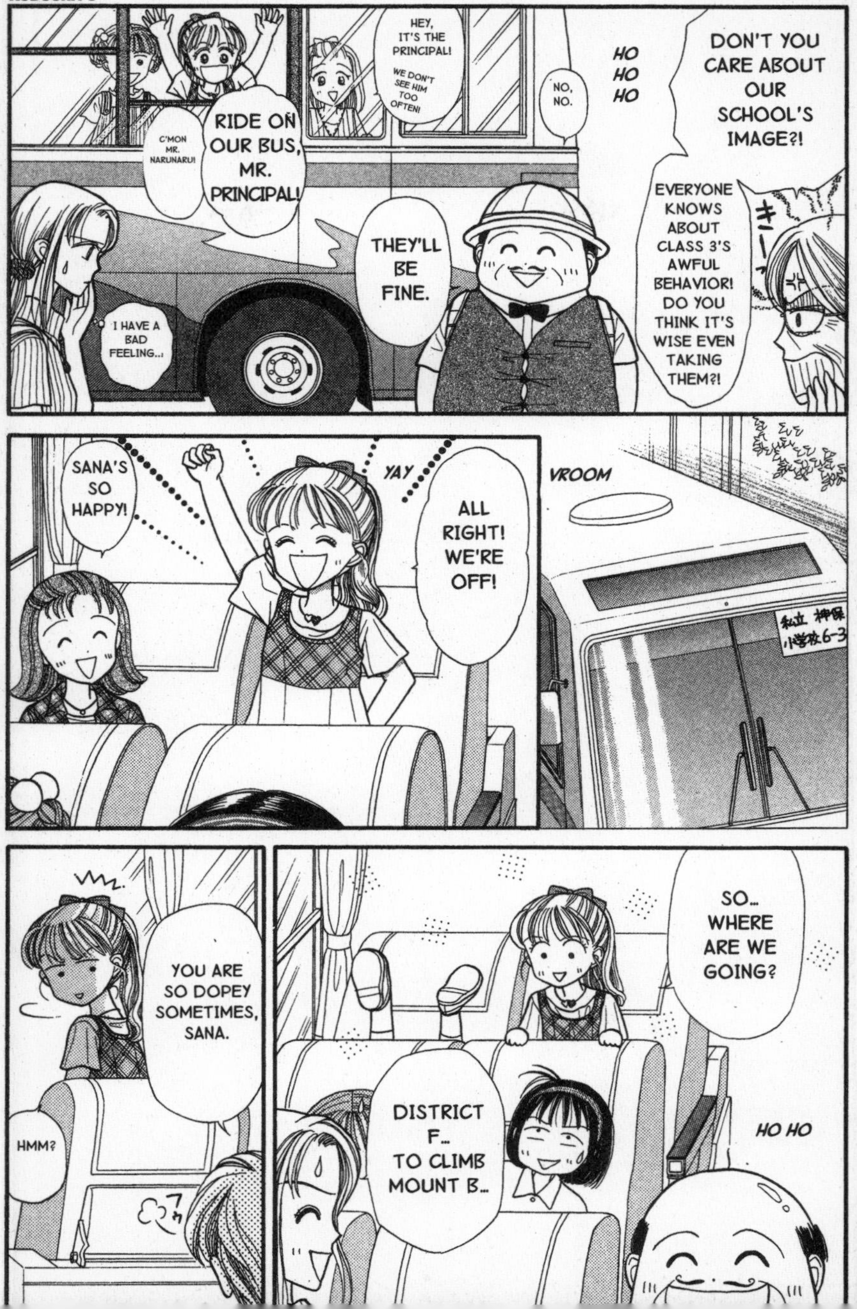
DON'T YOU CARE ABOUT OUR SCHOOL'S IMAGE?!
HO HO HO
NO, NO.
HEY, IT'S THE PRINCIPAL!
WE DON'T SEE HIM TOO OFTEN!
EVERYONE KNOWS ABOUT CLASS 3'S AWFUL BEHAVIOR! DO YOU THINK IT'S WISE EVEN TAKING THEM?!
RIDE ON OUR BUS, MR. PRINCIPAL!
C'MON MR. NARUNARU!
THEY'LL BE FINE.
I HAVE A BAD FEELING...
VROOM
私立 神保
小学校6-3
ALL RIGHT! WE'RE OFF!
YAY
SANA'S SO HAPPY!
SO... WHERE ARE WE GOING?
HO HO
DISTRICT F... TO CLIMB MOUNT B...
YOU ARE SO DOPEY SOMETIMES, SANA.
HMM?

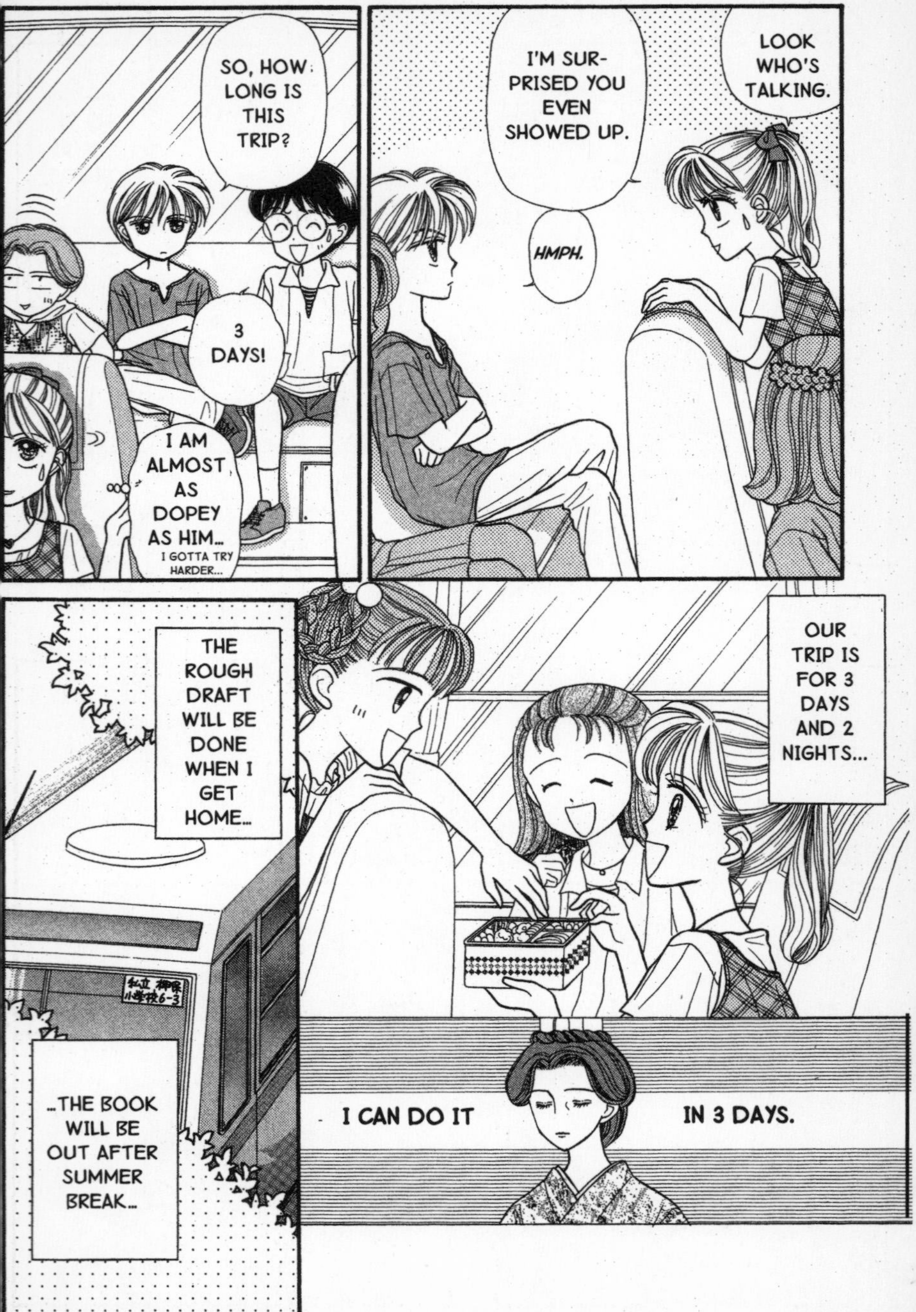
I'M SURPRISED YOU EVEN SHOWED UP.
LOOK WHO'S TALKING.
HMPH.
SO, HOW LONG IS THIS TRIP?
3 DAYS!
I AM ALMOST AS DOPEY AS HIM...
I GOTTA TRY HARDER...
OUR TRIP IS FOR 3 DAYS AND 2 NIGHTS...
I CAN DO IT IN 3 DAYS.
THE ROUGH DRAFT WILL BE DONE WHEN I GET HOME...
...THE BOOK WILL BE OUT AFTER SUMMER BREAK...

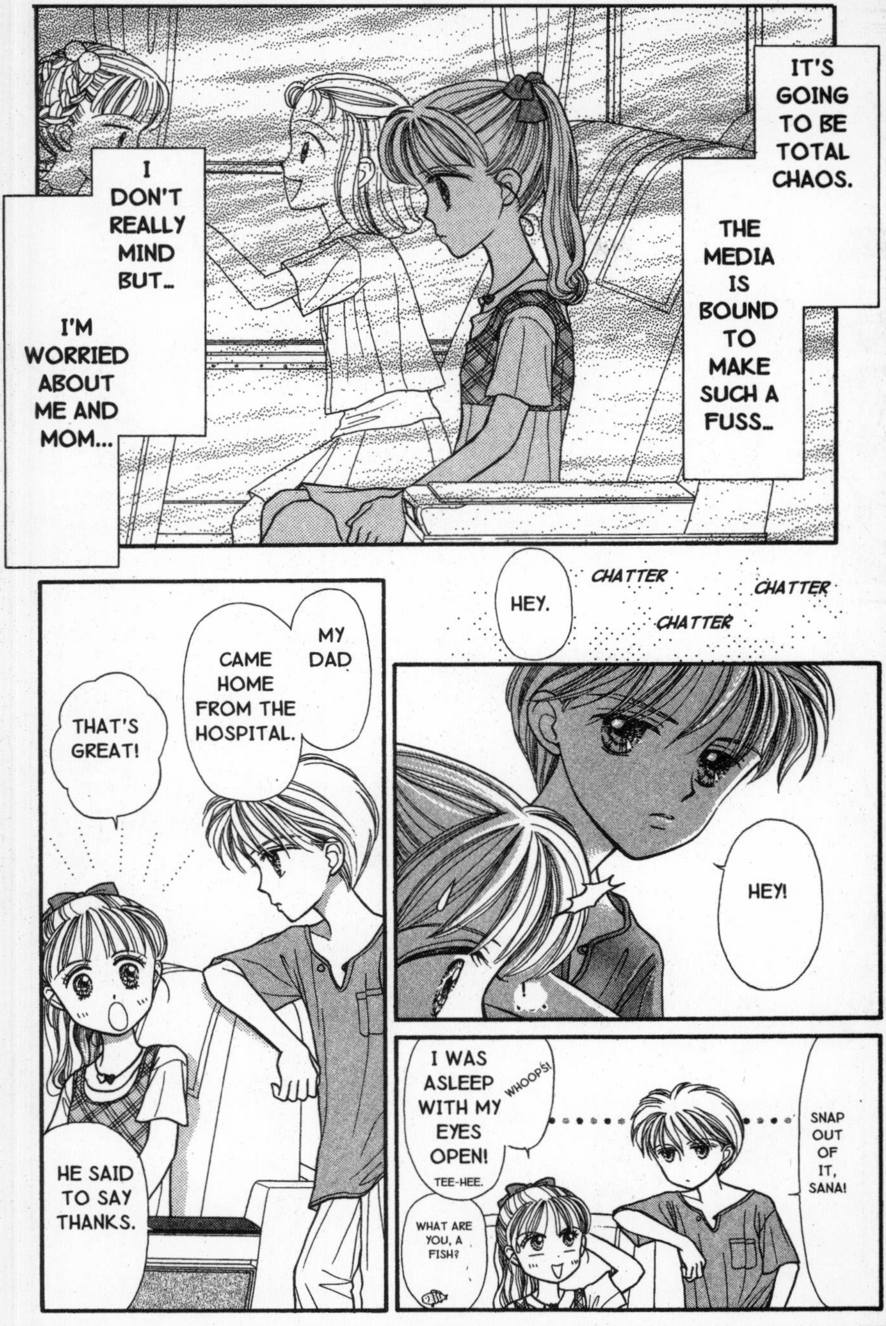
IT'S GOING TO BE TOTAL CHAOS.
THE MEDIA IS BOUND TO MAKE SUCH A FUSS...
I DON'T REALLY MIND BUT...
I'M WORRIED ABOUT ME AND MOM...
HEY.
CHATTER
CHATTER
CHATTER
HEY!
SNAP OUT OF IT, SANA!
WHOOPS!
I WAS ASLEEP WITH MY EYES OPEN!
TEE-HEE.
WHAT ARE YOU, A FISH?
MY DAD CAME HOME FROM THE HOSPITAL.
THAT'S GREAT!
HE SAID TO SAY THANKS.

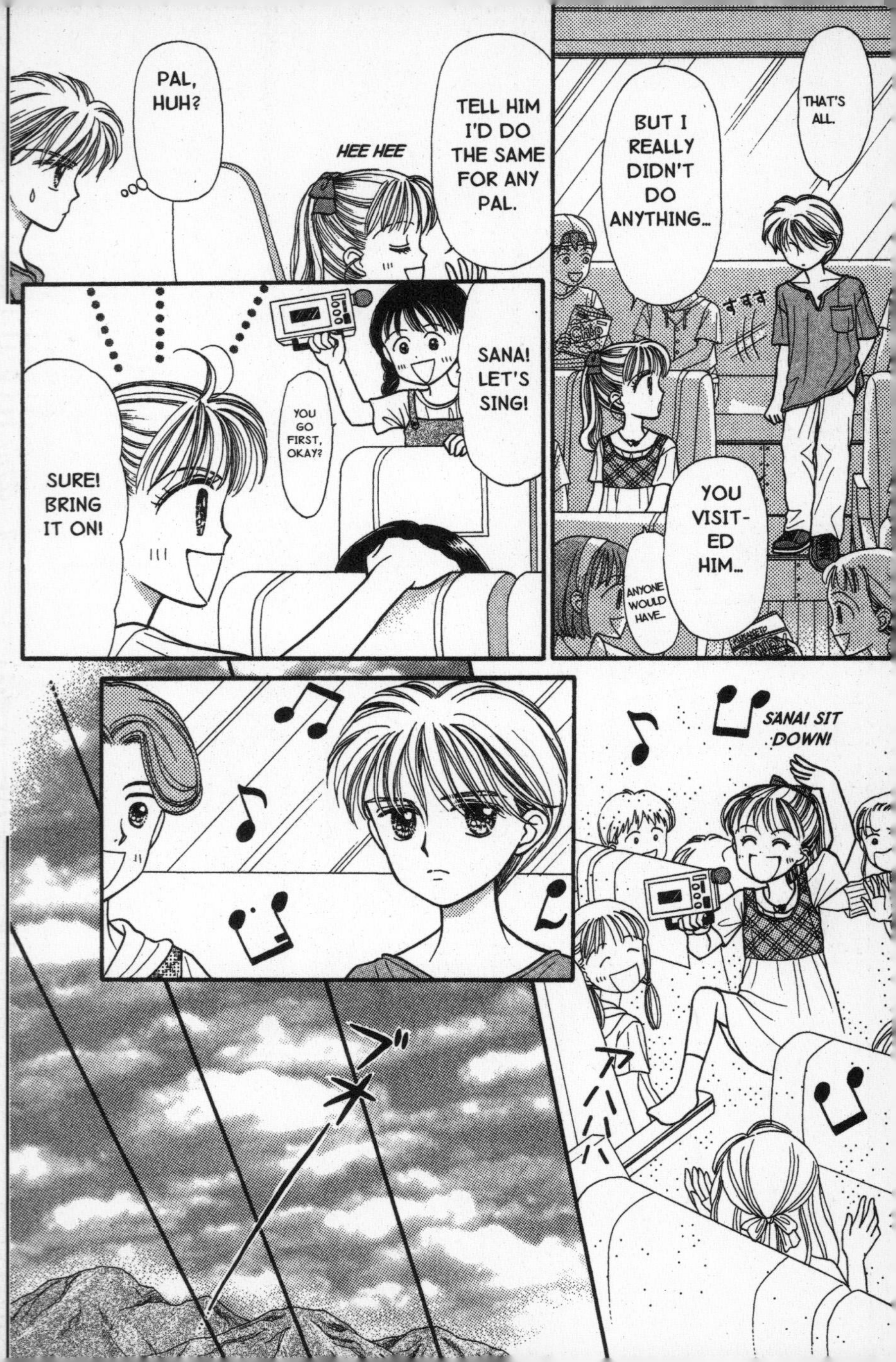
THAT'S ALL.
BUT I REALLY DIDN'T DO ANYTHING...
すすす
YOU VISIT-ED HIM...
ANYONE WOULD HAVE...
TELL HIM I'D DO THE SAME FOR ANY PAL.
HEE HEE
PAL, HUH?
SANA! LET'S SING!
YOU GO FIRST, OKAY?
SURE! BRING IT ON!
SANA! SIT DOWN!

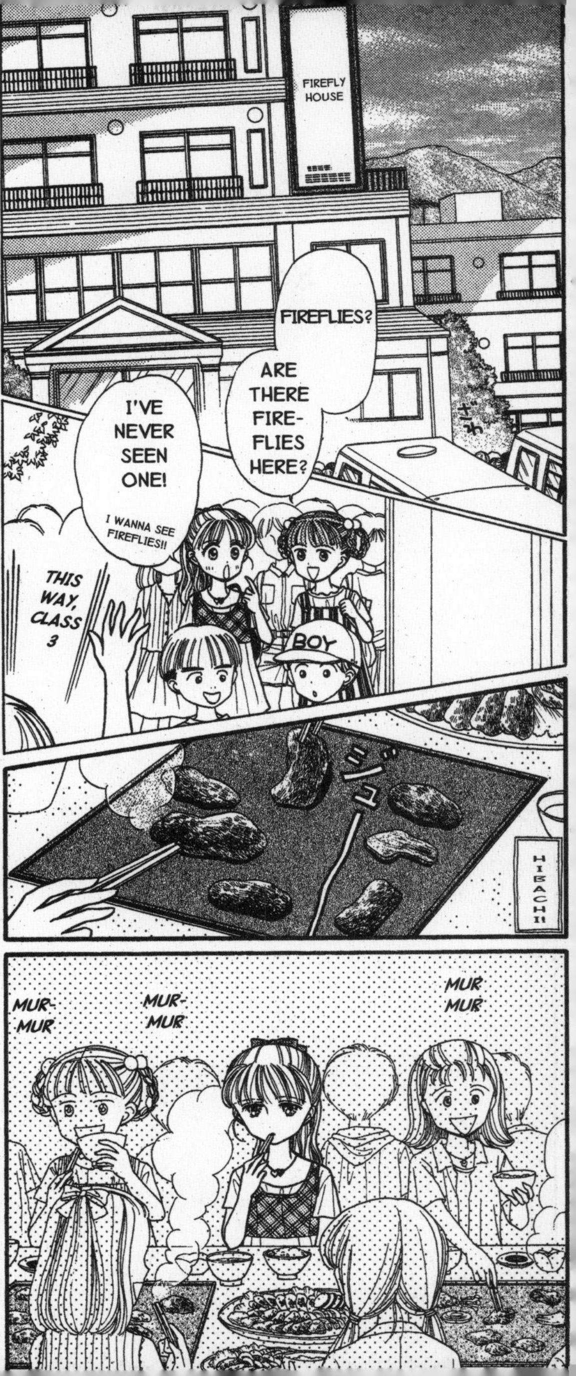
FIREFLY HOUSE
FIREFLIES?
ARE THERE FIRE-FLIES HERE?
I'VE NEVER SEEN ONE!
I WANNA SEE FIREFLIES!!
THIS WAY, CLASS 3
BOY
HIBACHI!!
ジュ
MUR MUR
MUR-MUR
MUR-MUR

All About Chipmunks Pt. 2

My mom said, "Those chipmunks are so cute, you should have them talking! That would be great!" I told her I didn't think it would be so great...

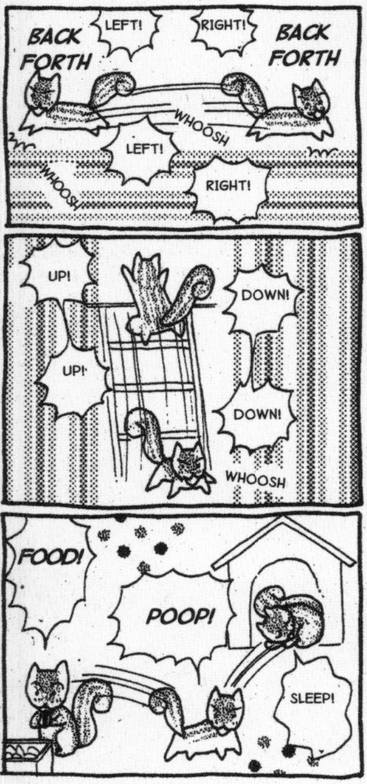
BACK FORTH
RIGHT!
LEFT!
BACK FORTH
WHOOSH
RIGHT!
LEFT!
WHOOSH
DOWN!
UP!
DOWN!
UP!
WHOOSH
POOP!
FOOD!
SLEEP!

because that's what it would be like.

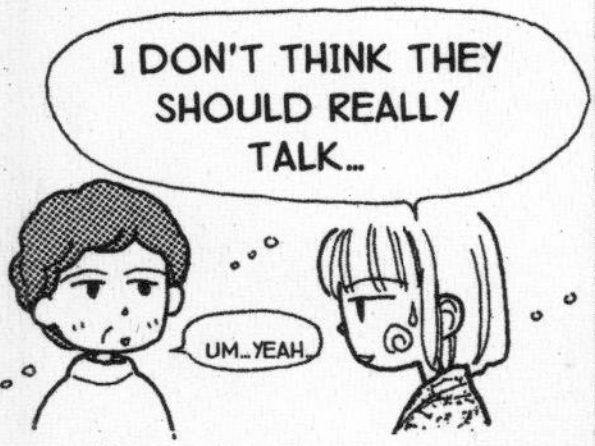
I DON'T THINK THEY SHOULD REALLY TALK...
UM...YEAH.

That's what I told my mom.

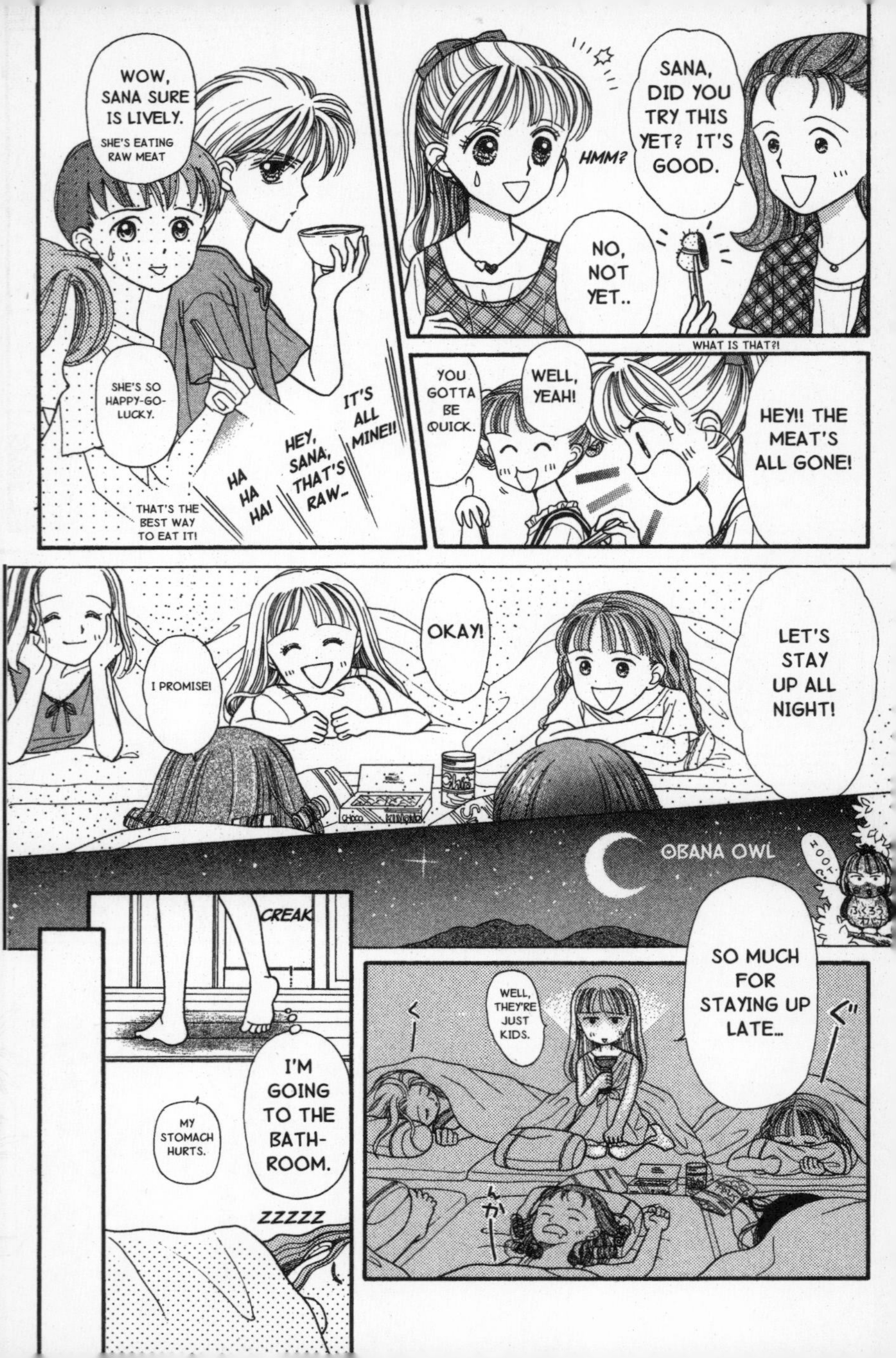
SANA, DID YOU TRY THIS YET? IT'S GOOD.
HMM?
NO, NOT YET..
WHAT IS THAT?!
HEY!! THE MEAT'S ALL GONE!
WELL, YEAH!
YOU GOTTA BE QUICK.
WOW, SANA SURE IS LIVELY.
SHE'S EATING RAW MEAT
IT'S ALL MINE!!
HEY, SANA, THAT'S RAW..
HA HA HA!
SHE'S SO HAPPY-GO-LUCKY.
THAT'S THE BEST WAY TO EAT IT!
LET'S STAY UP ALL NIGHT!
OKAY!
I PROMISE!
OBANA OWL
HOOT
SO MUCH FOR STAYING UP LATE...
WELL, THEY'RE JUST KIDS.
CREAK
I'M GOING TO THE BATHROOM.
MY STOMACH HURTS.
ZZZZZ

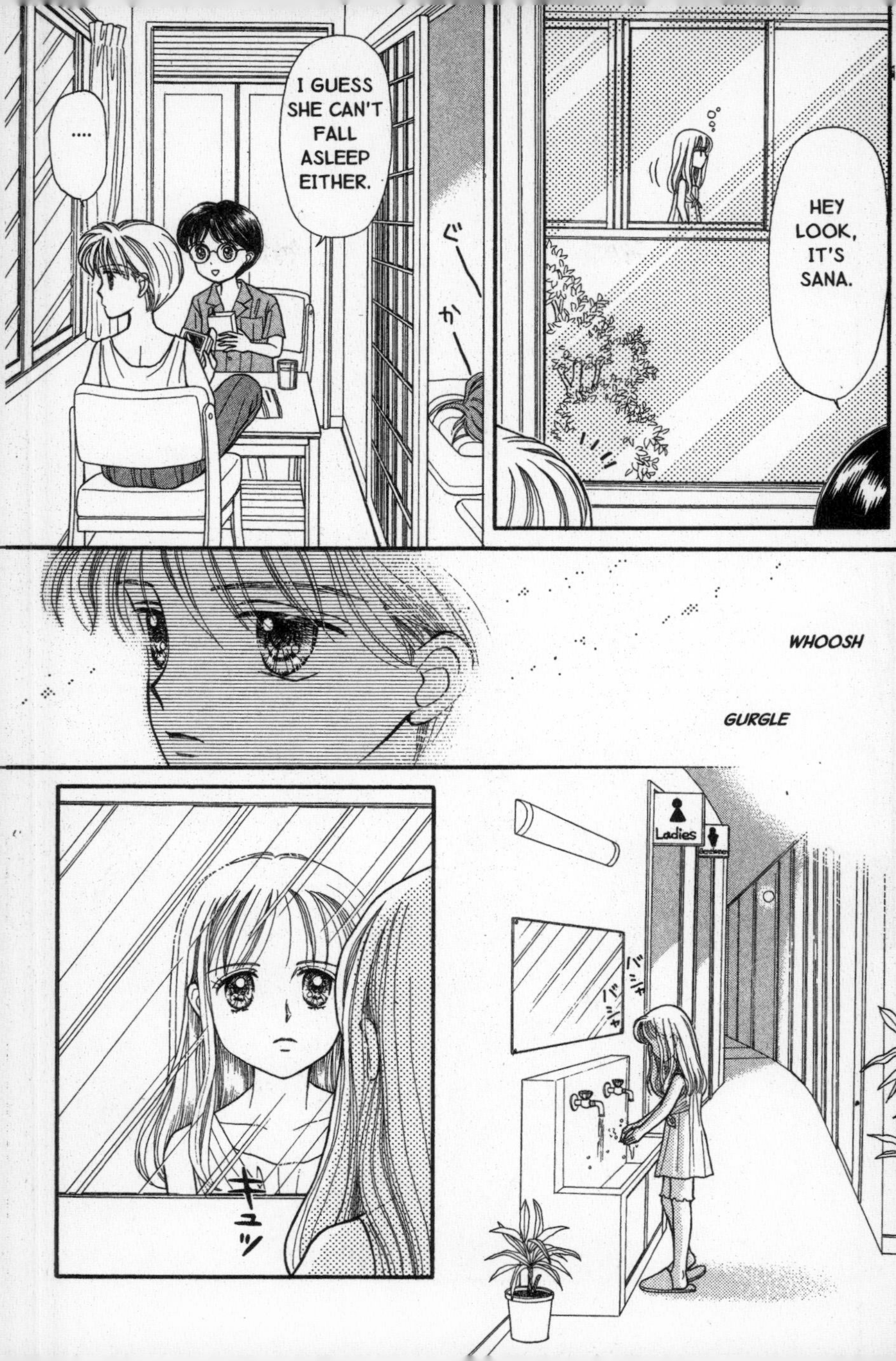
HEY LOOK, IT'S SANA.
I GUESS SHE CAN'T FALL ASLEEP EITHER.
....
ぐー
かー
WHOOSH
GURGLE
Ladies
バシャ
バシャ
キュッ

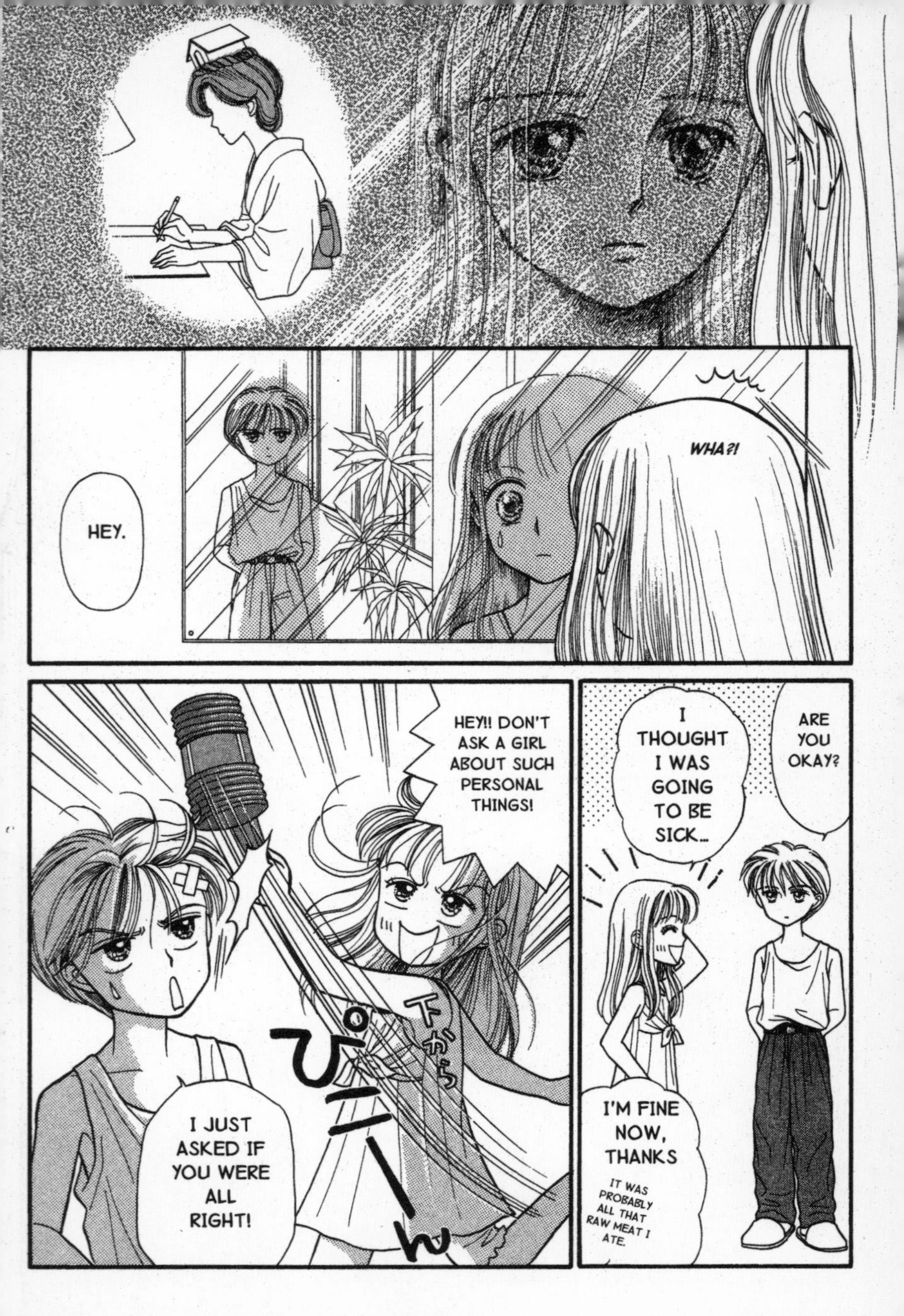
WHA?!
HEY.
ARE YOU OKAY?
I THOUGHT I WAS GOING TO BE SICK...
I'M FINE NOW, THANKS
IT WAS PROBABLY ALL THAT RAW MEAT I ATE.
HEY!! DON'T ASK A GIRL ABOUT SUCH PERSONAL THINGS!
下から
I JUST ASKED IF YOU WERE ALL RIGHT!

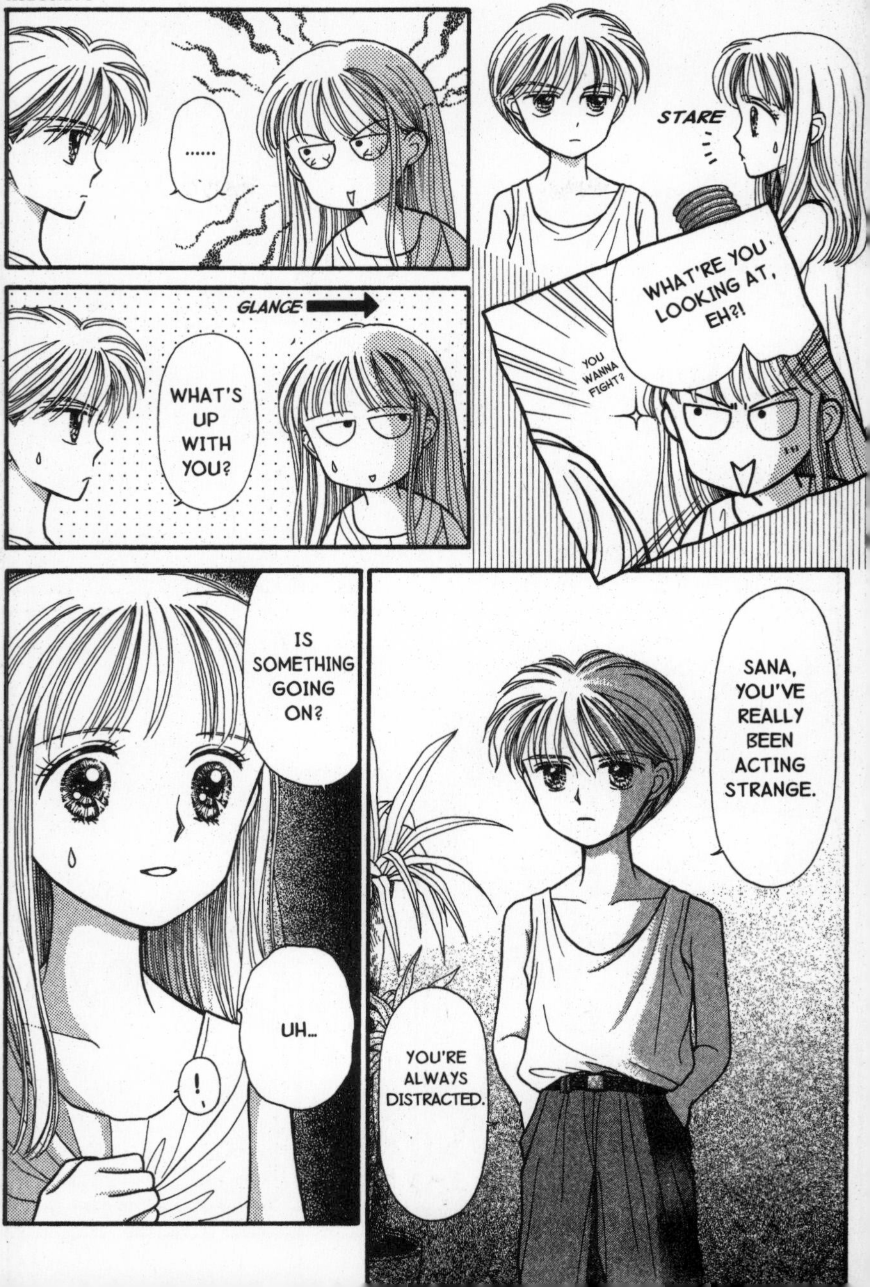
STARE
WHAT'RE YOU LOOKING AT, EH?!
YOU WANNA FIGHT?
......
GLANCE
WHAT'S UP WITH YOU?
SANA, YOU'VE REALLY BEEN ACTING STRANGE.
YOU'RE ALWAYS DISTRACTED.
IS SOMETHING GOING ON?
UH...
!

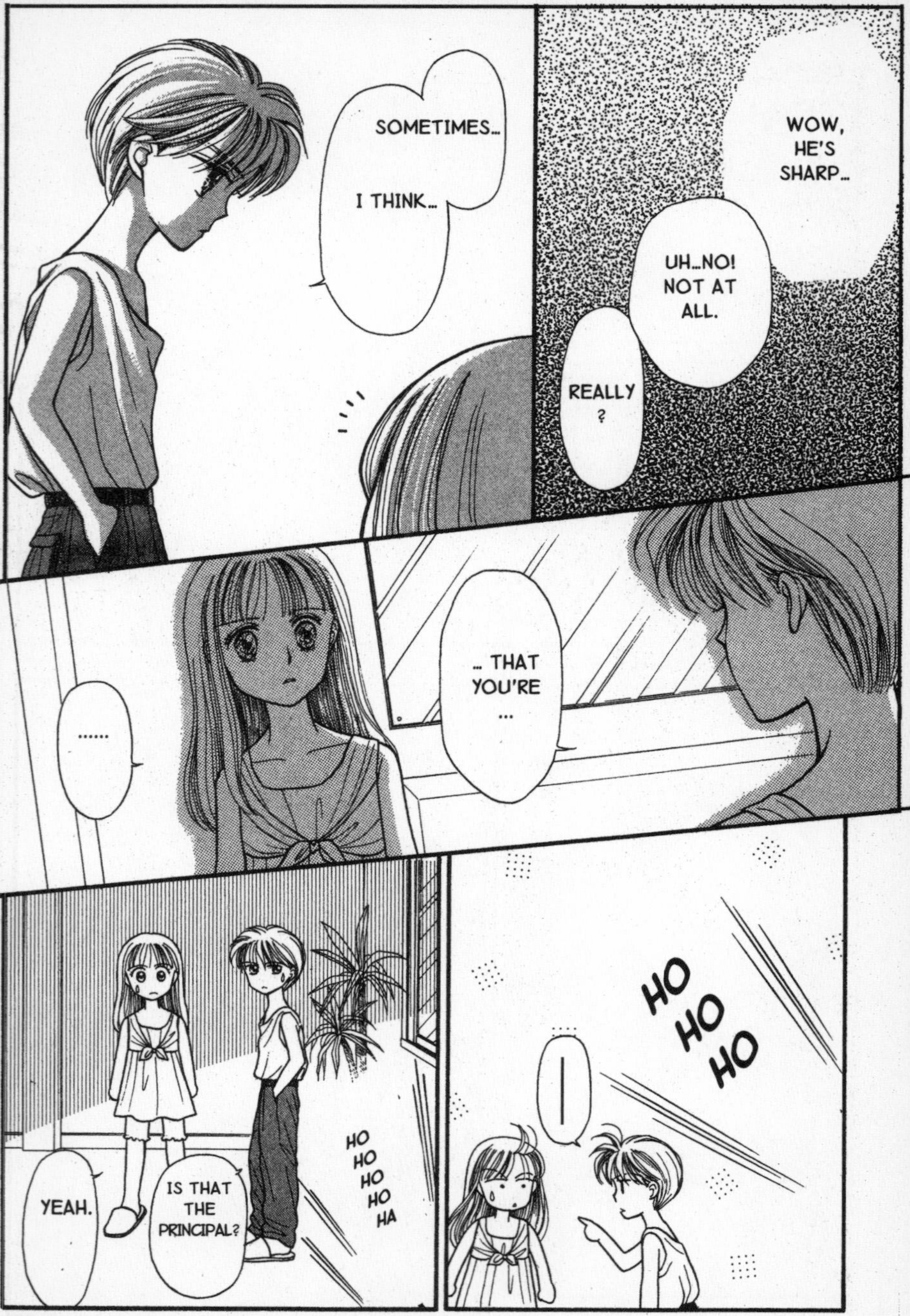
WOW, HE'S SHARP...
UH...NO! NOT AT ALL.
REALLY?
SOMETIMES...
I THINK...
... THAT YOU'RE ...
......
HO HO HO
!
HO HO HO HO HA
IS THAT THE PRINCIPAL?
YEAH.

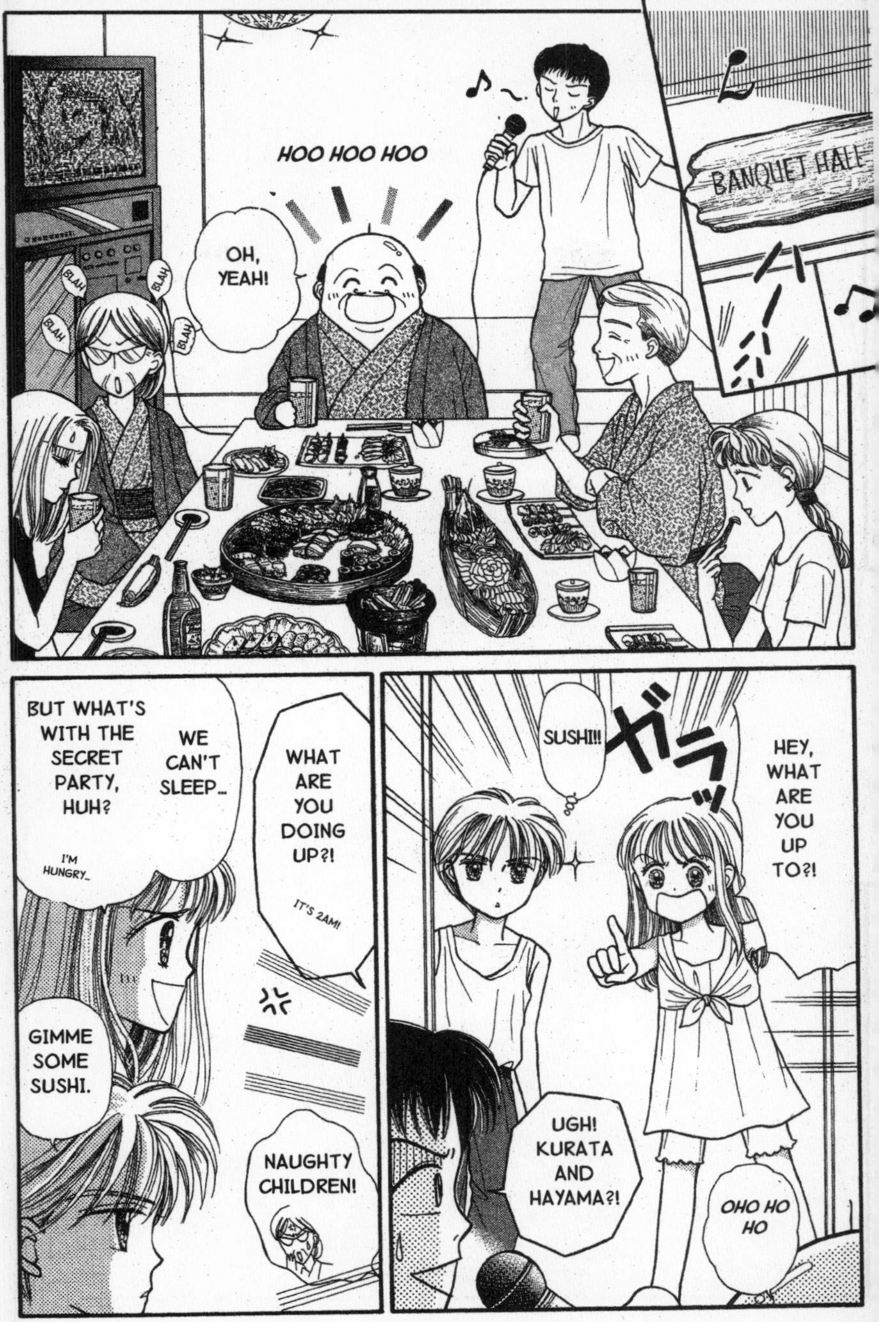
BANQUET HALL
HOO HOO HOO
OH, YEAH!
BLAH
BLAH
BLAH
BLAH
HEY, WHAT ARE YOU UP TO?!
ガラッ
SUSHI!!
UGH! KURATA AND HAYAMA?!
OHO HO HO
WHAT ARE YOU DOING UP?!
IT'S 2AM!
WE CAN'T SLEEP...
BUT WHAT'S WITH THE SECRET PARTY, HUH?
I'M HUNGRY...
GIMME SOME SUSHI.
NAUGHTY CHILDREN!

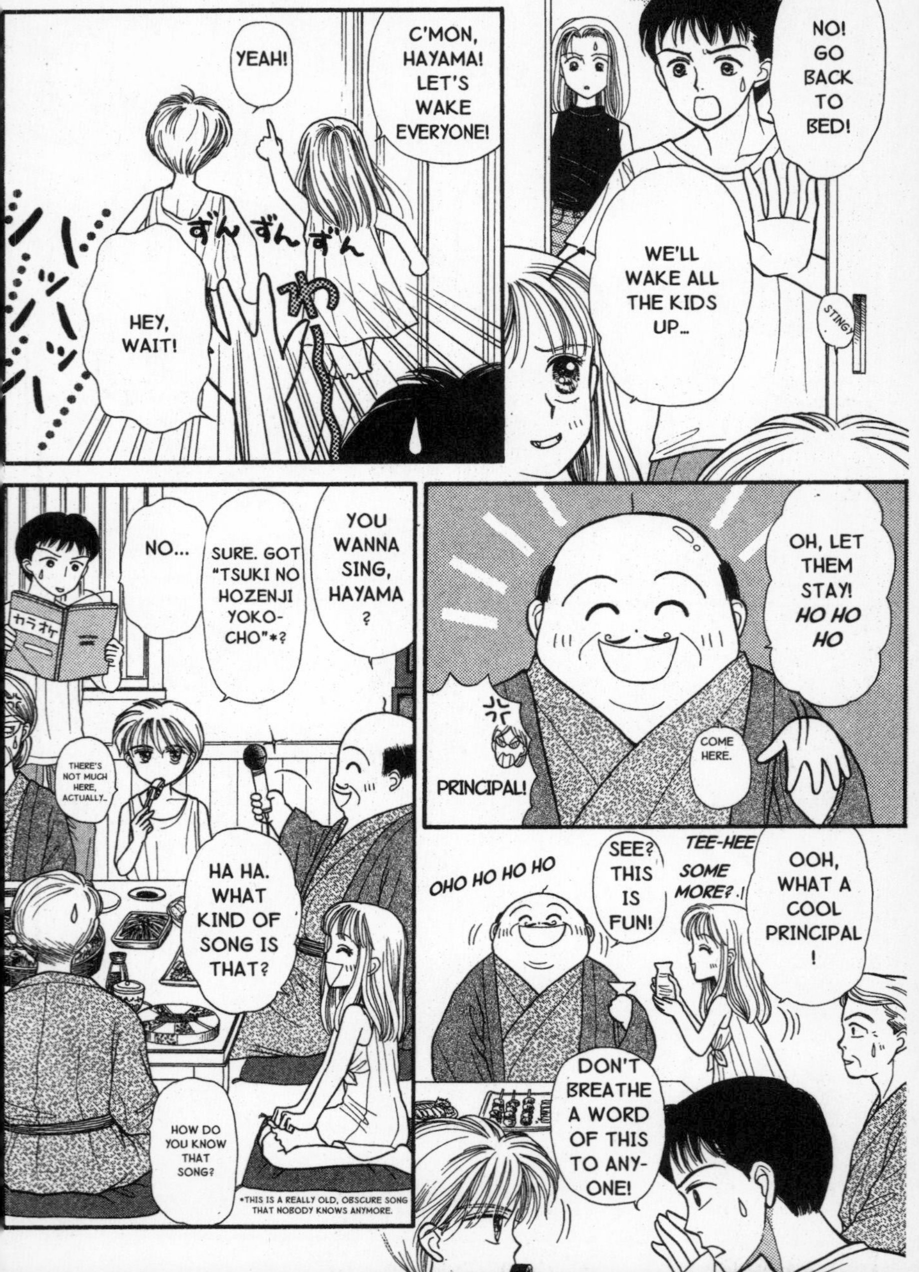
NO! GO BACK TO BED!
WE'LL WAKE ALL THE KIDS UP...
STINGY
C'MON, HAYAMA! LET'S WAKE EVERYONE!
YEAH!
ずんずんずん
HEY, WAIT!
OH, LET THEM STAY! HO HO HO
COME HERE.
PRINCIPAL!
OOH, WHAT A COOL PRINCIPAL!
TEE-HEE
SOME MORE?
SEE? THIS IS FUN!
OHO HO HO HO
DON'T BREATHE A WORD OF THIS TO ANY-ONE!
YOU WANNA SING, HAYAMA?
SURE. GOT "TSUKI NO HOZENJI YOKO-CHO"*?
NO...
カラオケ
THERE'S NOT MUCH HERE, ACTUALLY...
HA HA. WHAT KIND OF SONG IS THAT?
HOW DO YOU KNOW THAT SONG?
*THIS IS A REALLY OLD, OBSCURE SONG THAT NOBODY KNOWS ANYMORE.

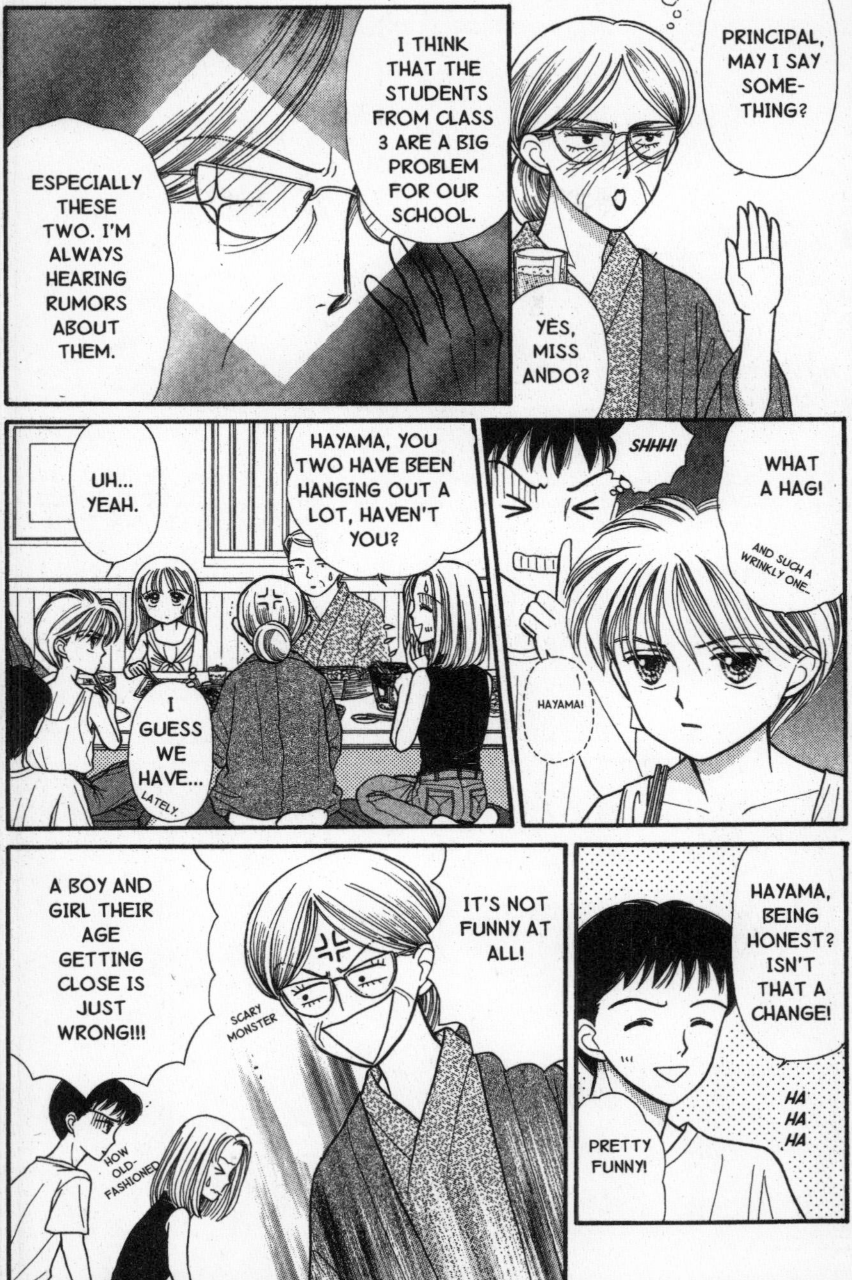
PRINCIPAL, MAY I SAY SOME-THING?
YES, MISS ANDO?
I THINK THAT THE STUDENTS FROM CLASS 3 ARE A BIG PROBLEM FOR OUR SCHOOL.
ESPECIALLY THESE TWO. I'M ALWAYS HEARING RUMORS ABOUT THEM.
WHAT A HAG!
AND SUCH A WRINKLY ONE...
SHHH!
HAYAMA!
HAYAMA, YOU TWO HAVE BEEN HANGING OUT A LOT, HAVEN'T YOU?
UH... YEAH.
I GUESS WE HAVE...
LATELY.
HAYAMA, BEING HONEST? ISN'T THAT A CHANGE!
HA HA HA
PRETTY FUNNY!
IT'S NOT FUNNY AT ALL!
A BOY AND GIRL THEIR AGE GETTING CLOSE IS JUST WRONG!!!
SCARY MONSTER
HOW OLD-FASHIONED

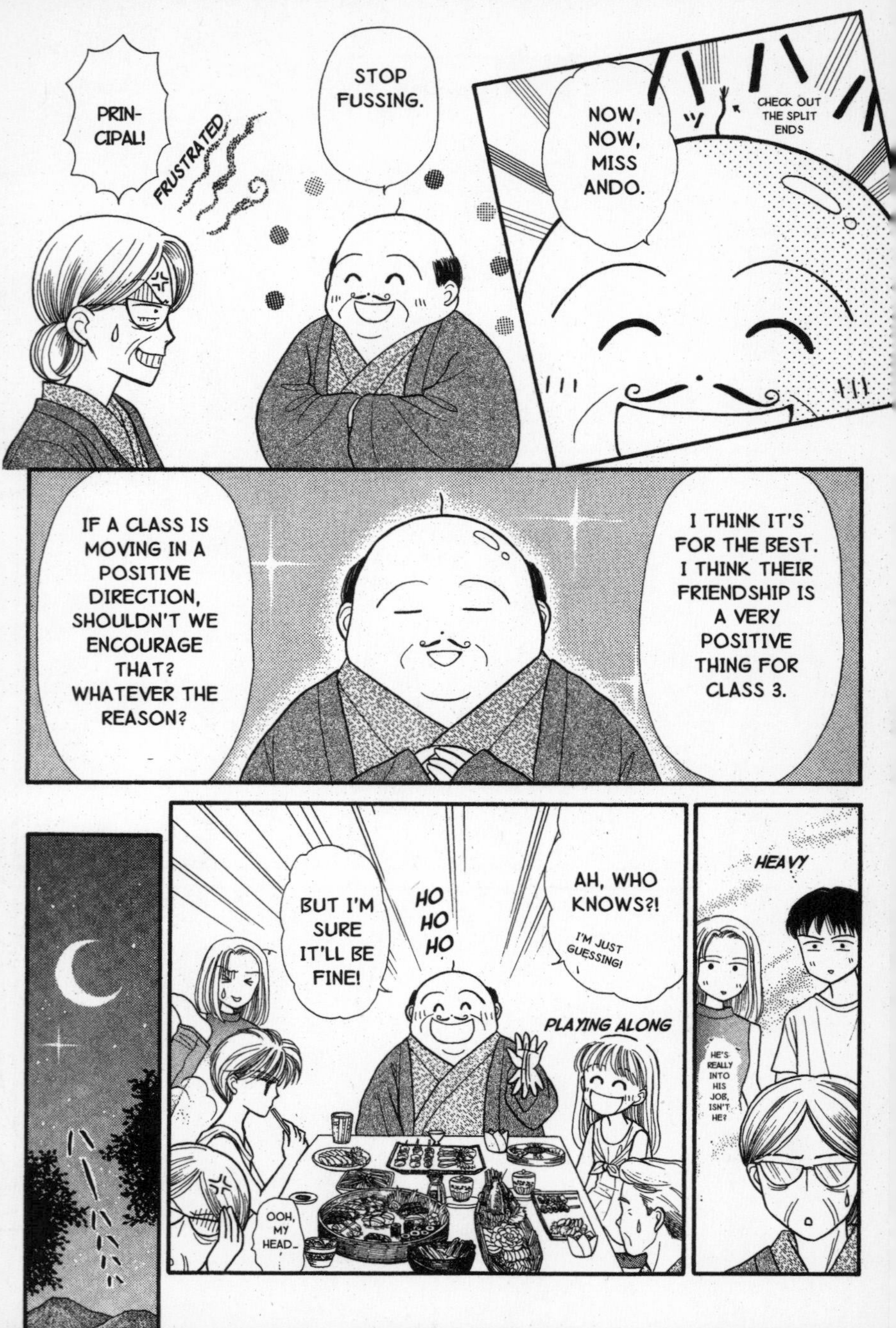
NOW, NOW, MISS ANDO.
CHECK OUT THE SPLIT ENDS
STOP FUSSING.
PRIN-CIPAL!
FRUSTRATED
I THINK IT'S FOR THE BEST. I THINK THEIR FRIENDSHIP IS A VERY POSITIVE THING FOR CLASS 3.
IF A CLASS IS MOVING IN A POSITIVE DIRECTION, SHOULDN'T WE ENCOURAGE THAT? WHATEVER THE REASON?
HEAVY
HE'S REALLY INTO HIS JOB, ISN'T HE?
AH, WHO KNOWS?!
I'M JUST GUESSING!
HO HO HO
BUT I'M SURE IT'LL BE FINE!
PLAYING ALONG
OOH, MY HEAD...

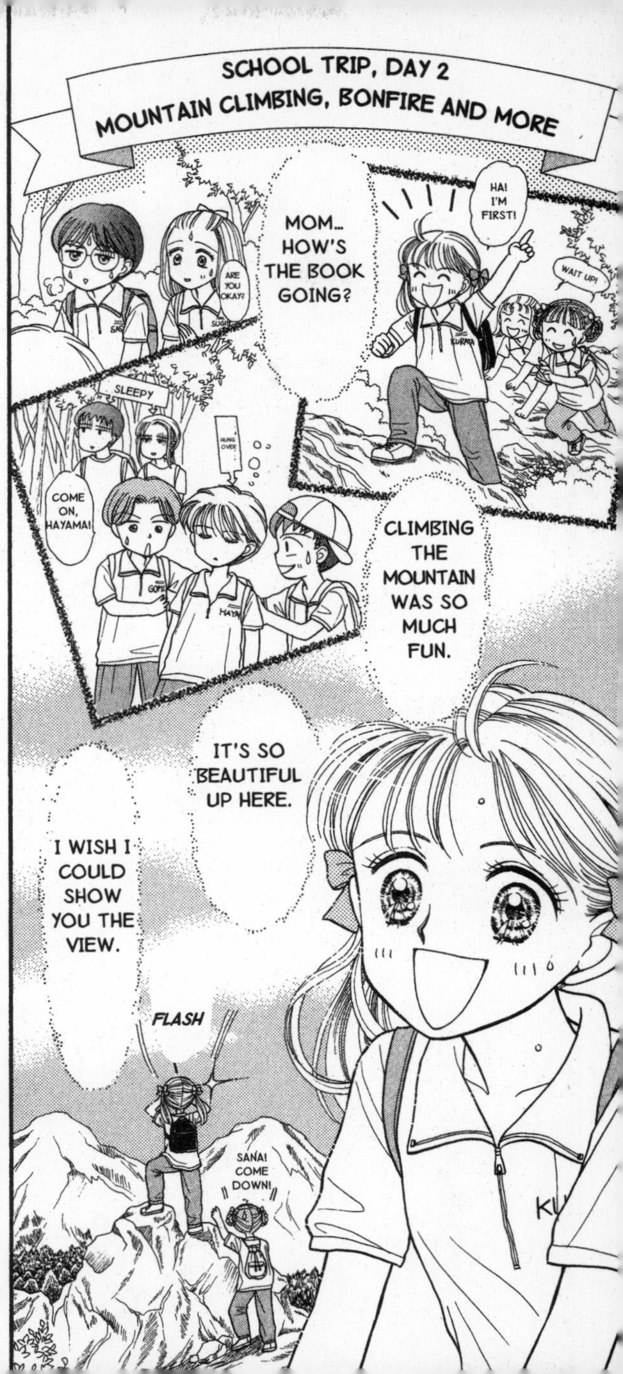
SCHOOL TRIP, DAY 2
MOUNTAIN CLIMBING, BONFIRE AND MORE
MOM... HOW'S THE BOOK GOING?
HA! I'M FIRST!
WAIT UP!
ARE YOU OKAY?
SLEEPY
HUNG OVER
COME ON, HAYAMA!
CLIMBING THE MOUNTAIN WAS SO MUCH FUN.
IT'S SO BEAUTIFUL UP HERE.
I WISH I COULD SHOW YOU THE VIEW.
FLASH
SANA! COME DOWN!

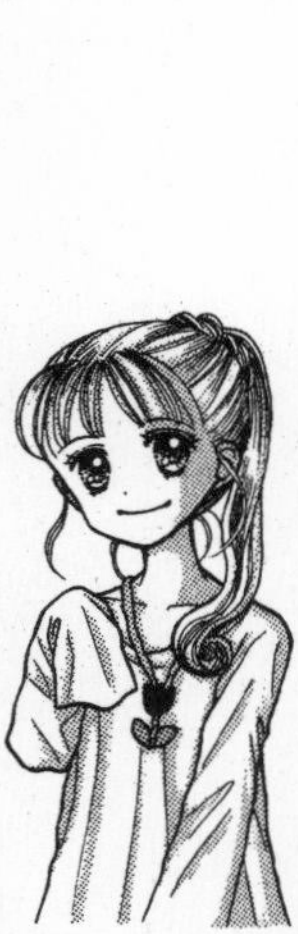

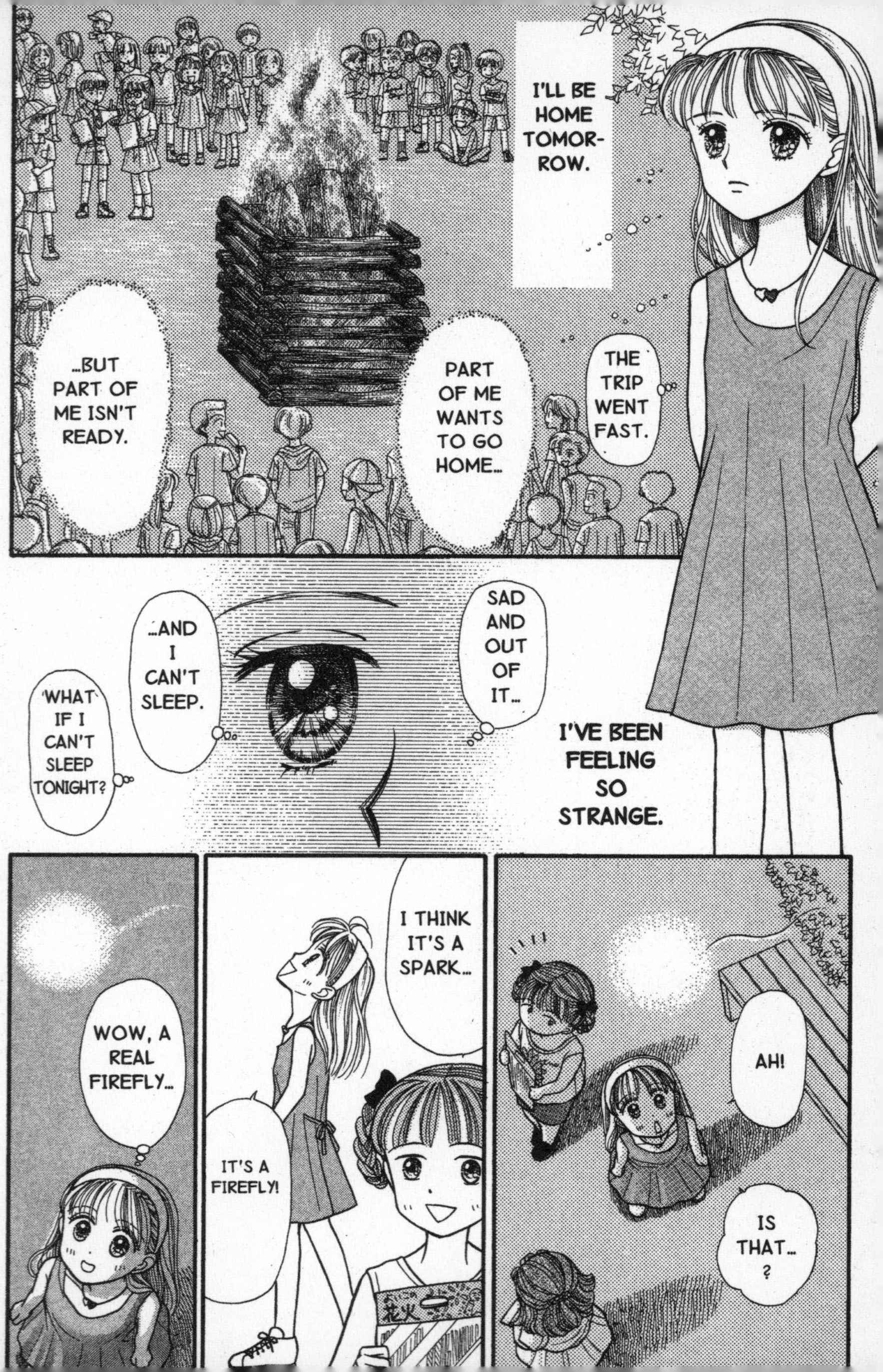

I'LL BE HOME TOMOR-ROW.
THE TRIP WENT FAST.
PART OF ME WANTS TO GO HOME...
...BUT PART OF ME ISN'T READY.
I'VE BEEN FEELING SO STRANGE.
SAD AND OUT OF IT...
...AND I CAN'T SLEEP.
WHAT IF I CAN'T SLEEP TONIGHT?
AH!
IS THAT... ?
I THINK IT'S A SPARK...
IT'S A FIREFLY!
花火
WOW, A REAL FIREFLY...

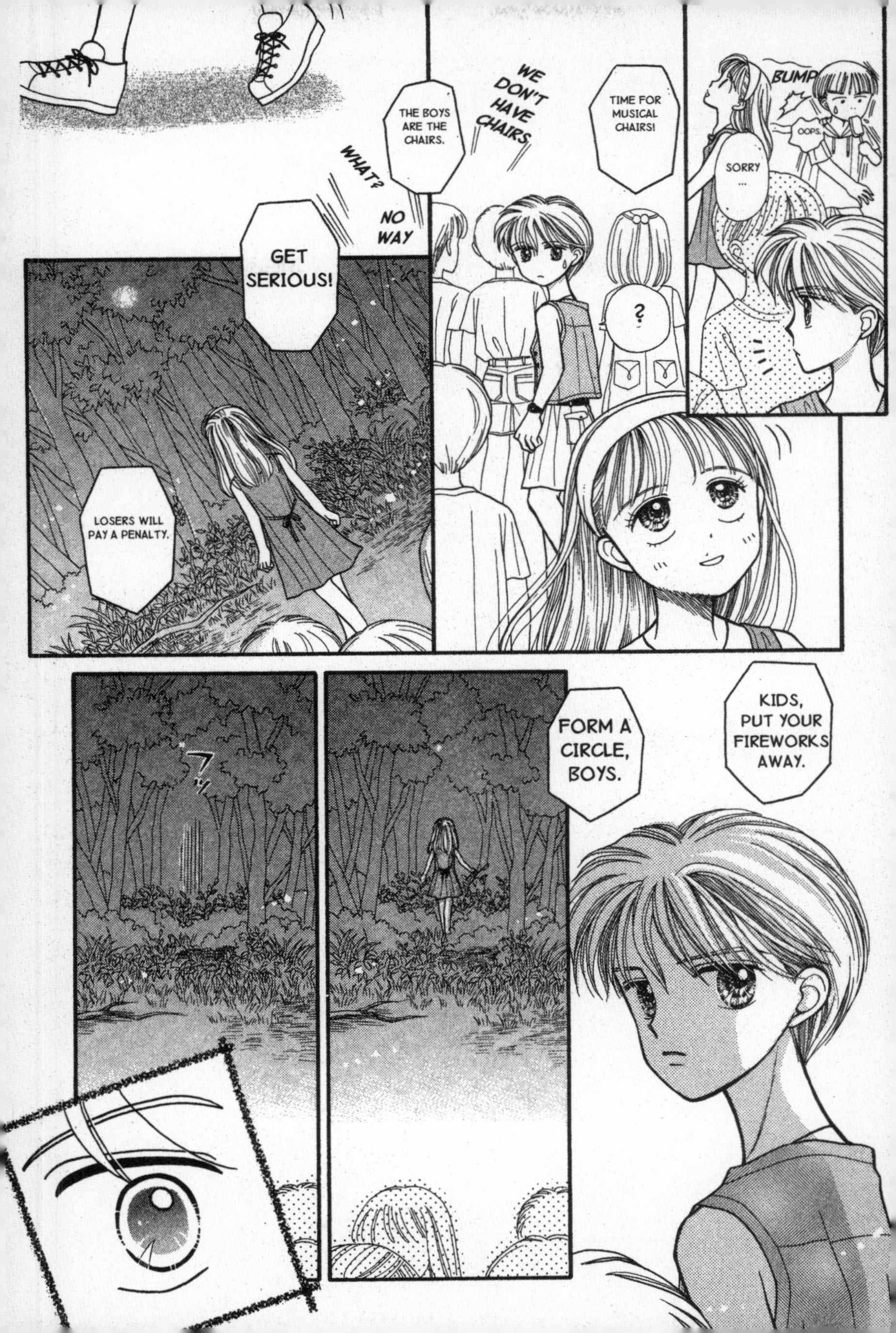
BUMP
OOPS.
SORRY ...
TIME FOR MUSICAL CHAIRS!
WE DON'T HAVE CHAIRS
THE BOYS ARE THE CHAIRS.
WHAT?
NO WAY
?
GET SERIOUS!
LOSERS WILL PAY A PENALTY.
KIDS, PUT YOUR FIREWORKS AWAY.
FORM A CIRCLE, BOYS.

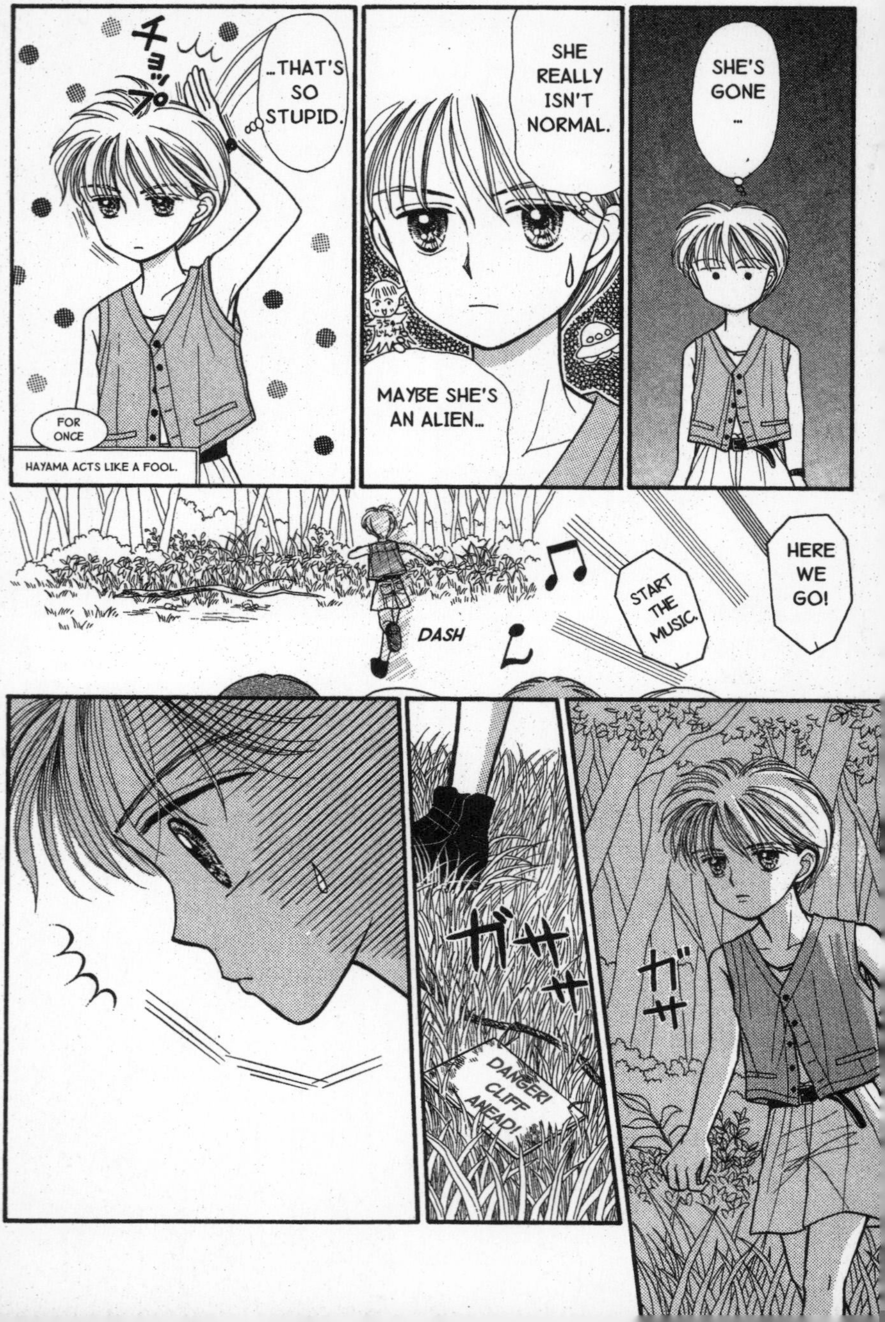
SHE'S GONE ...
SHE REALLY ISN'T NORMAL.
MAYBE SHE'S AN ALIEN...
チョップ
...THAT'S SO STUPID.
FOR ONCE
HAYAMA ACTS LIKE A FOOL.
HERE WE GO!
START THE MUSIC.
DASH
ガサ
ガサササ
DANGER! CLIFF AHEAD!

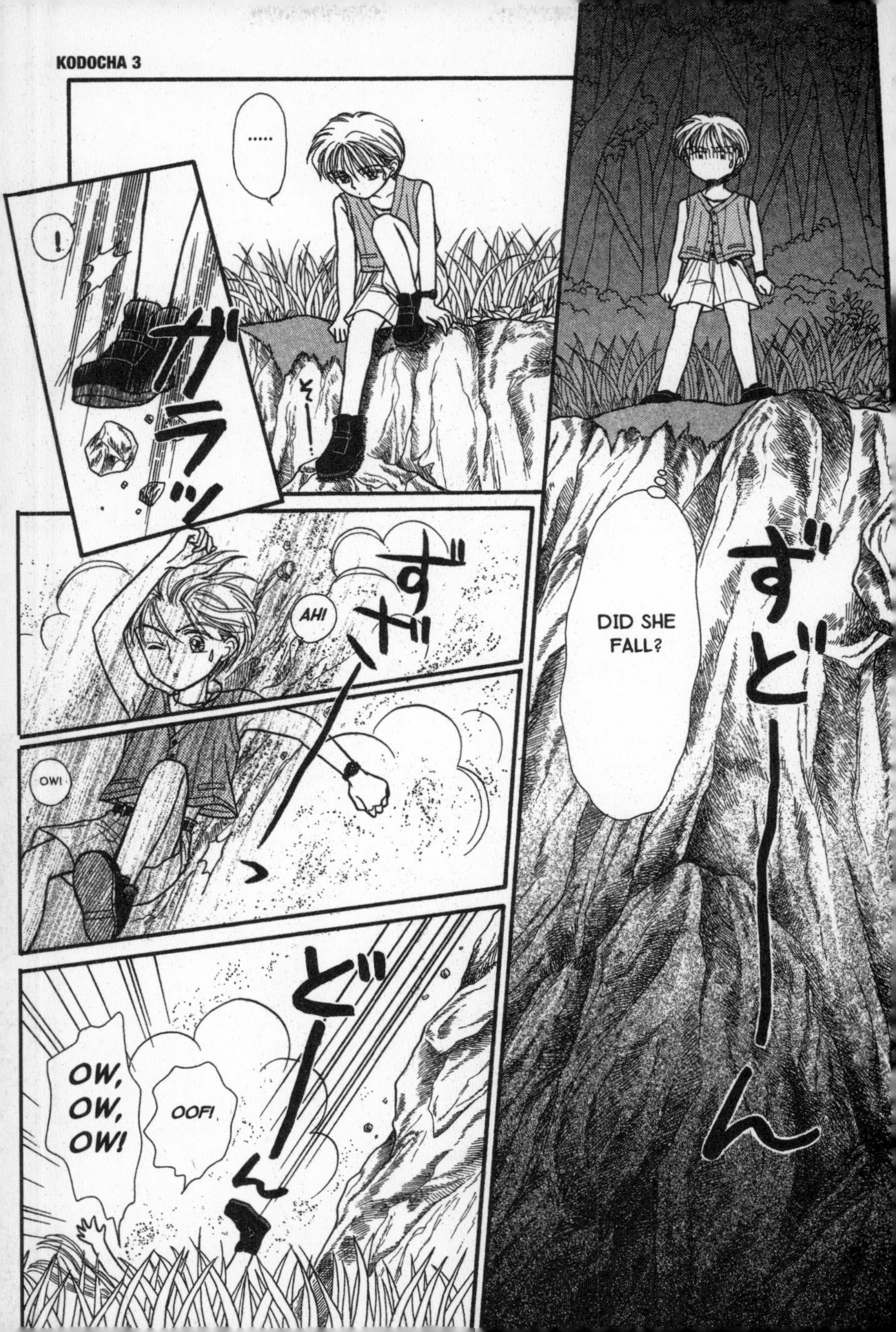
ずどーん
DID SHE FALL?
......
!
ガラッ
AH!
OW!
OOF!
OW, OW, OW!
どーん

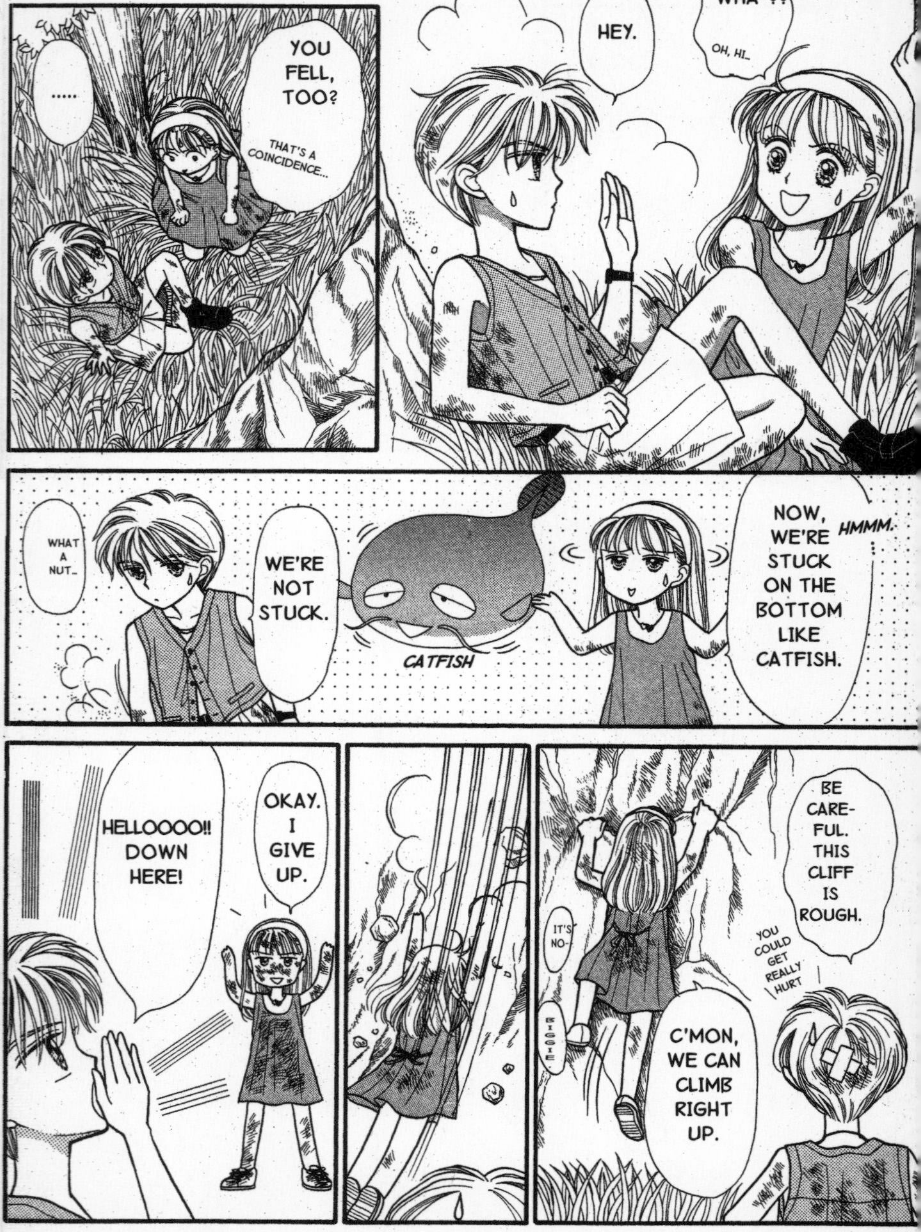
HEY.
WHA-??
OH, HI...
YOU FELL, TOO?
THAT'S A COINCIDENCE...
.....
NOW, WE'RE STUCK ON THE BOTTOM LIKE CATFISH.
HMMM.
CATFISH
WE'RE NOT STUCK.
WHAT A NUT...
BE CARE-FUL. THIS CLIFF IS ROUGH.
YOU COULD GET REALLY HURT
IT'S NO-
BIGGIE.
C'MON, WE CAN CLIMB RIGHT UP.
OKAY. I GIVE UP.
HELLOOOO!! DOWN HERE!

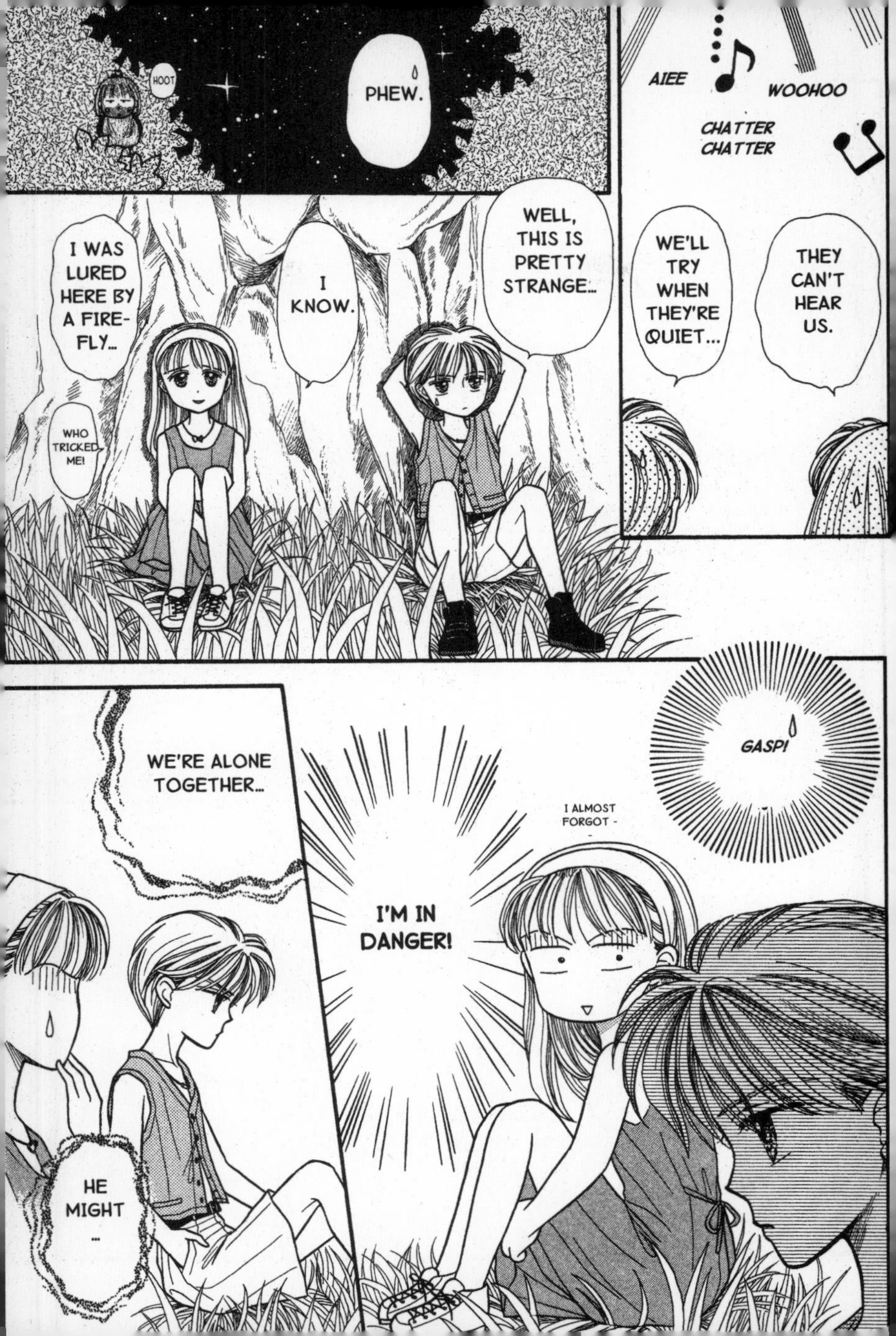

WOOHOO
AIEE
CHATTER CHATTER
THEY CAN'T HEAR US.
WE'LL TRY WHEN THEY'RE QUIET...
PHEW.
HOOT
WELL, THIS IS PRETTY STRANGE...
I KNOW.
I WAS LURED HERE BY A FIRE-FLY...
WHO TRICKED ME!
GASP!
I ALMOST FORGOT -
I'M IN DANGER!
WE'RE ALONE TOGETHER...
HE MIGHT ...

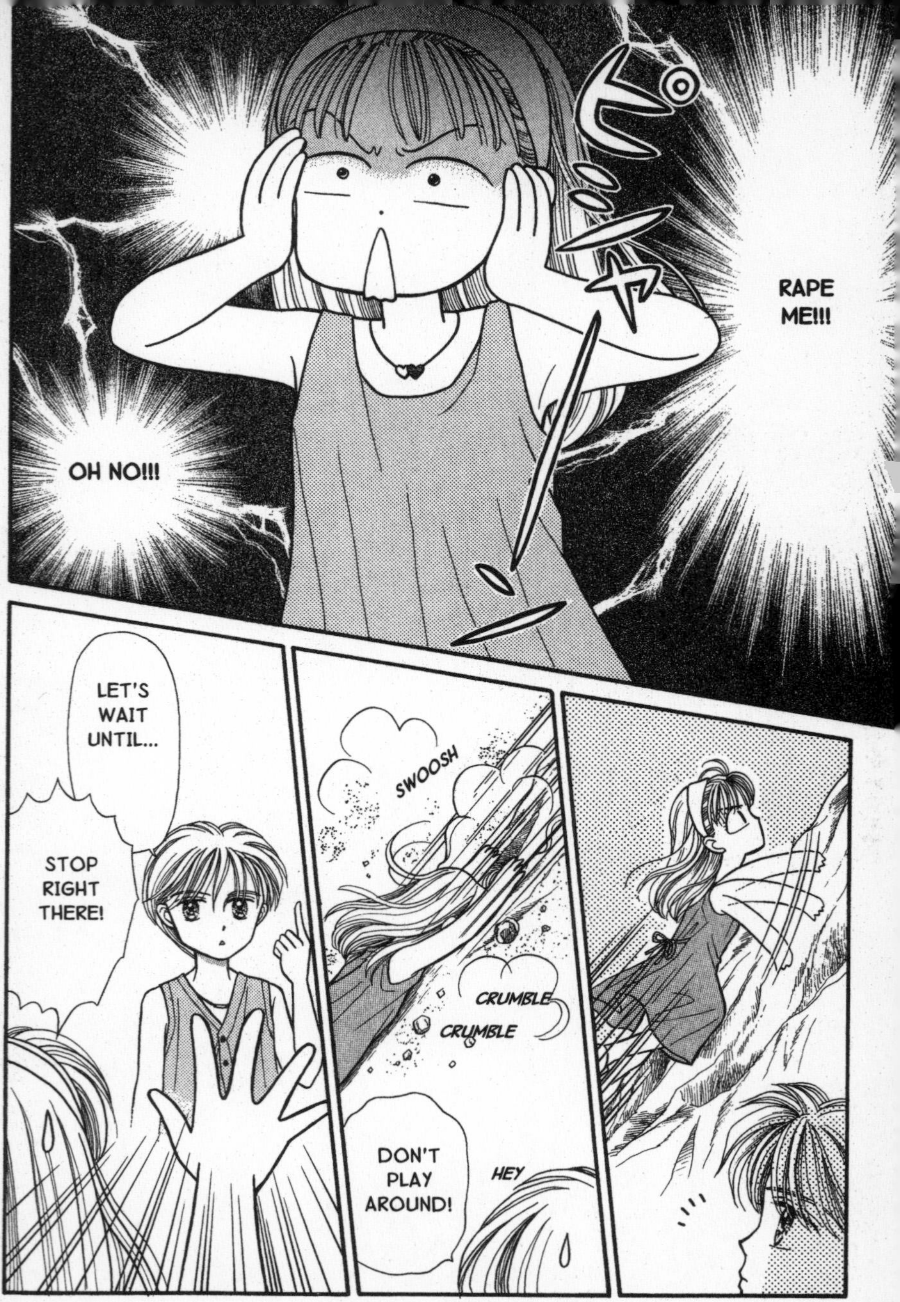
RAPE ME!!!
OH NO!!!
SWOOSH
CRUMBLE
CRUMBLE
DON'T PLAY AROUND!
HEY
LET'S WAIT UNTIL...
STOP RIGHT THERE!

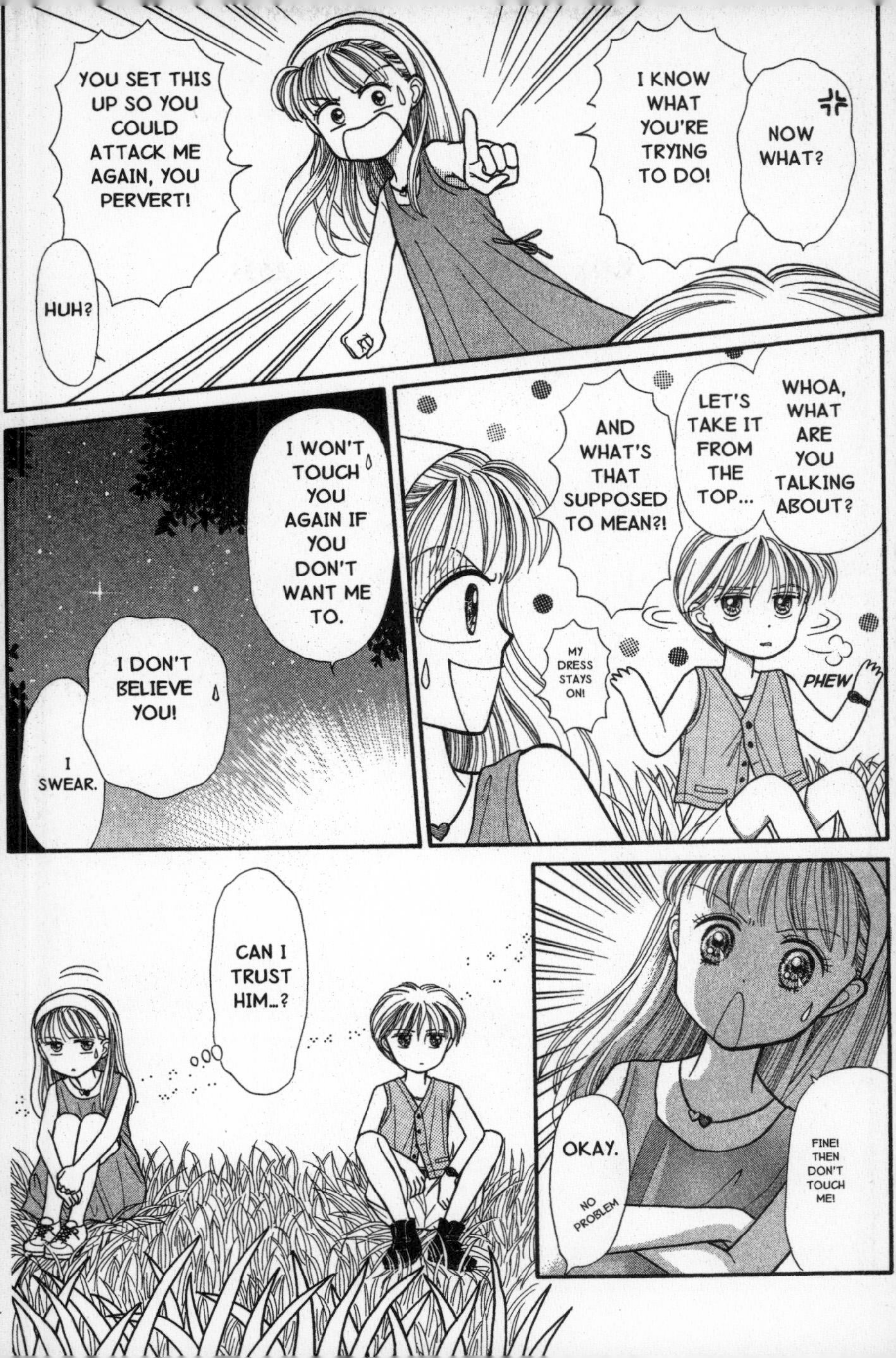
NOW WHAT?
I KNOW WHAT YOU'RE TRYING TO DO!
YOU SET THIS UP SO YOU COULD ATTACK ME AGAIN, YOU PERVERT!
HUH?
WHOA, WHAT ARE YOU TALKING ABOUT?
LET'S TAKE IT FROM THE TOP...
AND WHAT'S THAT SUPPOSED TO MEAN?!
PHEW
MY DRESS STAYS ON!
I WON'T TOUCH YOU AGAIN IF YOU DON'T WANT ME TO.
I DON'T BELIEVE YOU!
I SWEAR.
FINE! THEN DON'T TOUCH ME!
OKAY.
NO PROBLEM
CAN I TRUST HIM...?

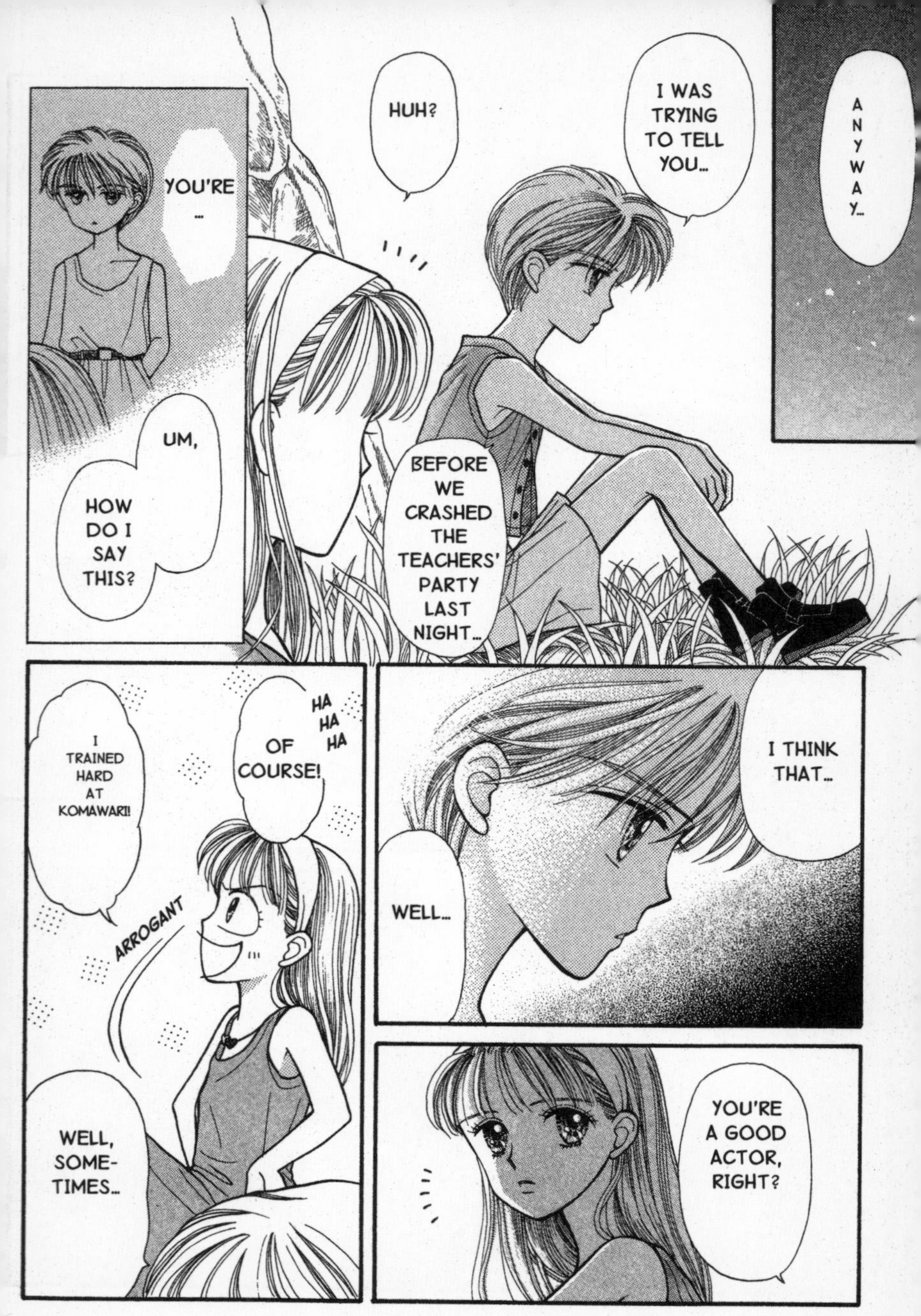
ANYWAY...
I WAS TRYING TO TELL YOU...
HUH?
BEFORE WE CRASHED THE TEACHERS' PARTY LAST NIGHT...
UM,
HOW DO I SAY THIS?
YOU'RE ...
I THINK THAT...
WELL...
YOU'RE A GOOD ACTOR, RIGHT?
HA HA HA
OF COURSE!
I TRAINED HARD AT KOMAWARI!
ARROGANT
WELL, SOMETIMES...

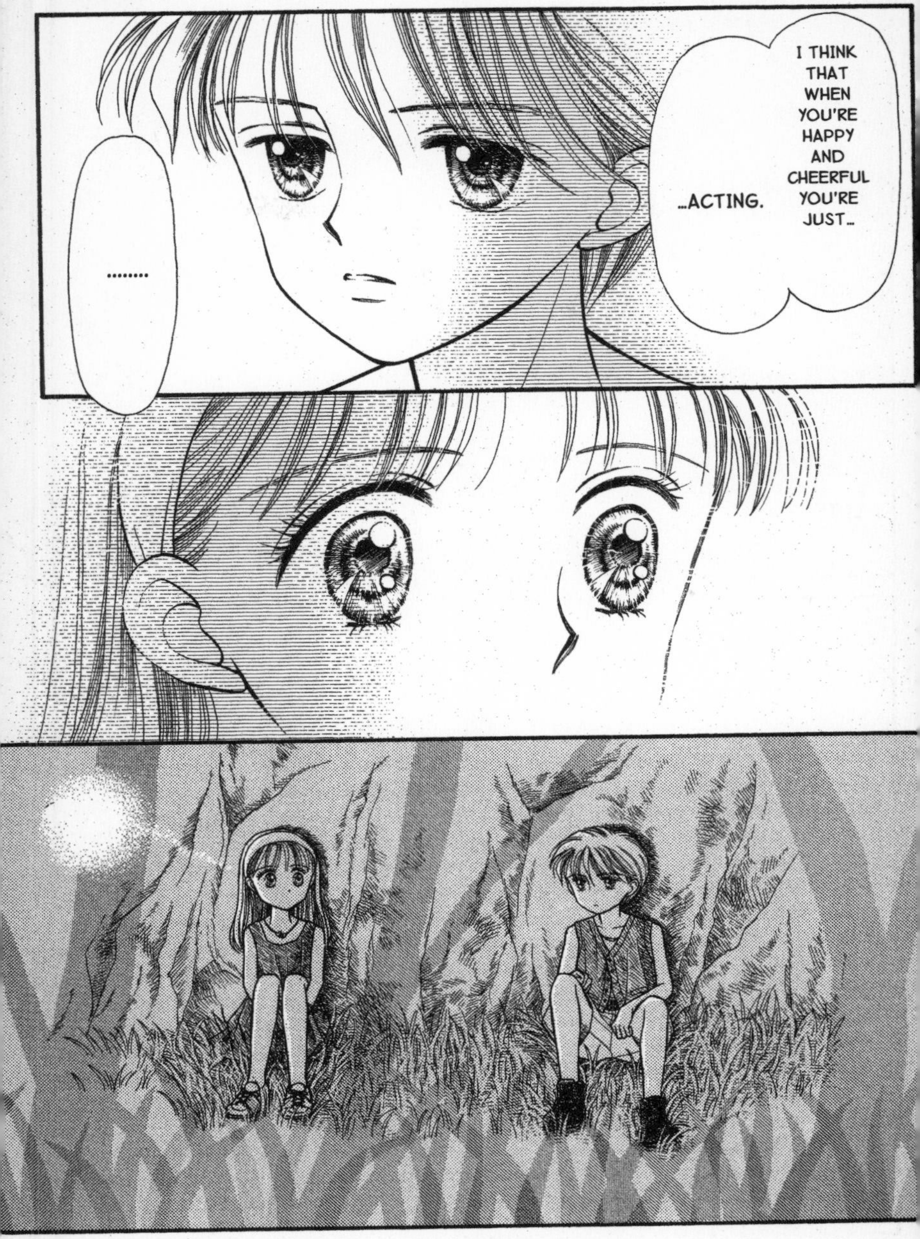
I THINK THAT WHEN YOU'RE HAPPY AND CHEERFUL YOU'RE JUST...
...ACTING.
....

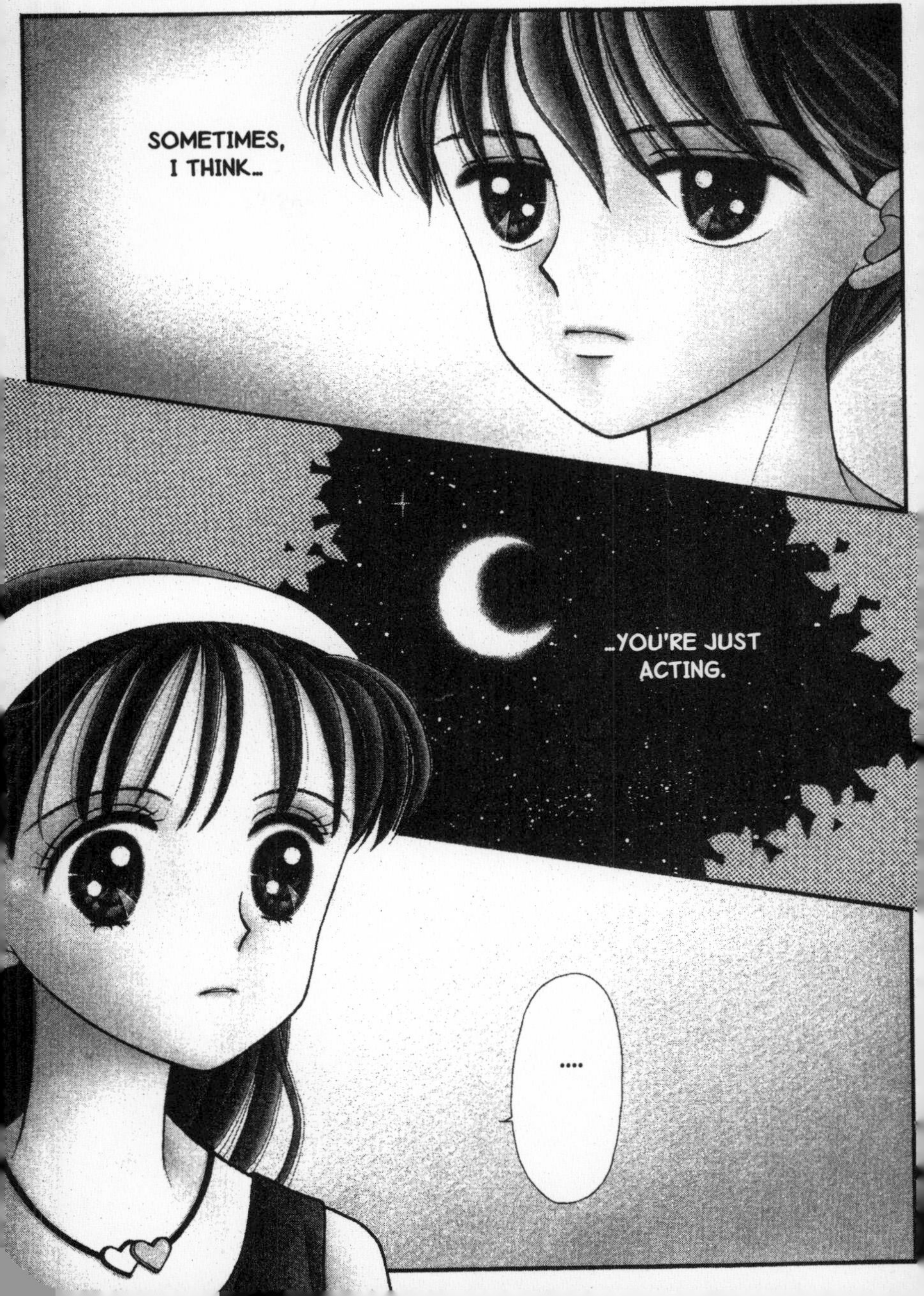
SOMETIMES, I THINK...
...YOU'RE JUST ACTING.
....

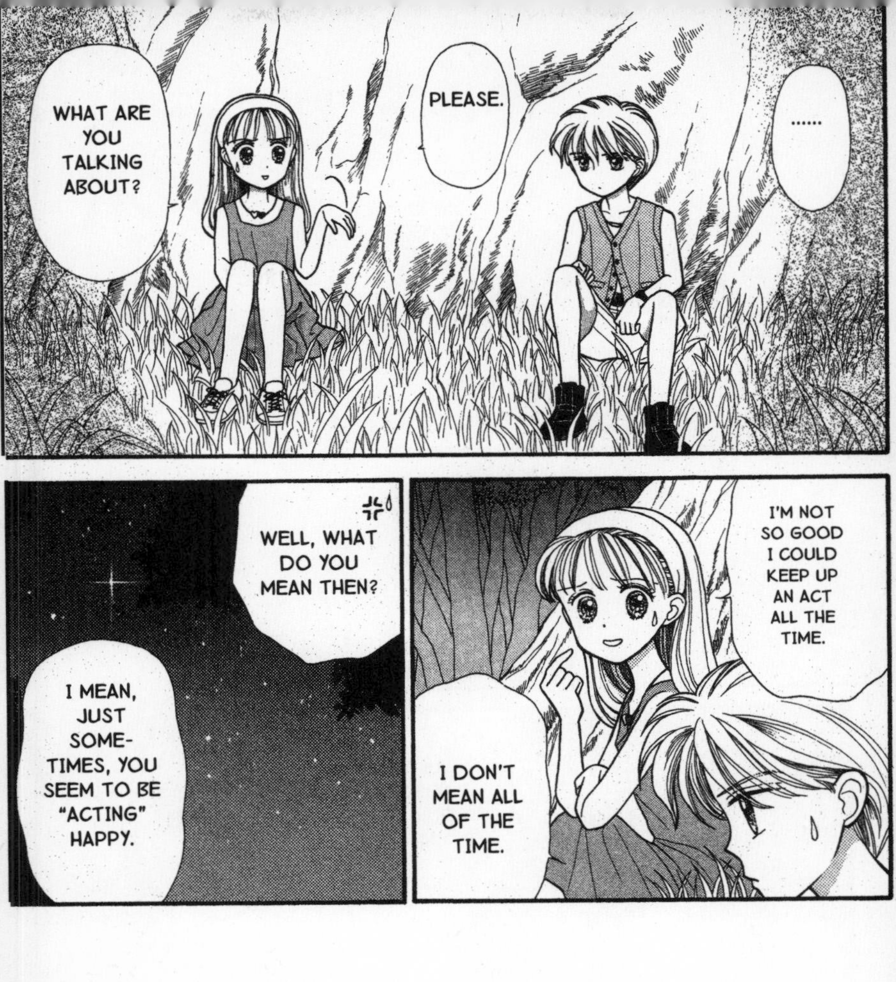
......
PLEASE.
WHAT ARE YOU TALKING ABOUT?
I'M NOT SO GOOD I COULD KEEP UP AN ACT ALL THE TIME.
I DON'T MEAN ALL OF THE TIME.
WELL, WHAT DO YOU MEAN THEN?
I MEAN, JUST SOME-TIMES, YOU SEEM TO BE "ACTING" HAPPY.

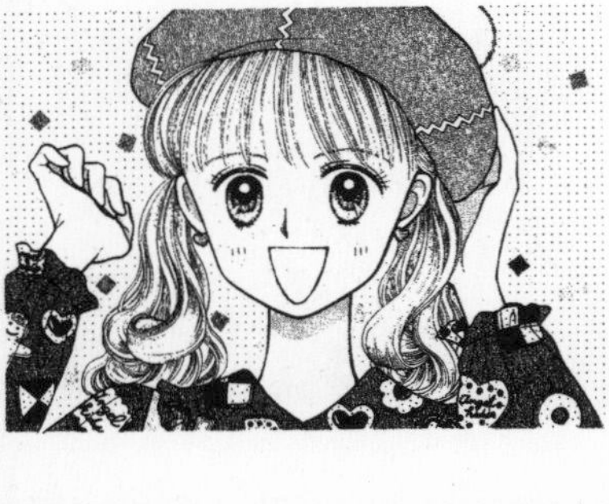

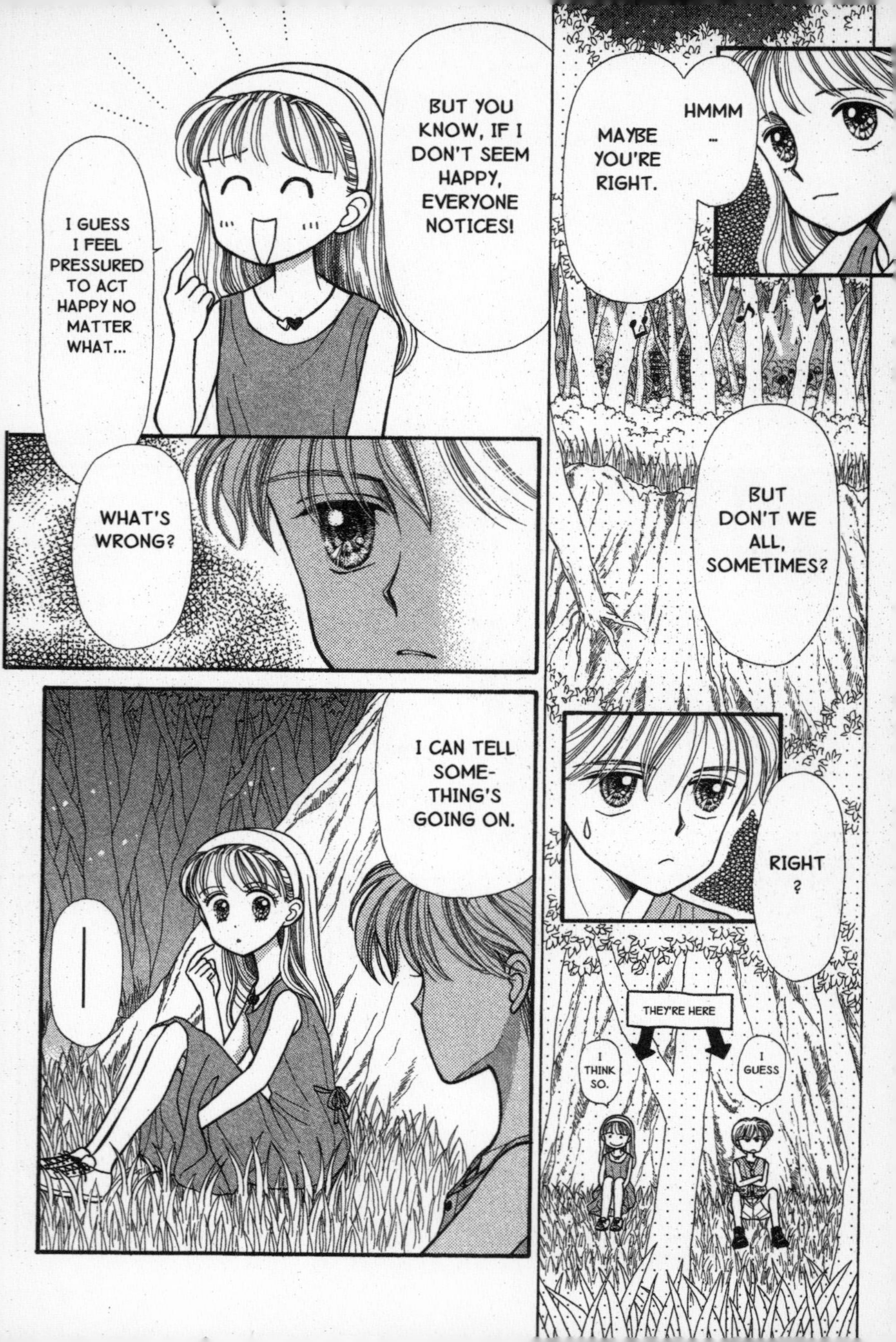
HMMM ...
MAYBE YOU'RE RIGHT.
BUT DON'T WE ALL, SOMETIMES?
RIGHT ?
THEY'RE HERE
I GUESS
I THINK SO.
BUT YOU KNOW, IF I DON'T SEEM HAPPY, EVERYONE NOTICES!
I GUESS I FEEL PRESSURED TO ACT HAPPY NO MATTER WHAT...
WHAT'S WRONG?
I CAN TELL SOME-THING'S GOING ON.

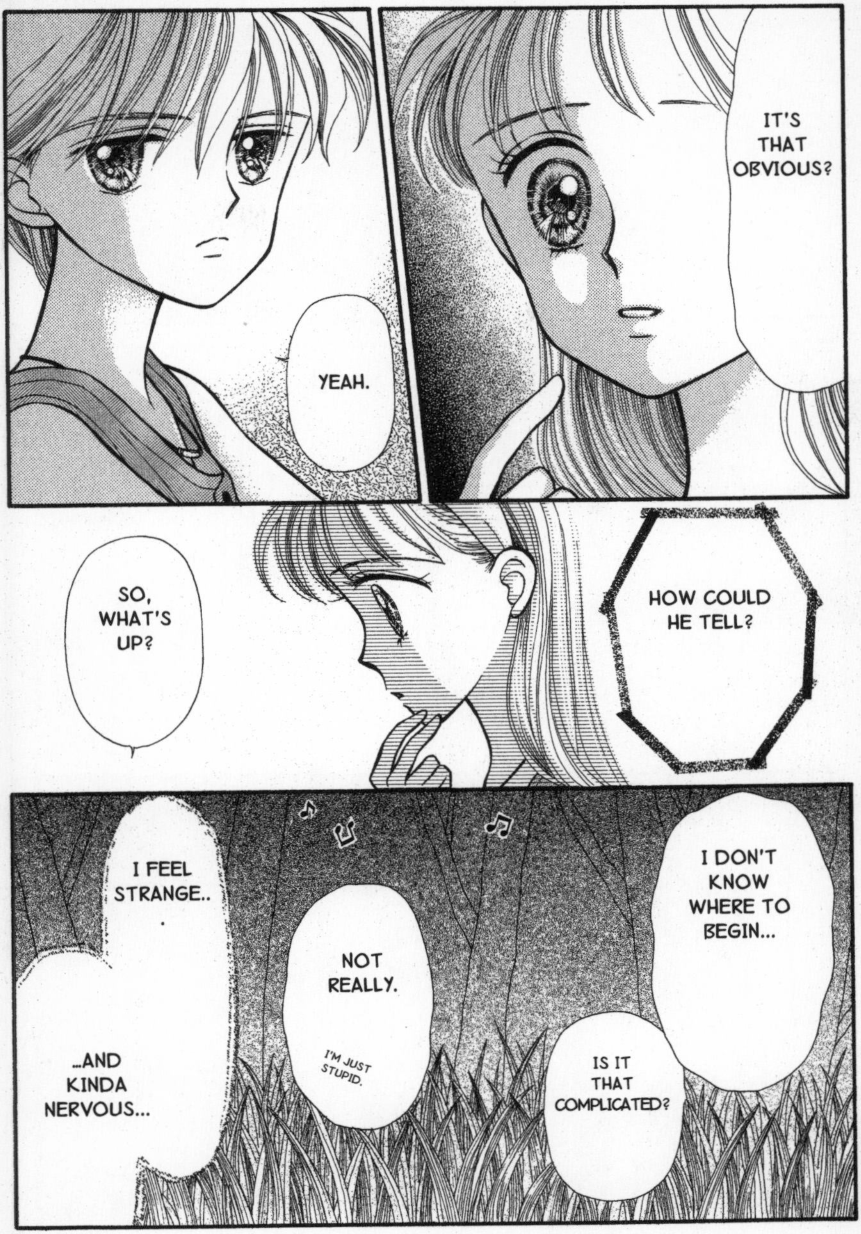
IT'S THAT OBVIOUS?
YEAH.
HOW COULD HE TELL?
SO, WHAT'S UP?
I DON'T KNOW WHERE TO BEGIN...
IS IT THAT COMPLICATED?
NOT REALLY.
I'M JUST STUPID.
I FEEL STRANGE...
...AND KINDA NERVOUS...

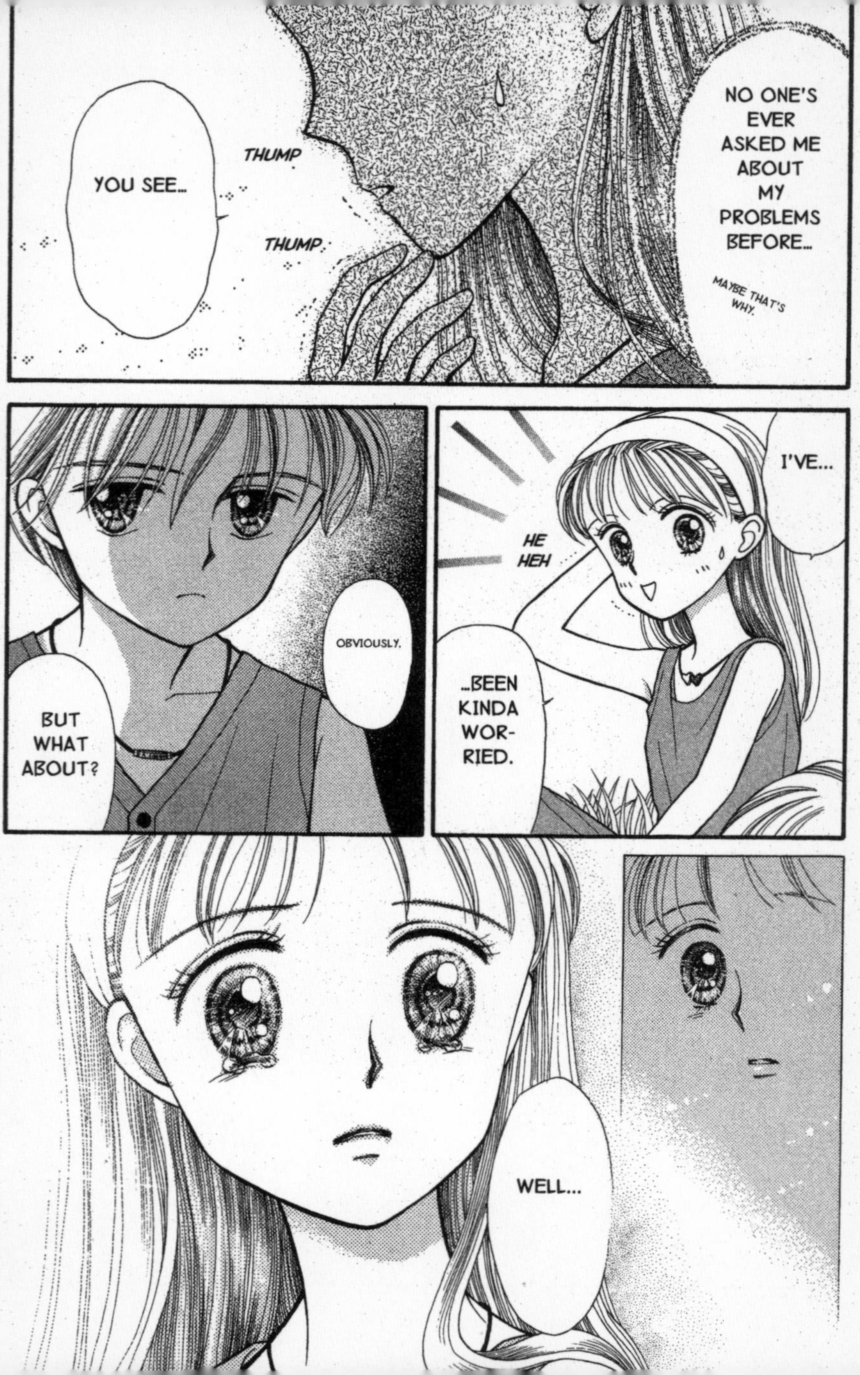
NO ONE'S EVER ASKED ME ABOUT MY PROBLEMS BEFORE...
MAYBE THAT'S WHY.
THUMP
THUMP
YOU SEE...
I'VE...
HE HEH
...BEEN KINDA WOR-RIED.
OBVIOUSLY.
BUT WHAT ABOUT?
WELL...

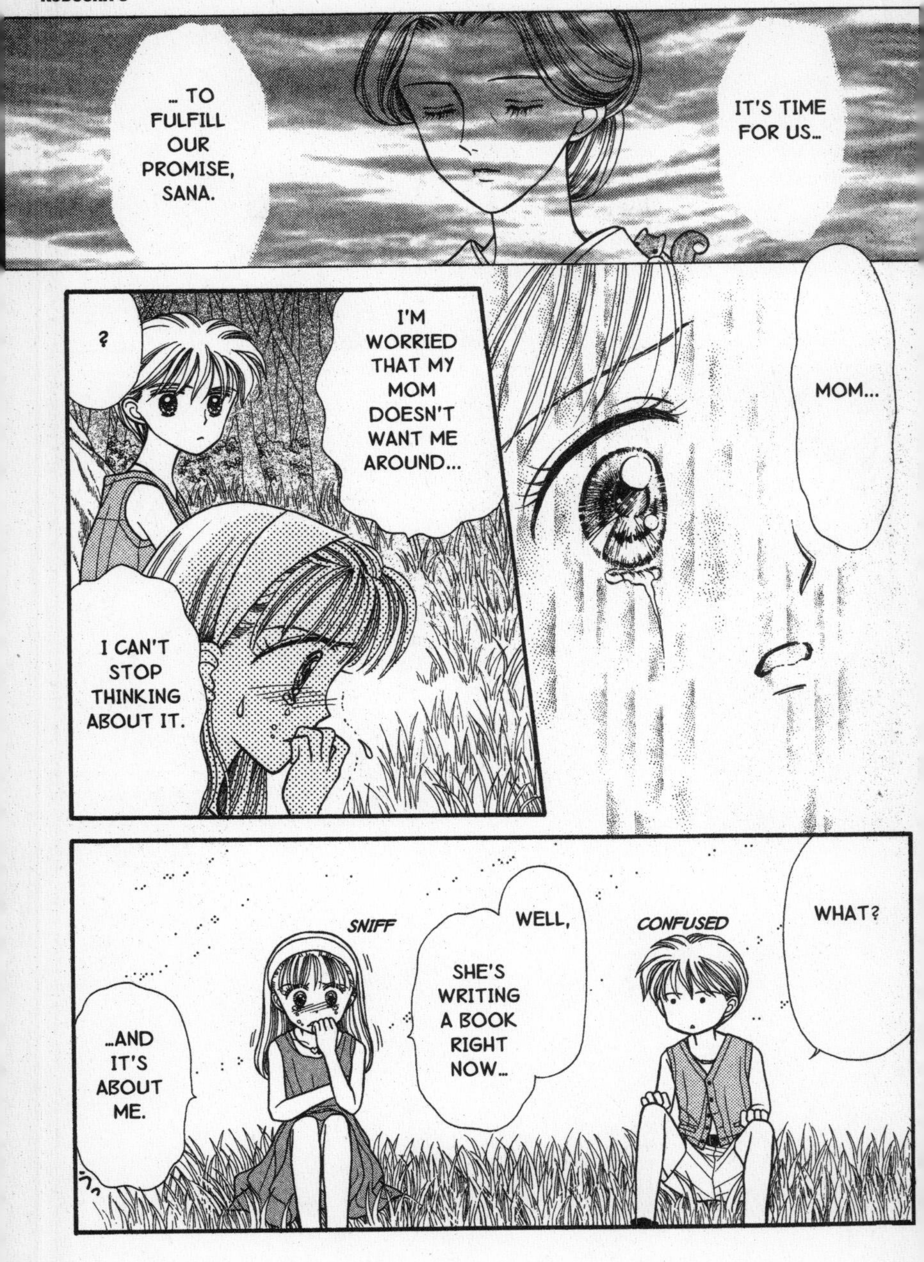
IT'S TIME FOR US...
... TO FULFILL OUR PROMISE, SANA.
MOM...
I'M WORRIED THAT MY MOM DOESN'T WANT ME AROUND...
?
I CAN'T STOP THINKING ABOUT IT.
WHAT?
CONFUSED
WELL,
SHE'S WRITING A BOOK RIGHT NOW...
SNIFF
...AND IT'S ABOUT ME.

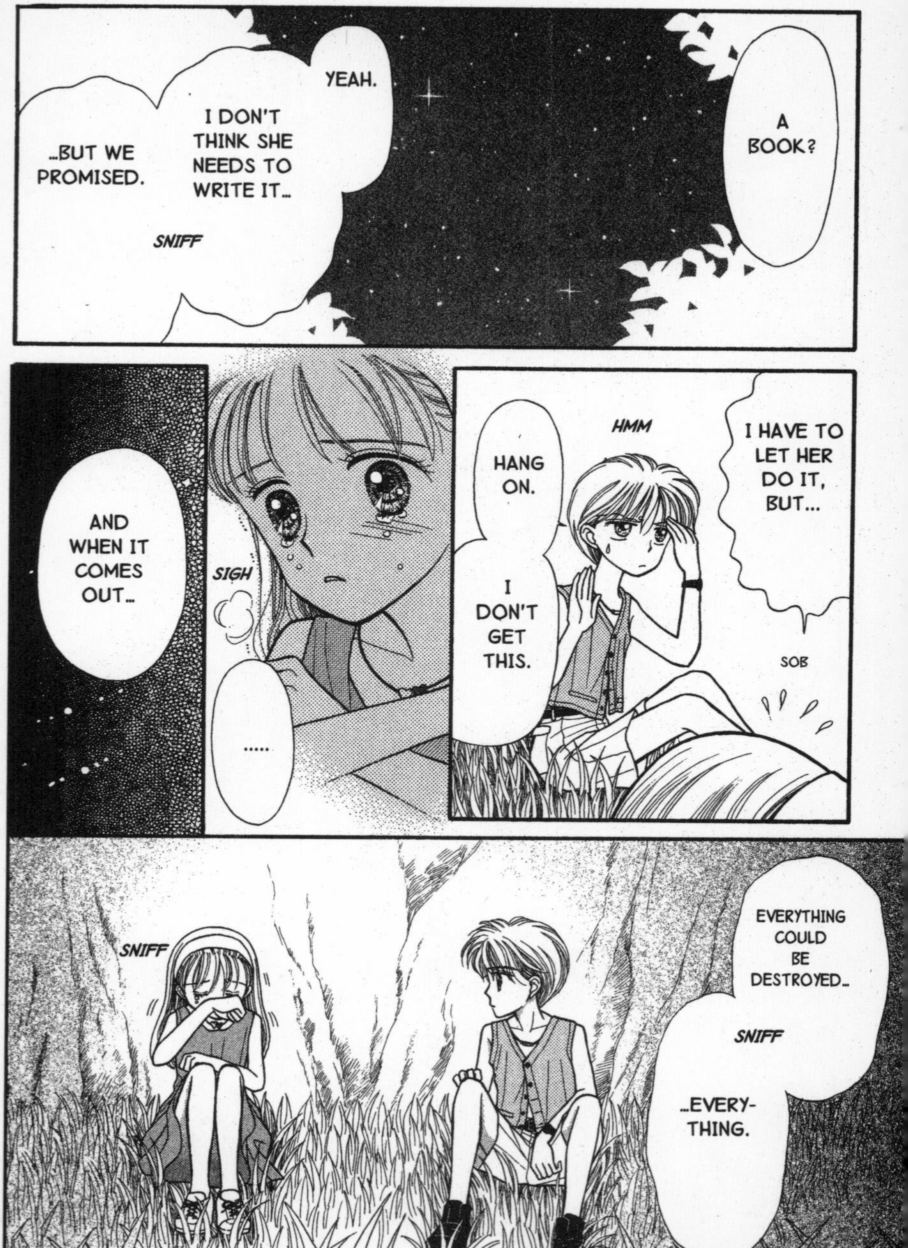

A BOOK?
YEAH.
I DON'T THINK SHE NEEDS TO WRITE IT...
...BUT WE PROMISED.
SNIFF
I HAVE TO LET HER DO IT, BUT...
HMM
HANG ON.
I DON'T GET THIS.
SOB
SIGH
.....
AND WHEN IT COMES OUT...
EVERYTHING COULD BE DESTROYED...
SNIFF
...EVERY-THING.
SNIFF

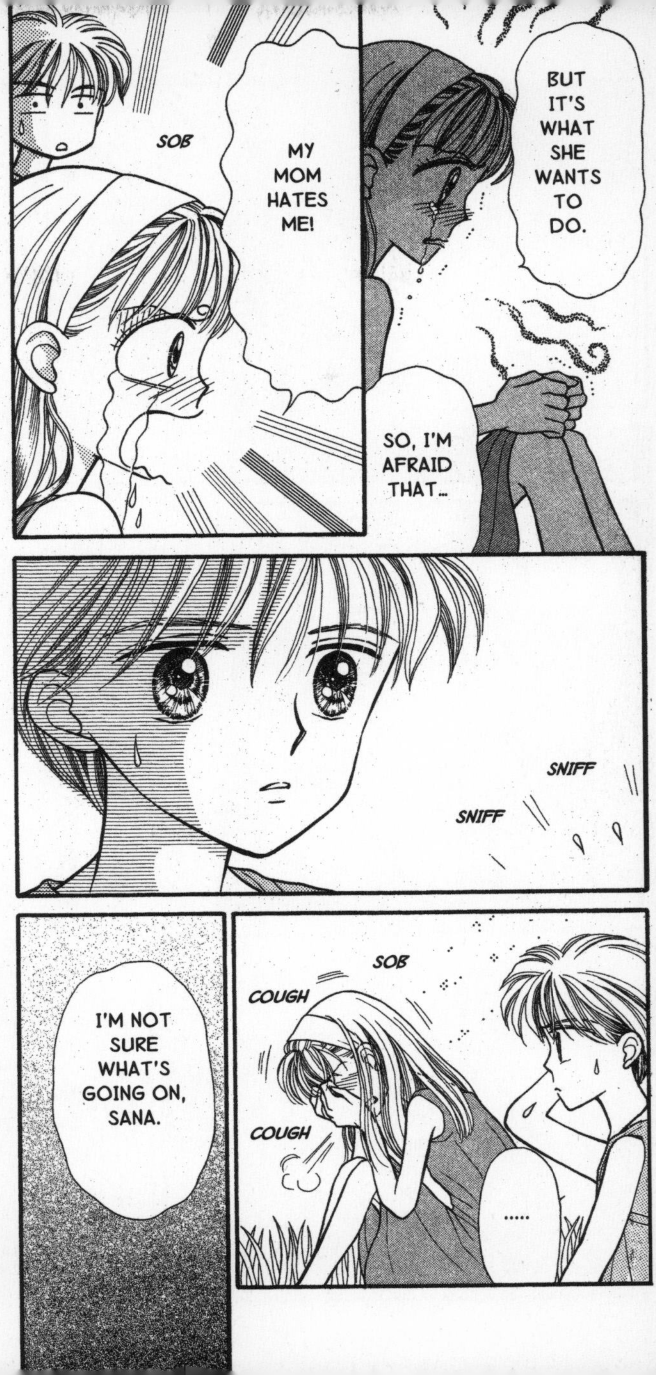
BUT IT'S WHAT SHE WANTS TO DO.
SO, I'M AFRAID THAT...
SOB
MY MOM HATES ME!
SNIFF
SNIFF
SOB
COUGH
COUGH
.....
I'M NOT SURE WHAT'S GOING ON, SANA.

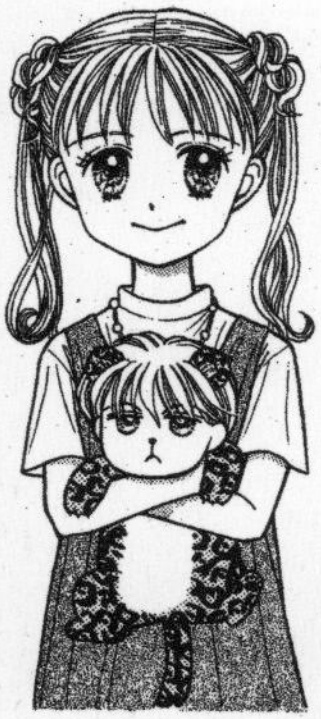

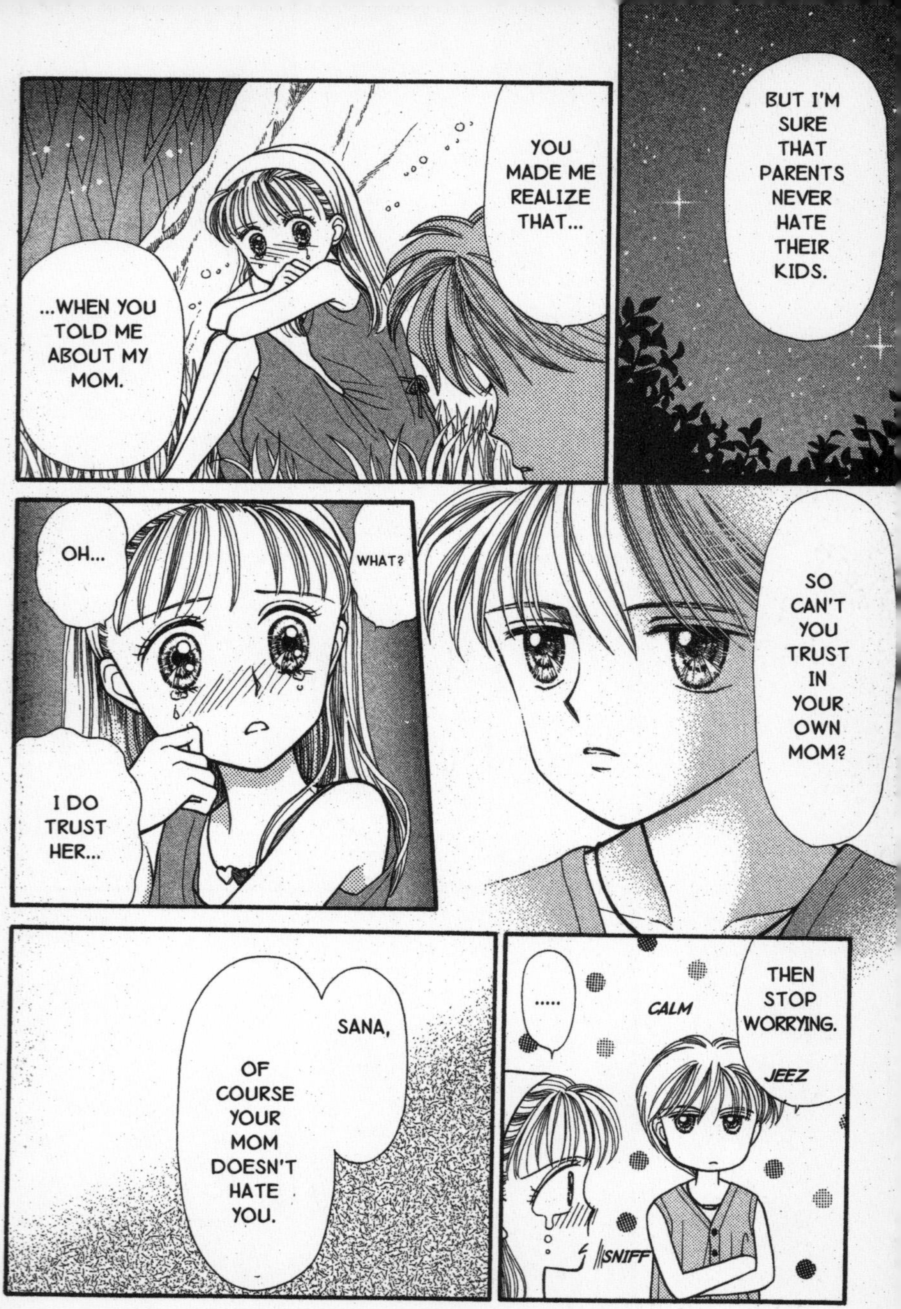
BUT I'M SURE THAT PARENTS NEVER HATE THEIR KIDS.
YOU MADE ME REALIZE THAT...
...WHEN YOU TOLD ME ABOUT MY MOM.
SO CAN'T YOU TRUST IN YOUR OWN MOM?
WHAT?
OH...
I DO TRUST HER...
THEN STOP WORRYING.
CALM
.....
JEEZ
SNIFF
SANA,
OF COURSE YOUR MOM DOESN'T HATE YOU.

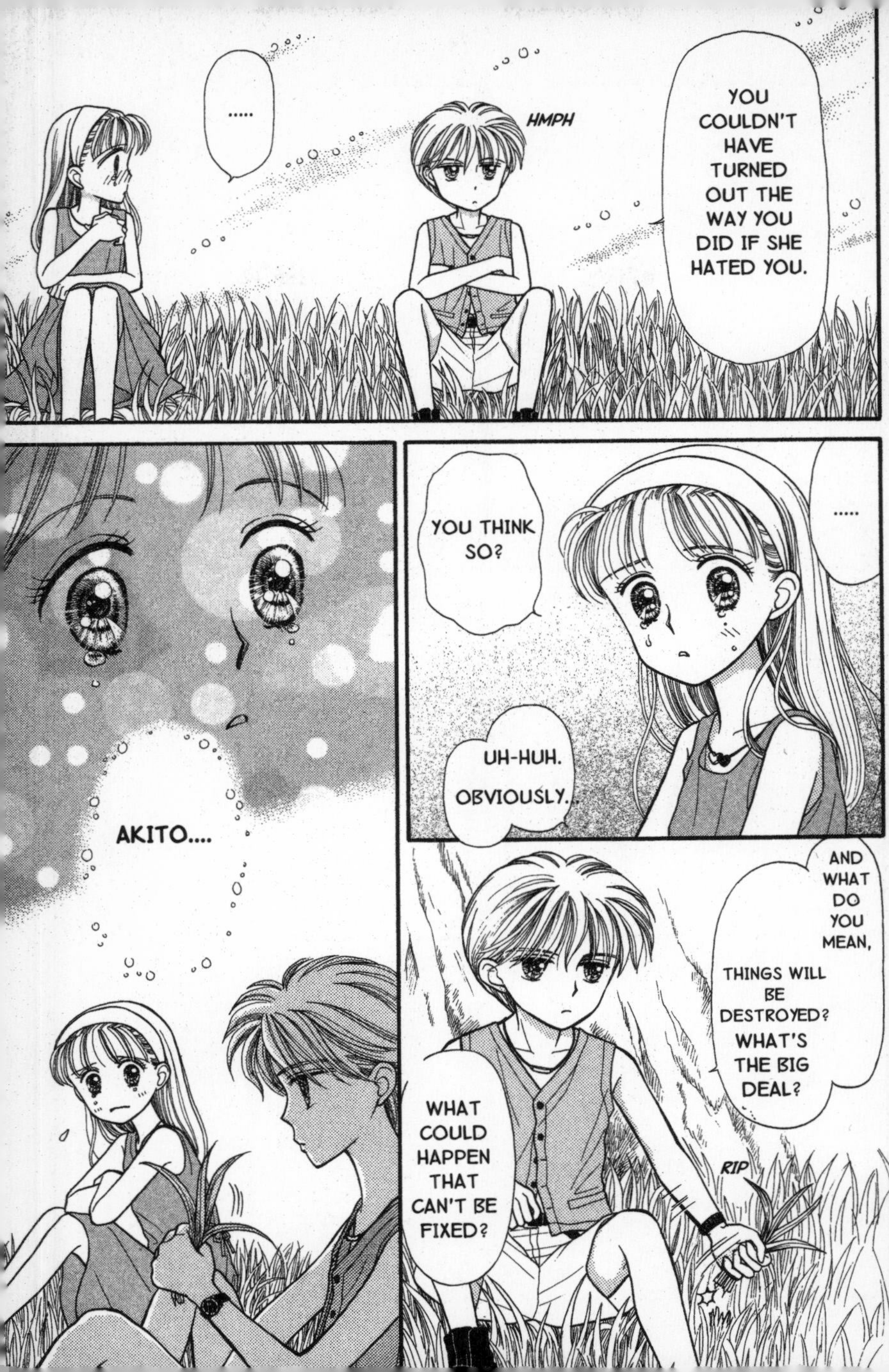
YOU COULDN'T HAVE TURNED OUT THE WAY YOU DID IF SHE HATED YOU.
HMPH
.....
.....
YOU THINK SO?
UH-HUH. OBVIOUSLY...
AND WHAT DO YOU MEAN, THINGS WILL BE DESTROYED? WHAT'S THE BIG DEAL?
RIP
WHAT COULD HAPPEN THAT CAN'T BE FIXED?
AKITO....

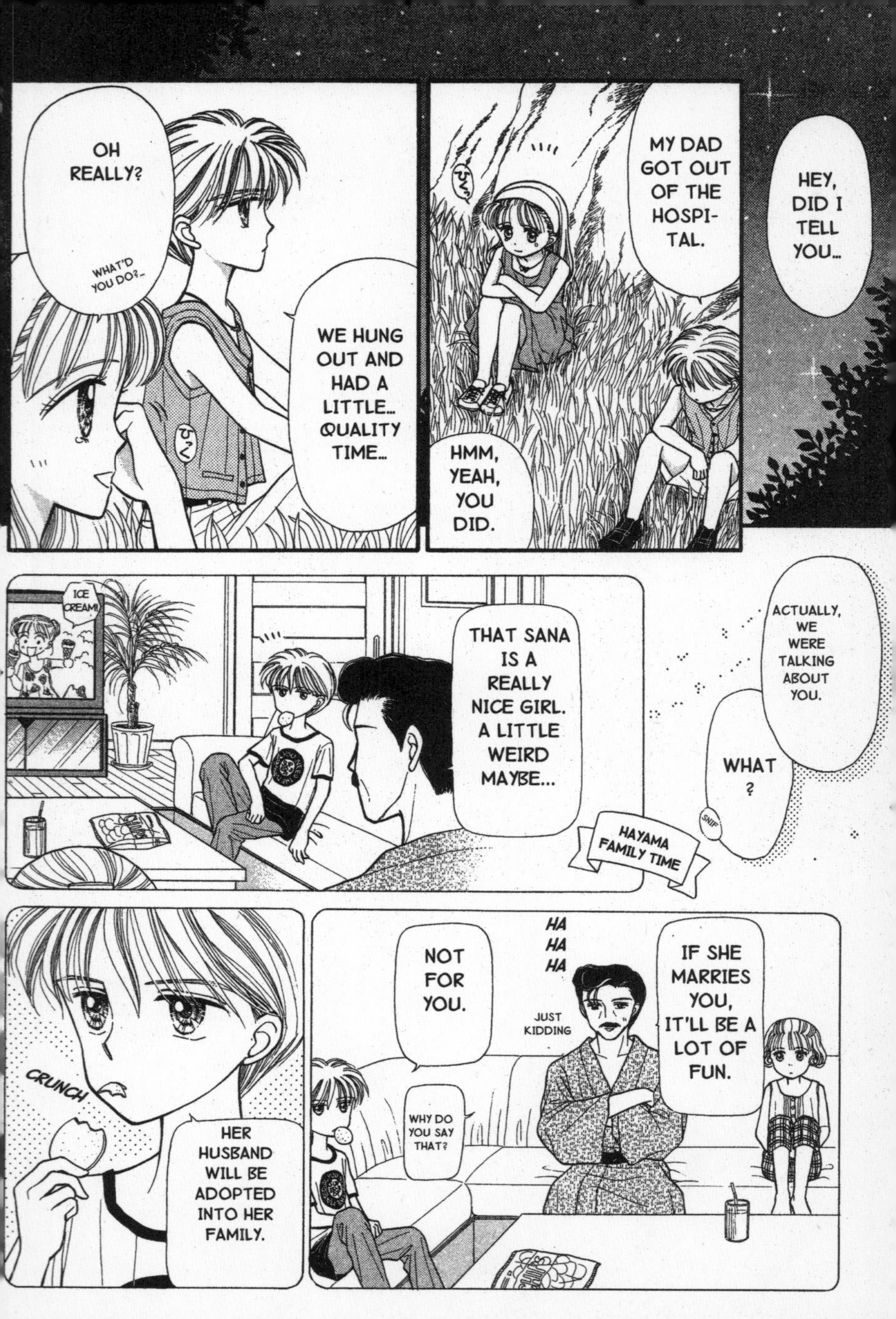
HEY, DID I TELL YOU...
MY DAD GOT OUT OF THE HOSPITAL.
HMM, YEAH, YOU DID.
OH REALLY?
WHAT'D YOU DO?..
WE HUNG OUT AND HAD A LITTLE... QUALITY TIME...
ACTUALLY, WE WERE TALKING ABOUT YOU.
WHAT?
SNIF
HAYAMA FAMILY TIME
THAT SANA IS A REALLY NICE GIRL. A LITTLE WEIRD MAYBE...
ICE CREAM!
IF SHE MARRIES YOU, IT'LL BE A LOT OF FUN.
HA HA HA
JUST KIDDING
NOT FOR YOU.
WHY DO YOU SAY THAT?
HER HUSBAND WILL BE ADOPTED INTO HER FAMILY.
CRUNCH

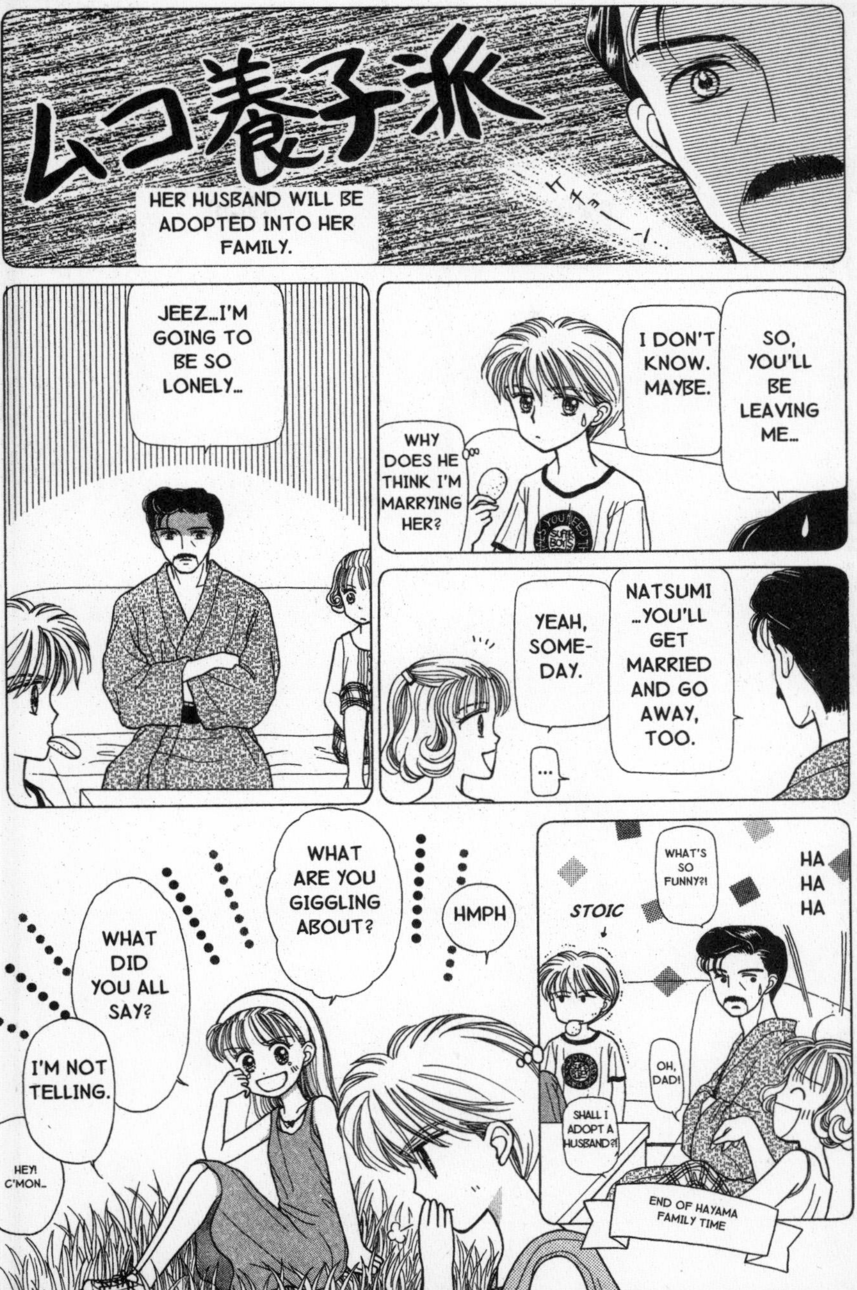
ムコ養子派
HER HUSBAND WILL BE ADOPTED INTO HER FAMILY.
SO, YOU'LL BE LEAVING ME...
I DON'T KNOW. MAYBE.
WHY DOES HE THINK I'M MARRYING HER?
NATSUMI ...YOU'LL GET MARRIED AND GO AWAY, TOO.
YEAH, SOME-DAY.
...
JEEZ...I'M GOING TO BE SO LONELY...
HA HA HA
WHAT'S SO FUNNY?!
STOIC
OH, DAD!
SHALL I ADOPT A HUSBAND?!
END OF HAYAMA FAMILY TIME
HMPH
WHAT ARE YOU GIGGLING ABOUT?
WHAT DID YOU ALL SAY?
I'M NOT TELLING.
HEY! C'MON...

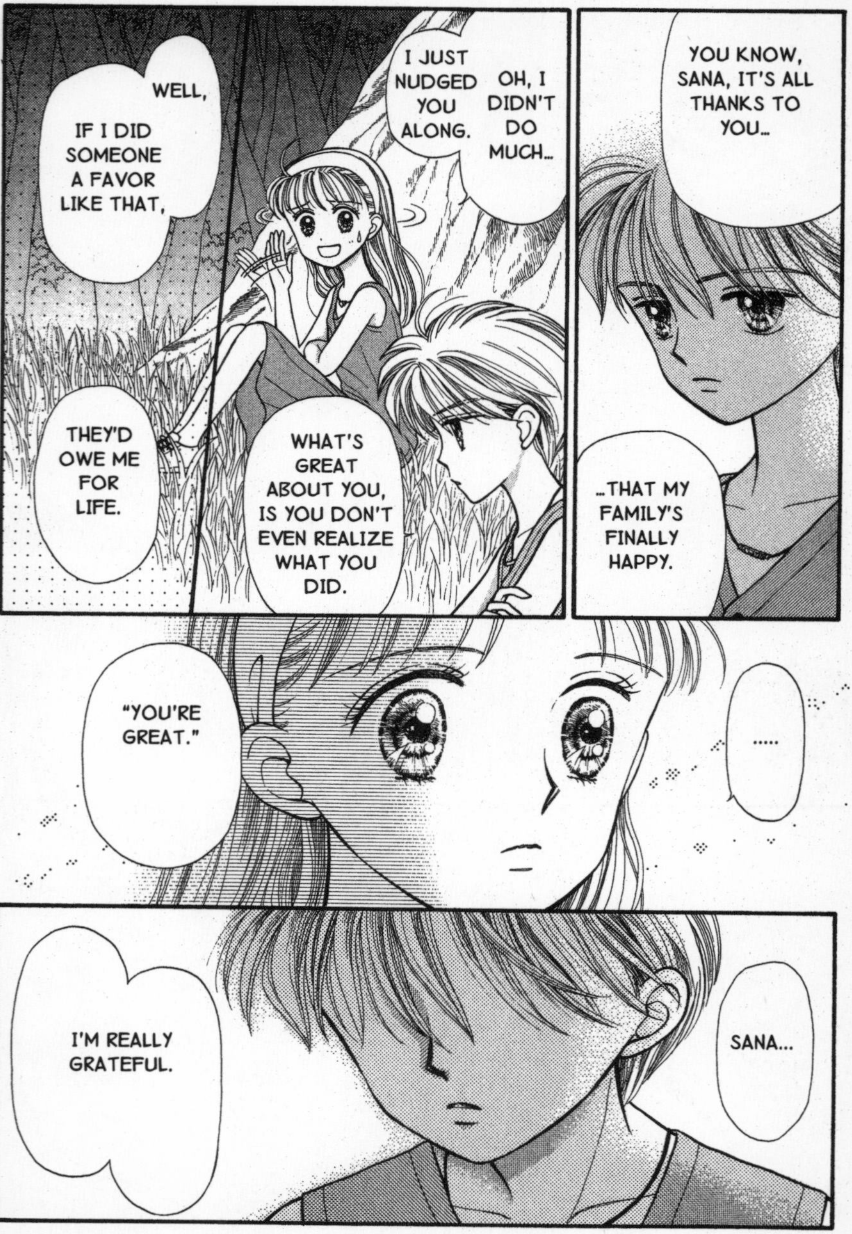
YOU KNOW, SANA, IT'S ALL THANKS TO YOU...
...THAT MY FAMILY'S FINALLY HAPPY.
OH, I DIDN'T DO MUCH...
I JUST NUDGED YOU ALONG.
WHAT'S GREAT ABOUT YOU, IS YOU DON'T EVEN REALIZE WHAT YOU DID.
WELL, IF I DID SOMEONE A FAVOR LIKE THAT,
THEY'D OWE ME FOR LIFE.
.....
"YOU'RE GREAT."
SANA...
I'M REALLY GRATEFUL.

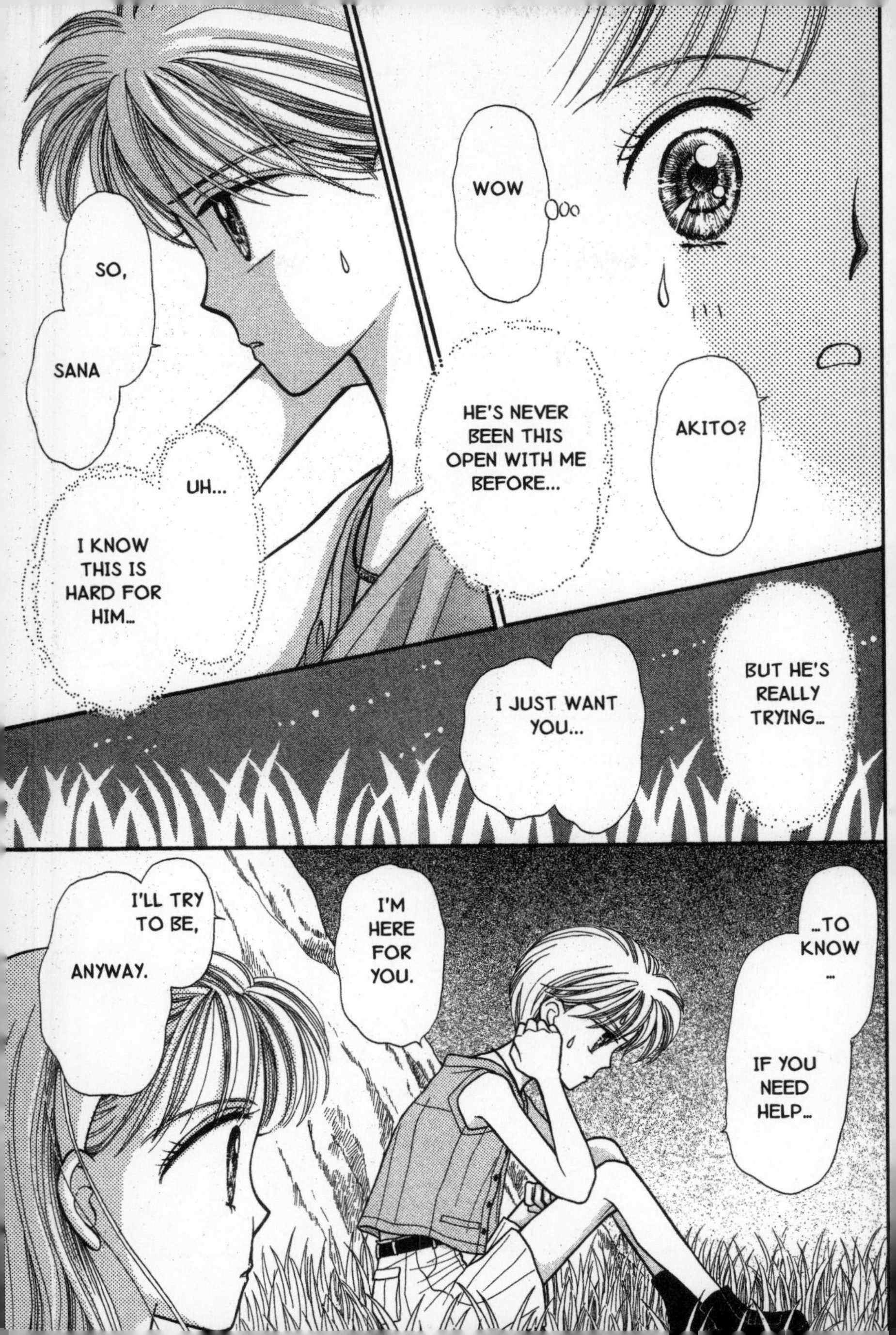
AKITO?
WOW
HE'S NEVER BEEN THIS OPEN WITH ME BEFORE...
SO, SANA
UH...
I KNOW THIS IS HARD FOR HIM...
BUT HE'S REALLY TRYING...
I JUST WANT YOU...
...TO KNOW ... IF YOU NEED HELP...
I'M HERE FOR YOU.
I'LL TRY TO BE, ANYWAY.

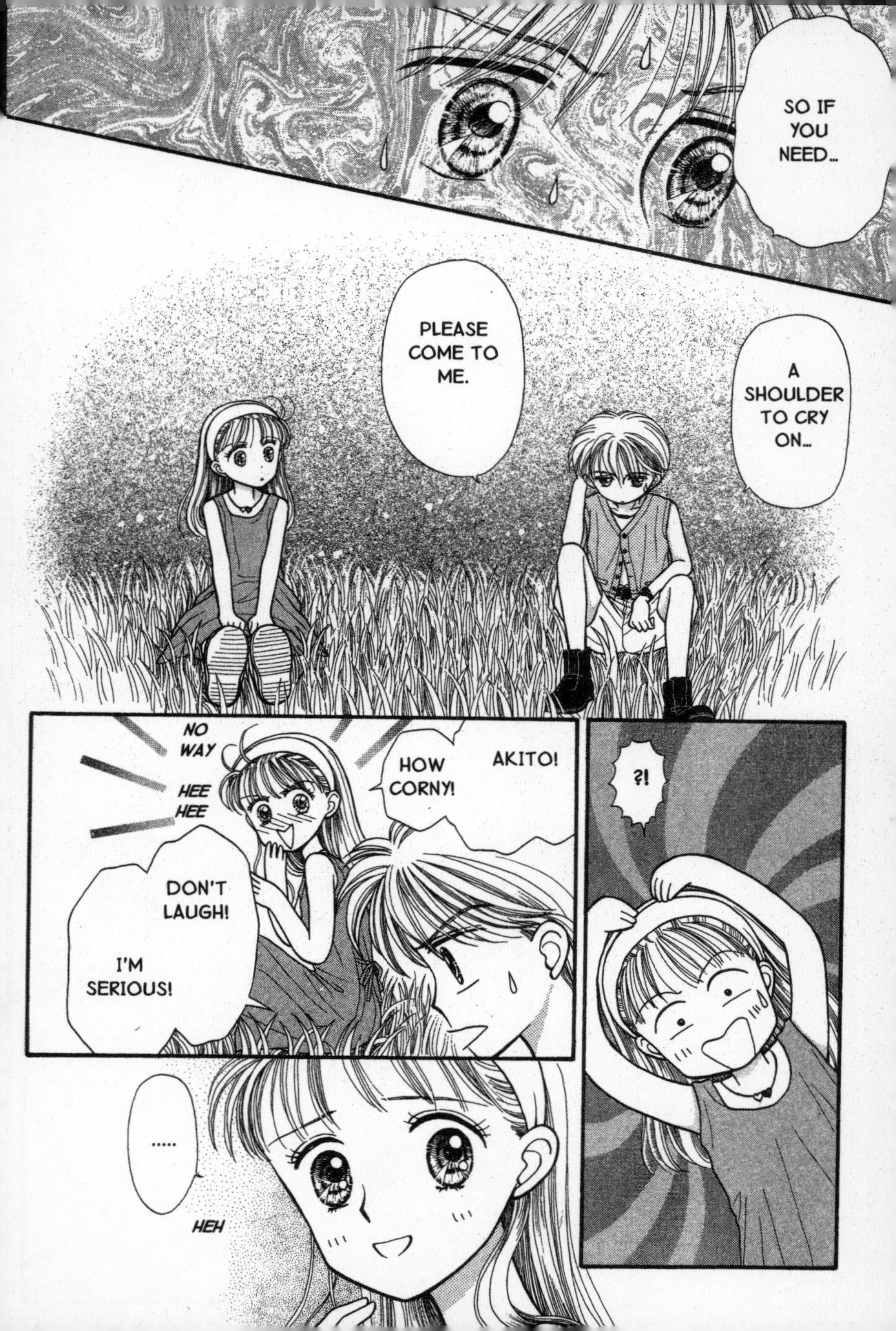
SO IF YOU NEED...
A SHOULDER TO CRY ON...
PLEASE COME TO ME.
?!
AKITO!
HOW CORNY!
NO WAY
HEE HEE
DON'T LAUGH!
I'M SERIOUS!
.....
HEH

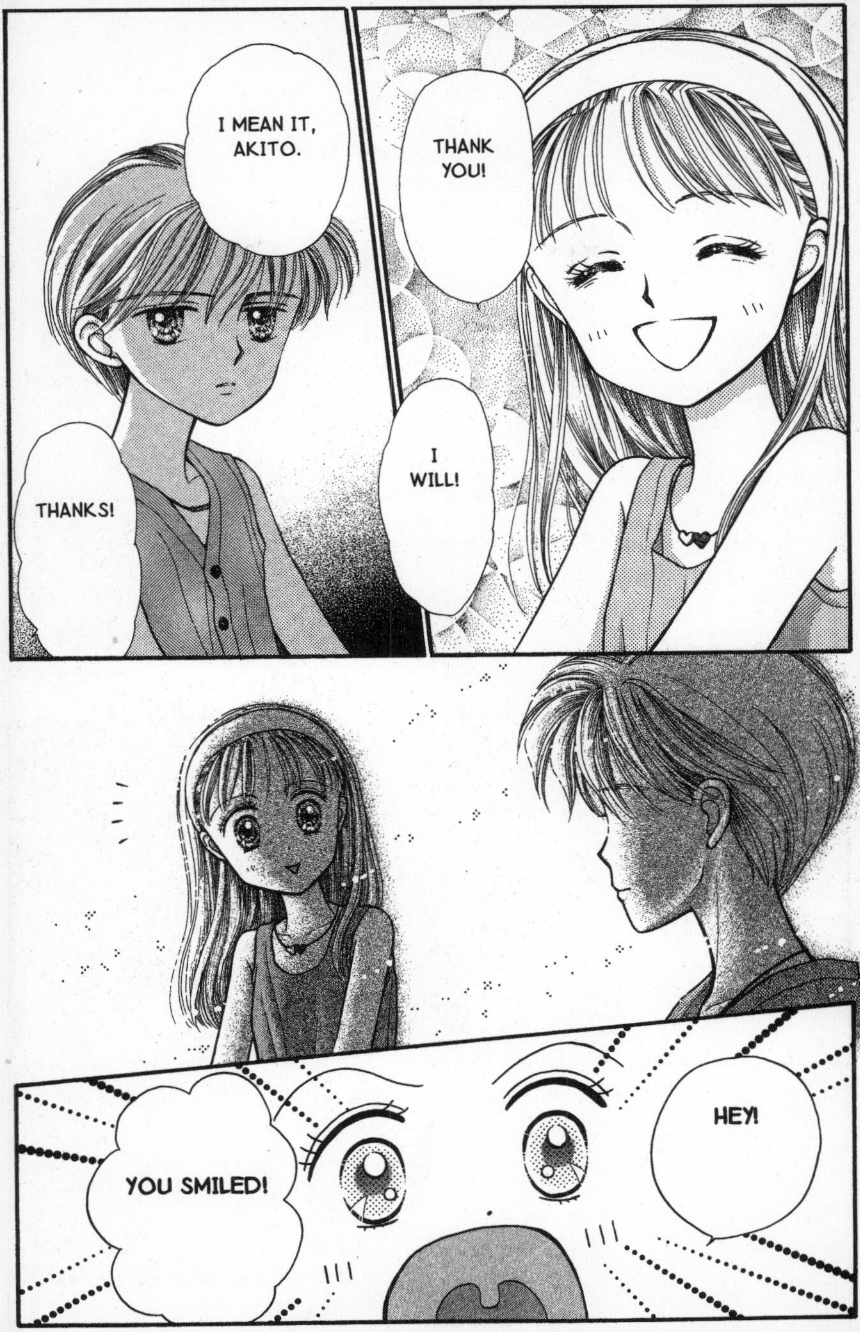
THANK YOU!
I WILL!
I MEAN IT, AKITO.
THANKS!
HEY!
YOU SMILED!

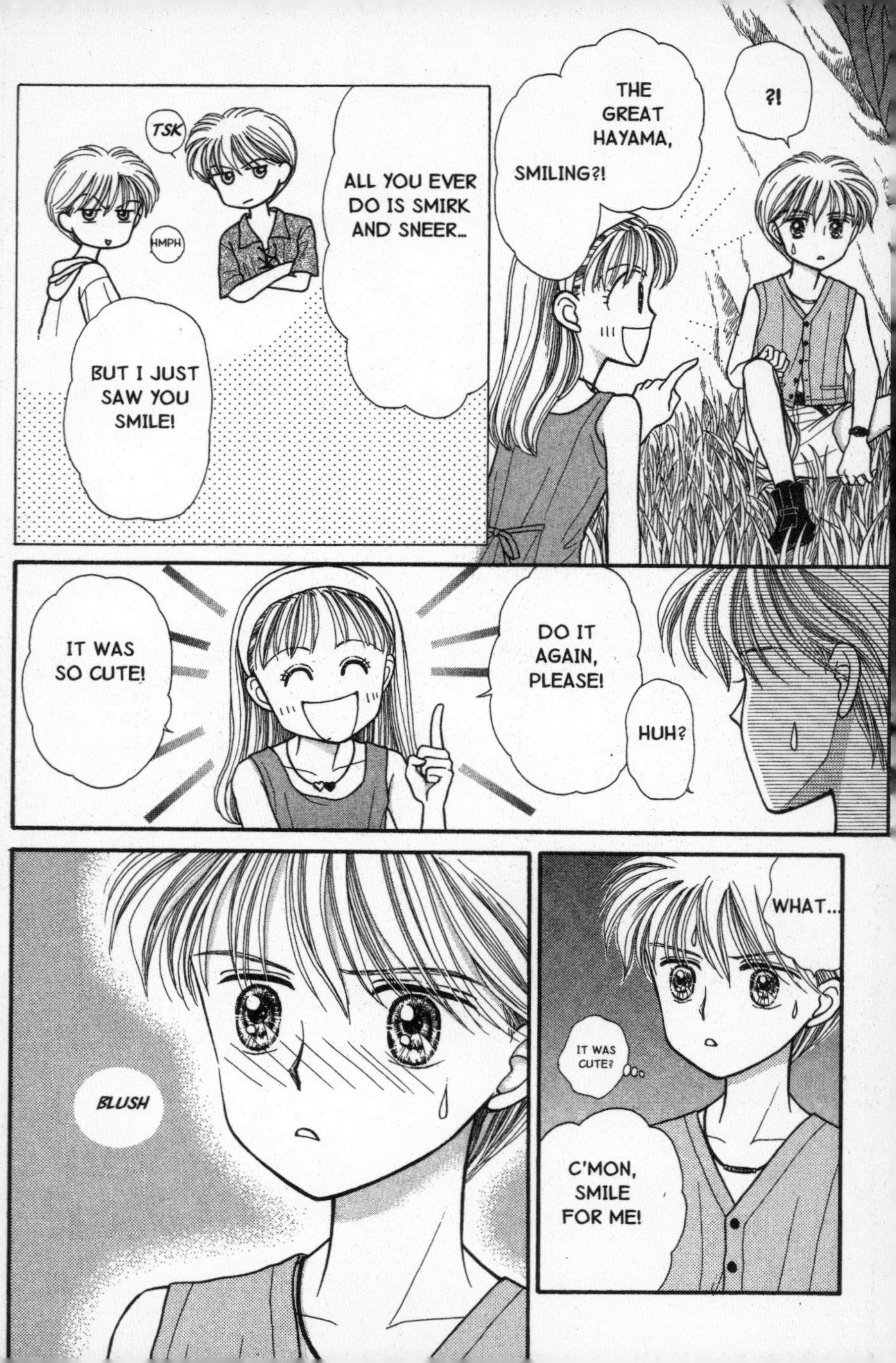
?!
THE GREAT HAYAMA, SMILING?!
ALL YOU EVER DO IS SMIRK AND SNEER...
TSK
HMPH
BUT I JUST SAW YOU SMILE!
DO IT AGAIN, PLEASE!
HUH?
IT WAS SO CUTE!
WHAT...
IT WAS CUTE?
C'MON, SMILE FOR ME!
BLUSH

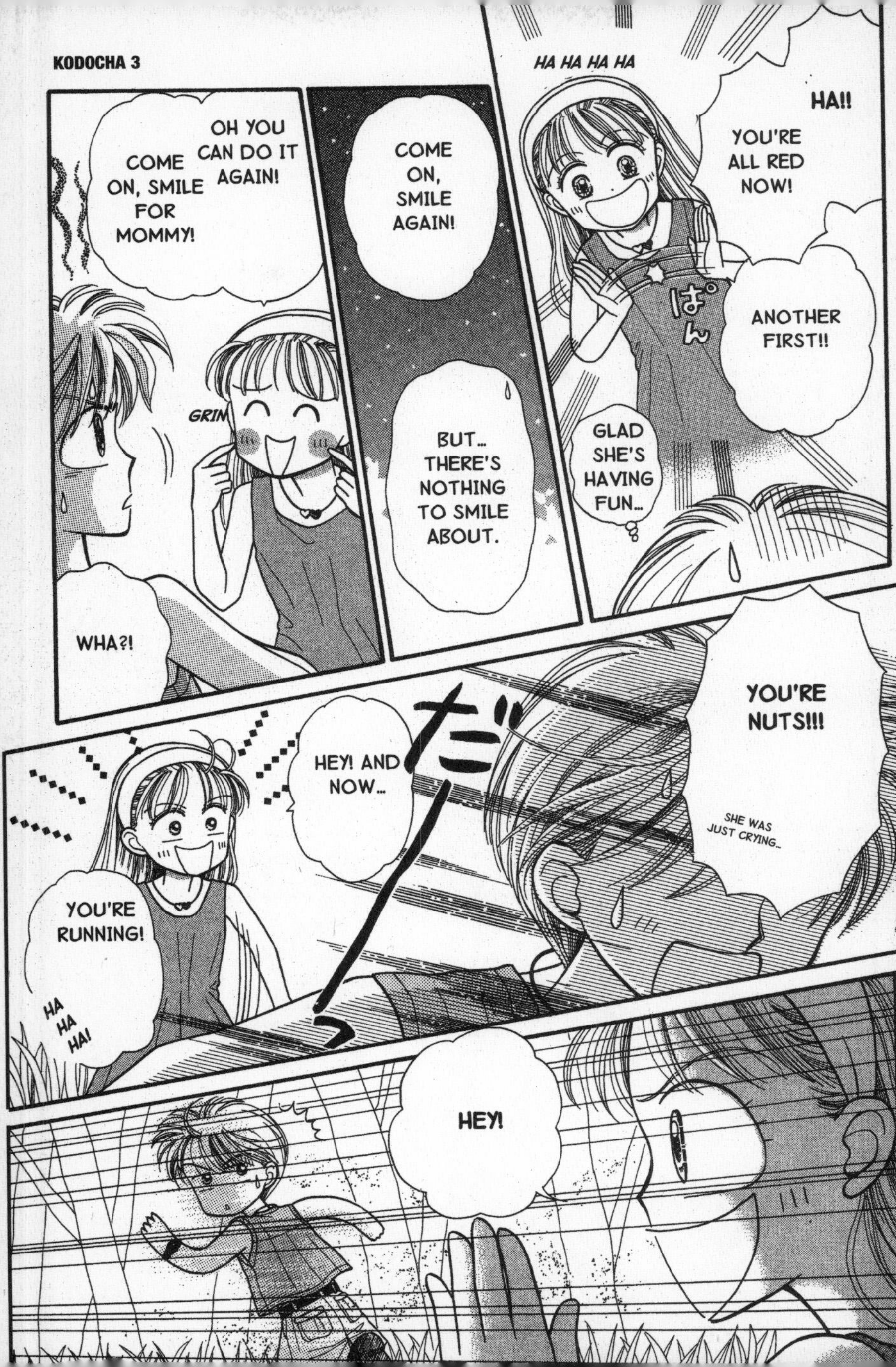
HA HA HA HA
HA!!
YOU'RE ALL RED NOW!
ぱん
ANOTHER FIRST!!
GLAD SHE'S HAVING FUN...
COME ON, SMILE AGAIN!
BUT... THERE'S NOTHING TO SMILE ABOUT.
OH YOU CAN DO IT AGAIN!
COME ON, SMILE FOR MOMMY!
GRIN
WHA?!
YOU'RE NUTS!!!
SHE WAS JUST CRYING...
だっ
HEY! AND NOW...
YOU'RE RUNNING!
HA HA HA!
HEY!

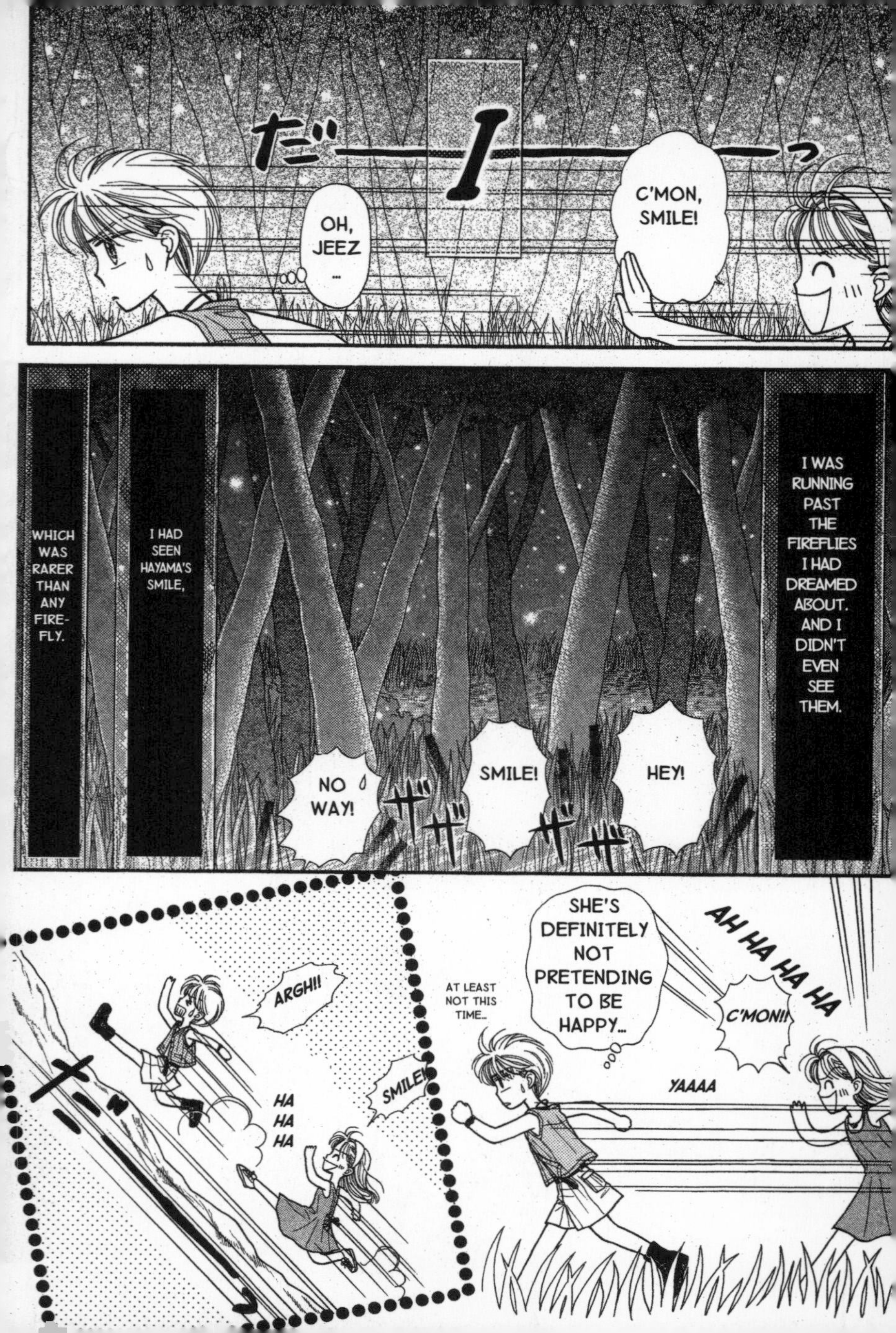
だーーーっ
C'MON, SMILE!
OH, JEEZ ...
I WAS RUNNING PAST THE FIREFLIES I HAD DREAMED ABOUT. AND I DIDN'T EVEN SEE THEM.
HEY!
ザザ
SMILE!
ザザ
NO WAY!
I HAD SEEN HAYAMA'S SMILE,
WHICH WAS RARER THAN ANY FIRE-FLY.
AH HA HA HA
C'MON!!
YAAAA
SHE'S DEFINITELY NOT PRETENDING TO BE HAPPY...
AT LEAST NOT THIS TIME...
ARGH!!
SMILE!
HA HA HA

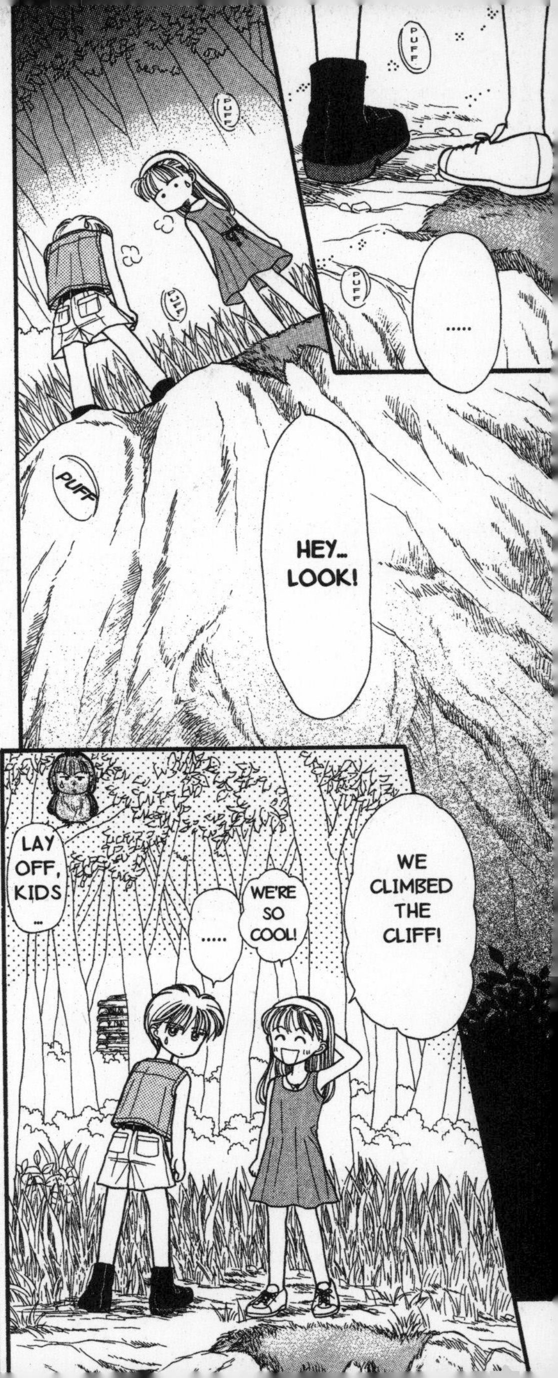
PUFF
PUFF
.....
PUFF
PUFF
PUFF
PUFF
HEY... LOOK!
WE CLIMBED THE CLIFF!
WE'RE SO COOL!
.....
LAY OFF, KIDS ...

All About Chipmunks Pt. 3

Speaking of chipmunks, my little chipmunk, "Mame-no-suke" is my second one. My first pet chipmunk was named Banner. I named him after this old cartoon, "Banner the Chipmunk". At least, I think I did, but I'm not sure. (If you have any idea what I'm talking about, please let me know!)
So, on the show, Banner wore a cute green vest. So, I made a felt vest and forced it on my Banner! Banner hated it...

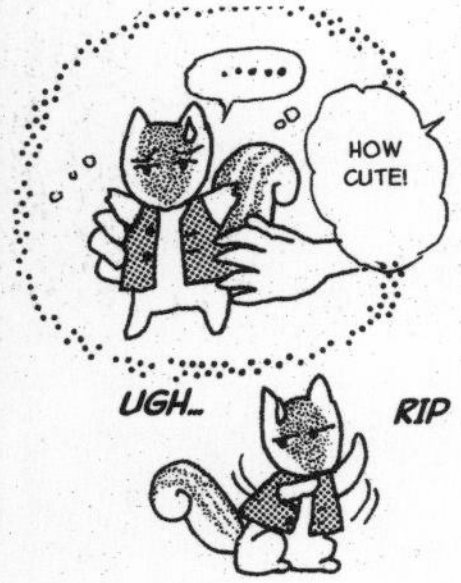
.....
HOW CUTE!
UGH...
RIP

...and tore it to pieces.

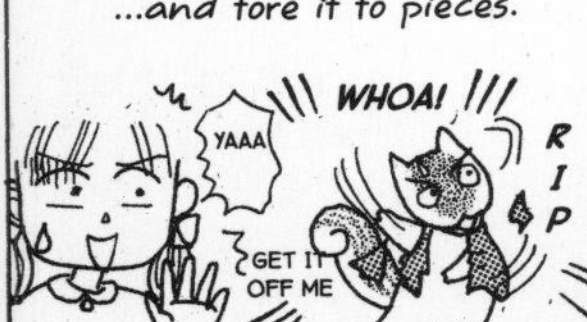
YAAA
WHOA!
RIP
GET IT OFF ME

I was sorry he wouldn't wear it, but I shouldn't have forced it, I guess!

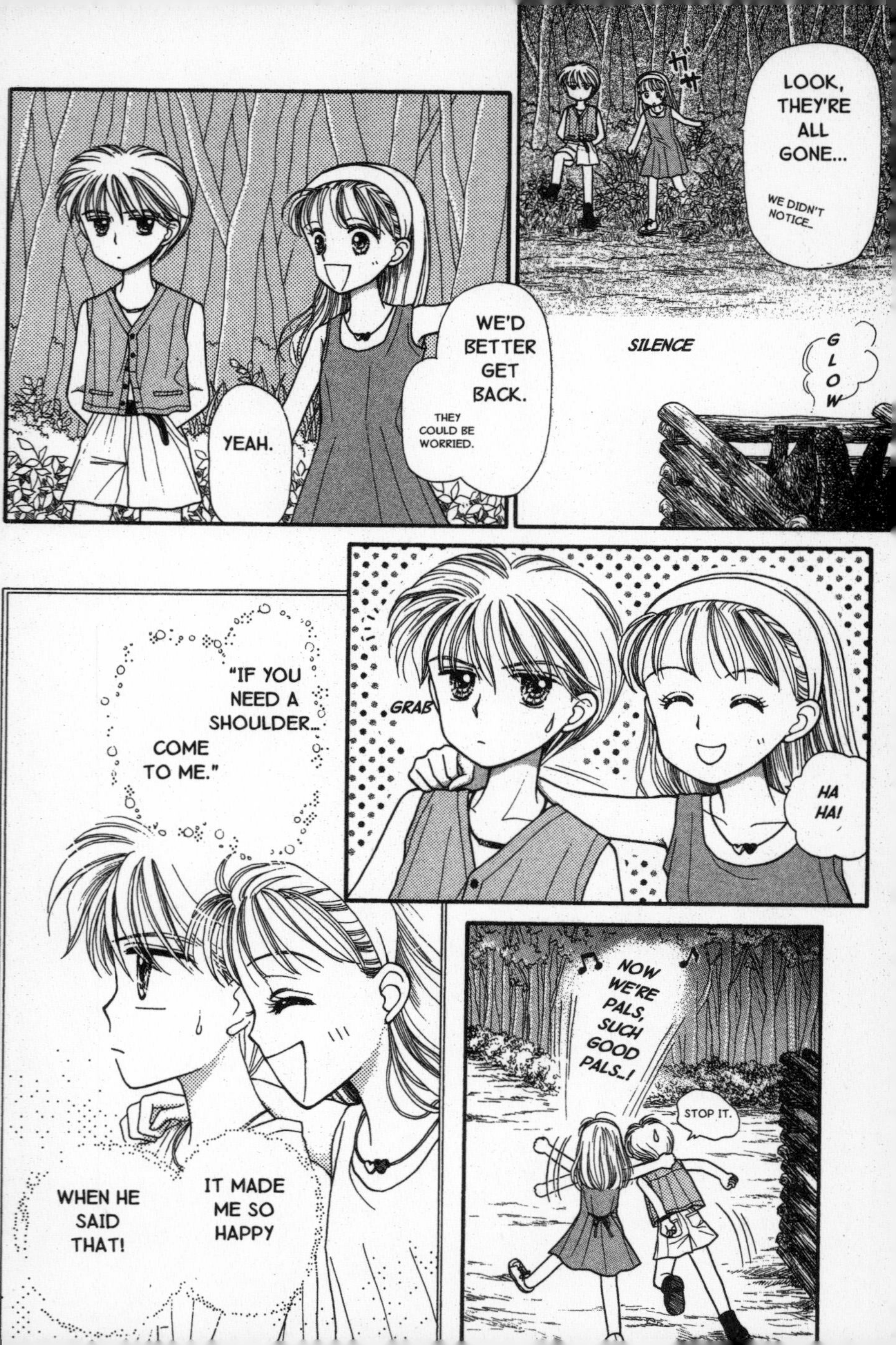
LOOK, THEY'RE ALL GONE...
WE DIDN'T NOTICE...
SILENCE
GLOW
WE'D BETTER GET BACK.
THEY COULD BE WORRIED.
YEAH.
GRAB
HA HA!
NOW WE'RE PALS, SUCH GOOD PALS...!
STOP IT.
"IF YOU NEED A SHOULDER... COME TO ME."
IT MADE ME SO HAPPY
WHEN HE SAID THAT!

The Smoke Girl

Here's a tale from junior high:

One day at school I was in a terrible mood. So, on my way home, I picked up a firecracker at a store, thinking that blowing it up by the river would make me feel better.

The problem was, I was a good girl so I'd never bought firecrackers before and I didn't know what I was doing. (I'd only watched friends from a distance.)

So, I picked up something that looked good.

I went down to the river and lit it. Smoke came out. More smoke came out. Smoke kept coming out. It didn't do anything else.

I found out later that it was only a smoke bomb. (Shock!) It annoyed me, bored me and only made me feel worse afterwards.

But it made a cute little memory.

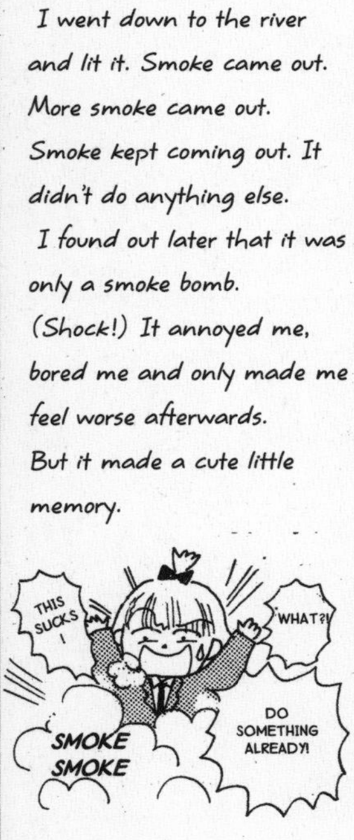
WHAT?!
THIS SUCKS!
DO SOMETHING ALREADY!
SMOKE SMOKE

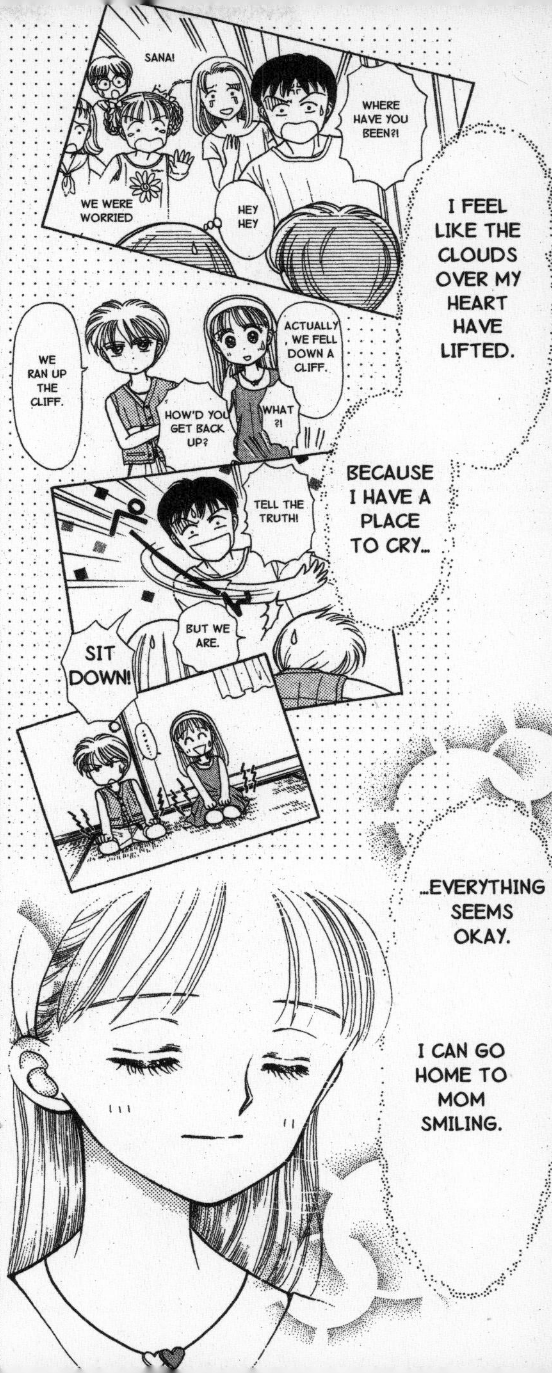
WHERE HAVE YOU BEEN?!
SANA!
HEY HEY
WE WERE WORRIED
I FEEL LIKE THE CLOUDS OVER MY HEART HAVE LIFTED.
ACTUALLY, WE FELL DOWN A CLIFF.
WHAT?!
HOW'D YOU GET BACK UP?
WE RAN UP THE CLIFF.
BECAUSE I HAVE A PLACE TO CRY...
TELL THE TRUTH!
BUT WE ARE.
SIT DOWN!
...
...EVERYTHING SEEMS OKAY.
I CAN GO HOME TO MOM SMILING.

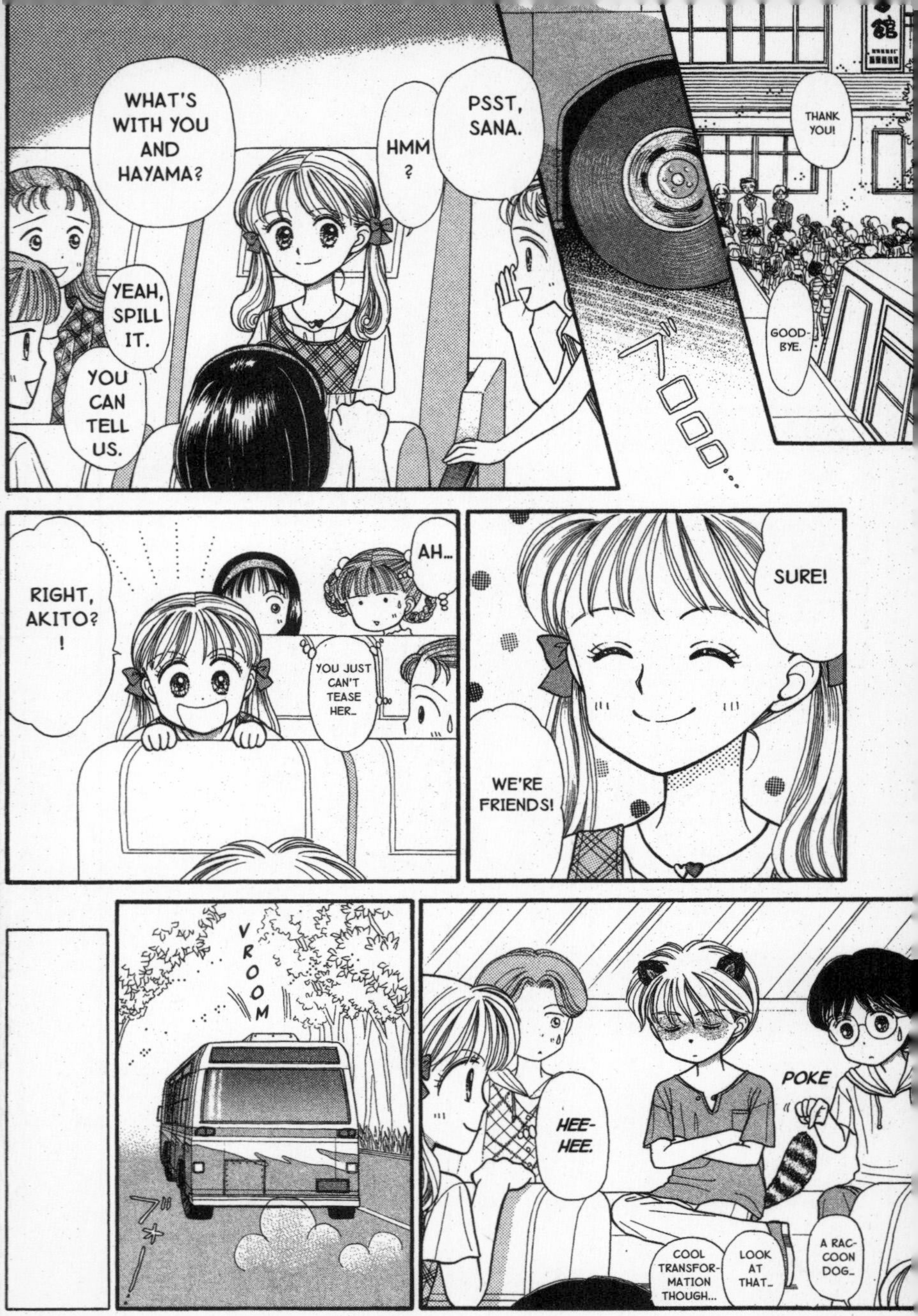
THANK YOU!
GOOD-BYE.
PSST, SANA.
HMM?
WHAT'S WITH YOU AND HAYAMA?
YEAH, SPILL IT.
YOU CAN TELL US.
SURE!
WE'RE FRIENDS!
AH...
YOU JUST CAN'T TEASE HER...
RIGHT, AKITO?!
A RAC-COON DOG...
POKE
LOOK AT THAT...
COOL TRANSFORMATION THOUGH...
HEE-HEE.
VROOM

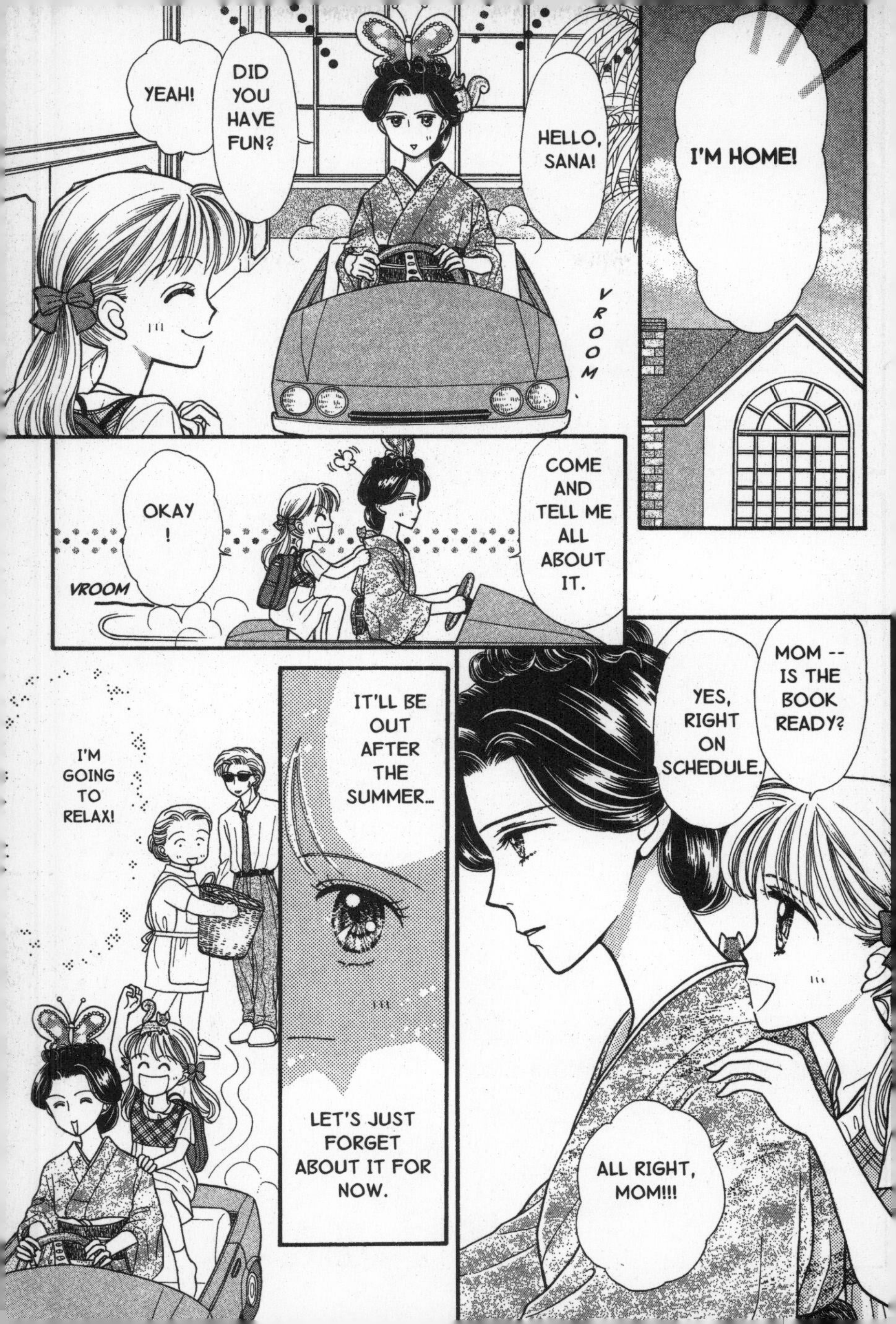
I'M HOME!
HELLO, SANA!
DID YOU HAVE FUN?
YEAH!
VROOM
COME AND TELL ME ALL ABOUT IT.
OKAY !
VROOM
MOM -- IS THE BOOK READY?
YES, RIGHT ON SCHEDULE.
ALL RIGHT, MOM!!!
IT'LL BE OUT AFTER THE SUMMER...
LET'S JUST FORGET ABOUT IT FOR NOW.
I'M GOING TO RELAX!

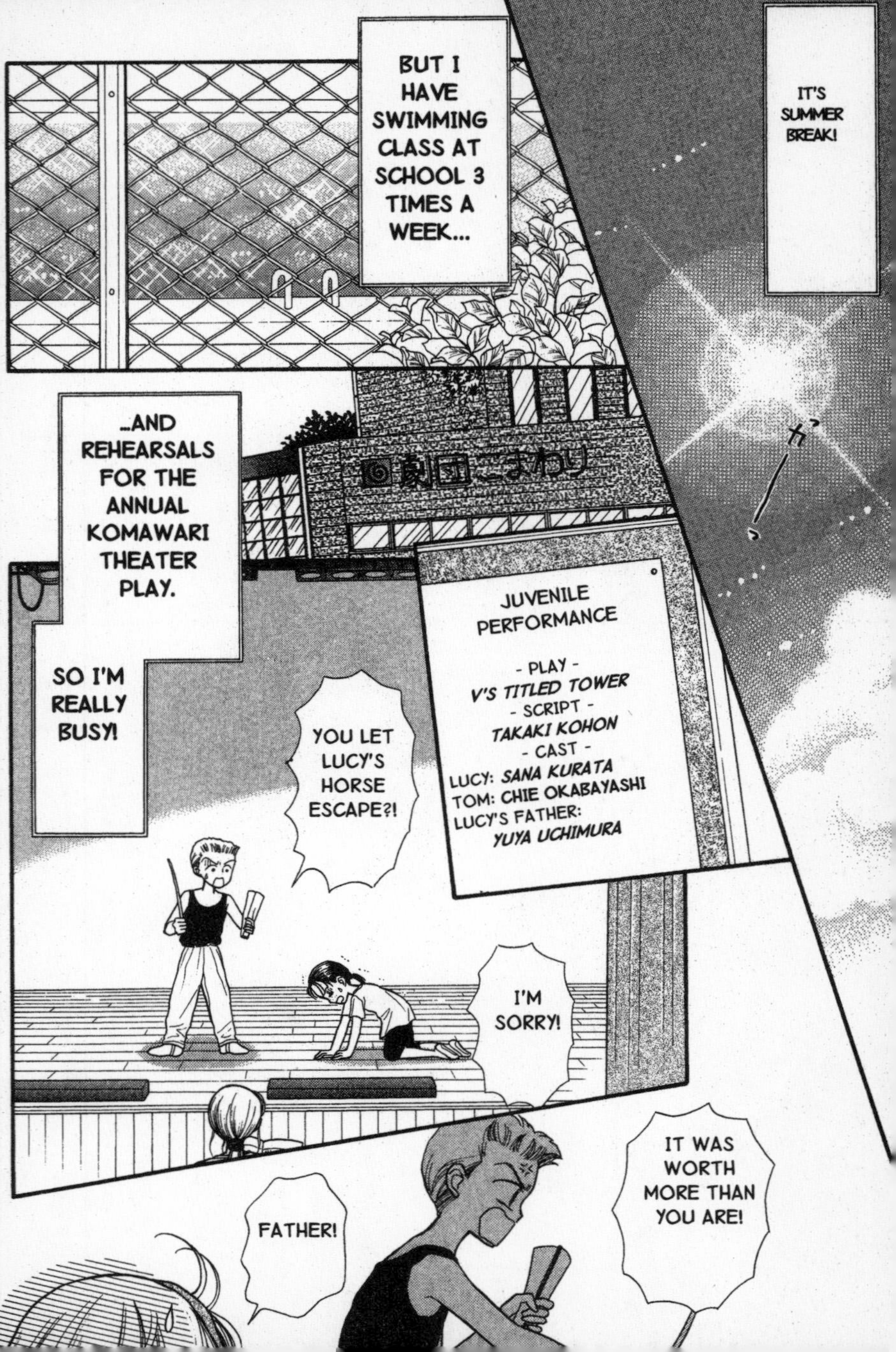
IT'S SUMMER BREAK!
ガー
BUT I HAVE SWIMMING CLASS AT SCHOOL 3 TIMES A WEEK...
劇団こまわり
...AND REHEARSALS FOR THE ANNUAL KOMAWARI THEATER PLAY.
JUVENILE PERFORMANCE
- PLAY -
V'S TITLED TOWER
- SCRIPT -
TAKAKI KOHON
- CAST -
LUCY: SANA KURATA
TOM: CHIE OKABAYASHI
LUCY'S FATHER: YUYA UCHIMURA
SO I'M REALLY BUSY!
YOU LET LUCY'S HORSE ESCAPE?!
I'M SORRY!
IT WAS WORTH MORE THAN YOU ARE!
FATHER!

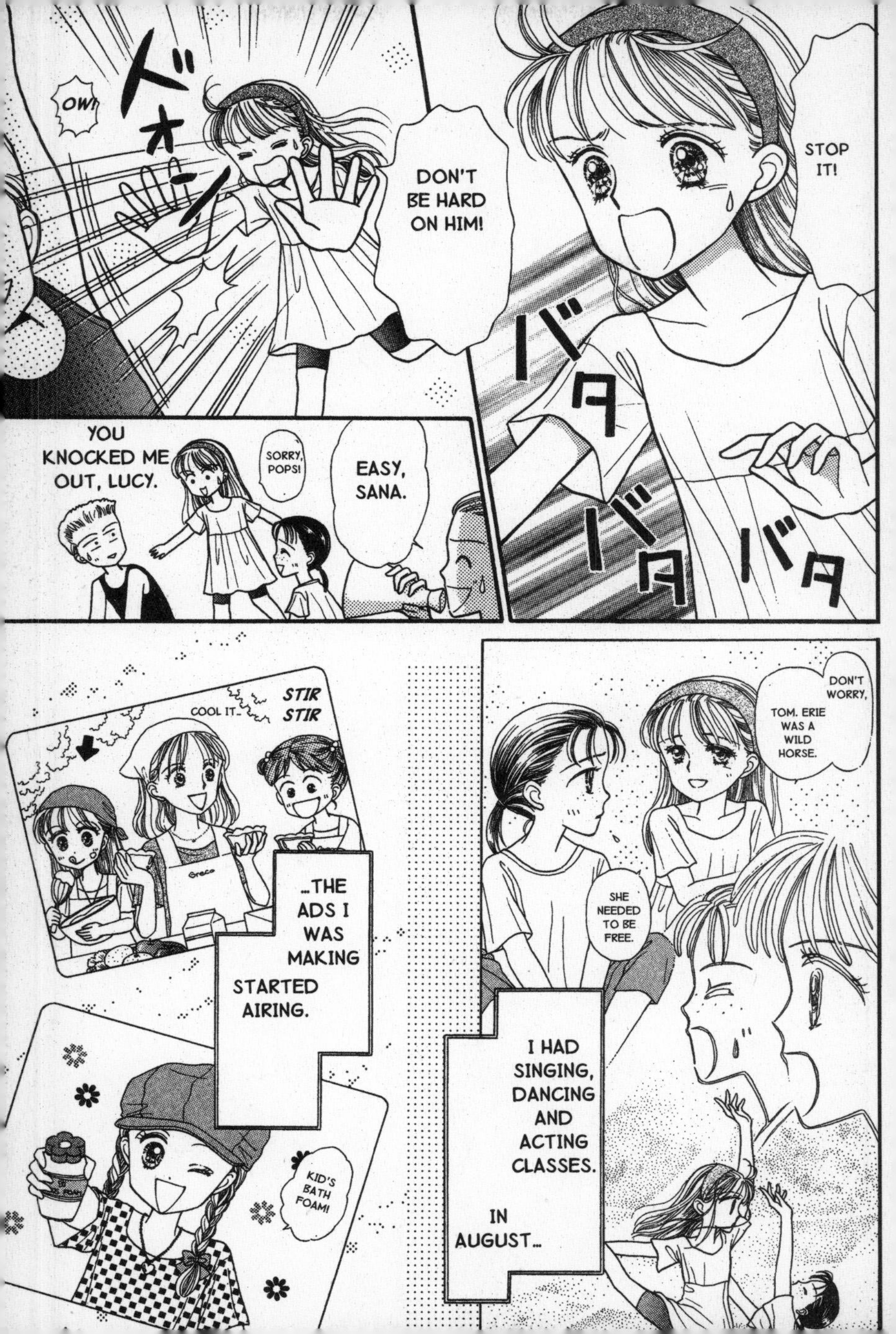
STOP IT!
バタ
バタ
バタ
DON'T BE HARD ON HIM!
ドオーン
OW!
EASY, SANA.
SORRY, POPS!
YOU KNOCKED ME OUT, LUCY.
DON'T WORRY, TOM. ERIE WAS A WILD HORSE.
SHE NEEDED TO BE FREE.
I HAD SINGING, DANCING AND ACTING CLASSES.
IN AUGUST...
STIR STIR
COOL IT...
...THE ADS I WAS MAKING STARTED AIRING.
KID'S BATH FOAM!

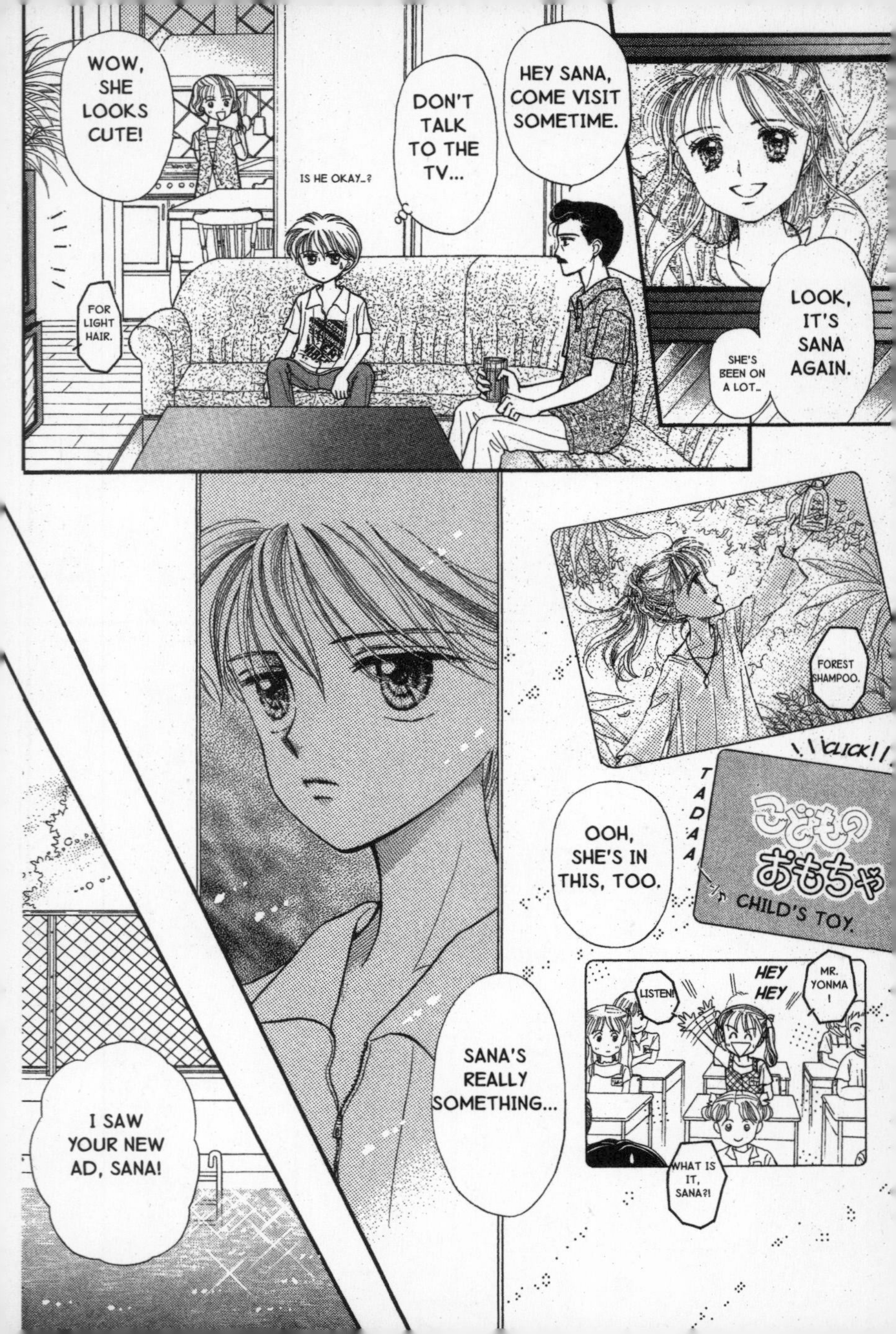
LOOK, IT'S SANA AGAIN.
SHE'S BEEN ON A LOT...
HEY SANA, COME VISIT SOMETIME.
DON'T TALK TO THE TV...
IS HE OKAY...?
WOW, SHE LOOKS CUTE!
FOR LIGHT HAIR.
FOREST SHAMPOO.
CLICK!
TADAAA
こどものおもちゃ
CHILD'S TOY.
OOH, SHE'S IN THIS, TOO.
HEY HEY
MR. YONMA!
LISTEN!
WHAT IS IT, SANA?!
SANA'S REALLY SOMETHING...
I SAW YOUR NEW AD, SANA!

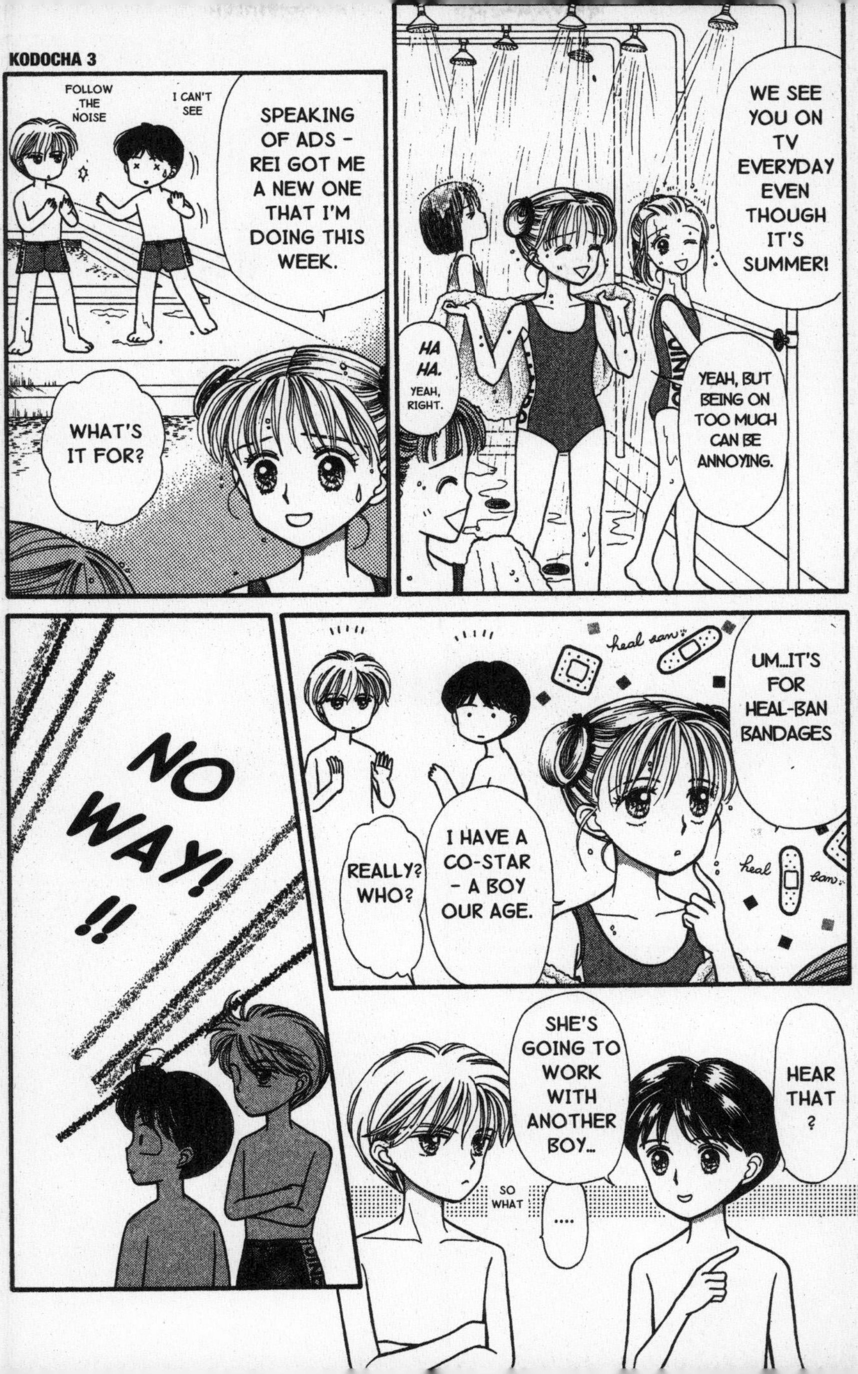
WE SEE YOU ON TV EVERYDAY EVEN THOUGH IT'S SUMMER!
YEAH, BUT BEING ON TOO MUCH CAN BE ANNOYING.
HA HA.
YEAH, RIGHT.
SPEAKING OF ADS - REI GOT ME A NEW ONE THAT I'M DOING THIS WEEK.
I CAN'T SEE
FOLLOW THE NOISE
WHAT'S IT FOR?
UM...IT'S FOR HEAL-BAN BANDAGES
heal ban
heal ban
I HAVE A CO-STAR - A BOY OUR AGE.
REALLY? WHO?
HEAR THAT?
SHE'S GOING TO WORK WITH ANOTHER BOY...
SO WHAT
....
NO WAY! !!

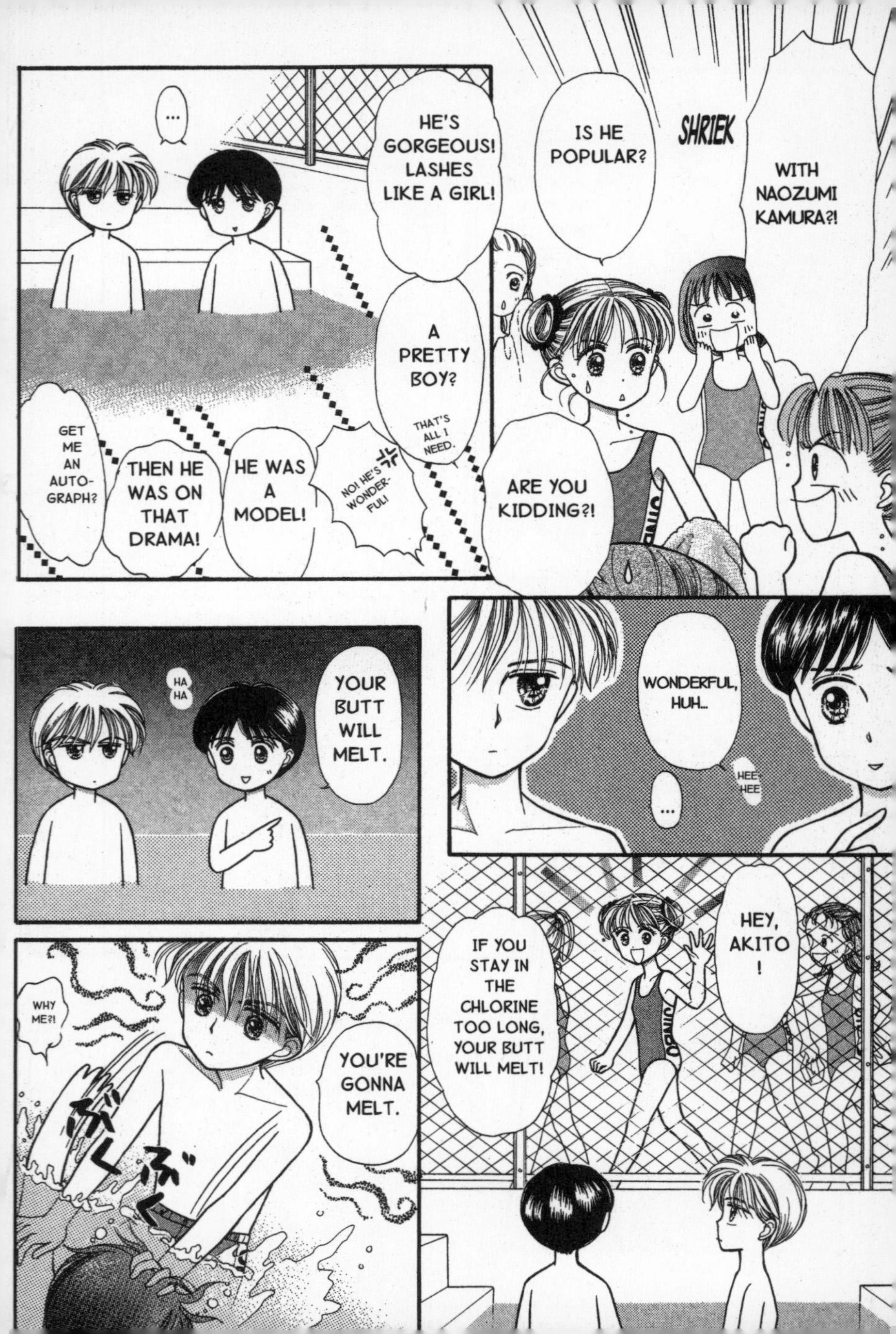
SHRIEK
WITH NAOZUMI KAMURA?!
IS HE POPULAR?
ARE YOU KIDDING?!
HE'S GORGEOUS! LASHES LIKE A GIRL!
A PRETTY BOY?
THAT'S ALL I NEED.
NO! HE'S WONDERFUL!
HE WAS A MODEL!
THEN HE WAS ON THAT DRAMA!
GET ME AN AUTOGRAPH?
...
WONDERFUL, HUH..
HEE HEE
...
YOUR BUTT WILL MELT.
HA HA
HEY, AKITO!
IF YOU STAY IN THE CHLORINE TOO LONG, YOUR BUTT WILL MELT!
YOU'RE GONNA MELT.
WHY ME?!
ぶくぶく

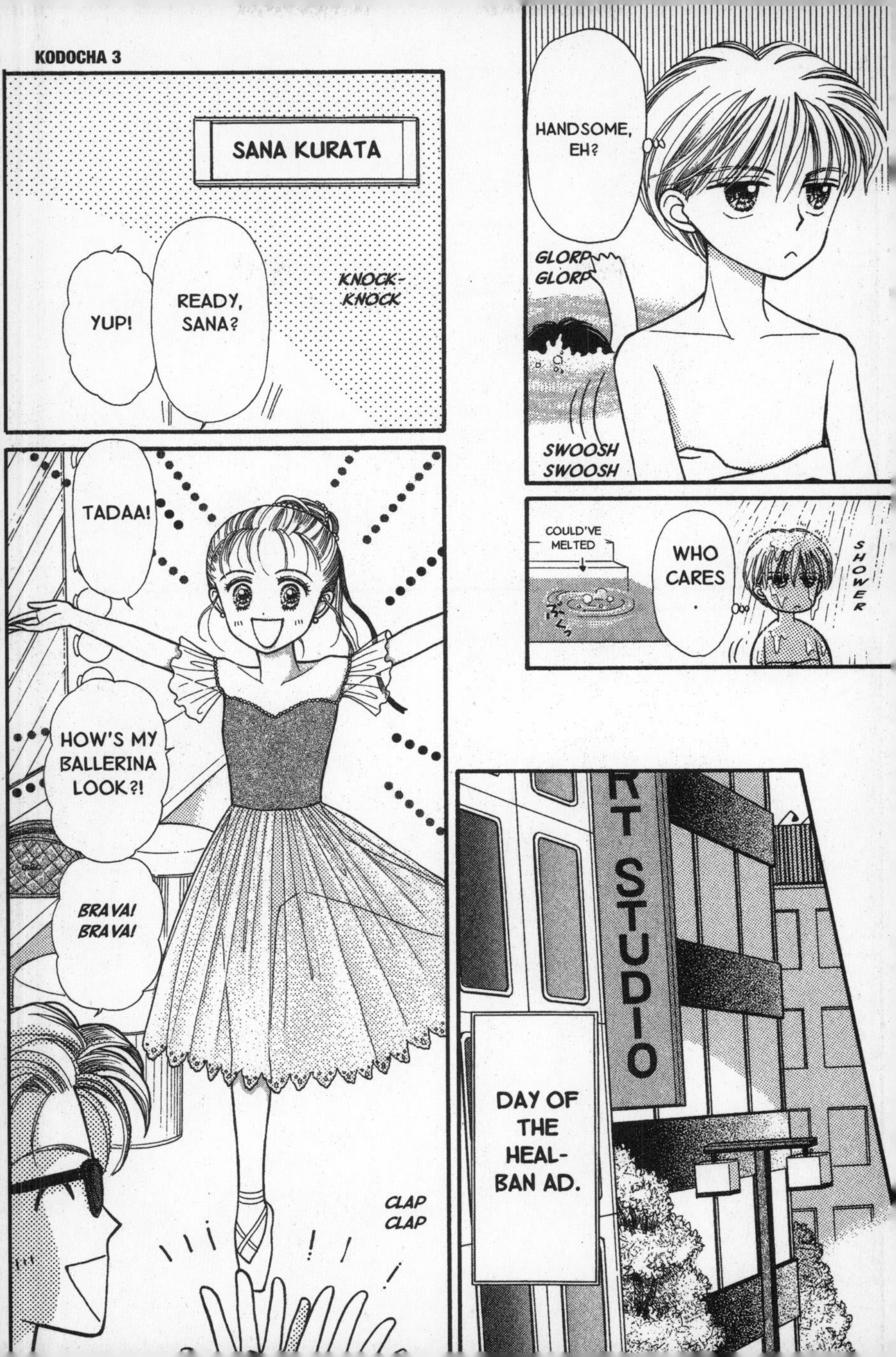
HANDSOME, EH?
GLORP GLORP
SWOOSH SWOOSH
COULD'VE MELTED
WHO CARES.
SHOWER
RT STUDIO
DAY OF THE HEAL-BAN AD.
SANA KURATA
KNOCK-KNOCK
READY, SANA?
YUP!
TADAA!
HOW'S MY BALLERINA LOOK?!
BRAVA! BRAVA!
CLAP CLAP

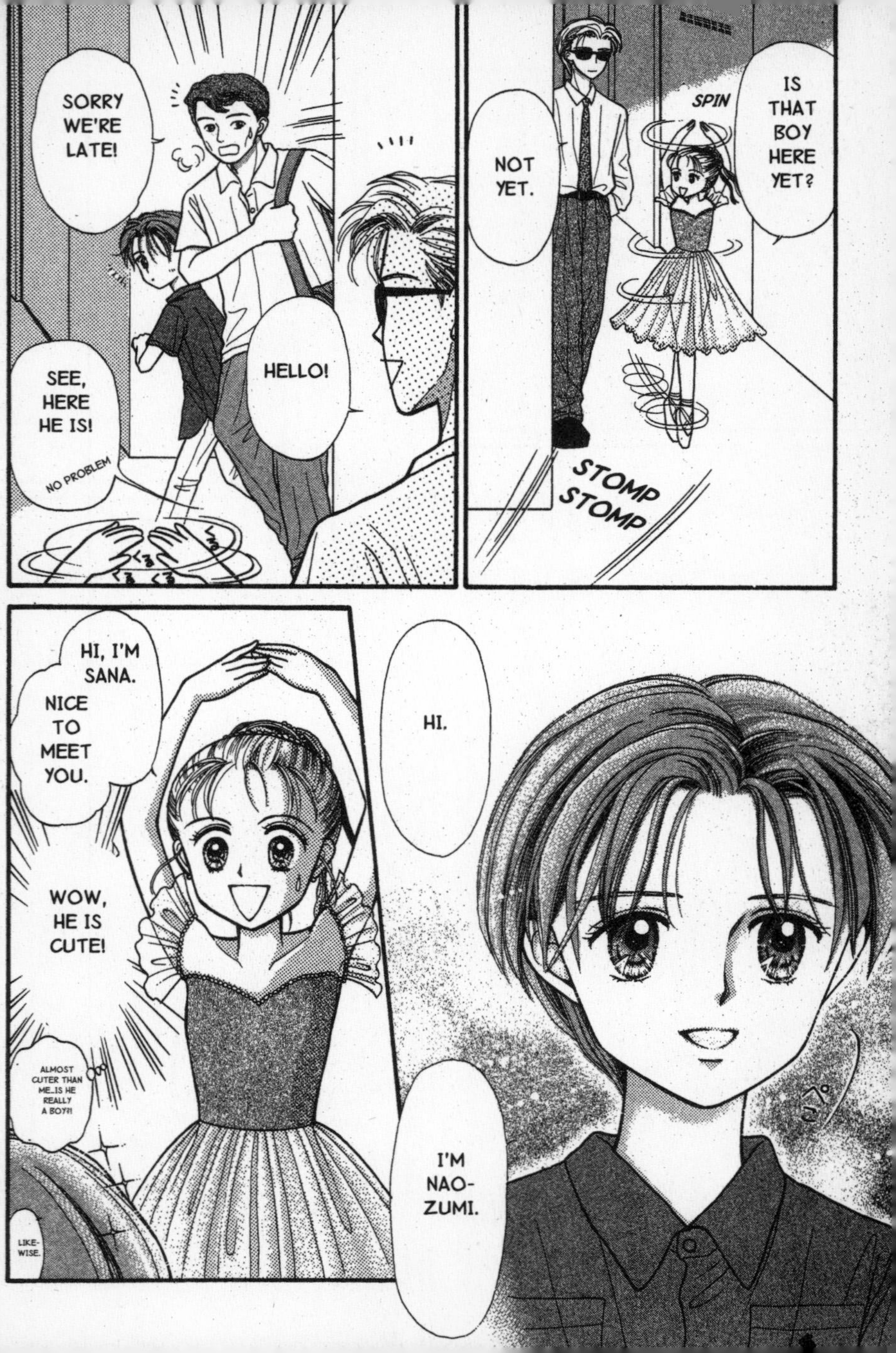

IS THAT BOY HERE YET?
SPIN
NOT YET.
STOMP STOMP
SORRY WE'RE LATE!
HELLO!
SEE, HERE HE IS!
NO PROBLEM
HI.
I'M NAO-ZUMI.
HI, I'M SANA. NICE TO MEET YOU.
WOW, HE IS CUTE!
ALMOST CUTER THAN ME...IS HE REALLY A BOY?!
LIKE-WISE.

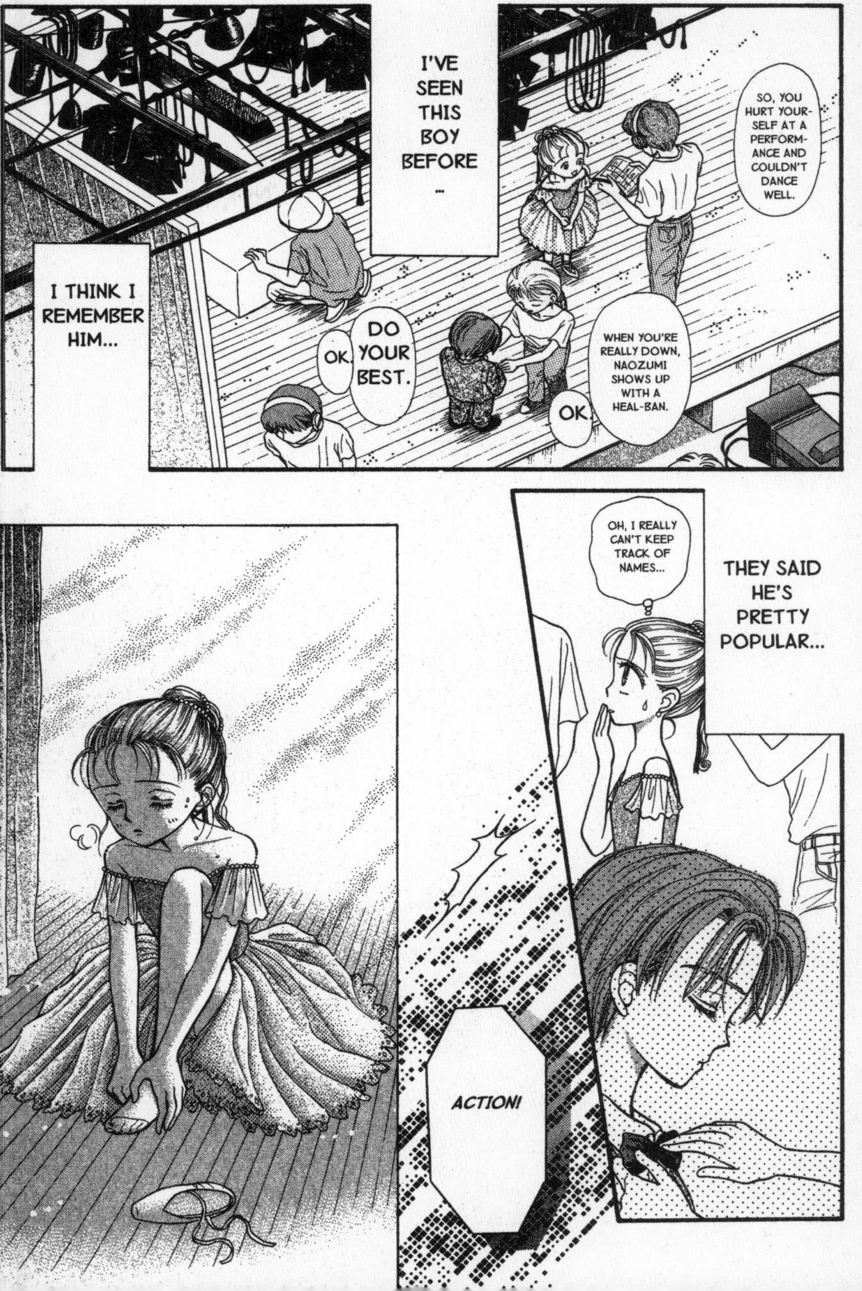
SO, YOU HURT YOURSELF AT A PERFORMANCE AND COULDN'T DANCE WELL.
I'VE SEEN THIS BOY BEFORE ...
WHEN YOU'RE REALLY DOWN, NAOZUMI SHOWS UP WITH A HEAL-BAN.
OK.
DO YOUR BEST.
OK.
I THINK I REMEMBER HIM...
THEY SAID HE'S PRETTY POPULAR...
OH, I REALLY CAN'T KEEP TRACK OF NAMES...
ACTION!

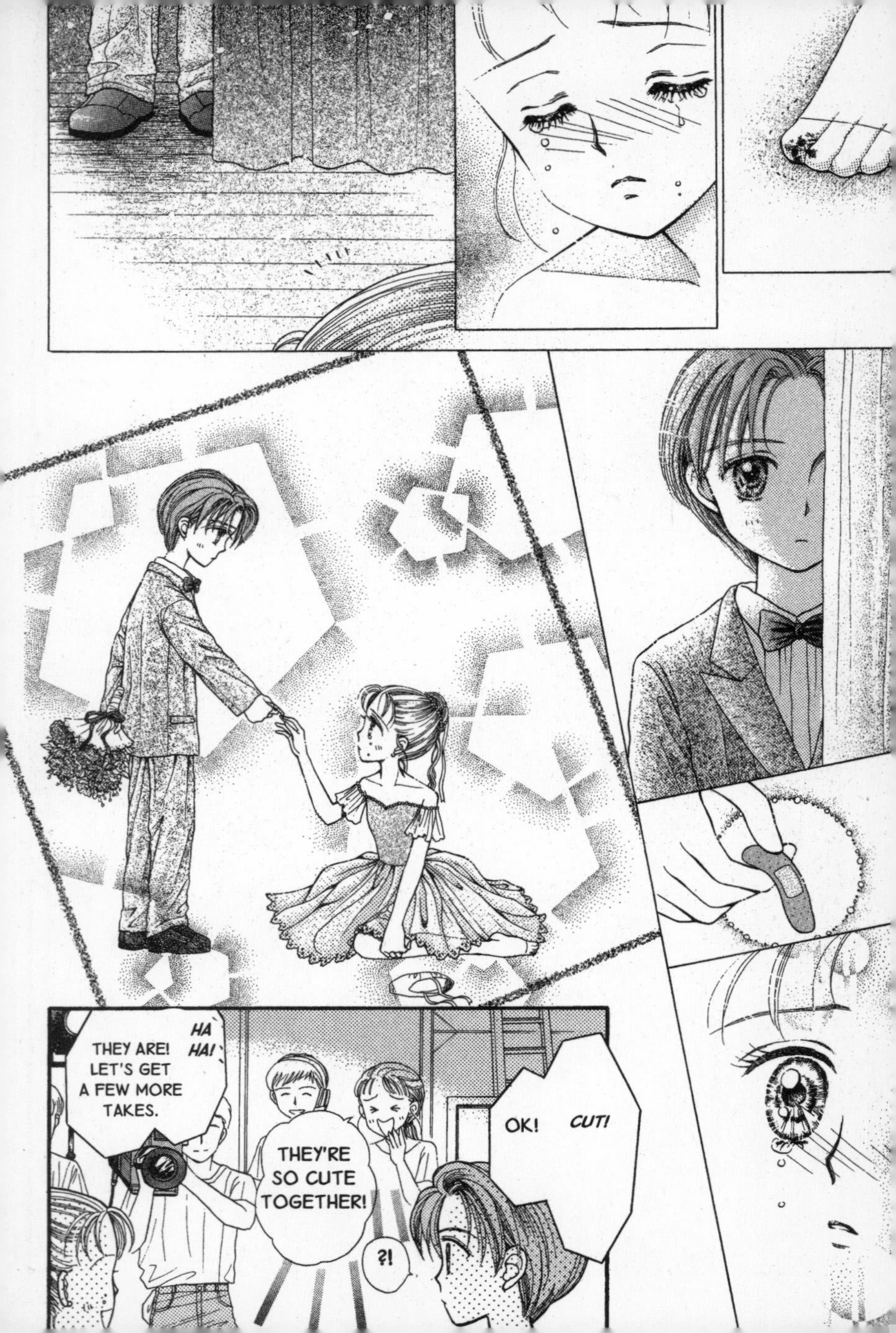
CUT!
OK!
HA HA!
THEY ARE! LET'S GET A FEW MORE TAKES.
THEY'RE SO CUTE TOGETHER!
?!

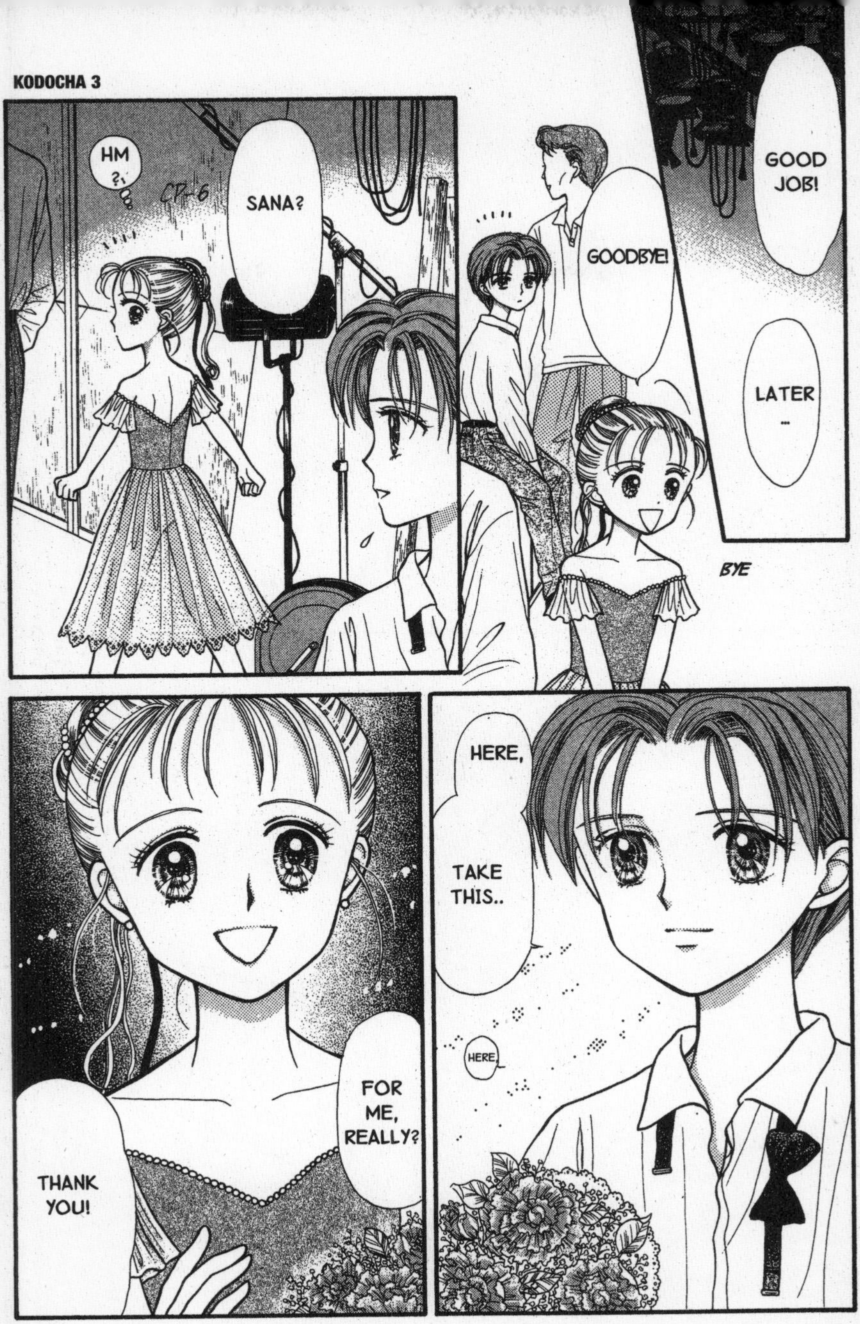
GOOD JOB!
LATER ...
GOODBYE!
BYE
SANA?
HM ?
HERE,
TAKE THIS..
HERE
FOR ME, REALLY?
THANK YOU!

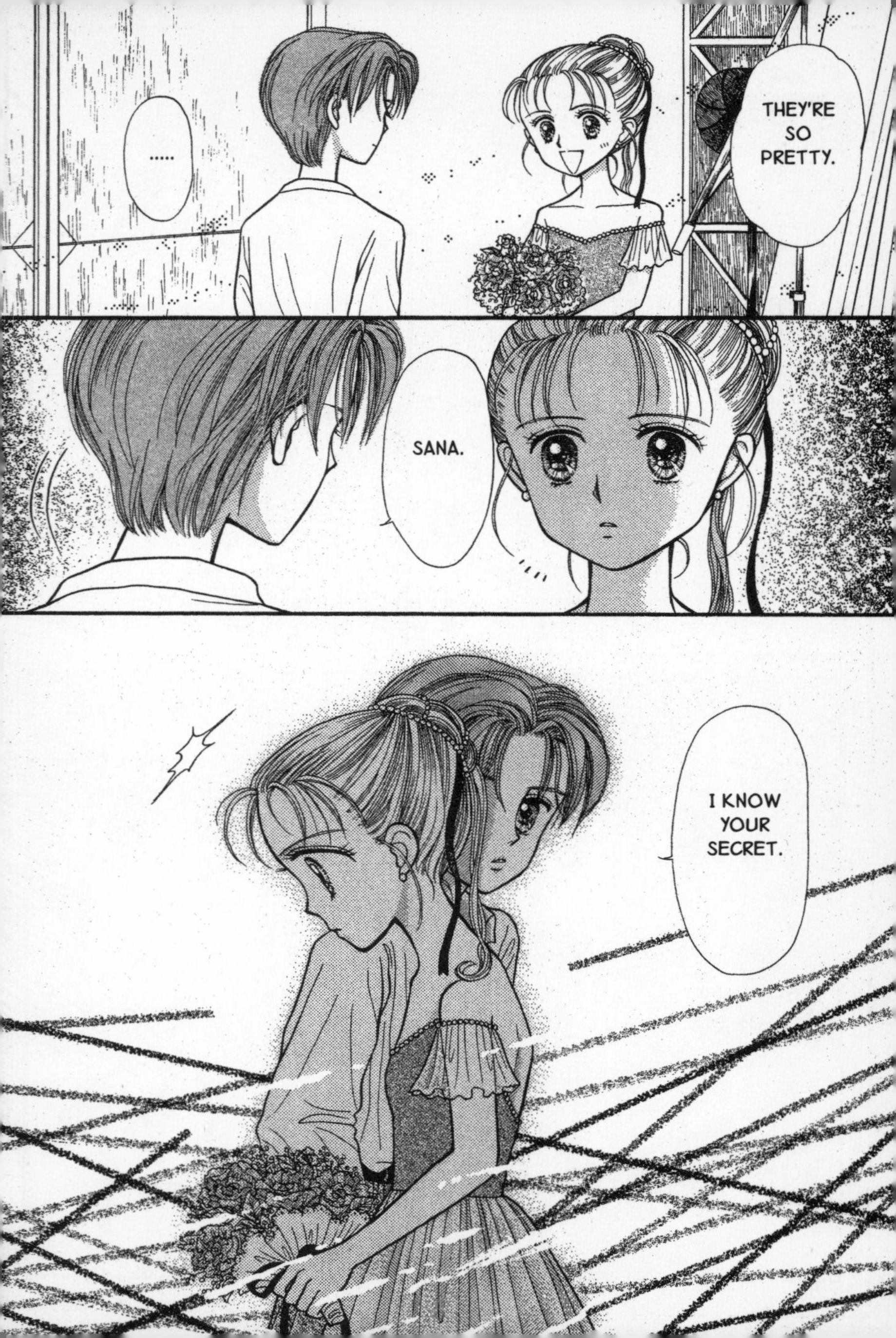
THEY'RE SO PRETTY.
.....
SANA.
I KNOW YOUR SECRET.

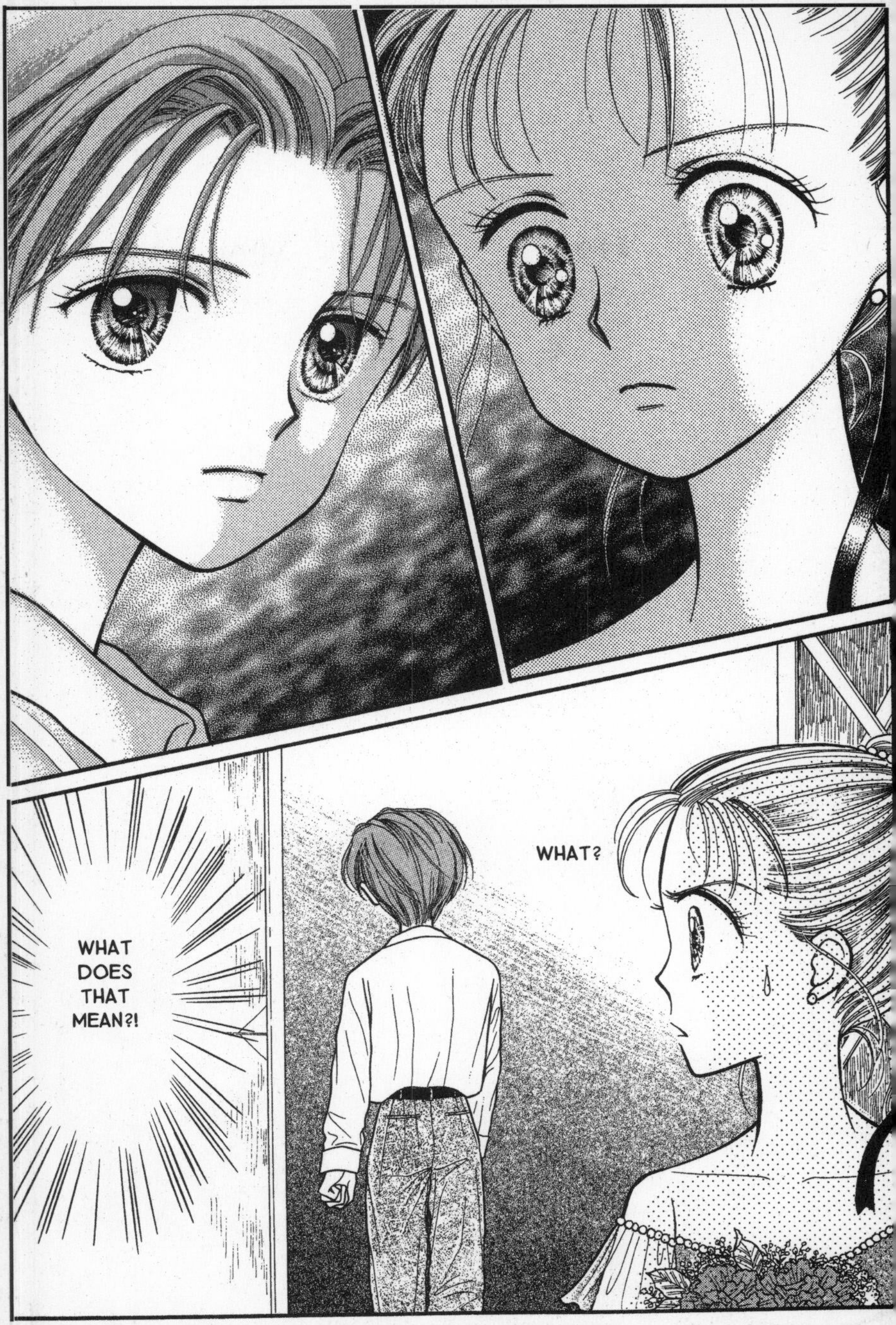
WHAT?
WHAT DOES THAT MEAN?!

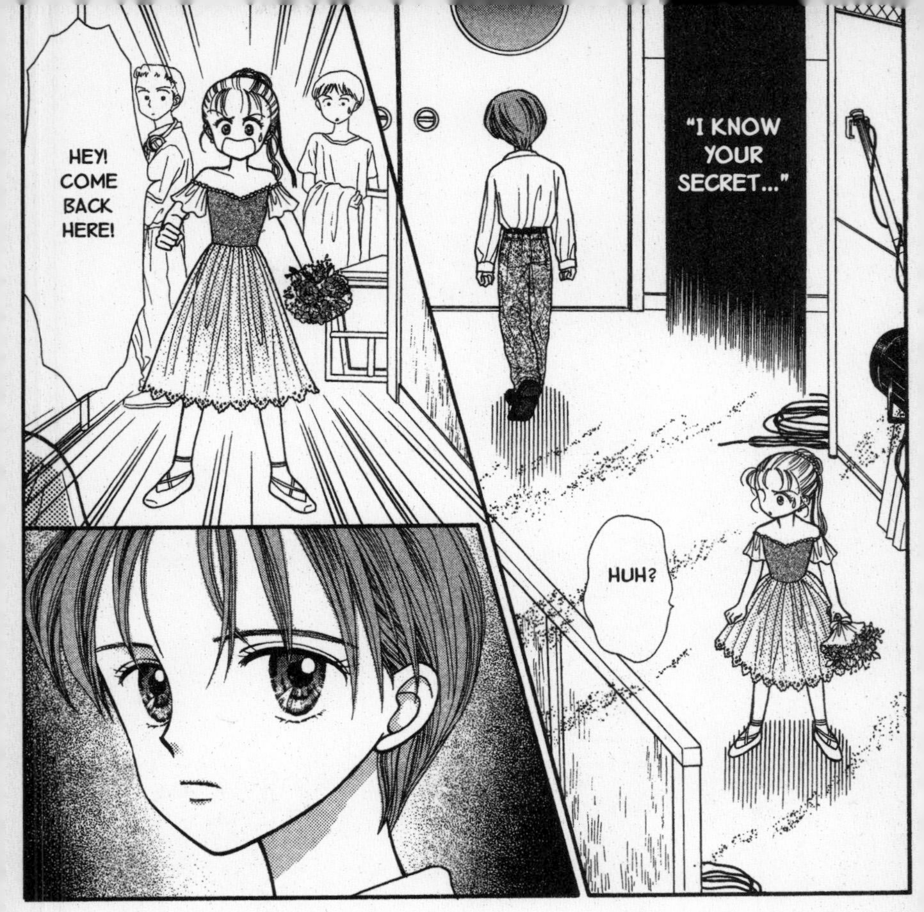
"I KNOW YOUR SECRET..."
HEY! COME BACK HERE!
HUH?

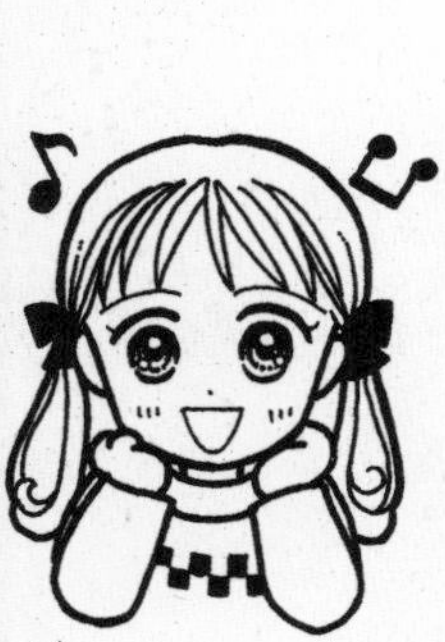

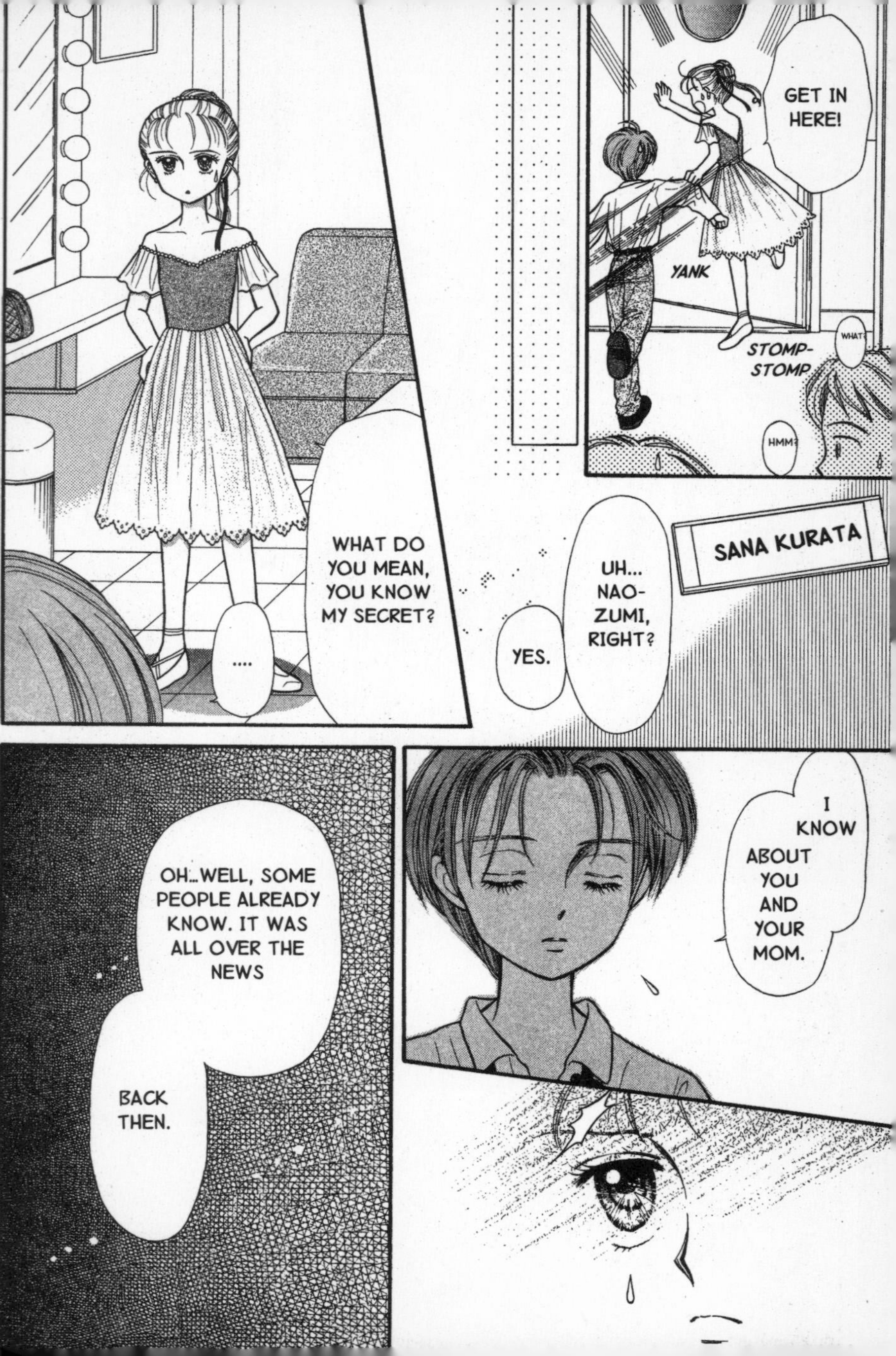
GET IN HERE!
YANK
STOMP-STOMP
WHAT?
HMM?
SANA KURATA
UH... NAO-ZUMI, RIGHT?
YES.
WHAT DO YOU MEAN, YOU KNOW MY SECRET?
....
I KNOW ABOUT YOU AND YOUR MOM.
OH...WELL, SOME PEOPLE ALREADY KNOW. IT WAS ALL OVER THE NEWS
BACK THEN.

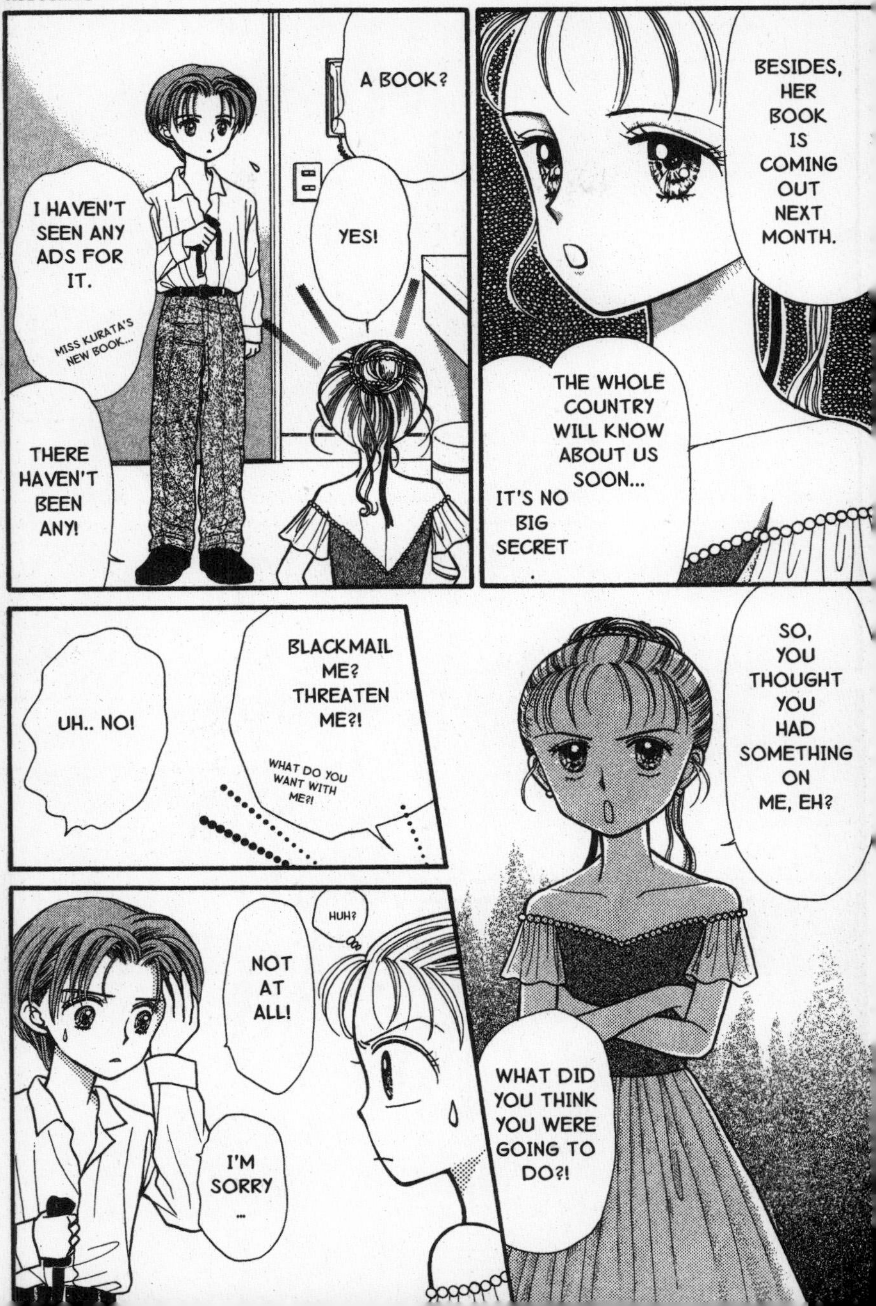
BESIDES, HER BOOK IS COMING OUT NEXT MONTH.
THE WHOLE COUNTRY WILL KNOW ABOUT US SOON...
IT'S NO BIG SECRET.
A BOOK?
YES!
I HAVEN'T SEEN ANY ADS FOR IT.
MISS KURATA'S NEW BOOK...
THERE HAVEN'T BEEN ANY!
SO, YOU THOUGHT YOU HAD SOMETHING ON ME, EH?
WHAT DID YOU THINK YOU WERE GOING TO DO?!
BLACKMAIL ME? THREATEN ME?!
WHAT DO YOU WANT WITH ME?!
UH.. NO!
HUH?
NOT AT ALL!
I'M SORRY ...

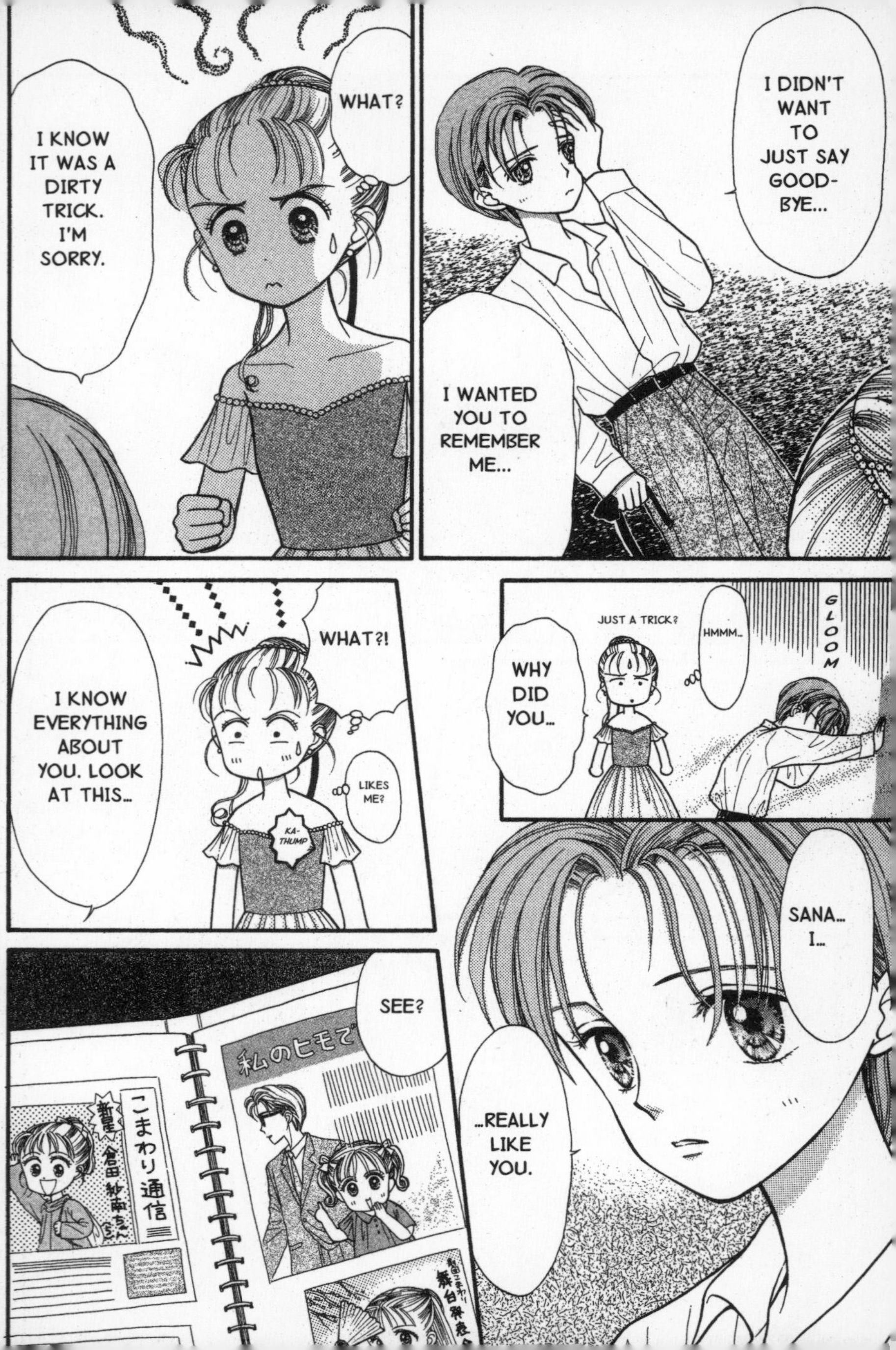
I DIDN'T WANT TO JUST SAY GOOD-BYE...
I WANTED YOU TO REMEMBER ME...
WHAT?
I KNOW IT WAS A DIRTY TRICK. I'M SORRY.
GLOOM
HMMM...
JUST A TRICK?
WHY DID YOU...
WHAT?!
LIKES ME?
KA-THUMP
I KNOW EVERYTHING ABOUT YOU. LOOK AT THIS...
SANA... I...
...REALLY LIKE YOU.
SEE?
私のヒモで
こまわり通信
新星
倉田紗南ちゃん

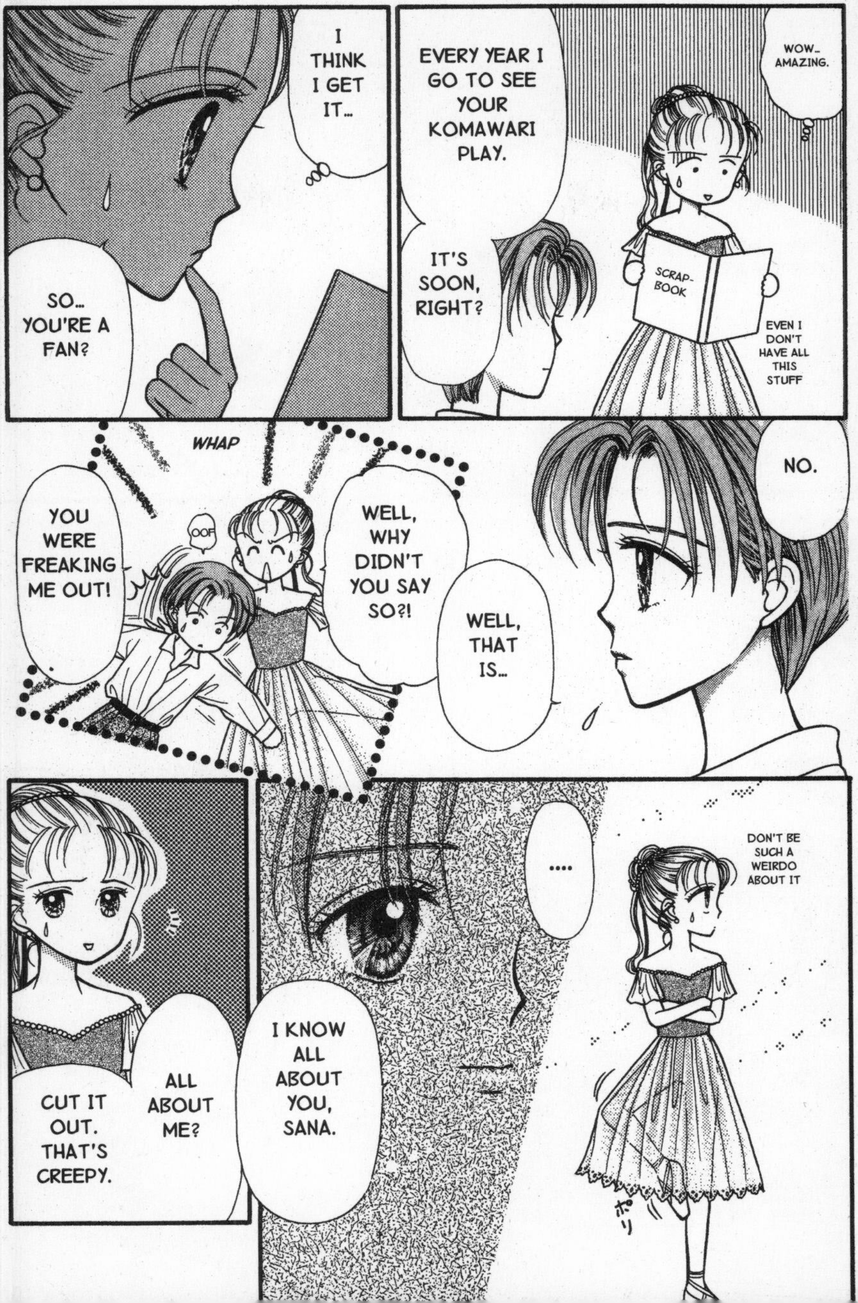
EVERY YEAR I GO TO SEE YOUR KOMAWARI PLAY.
WOW... AMAZING.
SCRAP-BOOK
EVEN I DON'T HAVE ALL THIS STUFF
IT'S SOON, RIGHT?
I THINK I GET IT...
SO... YOU'RE A FAN?
NO.
WELL, THAT IS...
WELL, WHY DIDN'T YOU SAY SO?!
WHAP
OOF
YOU WERE FREAKING ME OUT!
DON'T BE SUCH A WEIRDO ABOUT IT
....
ポリ
I KNOW ALL ABOUT YOU, SANA.
ALL ABOUT ME?
CUT IT OUT. THAT'S CREEPY.

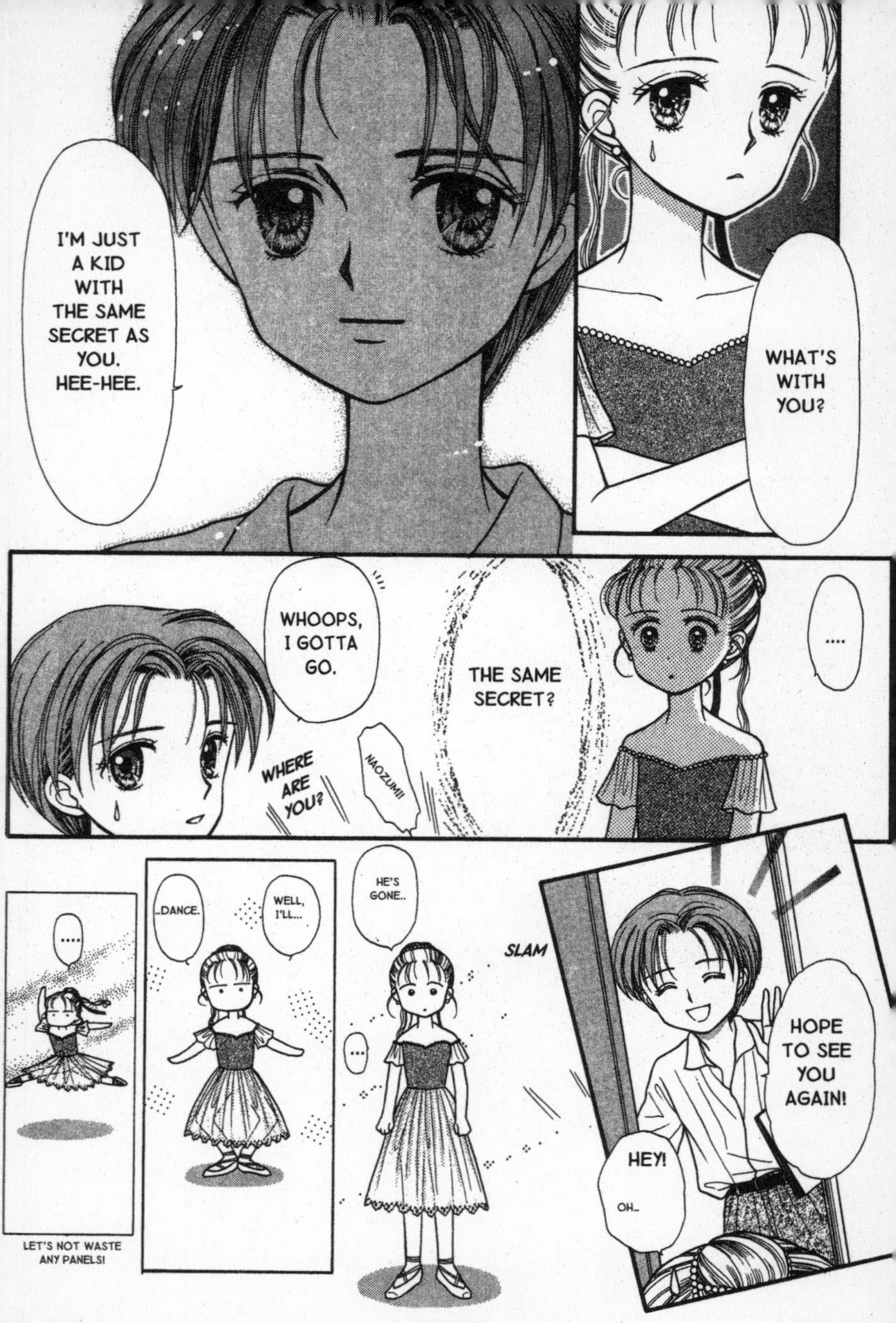
WHAT'S WITH YOU?
I'M JUST A KID WITH THE SAME SECRET AS YOU. HEE-HEE.
....
THE SAME SECRET?
WHOOPS, I GOTTA GO.
NAOZUMI!
WHERE ARE YOU?
HOPE TO SEE YOU AGAIN!
HEY!
OH..
SLAM
HE'S GONE..
....
WELL, I'LL...
..DANCE.
....
LET'S NOT WASTE ANY PANELS!

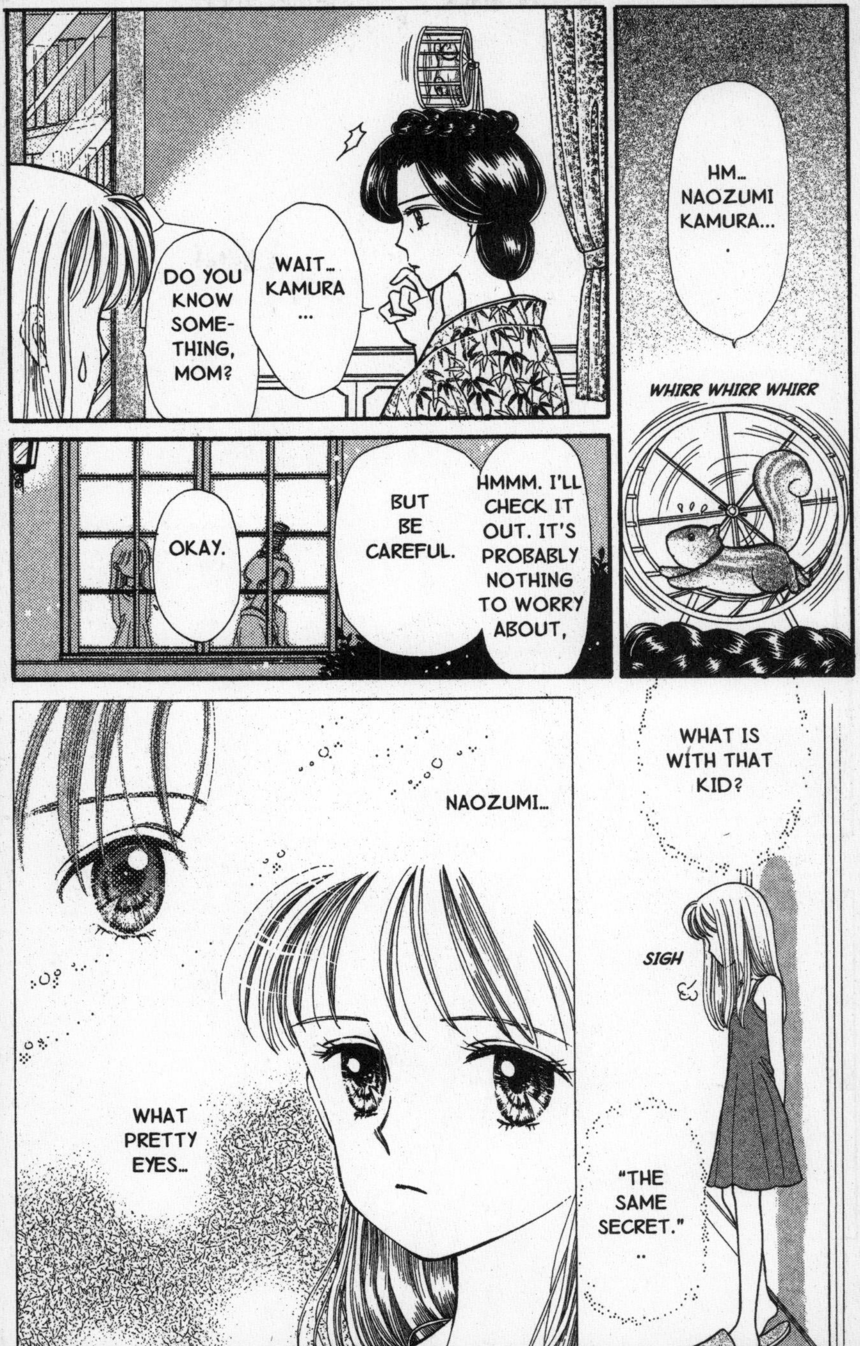
HM... NAOZUMI KAMURA....
WHIRR WHIRR WHIRR
WAIT... KAMURA...
DO YOU KNOW SOME-THING, MOM?
HMMM. I'LL CHECK IT OUT. IT'S PROBABLY NOTHING TO WORRY ABOUT,
BUT BE CAREFUL.
OKAY.
WHAT IS WITH THAT KID?
SIGH
"THE SAME SECRET." ..
NAOZUMI...
WHAT PRETTY EYES...

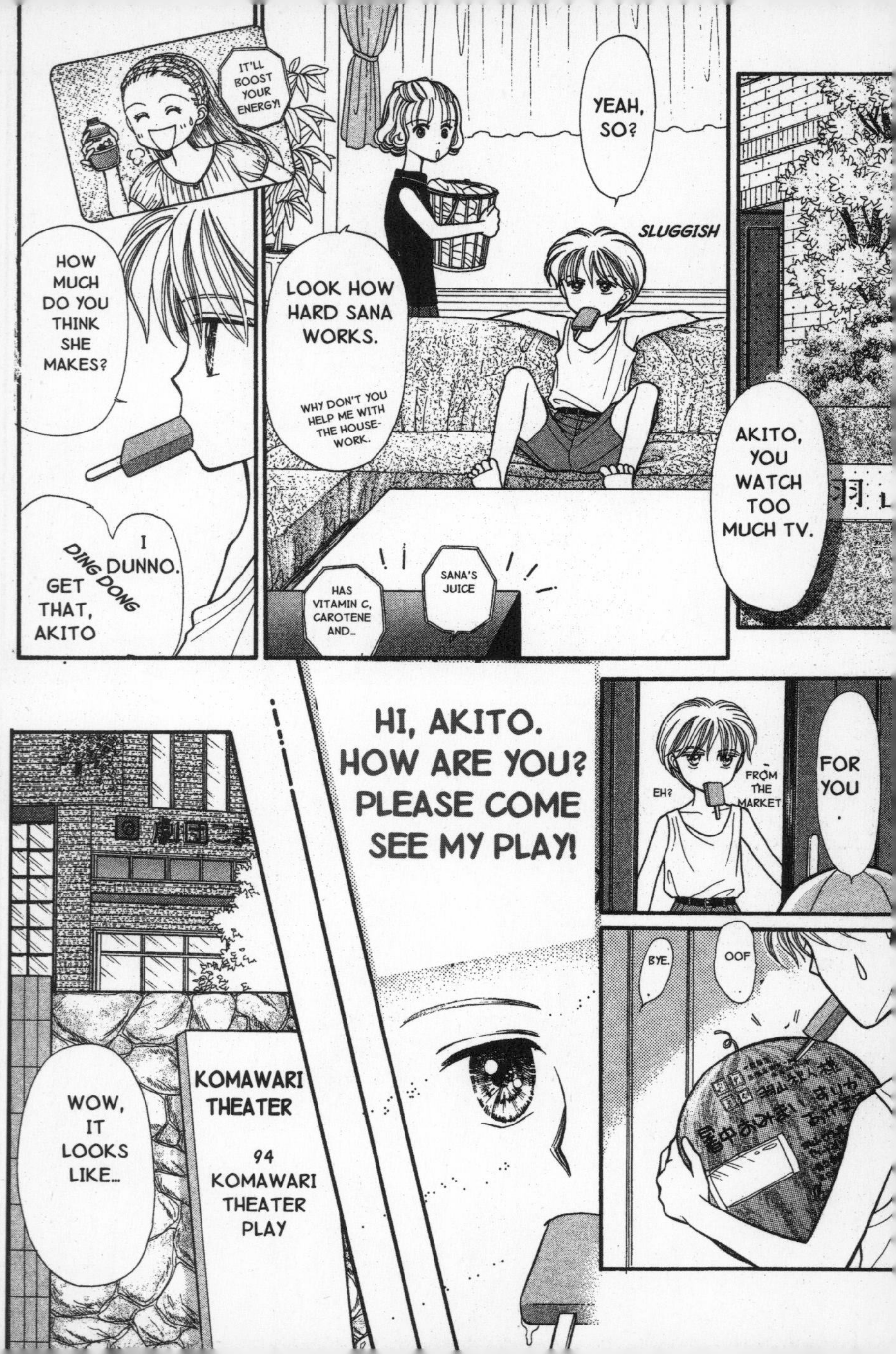
AKITO, YOU WATCH TOO MUCH TV.
YEAH, SO?
SLUGGISH
LOOK HOW HARD SANA WORKS.
WHY DON'T YOU HELP ME WITH THE HOUSE-WORK.
SANA'S JUICE
HAS VITAMIN C, CAROTENE AND...
IT'LL BOOST YOUR ENERGY!
HOW MUCH DO YOU THINK SHE MAKES?
I DUNNO.
DING DONG
GET THAT, AKITO
FOR YOU.
FROM THE MARKET
EH?
OOF
BYE.
HI, AKITO. HOW ARE YOU? PLEASE COME SEE MY PLAY!
KOMAWARI THEATER
94 KOMAWARI THEATER PLAY
WOW, IT LOOKS LIKE...

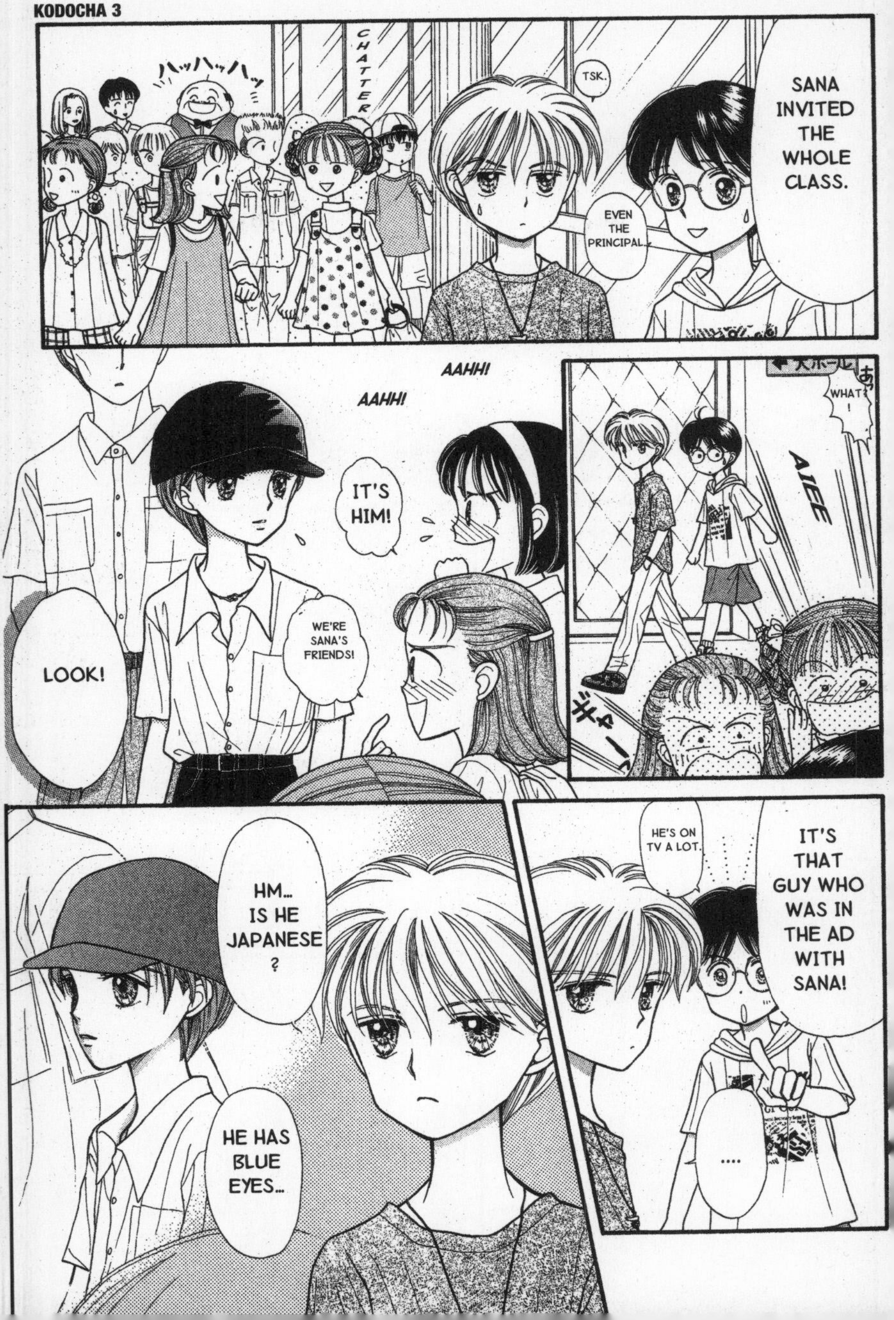
SANA INVITED THE WHOLE CLASS.
TSK.
EVEN THE PRINCIPAL.
CHATTER
ハッハッハッ
大ホール
WHAT!
AIEE
AAHH!
AAHH!
IT'S HIM!
WE'RE SANA'S FRIENDS!
LOOK!
IT'S THAT GUY WHO WAS IN THE AD WITH SANA!
HE'S ON TV A LOT.
....
HM... IS HE JAPANESE ?
HE HAS BLUE EYES...

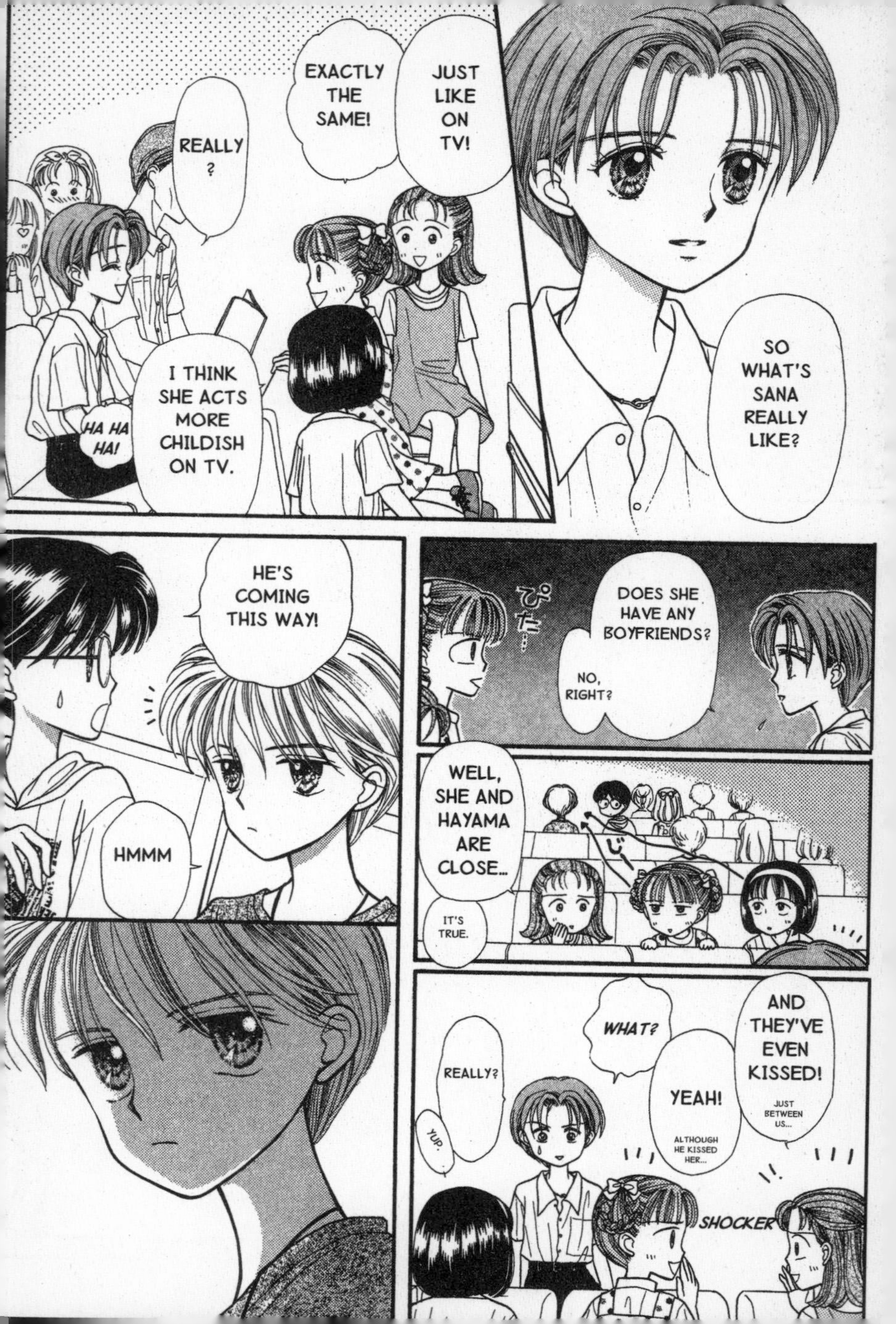
SO WHAT'S SANA REALLY LIKE?
JUST LIKE ON TV!
EXACTLY THE SAME!
REALLY?
I THINK SHE ACTS MORE CHILDISH ON TV.
HA HA HA!
ぴた…
DOES SHE HAVE ANY BOYFRIENDS?
NO, RIGHT?
WELL, SHE AND HAYAMA ARE CLOSE...
IT'S TRUE.
AND THEY'VE EVEN KISSED!
JUST BETWEEN US...
WHAT?
YEAH!
ALTHOUGH HE KISSED HER...
REALLY?
YUP.
SHOCKER
HE'S COMING THIS WAY!
HMMM

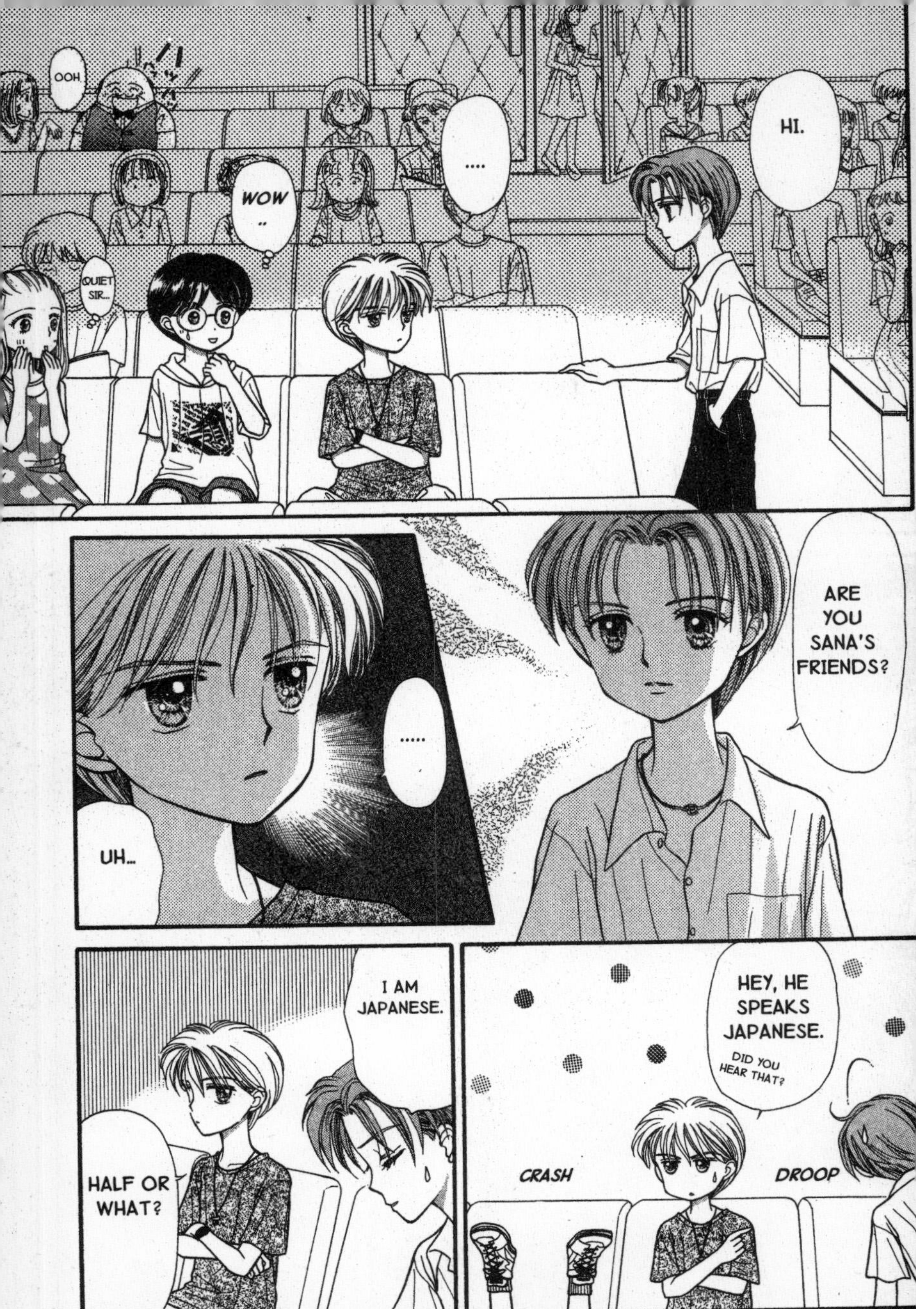
HI.
....
OOH.
WOW ..
QUIET SIR...
ARE YOU SANA'S FRIENDS?
.....
UH...
HEY, HE SPEAKS JAPANESE.
DID YOU HEAR THAT?
DROOP
CRASH
I AM JAPANESE.
HALF OR WHAT?

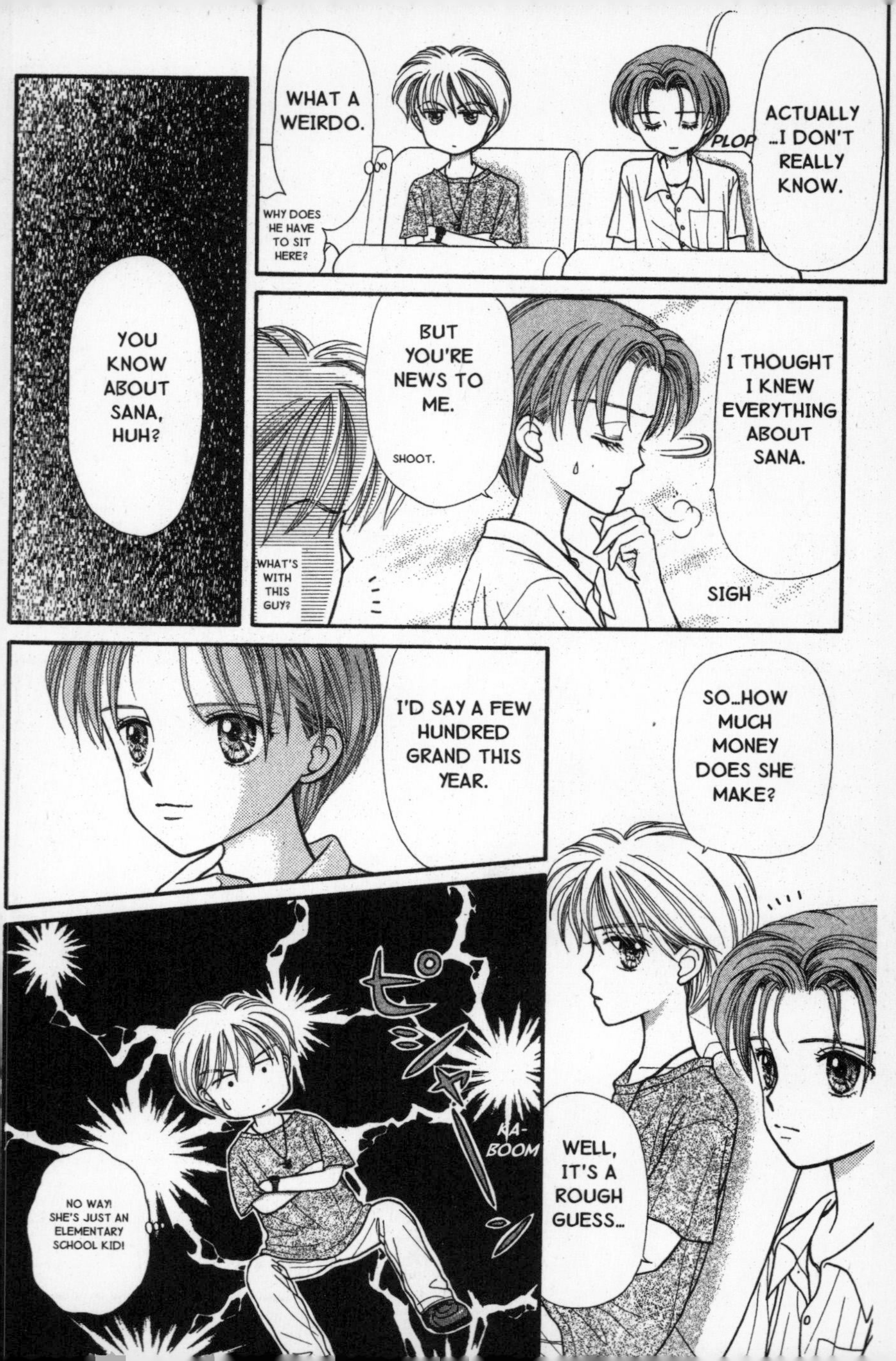
ACTUALLY ...I DON'T REALLY KNOW.
PLOP
WHAT A WEIRDO.
WHY DOES HE HAVE TO SIT HERE?
I THOUGHT I KNEW EVERYTHING ABOUT SANA.
SIGH
BUT YOU'RE NEWS TO ME.
SHOOT.
WHAT'S WITH THIS GUY?
YOU KNOW ABOUT SANA, HUH?
SO...HOW MUCH MONEY DOES SHE MAKE?
WELL, IT'S A ROUGH GUESS...
I'D SAY A FEW HUNDRED GRAND THIS YEAR.
KA-BOOM
NO WAY! SHE'S JUST AN ELEMENTARY SCHOOL KID!

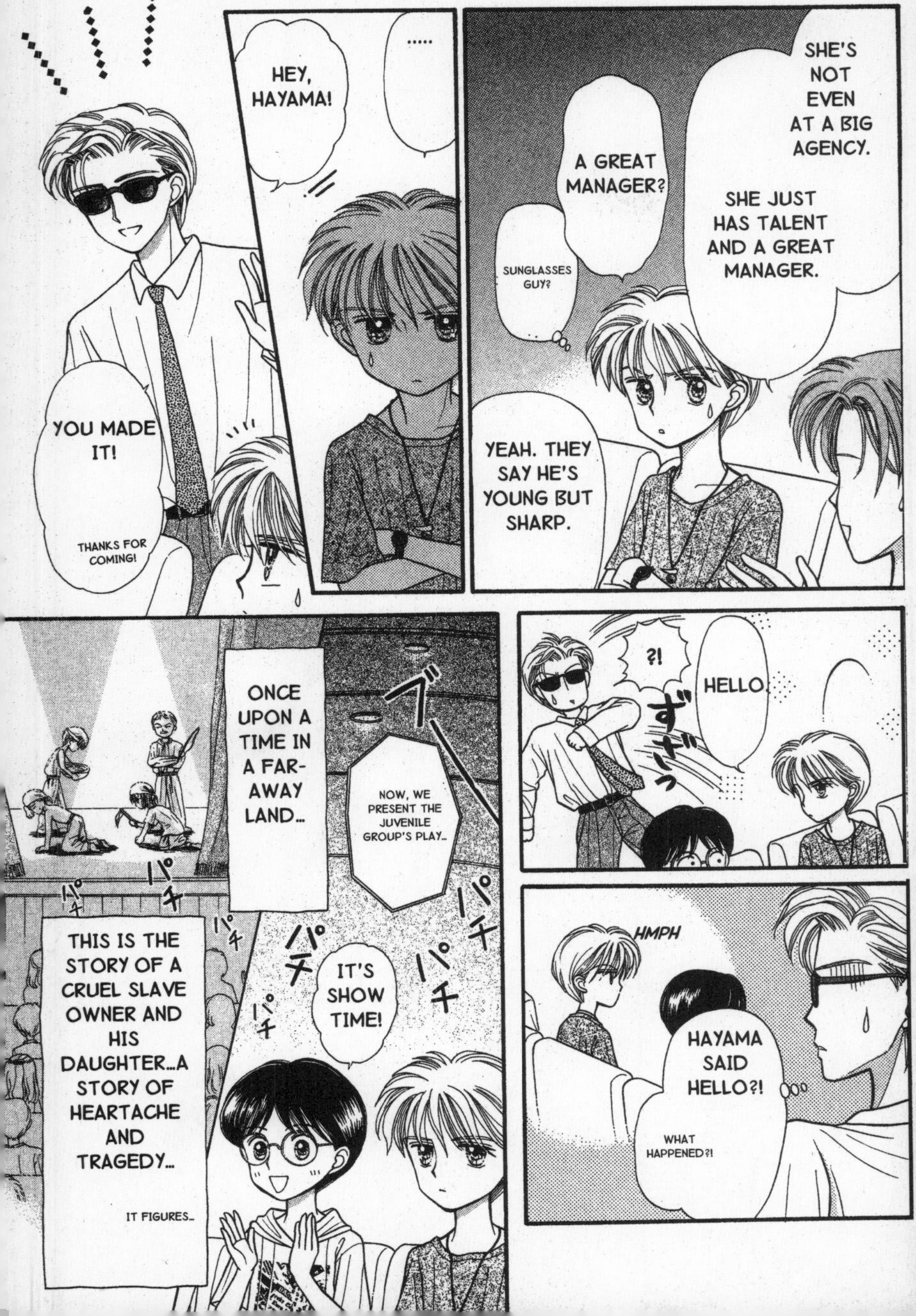
SHE'S NOT EVEN AT A BIG AGENCY.
SHE JUST HAS TALENT AND A GREAT MANAGER.
A GREAT MANAGER?
SUNGLASSES GUY?
YEAH. THEY SAY HE'S YOUNG BUT SHARP.
.....
HEY, HAYAMA!
YOU MADE IT!
THANKS FOR COMING!
HELLO.
?!
HMPH
HAYAMA SAID HELLO?!
WHAT HAPPENED?!
ONCE UPON A TIME IN A FAR-AWAY LAND...
NOW, WE PRESENT THE JUVENILE GROUP'S PLAY...
IT'S SHOW TIME!
THIS IS THE STORY OF A CRUEL SLAVE OWNER AND HIS DAUGHTER...A STORY OF HEARTACHE AND TRAGEDY...
IT FIGURES...

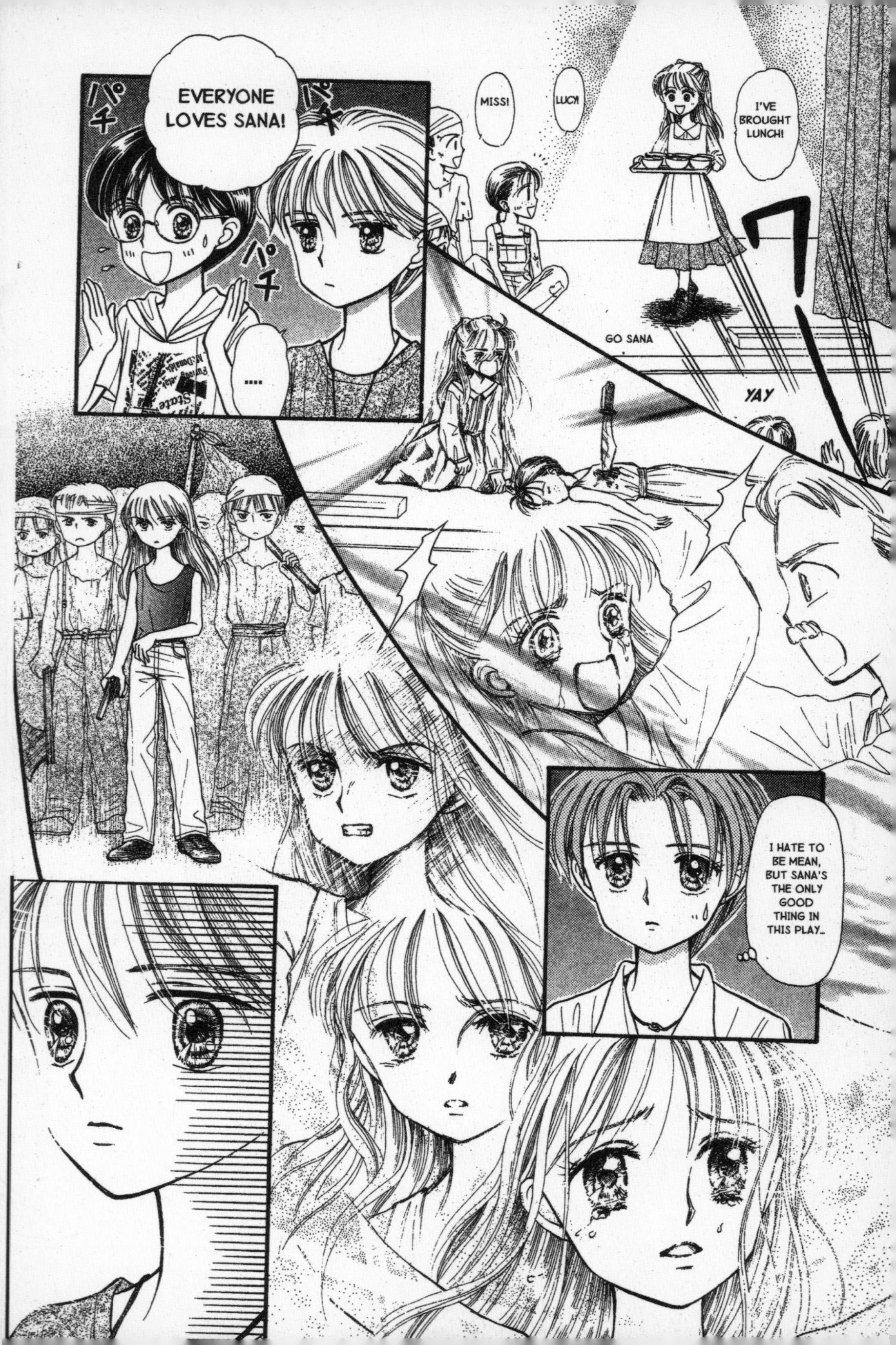
I'VE BROUGHT LUNCH!
LUCY!
MISS!
GO SANA
YAY
パチ
EVERYONE LOVES SANA!
パチ
パチ
....
I HATE TO BE MEAN, BUT SANA'S THE ONLY GOOD THING IN THIS PLAY...

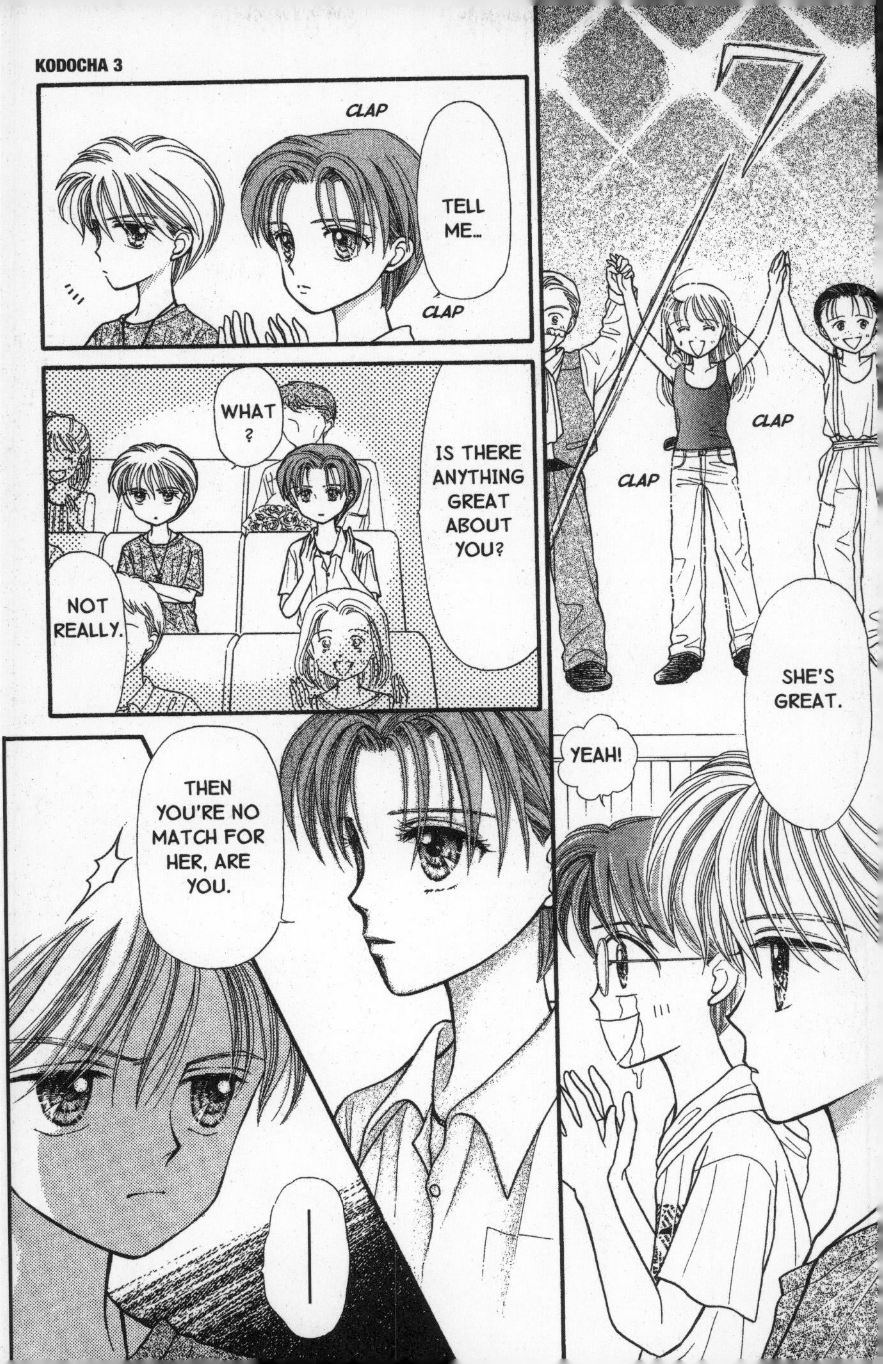
CLAP
CLAP
SHE'S GREAT.
YEAH!
CLAP
TELL ME...
CLAP
IS THERE ANYTHING GREAT ABOUT YOU?
WHAT ?
NOT REALLY.
THEN YOU'RE NO MATCH FOR HER, ARE YOU.

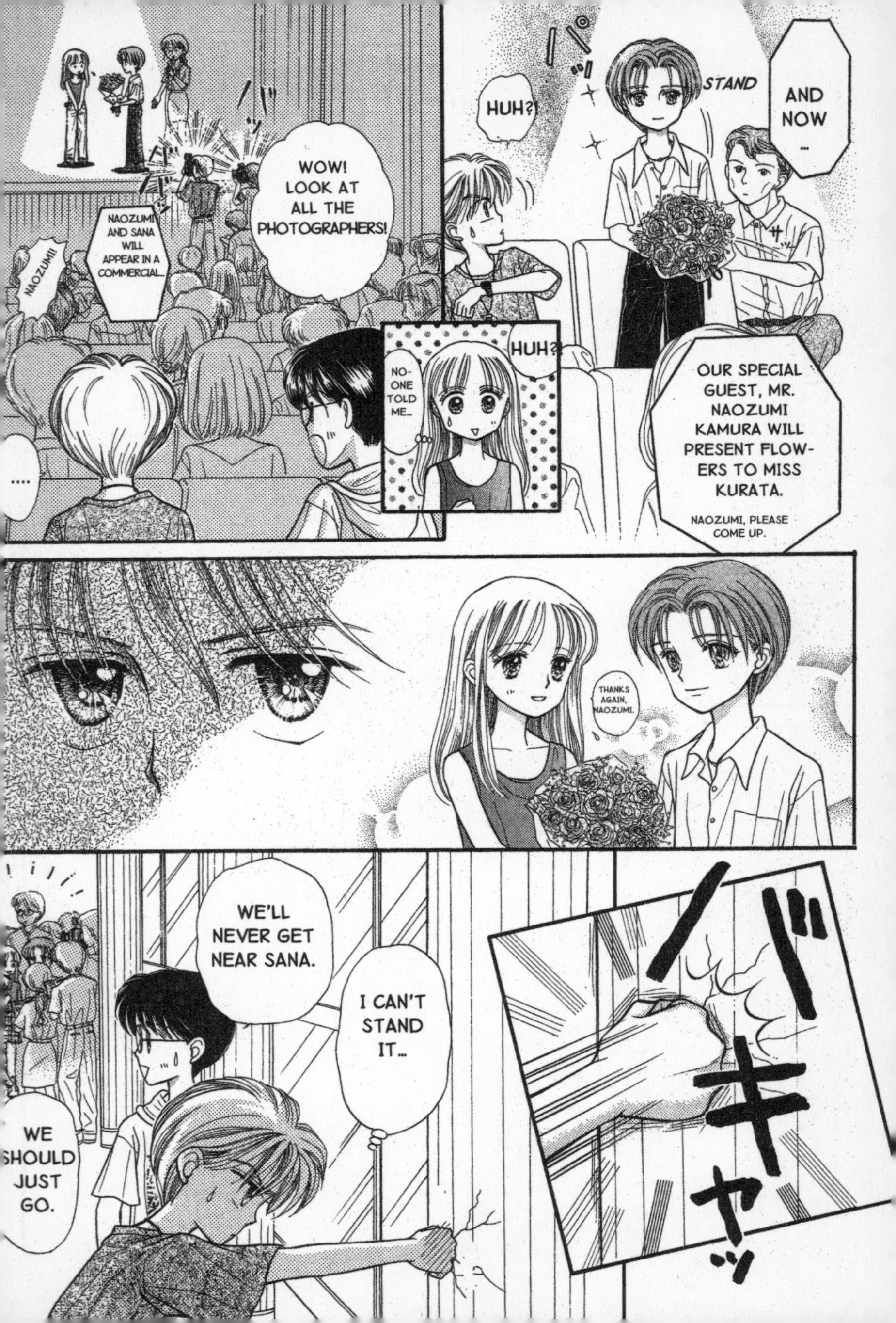
AND NOW ...
STAND
HUH?!
OUR SPECIAL GUEST, MR. NAOZUMI KAMURA WILL PRESENT FLOWERS TO MISS KURATA.
NAOZUMI, PLEASE COME UP.
HUH?!
NO-ONE TOLD ME...
WOW! LOOK AT ALL THE PHOTOGRAPHERS!
NAOZUMI AND SANA WILL APPEAR IN A COMMERCIAL...
NAOZUMI!
....
THANKS AGAIN, NAOZUMI.
バキャッ
WE'LL NEVER GET NEAR SANA.
I CAN'T STAND IT...
WE SHOULD JUST GO.

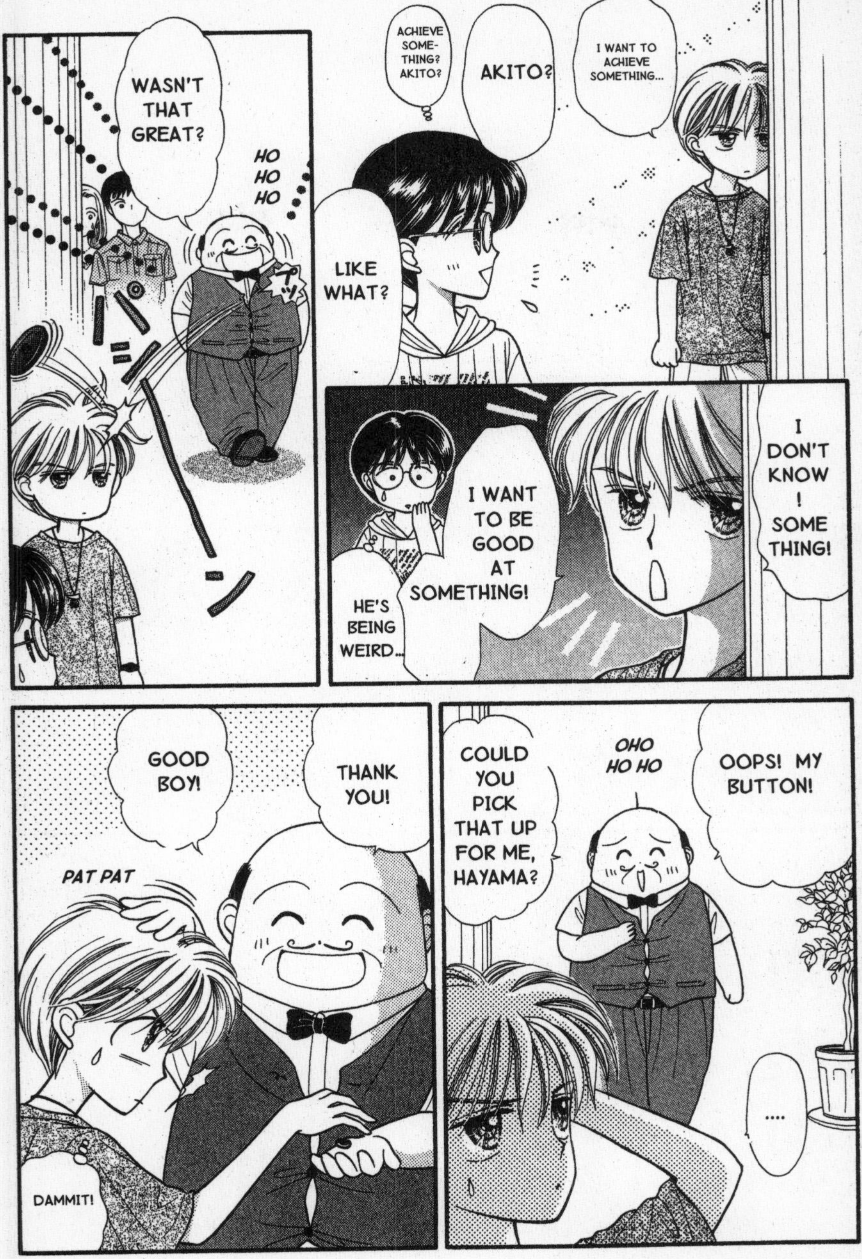
I WANT TO ACHIEVE SOMETHING...
AKITO?
ACHIEVE SOME-THING? AKITO?
LIKE WHAT?
I DON'T KNOW! SOME THING!
I WANT TO BE GOOD AT SOMETHING!
HE'S BEING WEIRD...
HO HO HO
WASN'T THAT GREAT?
OOPS! MY BUTTON!
OHO HO HO
COULD YOU PICK THAT UP FOR ME, HAYAMA?
....
THANK YOU!
GOOD BOY!
PAT PAT
DAMMIT!

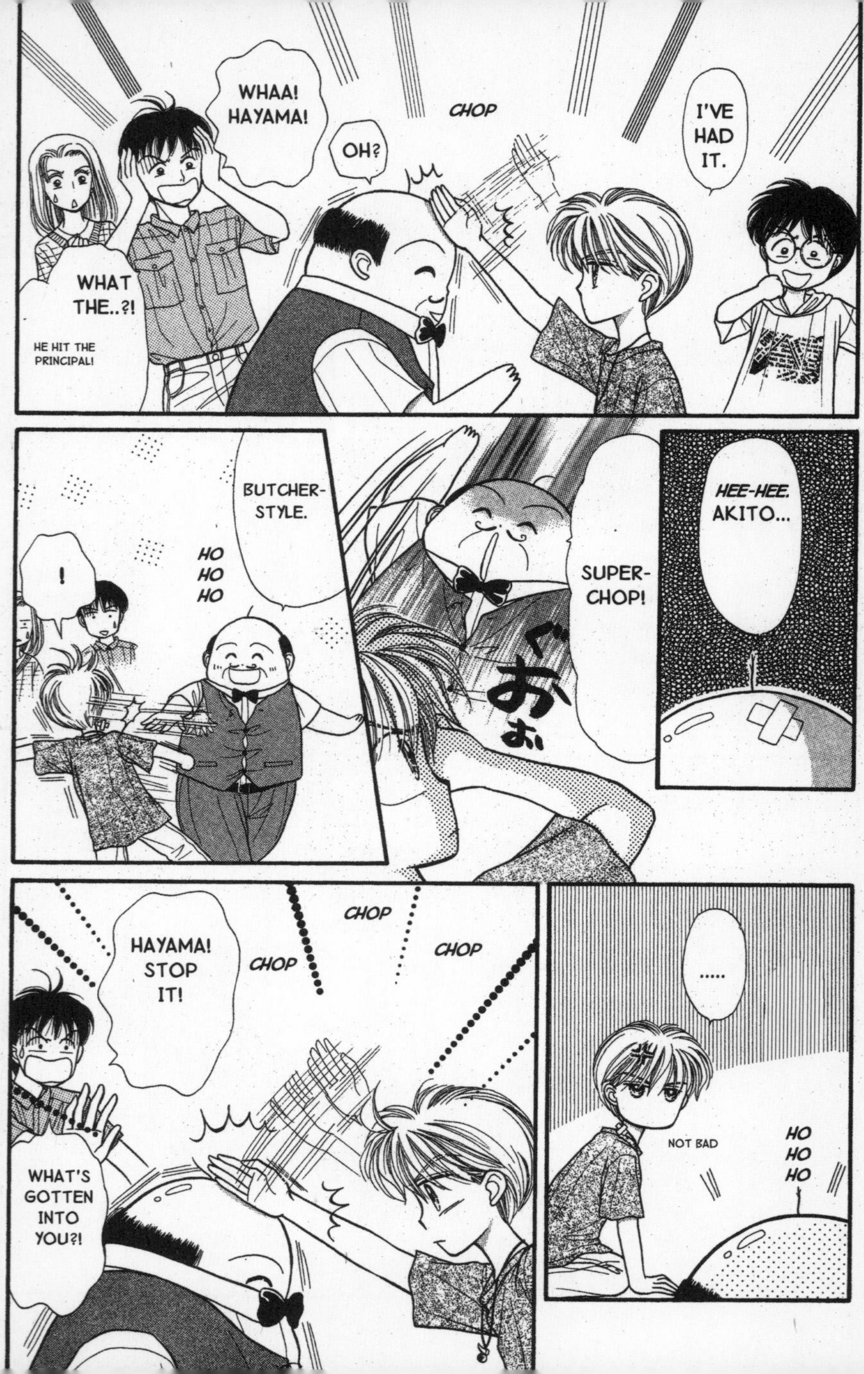
I'VE HAD IT.
CHOP
OH?
WHAA! HAYAMA!
WHAT THE..?!
HE HIT THE PRINCIPAL!
HEE-HEE. AKITO...
SUPER-CHOP!
ぐおぉ
BUTCHER-STYLE.
HO HO HO
!
.....
HO HO HO
NOT BAD
CHOP
CHOP
CHOP
HAYAMA! STOP IT!
WHAT'S GOTTEN INTO YOU?!

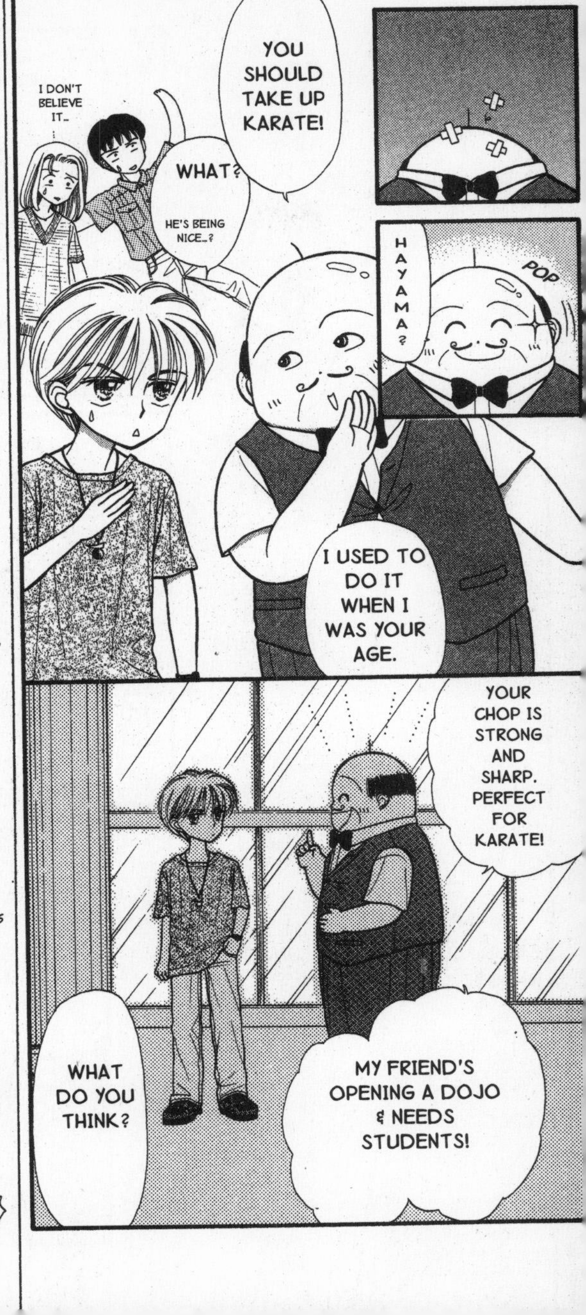
HAYAMA?
POP
YOU SHOULD TAKE UP KARATE!
WHAT?
I DON'T BELIEVE IT...
HE'S BEING NICE...?
I USED TO DO IT WHEN I WAS YOUR AGE.
YOUR CHOP IS STRONG AND SHARP. PERFECT FOR KARATE!
MY FRIEND'S OPENING A DOJO & NEEDS STUDENTS!
WHAT DO YOU THINK?

Cut the Red Tape!

I just finished moving. There was too much paperwork! I understand they need it all, but it was annoying. I also thought the house prices were way too expensive! Stray cats and dogs get their territories based on their size, so why do humans do it based on their bank accounts? If humans got their land based on their size, things would be much fairer. (Kinda corny, eh?) So, I wished I was born in the primitive age. Well, it must have been hard back then, too, but sometimes I think it still must have been much better than the complicated world we're living in. When I'm angry like this, I can come up with stories easily! So, here's my new idea - Kodocha: Primitive Version. It's the same story, but they talk like cave men.

I WISH I COULD THROW IT IN AS AN EXTRA SOMEDAY. MAYBE WHEN I HAVE MORE TIME...

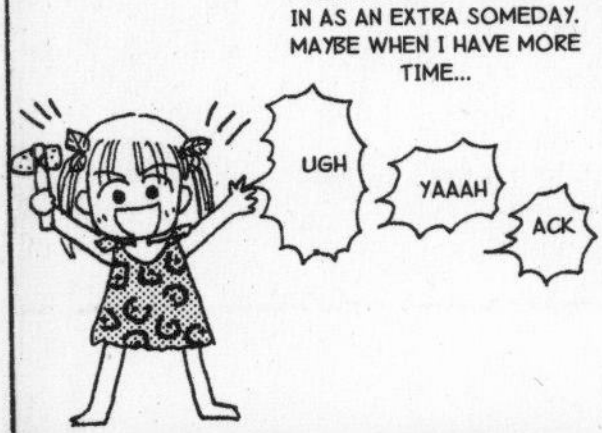
UGH
YAAAH
ACK

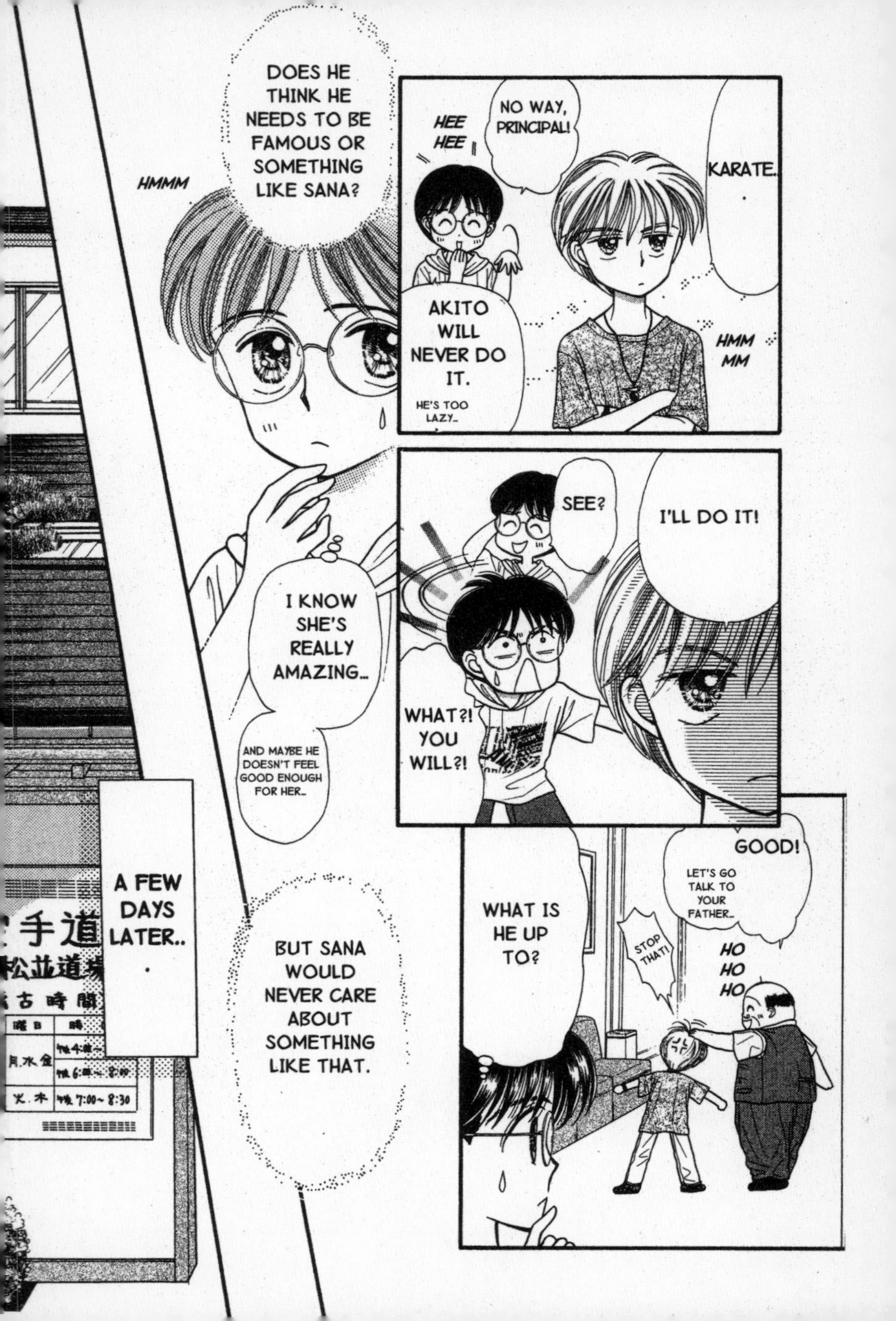

KARATE.
HMM MM
NO WAY, PRINCIPAL!
HEE HEE
AKITO WILL NEVER DO IT.
HE'S TOO LAZY...
I'LL DO IT!
SEE?
WHAT?! YOU WILL?!
GOOD!
LET'S GO TALK TO YOUR FATHER...
HO HO HO
STOP THAT!
WHAT IS HE UP TO?
DOES HE THINK HE NEEDS TO BE FAMOUS OR SOMETHING LIKE SANA?
HMMM
I KNOW SHE'S REALLY AMAZING...
AND MAYBE HE DOESN'T FEEL GOOD ENOUGH FOR HER...
A FEW DAYS LATER...
BUT SANA WOULD NEVER CARE ABOUT SOMETHING LIKE THAT.

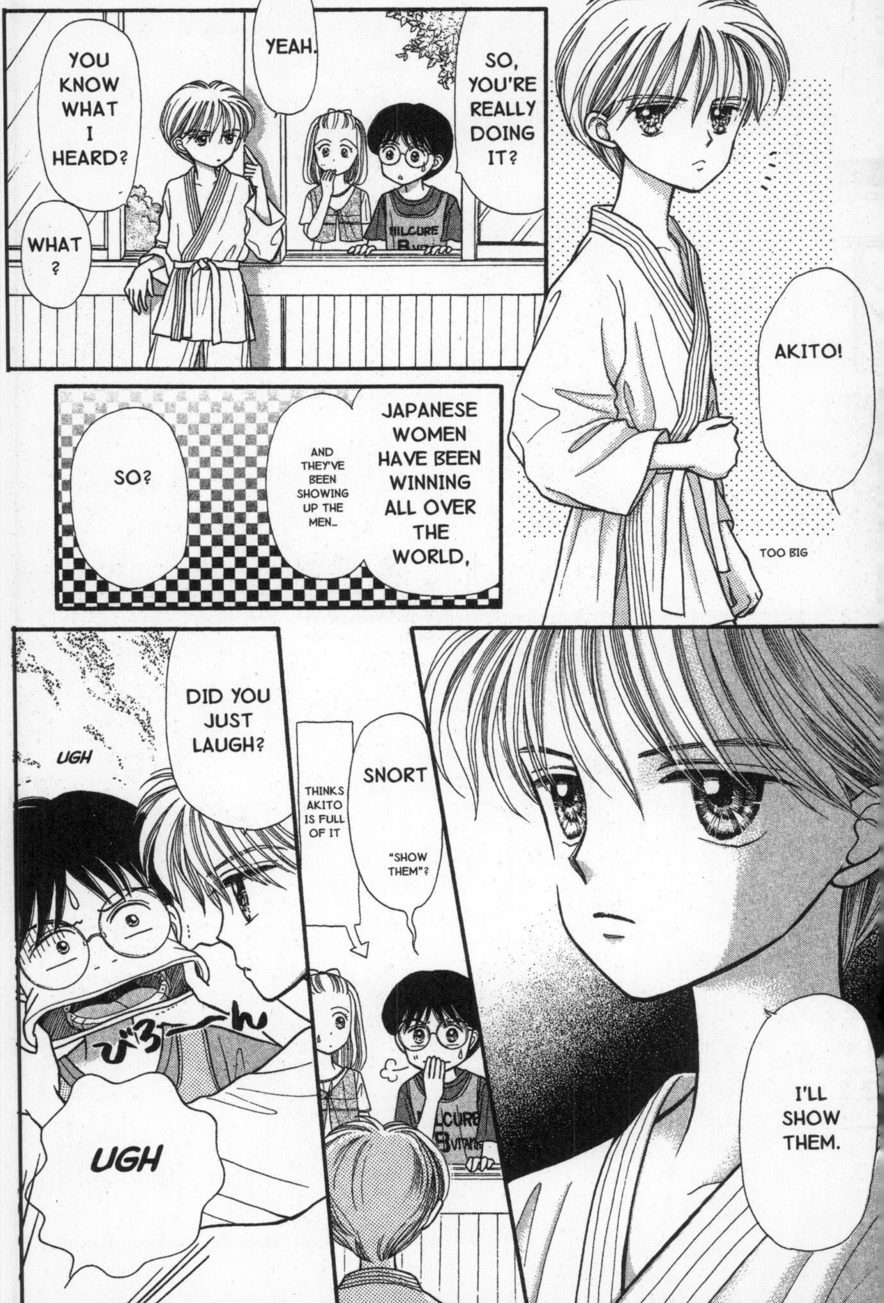
AKITO!
TOO BIG
SO, YOU'RE REALLY DOING IT?
YEAH.
YOU KNOW WHAT I HEARD?
WHAT?
JAPANESE WOMEN HAVE BEEN WINNING ALL OVER THE WORLD,
AND THEY'VE BEEN SHOWING UP THE MEN...
SO?
I'LL SHOW THEM.
SNORT
"SHOW THEM"?
THINKS AKITO IS FULL OF IT
DID YOU JUST LAUGH?
UGH
びろーん
UGH

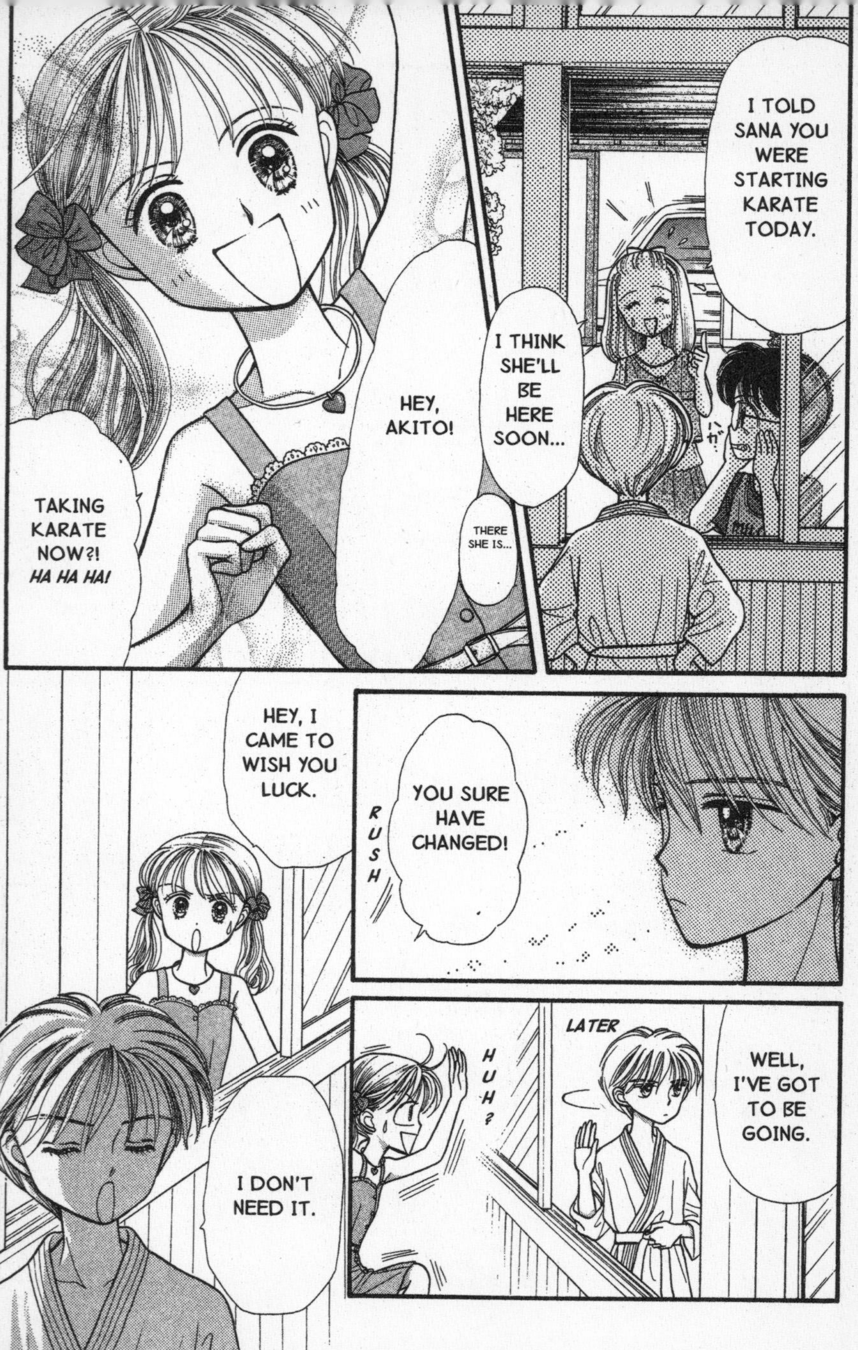
I TOLD SANA YOU WERE STARTING KARATE TODAY.
I THINK SHE'LL BE HERE SOON...
THERE SHE IS...
HEY, AKITO!
TAKING KARATE NOW?! HA HA HA!
YOU SURE HAVE CHANGED!
RUSH
WELL, I'VE GOT TO BE GOING.
LATER
HUH?
HEY, I CAME TO WISH YOU LUCK.
I DON'T NEED IT.

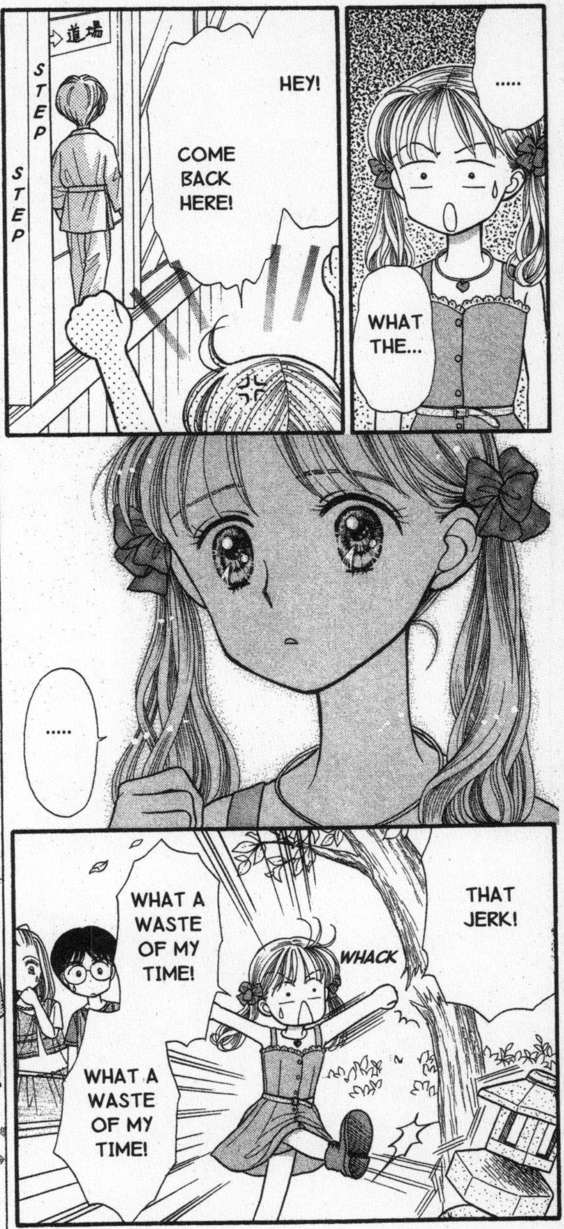
.....
WHAT THE...
HEY!
COME BACK HERE!
⇨道場
STEP STEP
.....
THAT JERK!
WHACK
WHAT A WASTE OF MY TIME!
WHAT A WASTE OF MY TIME!

Home Sweet Home

So, moving was annoying, but I really like my new house. (It's not really new, just new to me.) I'm happy because I dreamed about living in a house, instead of an apartment, my whole life. My true dream was not to be a comic book artist, but to get a house and live an upper-middle-class life. Things are going well so far and I'm really happy. (I still feel poor though, so I always worry something's going to go wrong...)
I found out I have an attic, so I go up there to work on character names, drink and sleep. (And I caught a cold up there, too.) It's fun! I think I like small, dark spaces. It would be perfect if I just had a haystack to sleep on. (hee hee)

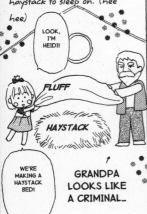

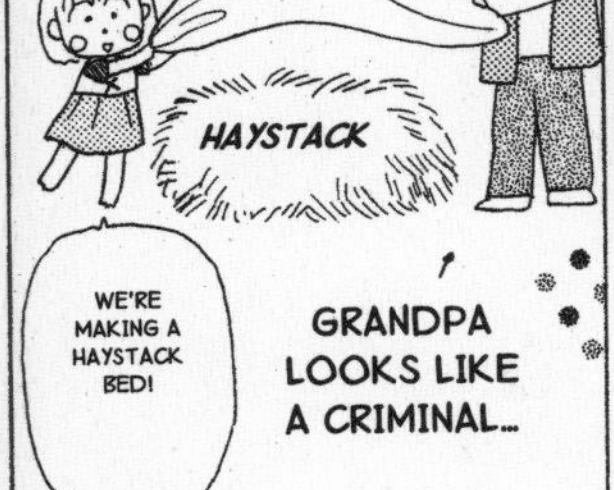
LOOK, I'M HEIDI!
FLUFF
HAYSTACK
WE'RE MAKING A HAYSTACK BED!
GRANDPA LOOKS LIKE A CRIMINAL...

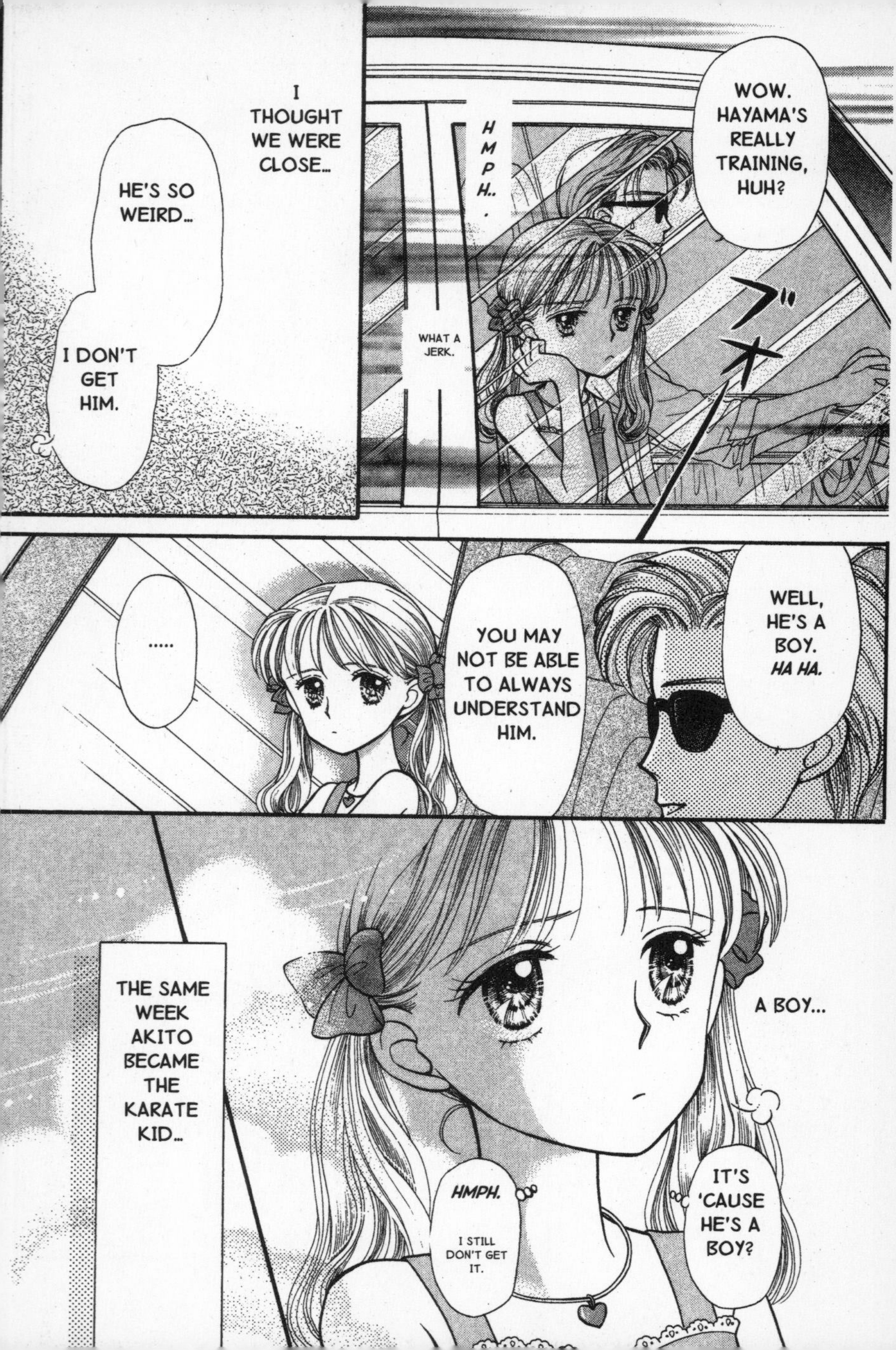
WOW. HAYAMA'S REALLY TRAINING, HUH?
ブオ
HMPH...
WHAT A JERK.
I THOUGHT WE WERE CLOSE...
HE'S SO WEIRD...
I DON'T GET HIM.
WELL, HE'S A BOY. HA HA.
YOU MAY NOT BE ABLE TO ALWAYS UNDERSTAND HIM.
.....
A BOY...
IT'S 'CAUSE HE'S A BOY?
HMPH.
I STILL DON'T GET IT.
THE SAME WEEK AKITO BECAME THE KARATE KID...

THE PRESS STARTED ACTING LIKE NAOZUMI AND I WERE A COUPLE.

WHAT A MESS...

SANA!

WHAT A CUTE AD!

HEY, THAT'S MINE!

I HAVE A PHOTO SHOOT TOMORROW.

WITH NAOZUMI...

I DON'T TRUST NAOZUMI YET.

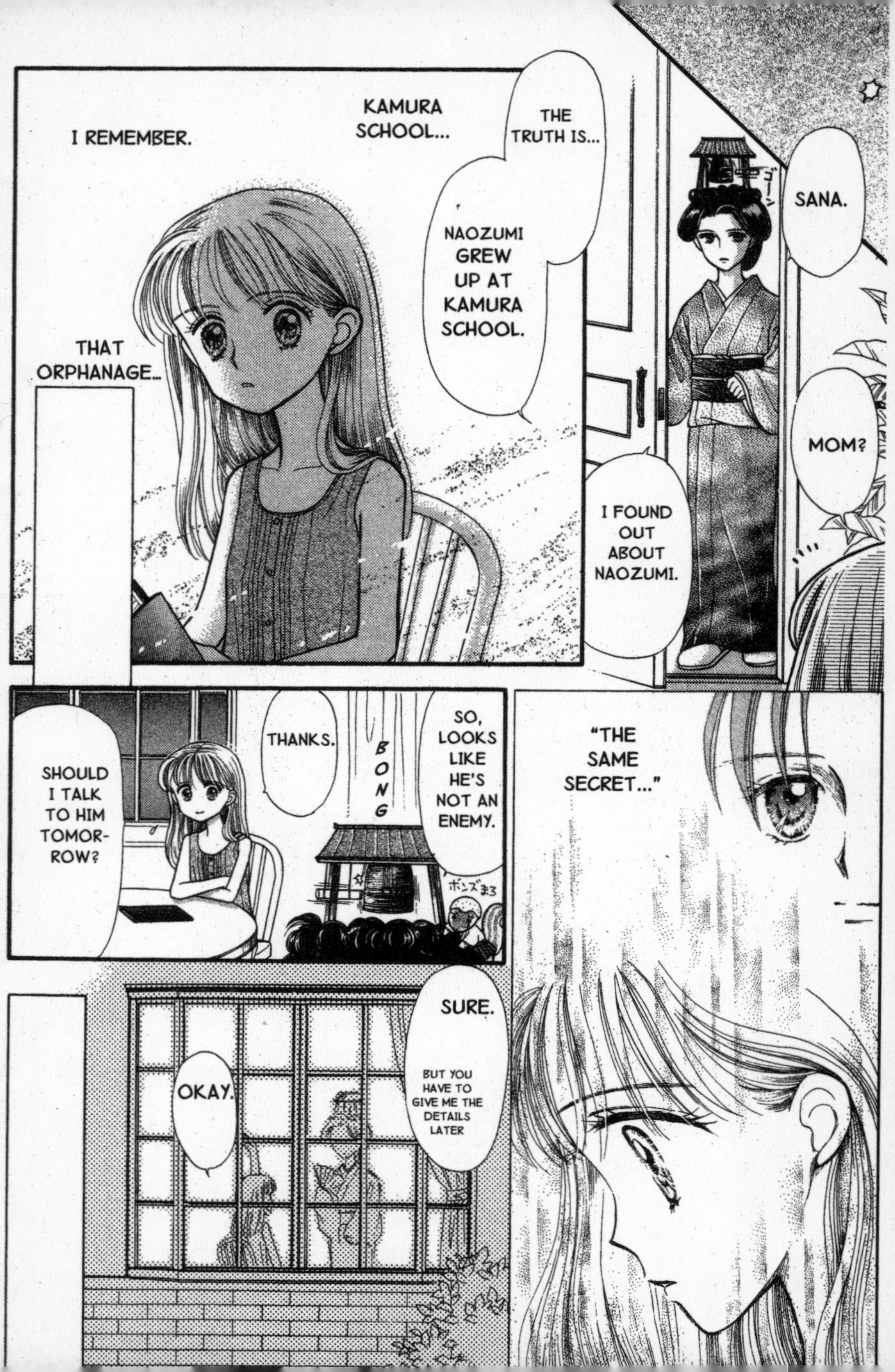
ゴーン
SANA.
MOM?
I FOUND OUT ABOUT NAOZUMI.
THE TRUTH IS...
NAOZUMI GREW UP AT KAMURA SCHOOL.
KAMURA SCHOOL...
I REMEMBER.
THAT ORPHANAGE...
"THE SAME SECRET..."
SO, LOOKS LIKE HE'S NOT AN ENEMY.
BONG
THANKS.
ポンズまろ
SHOULD I TALK TO HIM TOMOR-ROW?
SURE.
BUT YOU HAVE TO GIVE ME THE DETAILS LATER
OKAY.

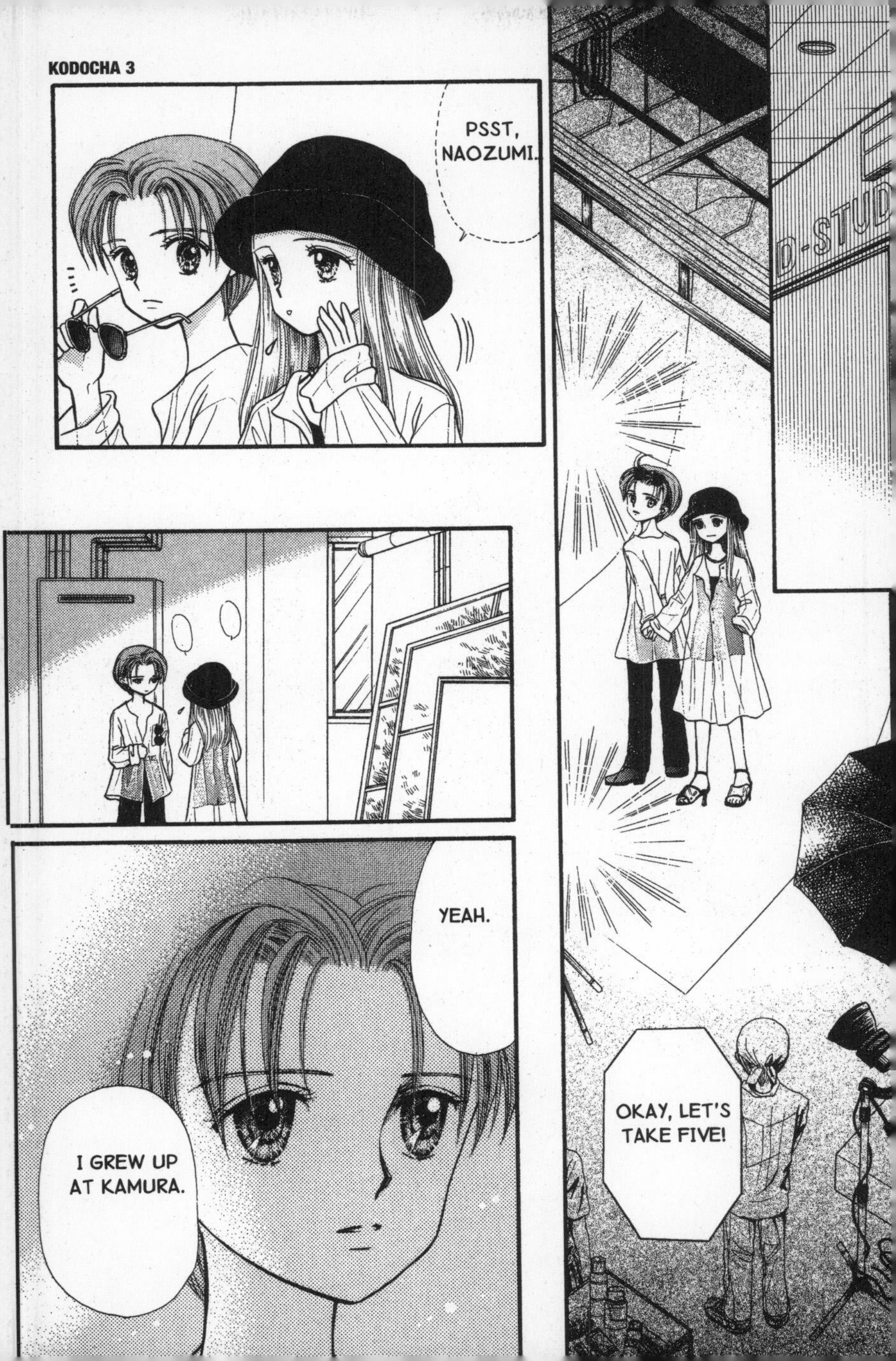
OKAY, LET'S TAKE FIVE!
PSST, NAOZUMI...
YEAH.
I GREW UP AT KAMURA.

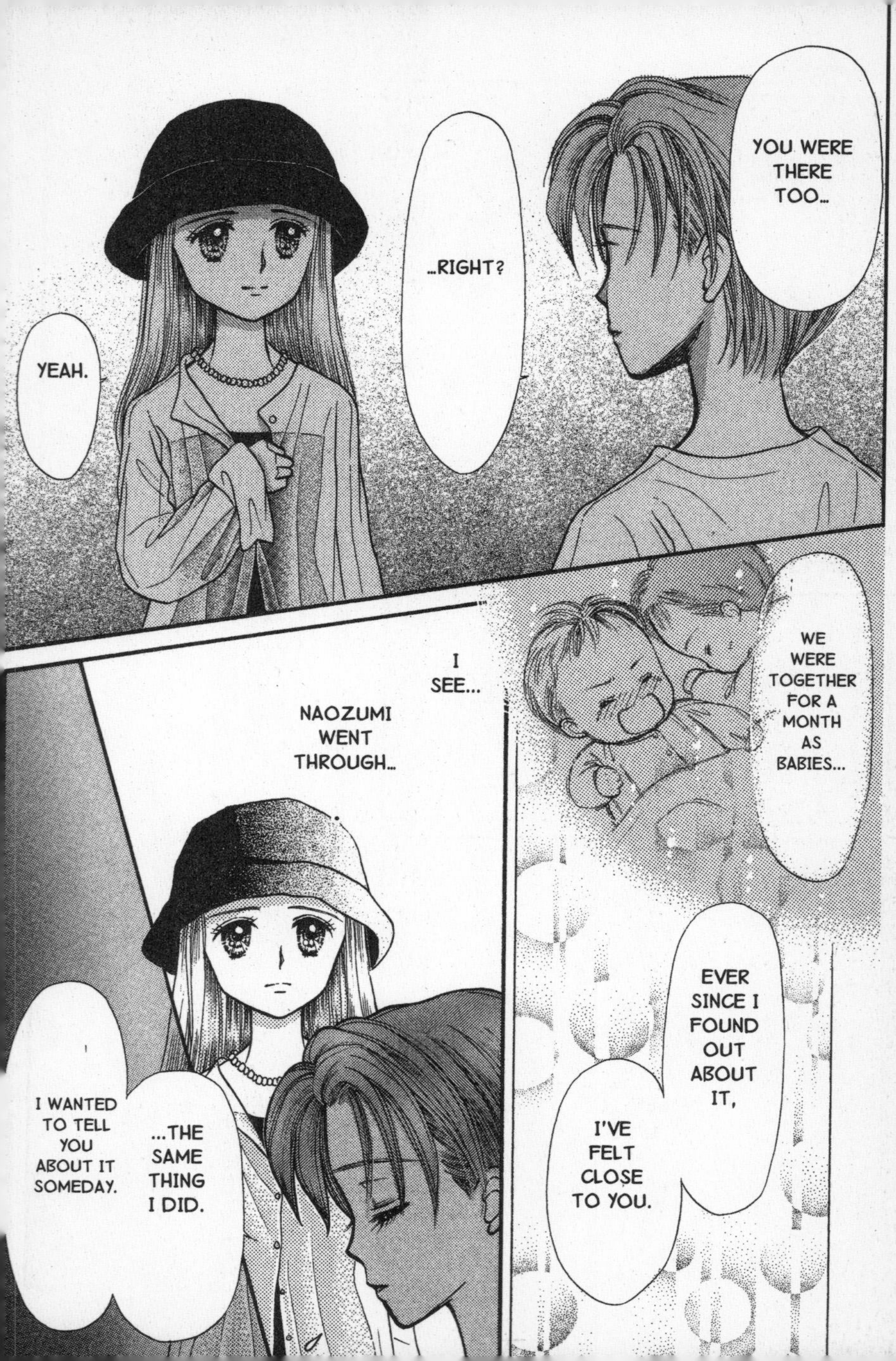
YOU WERE THERE TOO...
...RIGHT?
YEAH.
WE WERE TOGETHER FOR A MONTH AS BABIES...
EVER SINCE I FOUND OUT ABOUT IT,
I'VE FELT CLOSE TO YOU.
I SEE...
NAOZUMI WENT THROUGH...
...THE SAME THING I DID.
I WANTED TO TELL YOU ABOUT IT SOMEDAY.

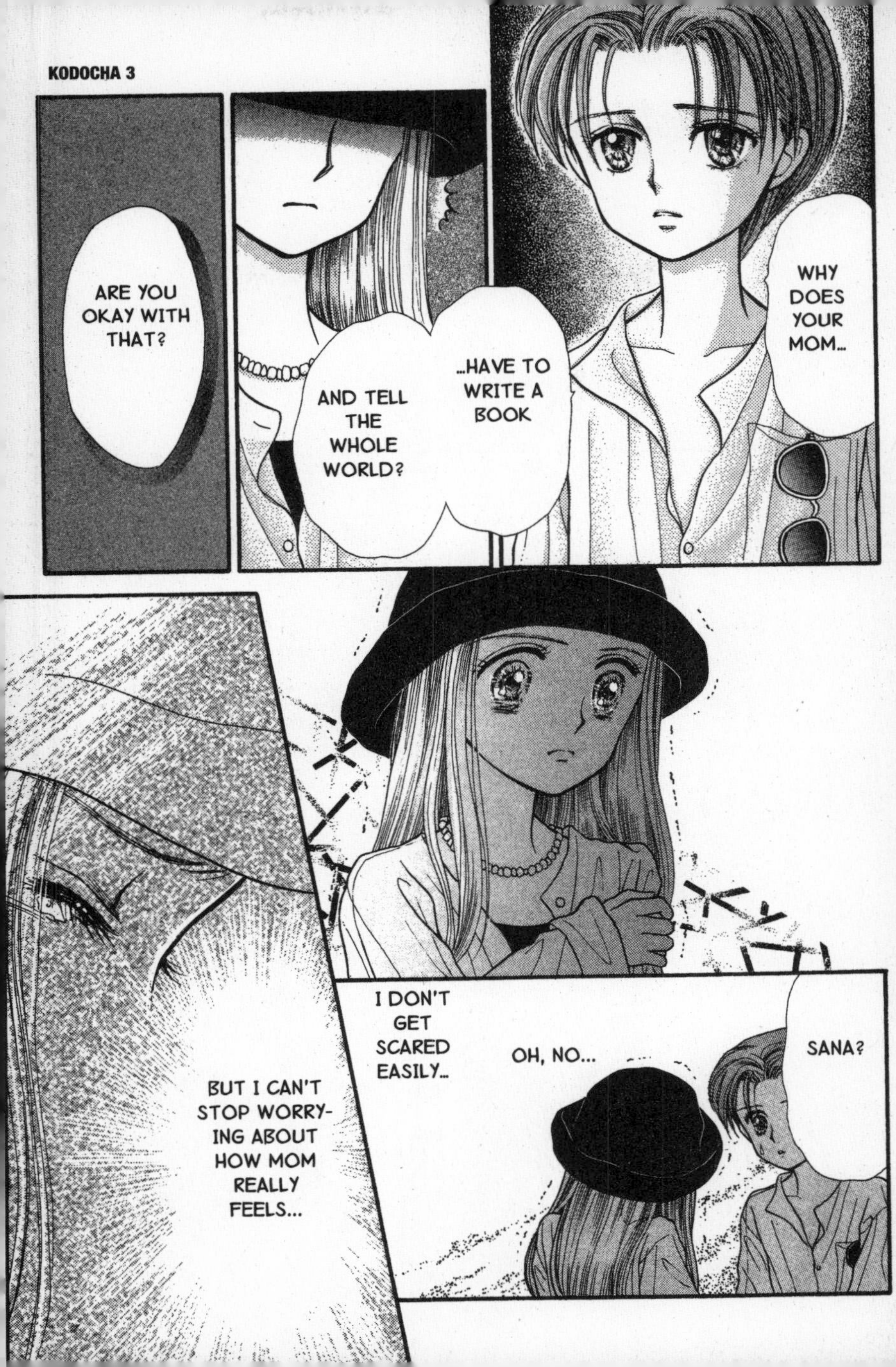
WHY DOES YOUR MOM...
...HAVE TO WRITE A BOOK
AND TELL THE WHOLE WORLD?
ARE YOU OKAY WITH THAT?
SANA?
OH, NO...
I DON'T GET SCARED EASILY...
BUT I CAN'T STOP WORRY-ING ABOUT HOW MOM REALLY FEELS...

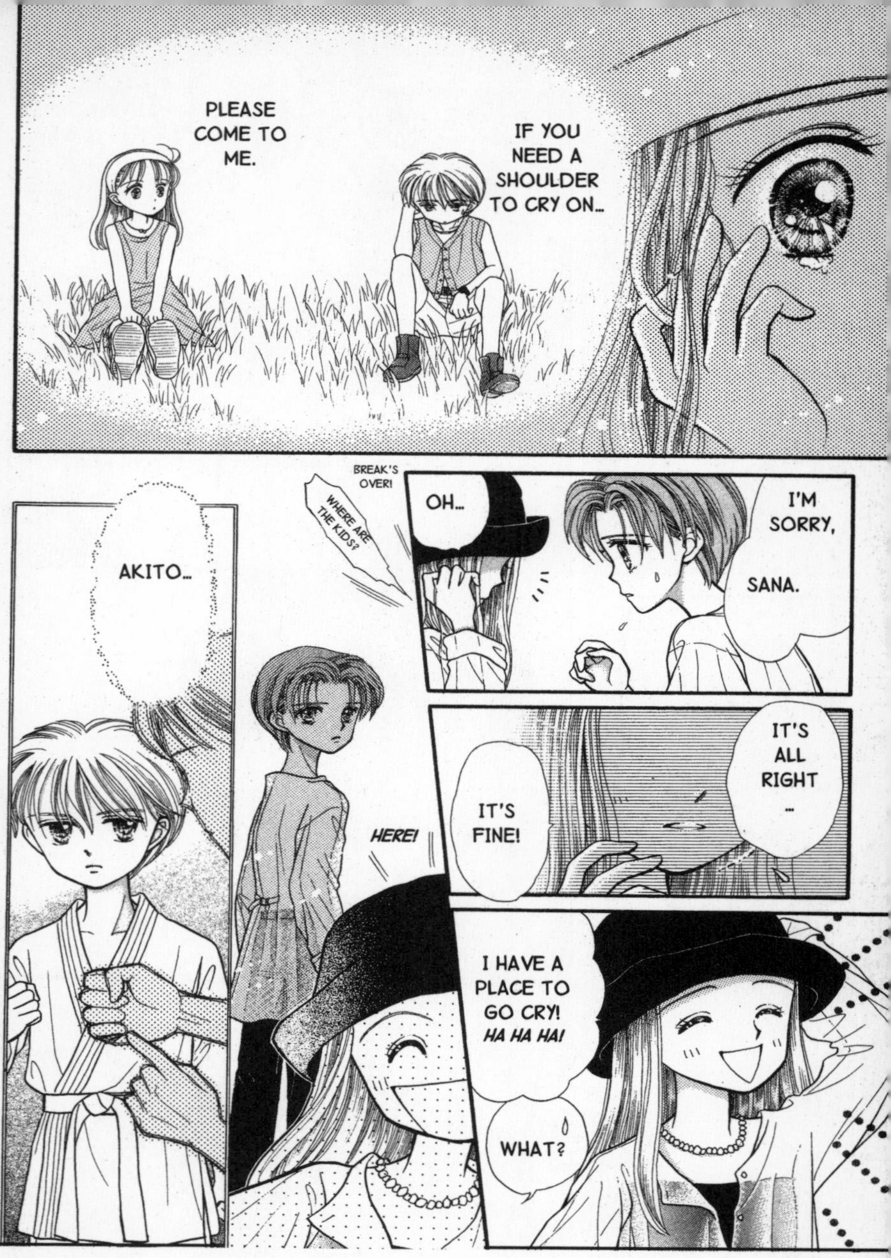
IF YOU NEED A SHOULDER TO CRY ON...
PLEASE COME TO ME.
I'M SORRY,
SANA.
OH...
BREAK'S OVER!
WHERE ARE THE KIDS?
IT'S ALL RIGHT ...
IT'S FINE!
I HAVE A PLACE TO GO CRY! HA HA HA!
WHAT?
HERE!
AKITO...

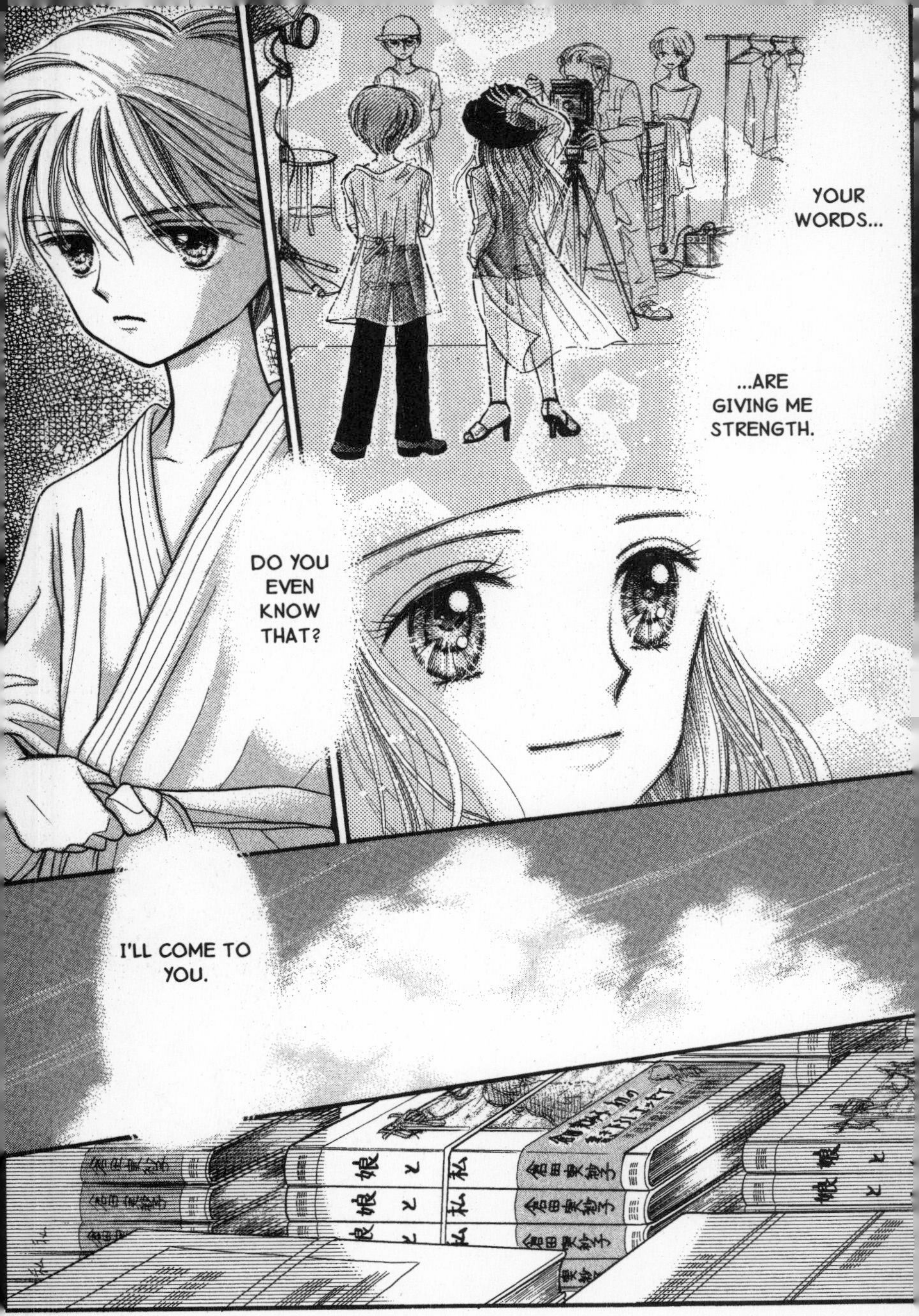
YOUR WORDS...
...ARE GIVING ME STRENGTH.
DO YOU EVEN KNOW THAT?
I'LL COME TO YOU.

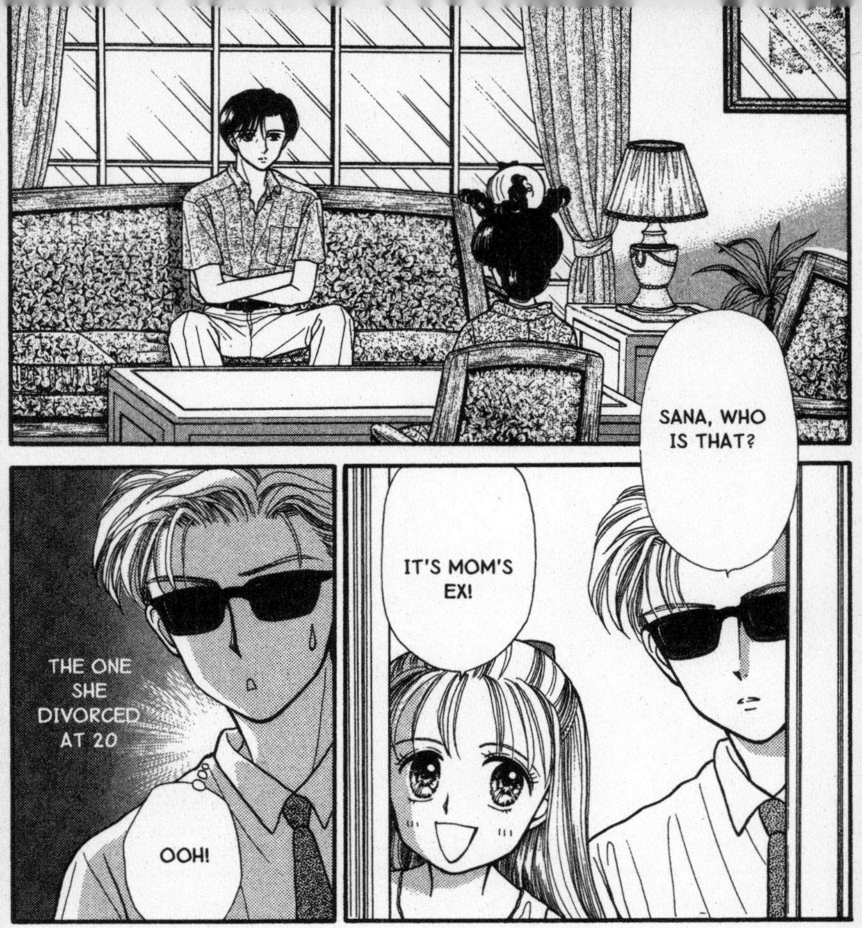
SANA, WHO IS THAT?
IT'S MOM'S EX!
THE ONE SHE DIVORCED AT 20
OOH!

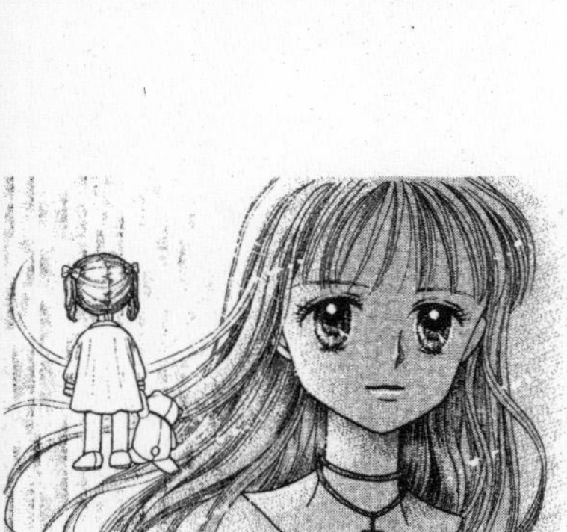

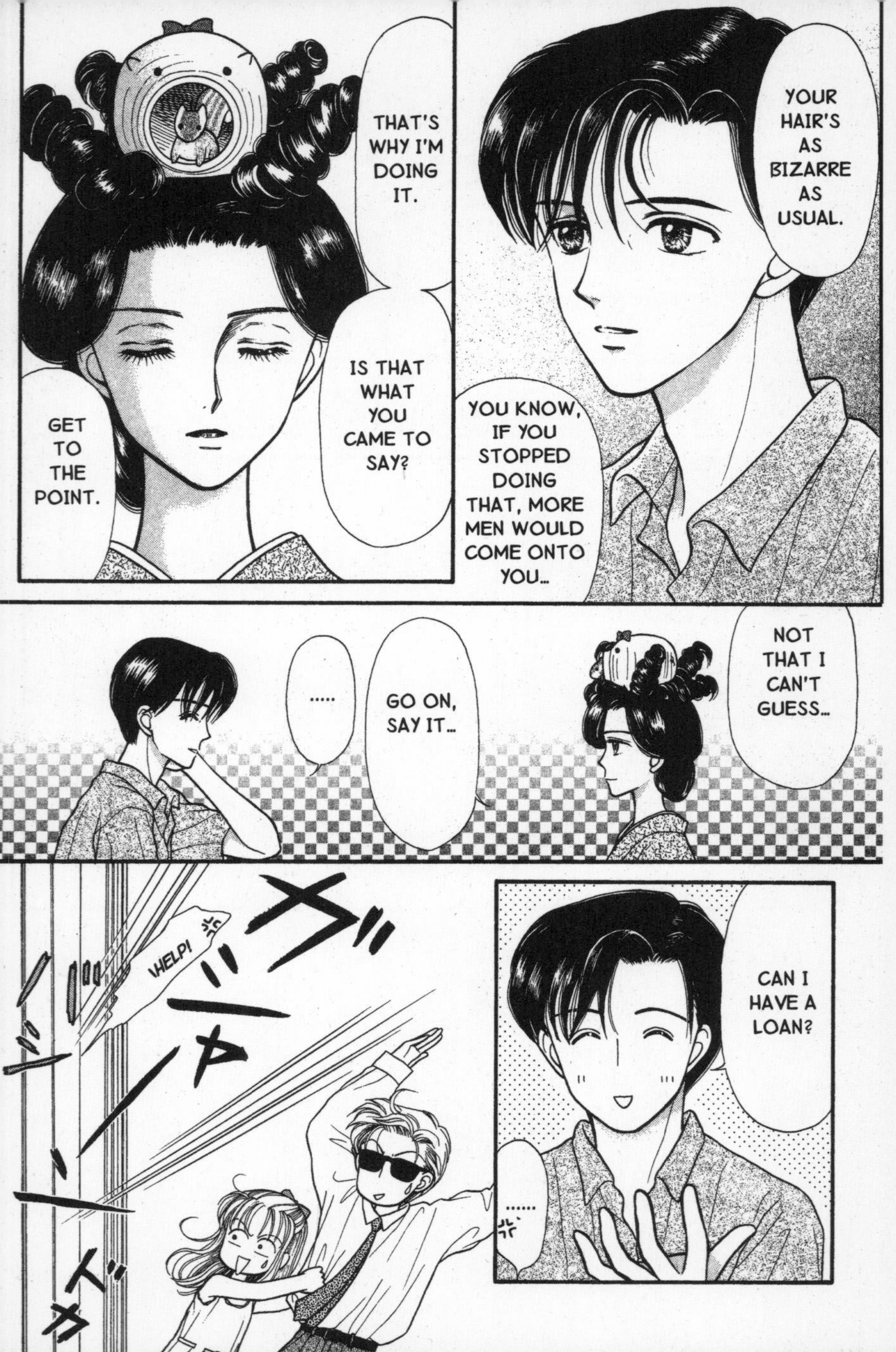
YOUR HAIR'S AS BIZARRE AS USUAL.
YOU KNOW, IF YOU STOPPED DOING THAT, MORE MEN WOULD COME ONTO YOU...
THAT'S WHY I'M DOING IT.
IS THAT WHAT YOU CAME TO SAY?
GET TO THE POINT.
NOT THAT I CAN'T GUESS...
GO ON, SAY IT...
.....
CAN I HAVE A LOAN?
......
HELP!

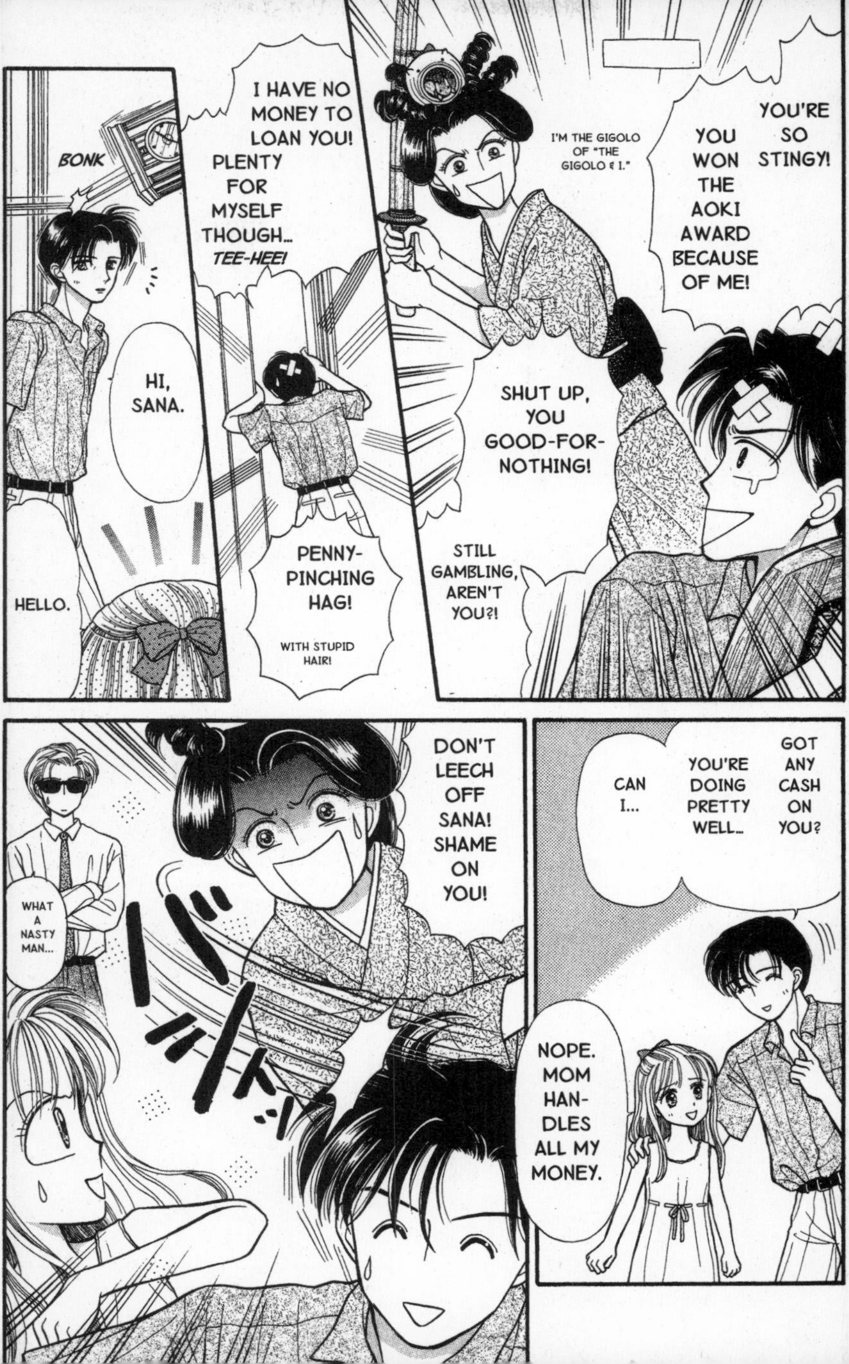
YOU'RE SO STINGY!
YOU WON THE AOKI AWARD BECAUSE OF ME!
I'M THE GIGOLO OF "THE GIGOLO & I."
SHUT UP, YOU GOOD-FOR-NOTHING!
STILL GAMBLING, AREN'T YOU?!
I HAVE NO MONEY TO LOAN YOU! PLENTY FOR MYSELF THOUGH... TEE-HEE!
PENNY-PINCHING HAG!
WITH STUPID HAIR!
BONK
HI, SANA.
HELLO.
GOT ANY CASH ON YOU?
YOU'RE DOING PRETTY WELL...
CAN I...
NOPE. MOM HANDLES ALL MY MONEY.
DON'T LEECH OFF SANA! SHAME ON YOU!
WHAT A NASTY MAN...

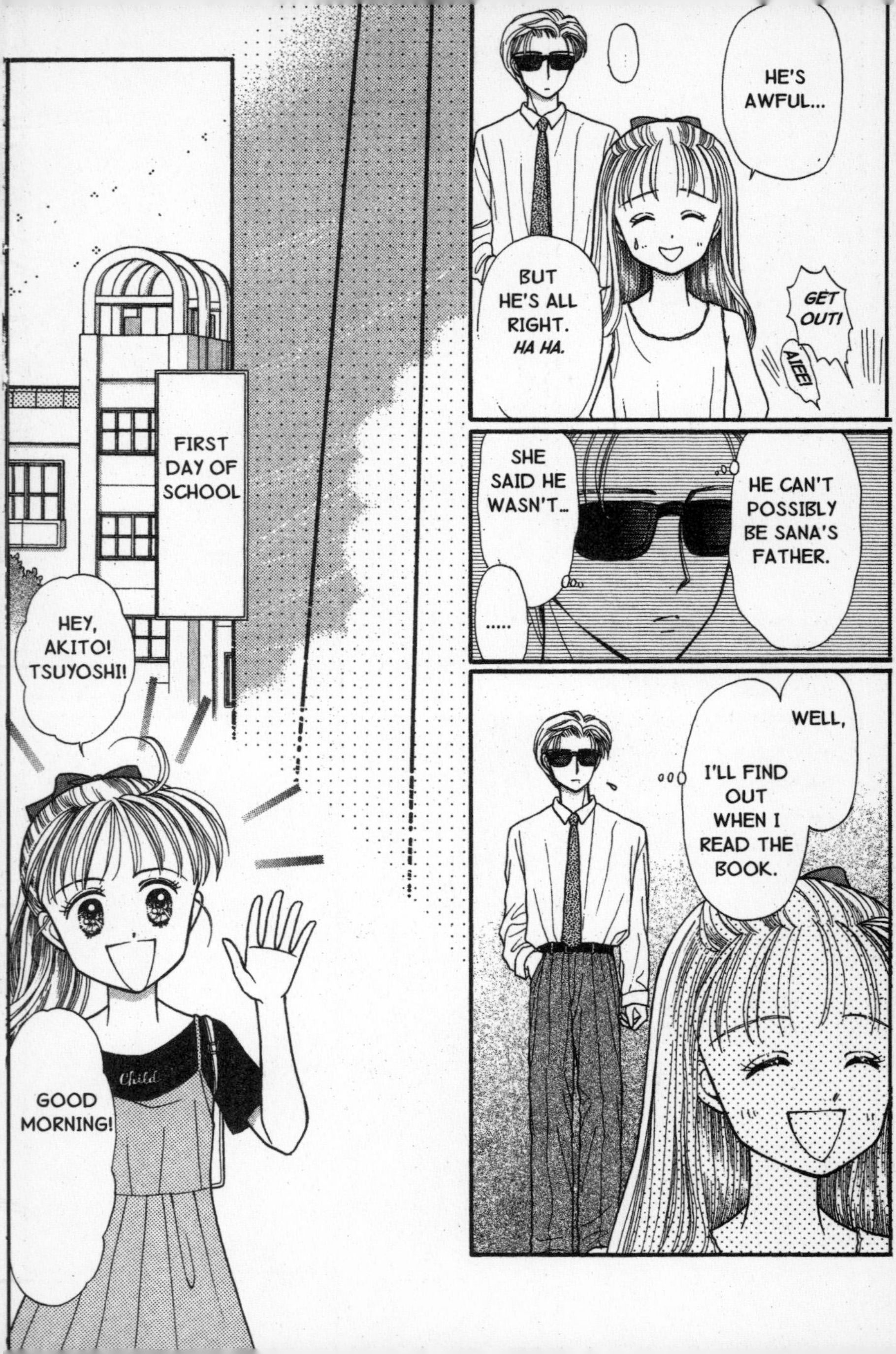

HE'S AWFUL...
...
GET OUT!
AIEE!
BUT HE'S ALL RIGHT. HA HA.
HE CAN'T POSSIBLY BE SANA'S FATHER.
SHE SAID HE WASN'T...
.....
WELL, I'LL FIND OUT WHEN I READ THE BOOK.
FIRST DAY OF SCHOOL
HEY, AKITO! TSUYOSHI!
Child
GOOD MORNING!

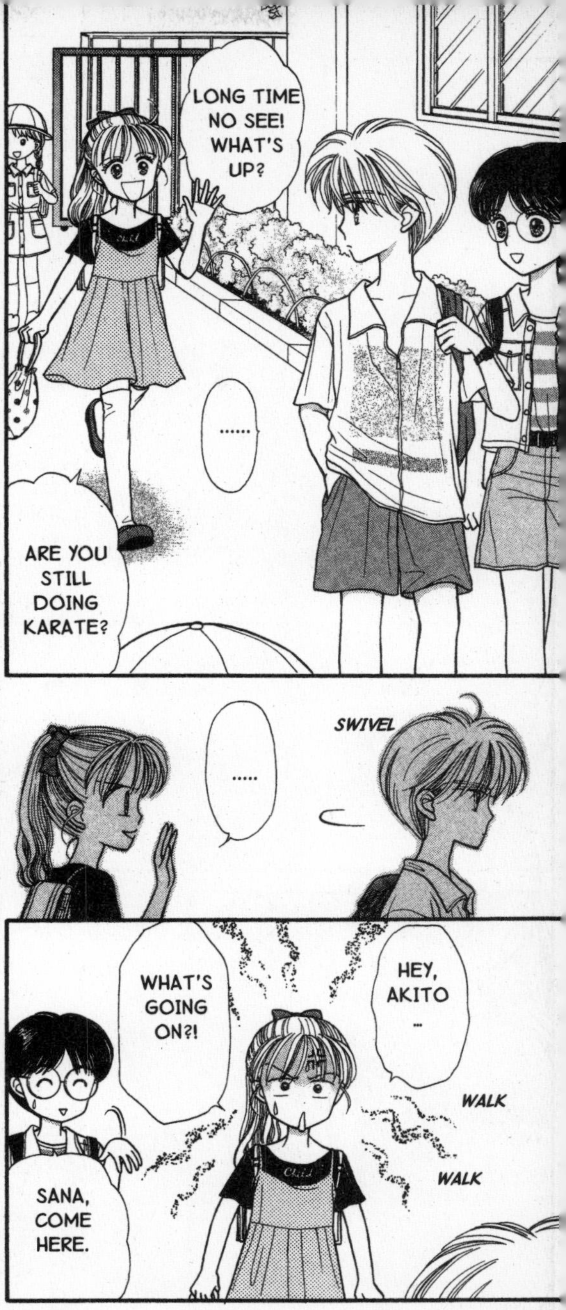
LONG TIME NO SEE! WHAT'S UP?
......
ARE YOU STILL DOING KARATE?
SWIVEL
.....
HEY, AKITO ...
WHAT'S GOING ON?!
WALK
WALK
SANA, COME HERE.

Cartoons and Such

The Kodocha cartoon will be starting on TV soon! (In April of 96.)

Wow. I'm too busy with the comics to be involved with the production, but as the creator I've checked over the script and characters. I think it looks pretty good! The way the characters play dumb has been really emphasized, which shows the staff really got the comic — that makes me happy. So try and check it out, guys! The show is being sponsored by the toy company, TOMY. I saw their line-up of planner toys for Kodocha, and it looked good. I'm looking forward to seeing them! (Since the title means "Child's Toy", the toys have to be good!)

My publisher's name is also Tomy, so it's kind of confusing. (hee hee)

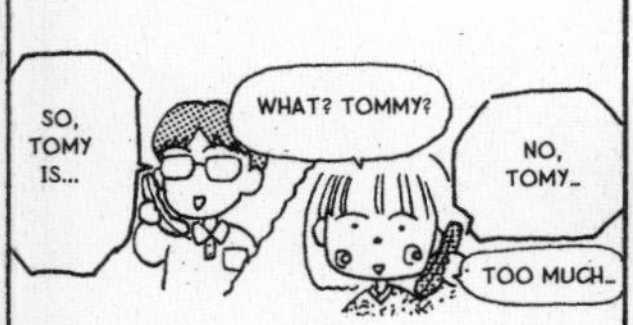
SO, TOMY IS...
WHAT? TOMMY?
NO, TOMY...
TOO MUCH...

By the way, the mole alarm clock I wrote about in book two was actually made by TOMY. In a meeting, a person from TOMY pointed it out to me.

I had no idea!

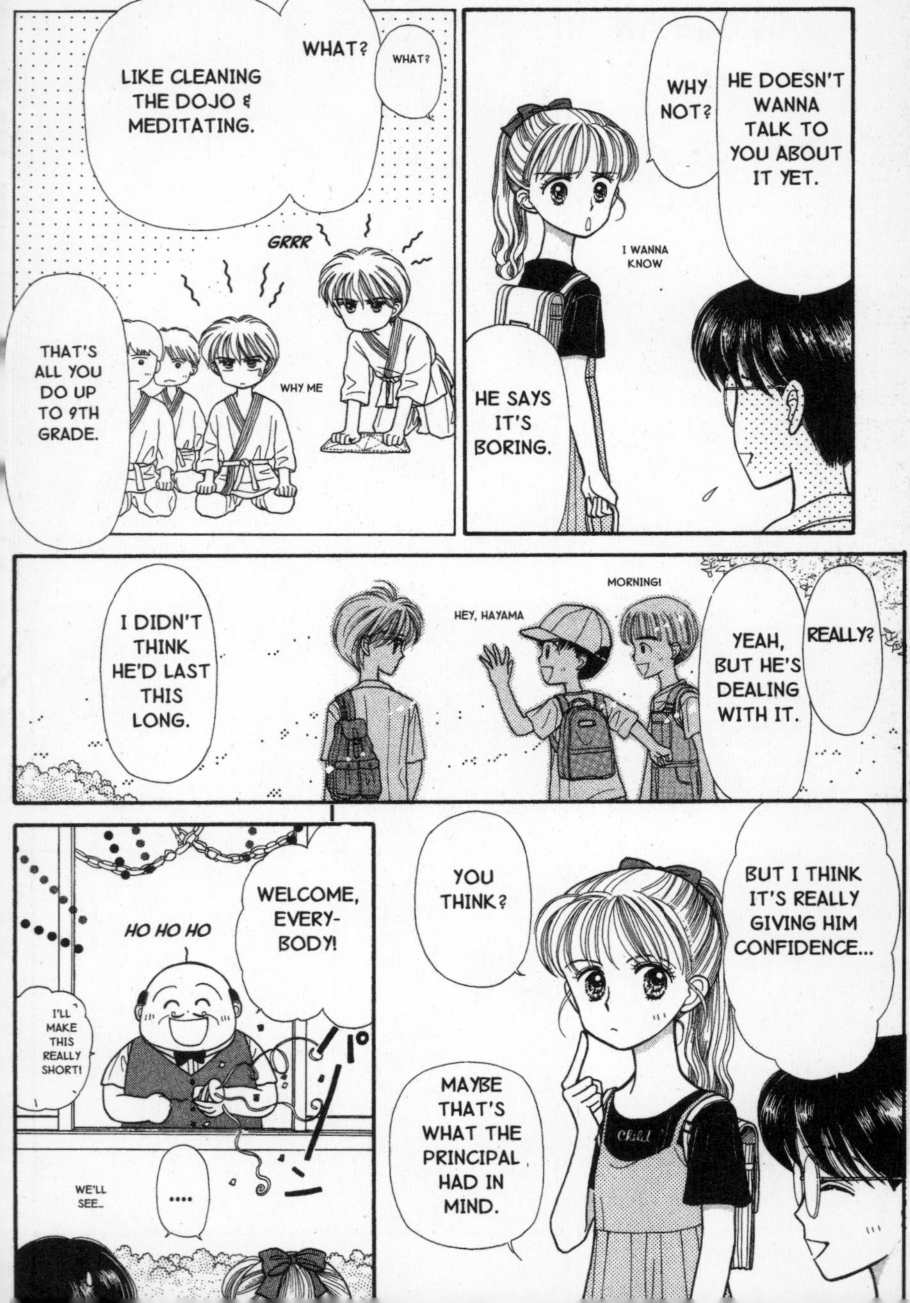
HE DOESN'T WANNA TALK TO YOU ABOUT IT YET.
WHY NOT?
I WANNA KNOW
HE SAYS IT'S BORING.
WHAT?
WHAT?
LIKE CLEANING THE DOJO & MEDITATING.
GRRR
WHY ME
THAT'S ALL YOU DO UP TO 9TH GRADE.
REALLY?
YEAH, BUT HE'S DEALING WITH IT.
MORNING!
HEY, HAYAMA
I DIDN'T THINK HE'D LAST THIS LONG.
BUT I THINK IT'S REALLY GIVING HIM CONFIDENCE...
YOU THINK?
MAYBE THAT'S WHAT THE PRINCIPAL HAD IN MIND.
WELCOME, EVERY-BODY!
HO HO HO
I'LL MAKE THIS REALLY SHORT!
....
WE'LL SEE...

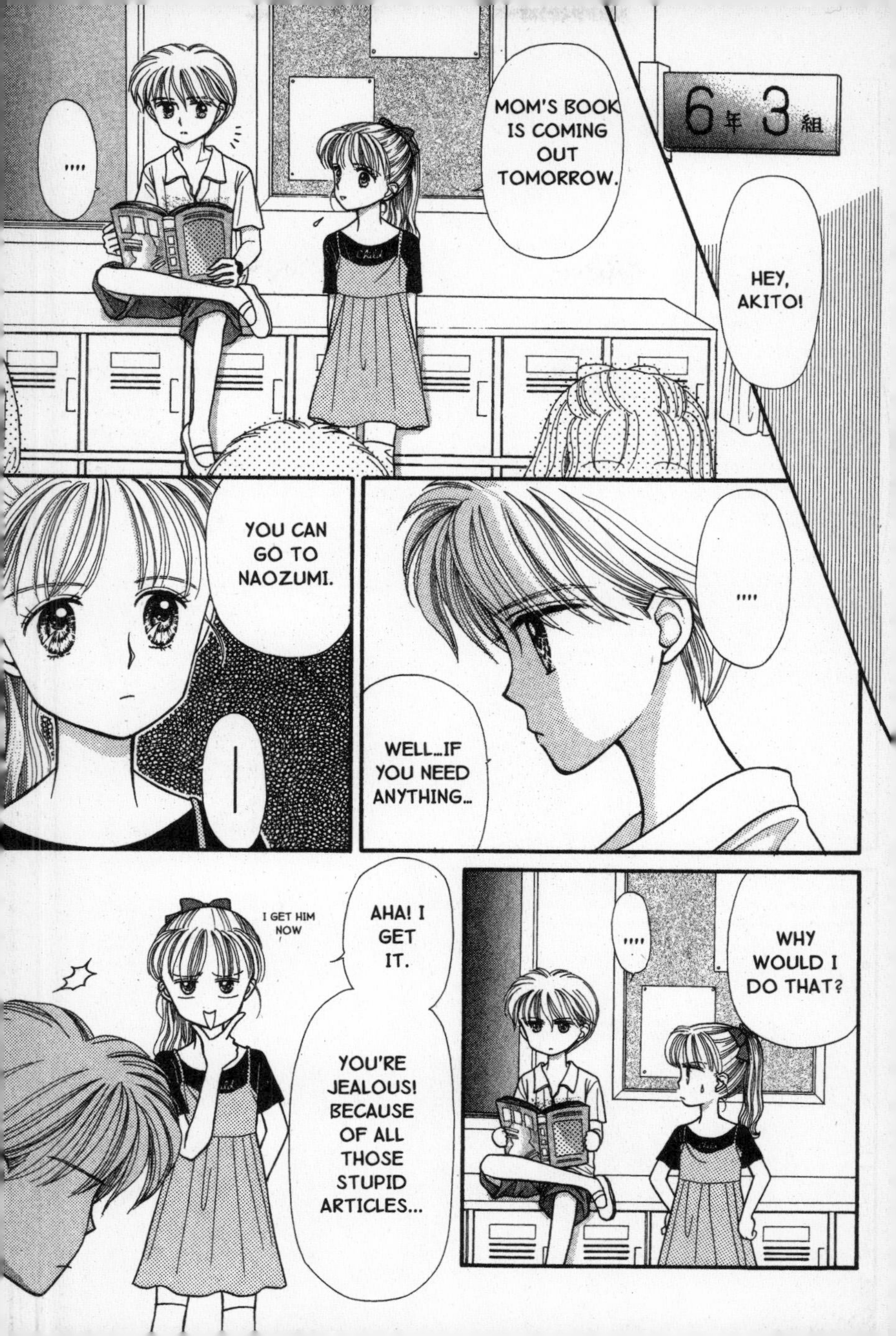
6年3組
HEY, AKITO!
MOM'S BOOK IS COMING OUT TOMORROW.
....
....
WELL...IF YOU NEED ANYTHING...
YOU CAN GO TO NAOZUMI.
WHY WOULD I DO THAT?
....
AHA! I GET IT.
I GET HIM NOW
YOU'RE JEALOUS! BECAUSE OF ALL THOSE STUPID ARTICLES...

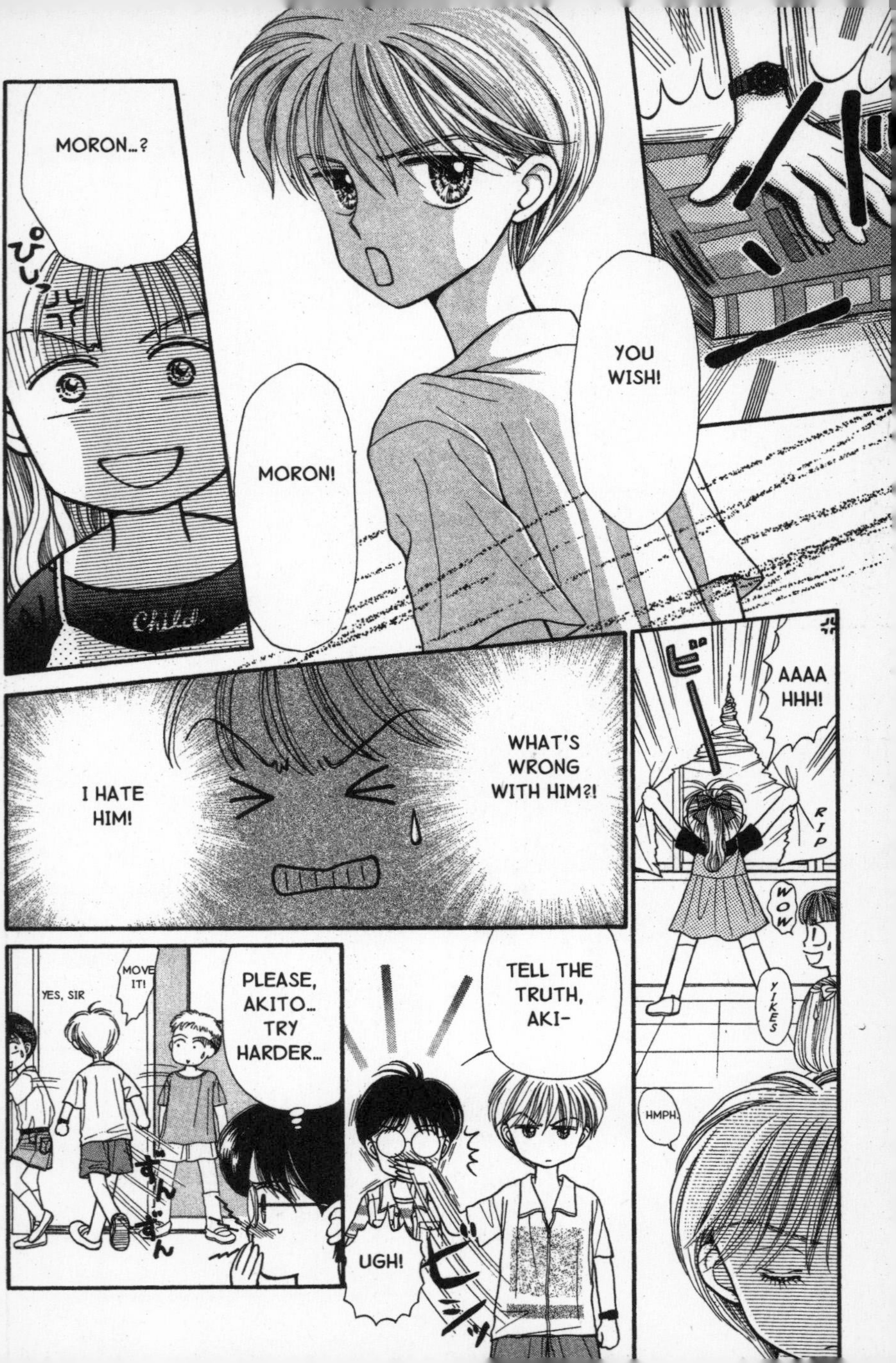
YOU WISH!
MORON!
MORON...?
AAAA HHH!
RIP
WOW
YIKES
WHAT'S WRONG WITH HIM?!
I HATE HIM!
HMPH.
TELL THE TRUTH, AKI-
UGH!
PLEASE, AKITO... TRY HARDER...
MOVE IT!
YES, SIR

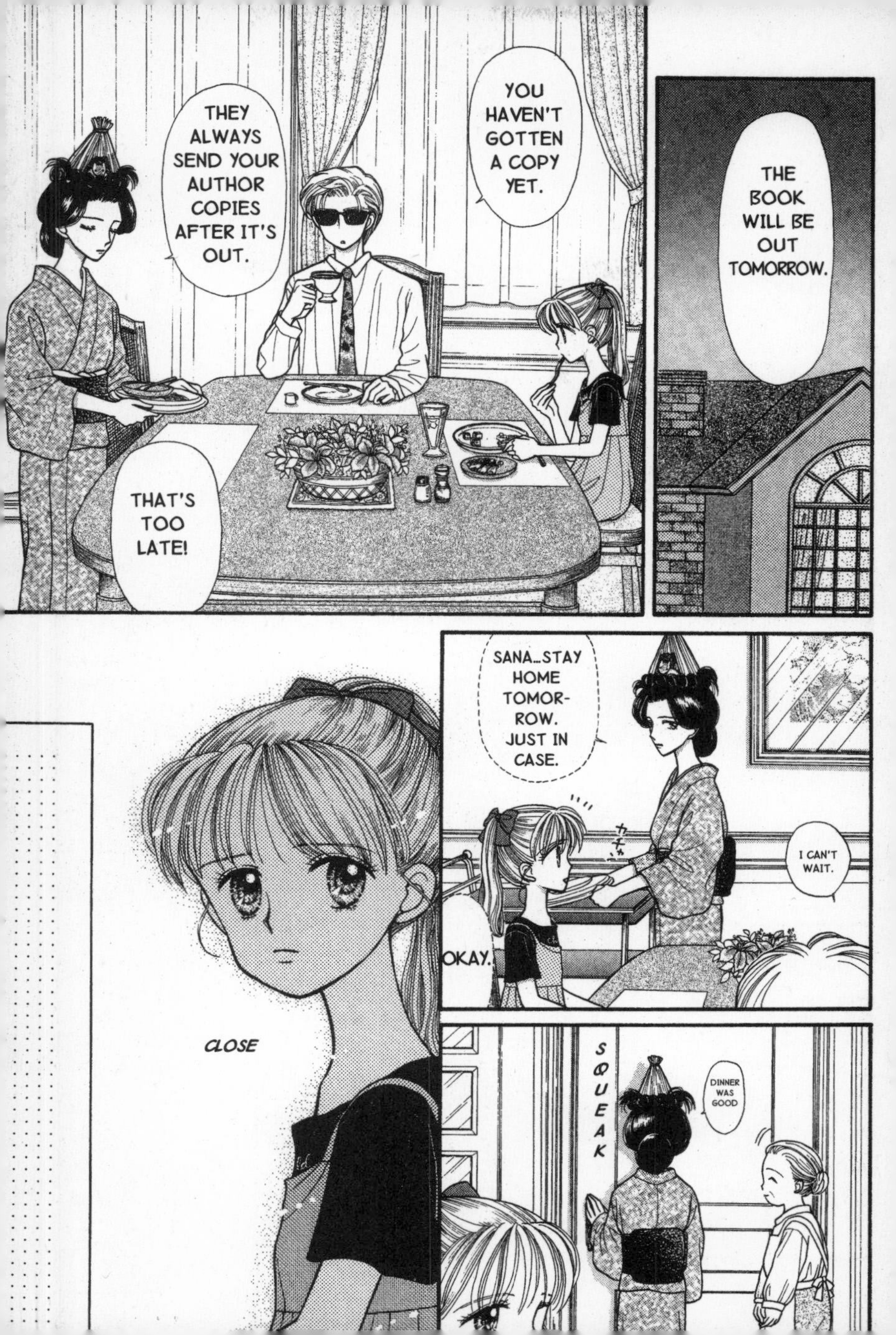
THE BOOK WILL BE OUT TOMORROW.
YOU HAVEN'T GOTTEN A COPY YET.
THEY ALWAYS SEND YOUR AUTHOR COPIES AFTER IT'S OUT.
THAT'S TOO LATE!
SANA...STAY HOME TOMOR-ROW. JUST IN CASE.
I CAN'T WAIT.
OKAY.
SQUEAK
DINNER WAS GOOD
CLOSE

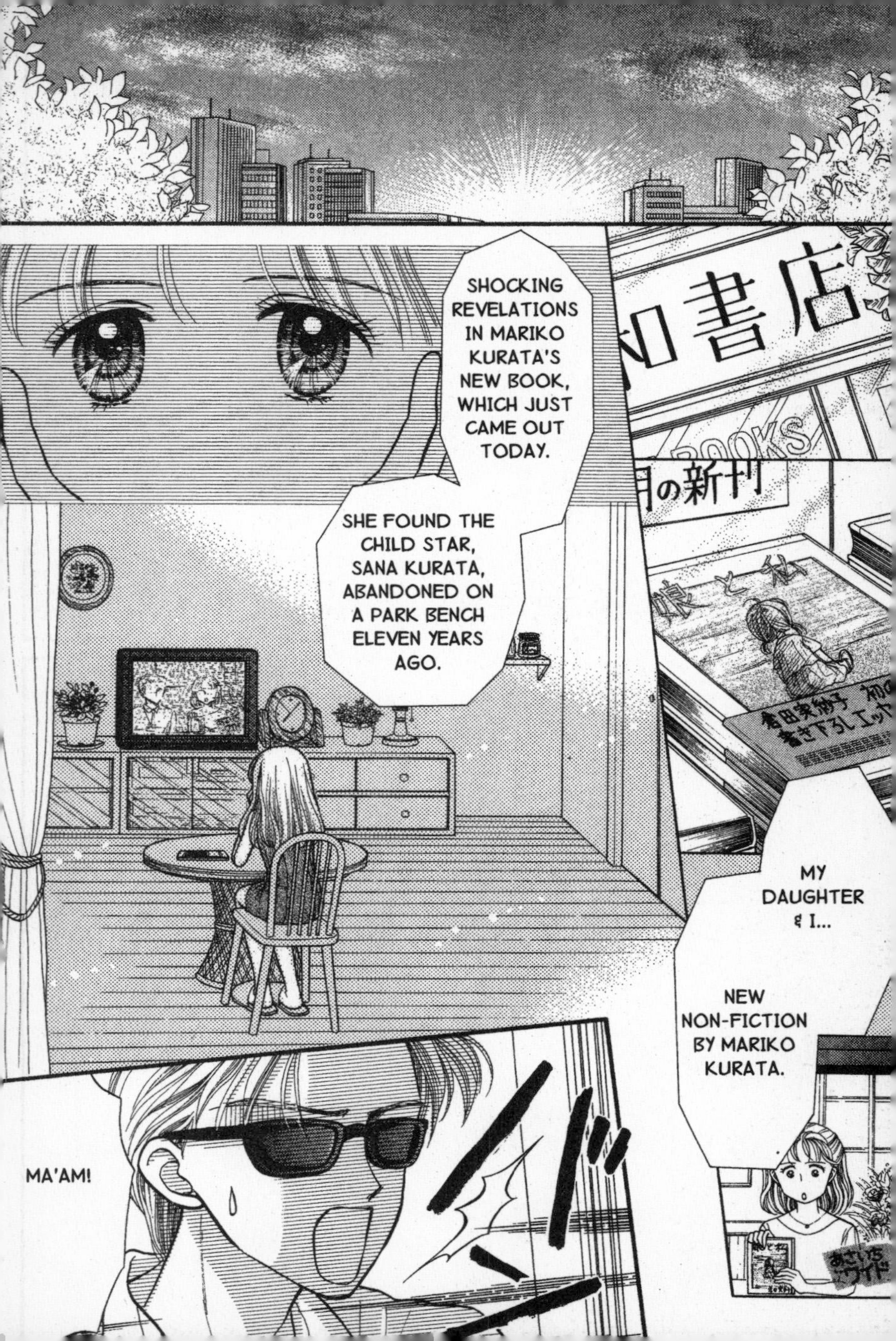
MY DAUGHTER & I...
NEW NON-FICTION BY MARIKO KURATA.
SHOCKING REVELATIONS IN MARIKO KURATA'S NEW BOOK, WHICH JUST CAME OUT TODAY.
SHE FOUND THE CHILD STAR, SANA KURATA, ABANDONED ON A PARK BENCH ELEVEN YEARS AGO.
MA'AM!

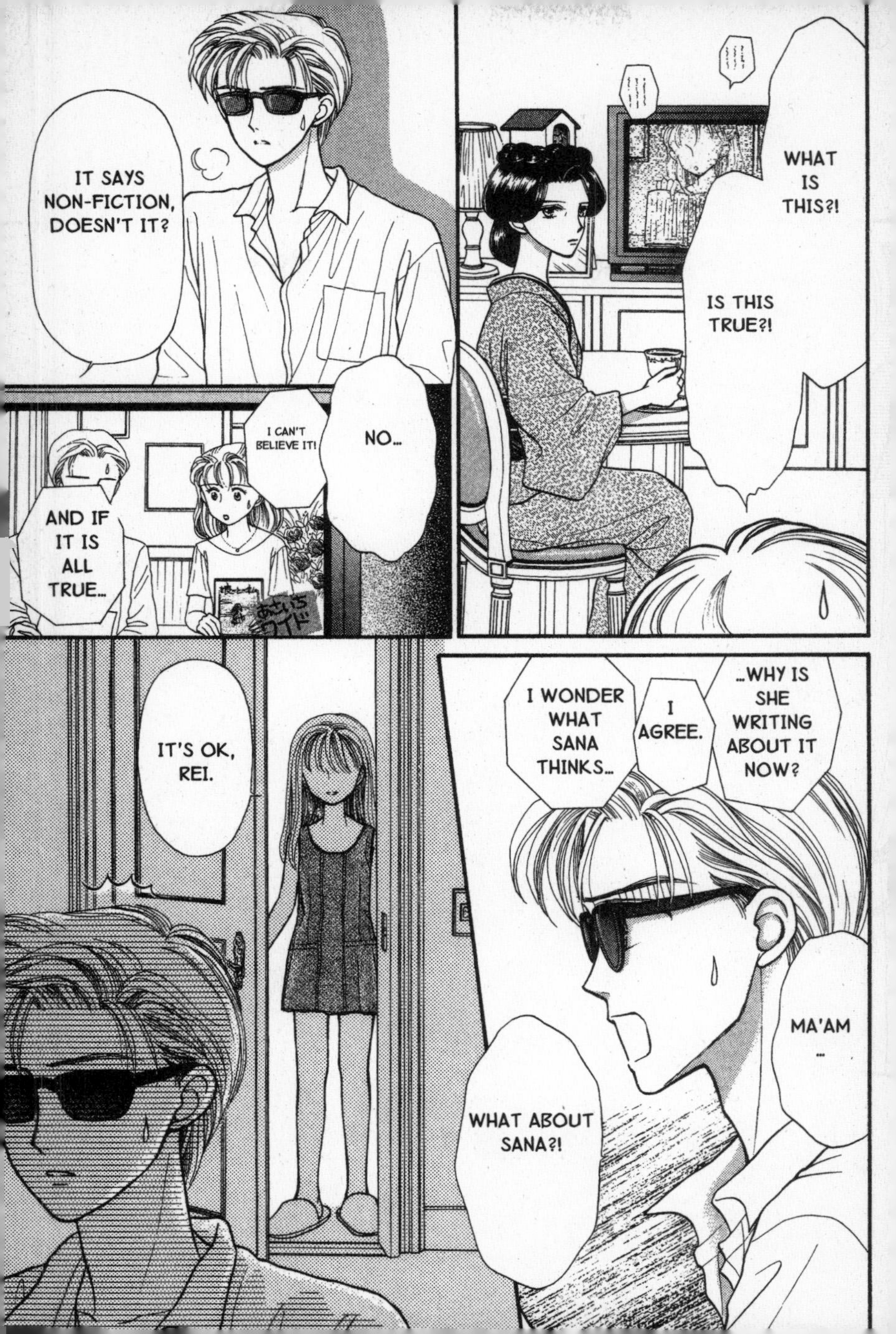
WHAT IS THIS?!
IS THIS TRUE?!
IT SAYS NON-FICTION, DOESN'T IT?
NO...
I CAN'T BELIEVE IT!
AND IF IT IS ALL TRUE...
...WHY IS SHE WRITING ABOUT IT NOW?
I AGREE.
I WONDER WHAT SANA THINKS...
MA'AM ...
WHAT ABOUT SANA?!
IT'S OK, REI.

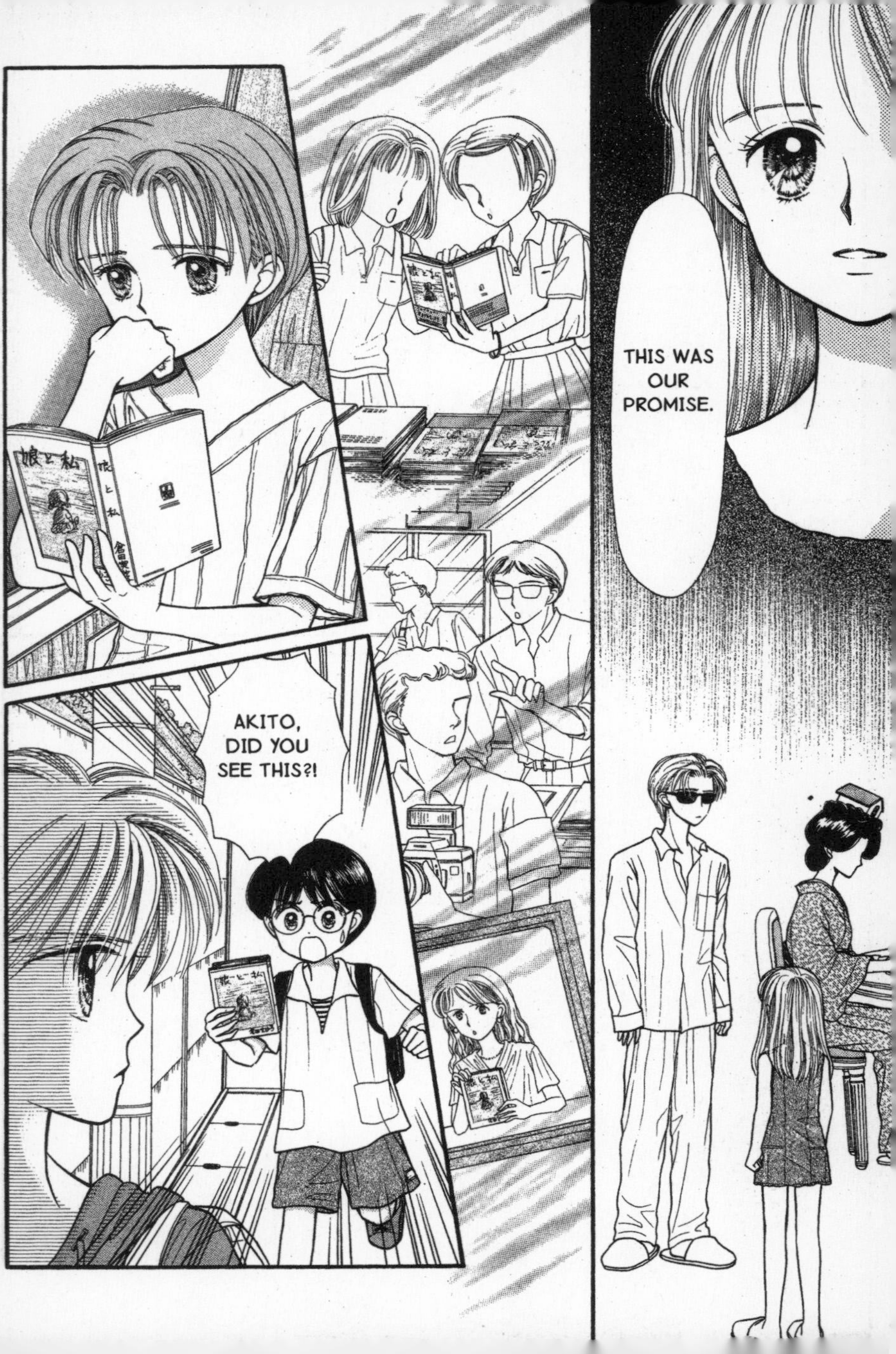
THIS WAS OUR PROMISE.
娘と私
AKITO, DID YOU SEE THIS?!

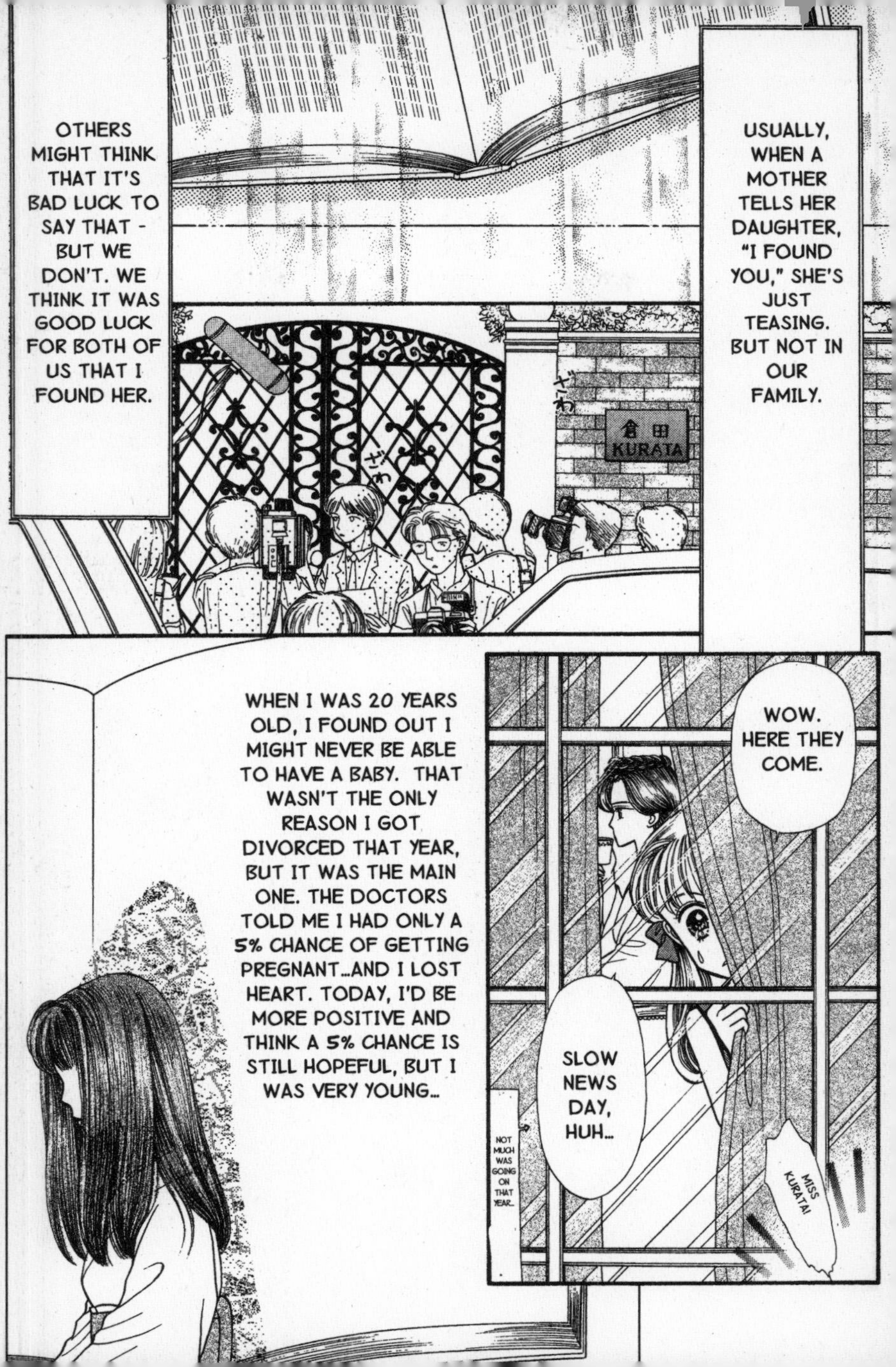
USUALLY, WHEN A MOTHER TELLS HER DAUGHTER, "I FOUND YOU," SHE'S JUST TEASING. BUT NOT IN OUR FAMILY.
倉田 KURATA
ざわ
ざわ
OTHERS MIGHT THINK THAT IT'S BAD LUCK TO SAY THAT - BUT WE DON'T. WE THINK IT WAS GOOD LUCK FOR BOTH OF US THAT I FOUND HER.
WOW. HERE THEY COME.
MISS KURATA!
SLOW NEWS DAY, HUH...
NOT MUCH WAS GOING ON THAT YEAR...
WHEN I WAS 20 YEARS OLD, I FOUND OUT I MIGHT NEVER BE ABLE TO HAVE A BABY. THAT WASN'T THE ONLY REASON I GOT DIVORCED THAT YEAR, BUT IT WAS THE MAIN ONE. THE DOCTORS TOLD ME I HAD ONLY A 5% CHANCE OF GETTING PREGNANT...AND I LOST HEART. TODAY, I'D BE MORE POSITIVE AND THINK A 5% CHANCE IS STILL HOPEFUL, BUT I WAS VERY YOUNG...

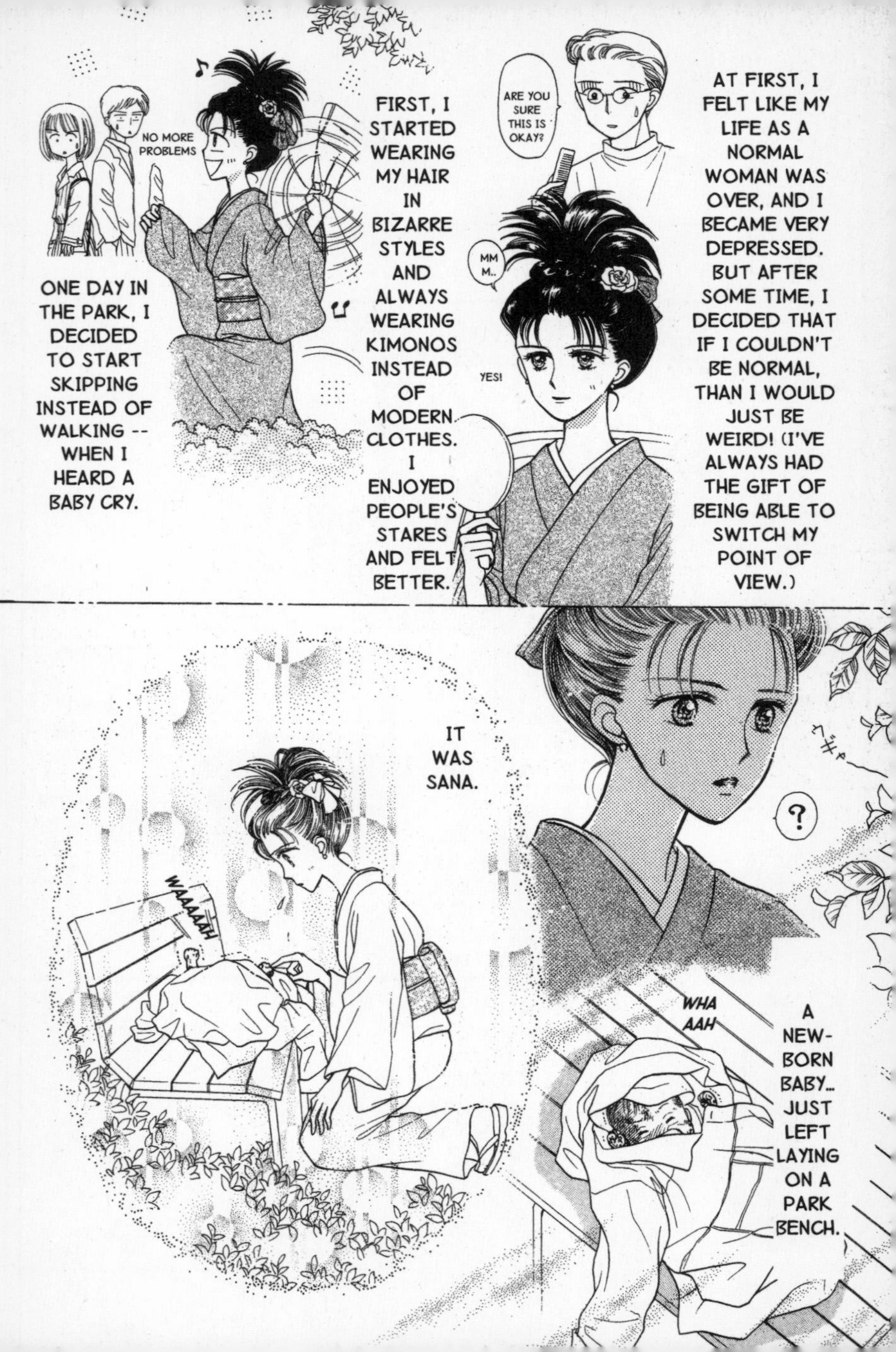
AT FIRST, I FELT LIKE MY LIFE AS A NORMAL WOMAN WAS OVER, AND I BECAME VERY DEPRESSED. BUT AFTER SOME TIME, I DECIDED THAT IF I COULDN'T BE NORMAL, THAN I WOULD JUST BE WEIRD! (I'VE ALWAYS HAD THE GIFT OF BEING ABLE TO SWITCH MY POINT OF VIEW.)
ARE YOU SURE THIS IS OKAY?
MM M..
YES!
FIRST, I STARTED WEARING MY HAIR IN BIZARRE STYLES AND ALWAYS WEARING KIMONOS INSTEAD OF MODERN CLOTHES. I ENJOYED PEOPLE'S STARES AND FELT BETTER.
NO MORE PROBLEMS
ONE DAY IN THE PARK, I DECIDED TO START SKIPPING INSTEAD OF WALKING -- WHEN I HEARD A BABY CRY.
?
WHA AAH
A NEW-BORN BABY... JUST LEFT LAYING ON A PARK BENCH.
IT WAS SANA.
WAAAAAH

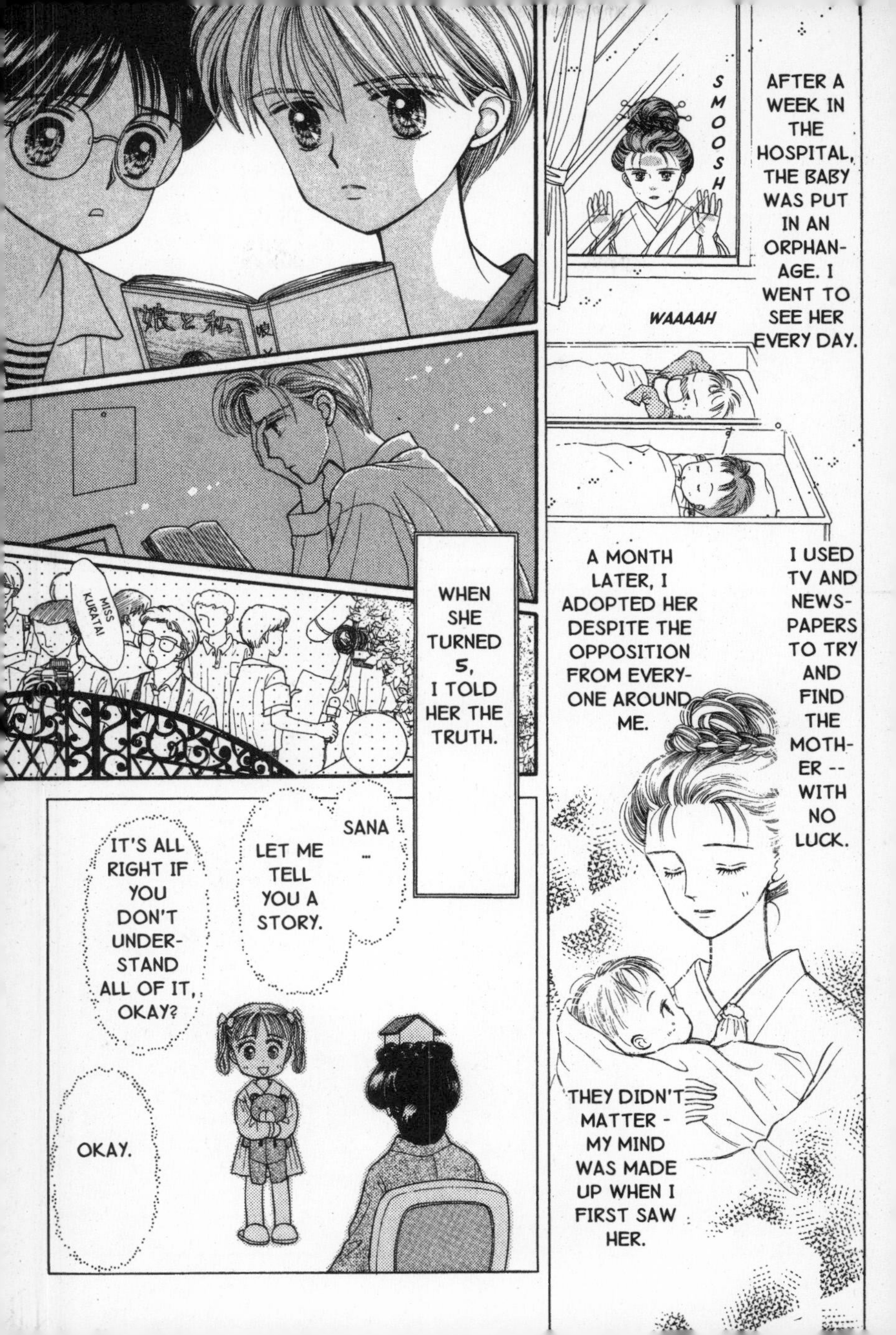
SMOOSH
AFTER A WEEK IN THE HOSPITAL, THE BABY WAS PUT IN AN ORPHANAGE. I WENT TO SEE HER EVERY DAY.
WAAAAH
I USED TV AND NEWSPAPERS TO TRY AND FIND THE MOTHER -- WITH NO LUCK.
A MONTH LATER, I ADOPTED HER DESPITE THE OPPOSITION FROM EVERYONE AROUND ME.
THEY DIDN'T MATTER - MY MIND WAS MADE UP WHEN I FIRST SAW HER.
娘と私
MISS KURATA!
WHEN SHE TURNED 5, I TOLD HER THE TRUTH.
SANA ...
LET ME TELL YOU A STORY.
IT'S ALL RIGHT IF YOU DON'T UNDERSTAND ALL OF IT, OKAY?
OKAY.

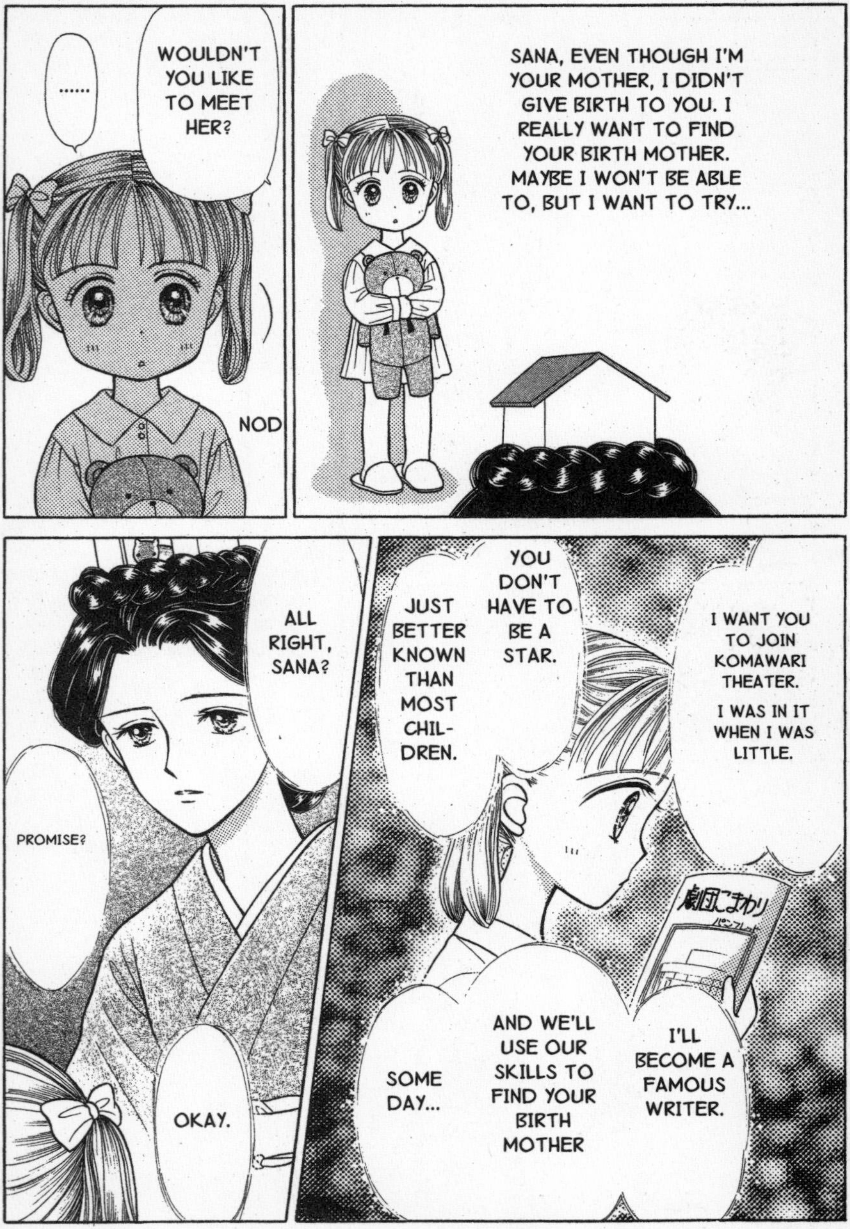
SANA, EVEN THOUGH I'M YOUR MOTHER, I DIDN'T GIVE BIRTH TO YOU. I REALLY WANT TO FIND YOUR BIRTH MOTHER. MAYBE I WON'T BE ABLE TO, BUT I WANT TO TRY...
WOULDN'T YOU LIKE TO MEET HER?
......
NOD
I WANT YOU TO JOIN KOMAWARI THEATER.
I WAS IN IT WHEN I WAS LITTLE.
YOU DON'T HAVE TO BE A STAR.
JUST BETTER KNOWN THAN MOST CHIL-DREN.
劇団こまわり
I'LL BECOME A FAMOUS WRITER.
AND WE'LL USE OUR SKILLS TO FIND YOUR BIRTH MOTHER
SOME DAY...
ALL RIGHT, SANA?
PROMISE?
OKAY.

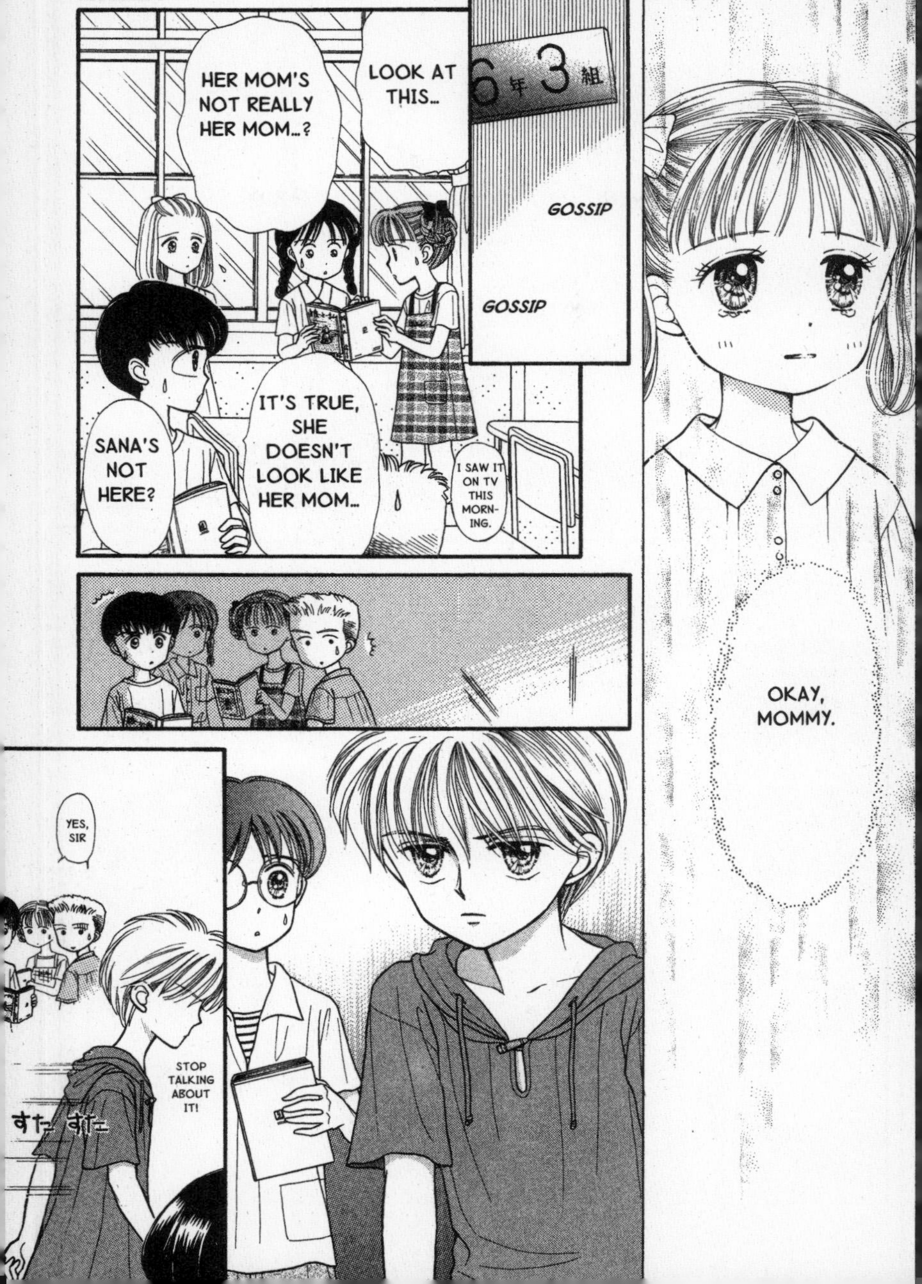
OKAY, MOMMY.
6年3組
GOSSIP
GOSSIP
LOOK AT THIS...
HER MOM'S NOT REALLY HER MOM...?
I SAW IT ON TV THIS MORN-ING.
IT'S TRUE, SHE DOESN'T LOOK LIKE HER MOM...
SANA'S NOT HERE?
STOP TALKING ABOUT IT!
YES, SIR
すた すた

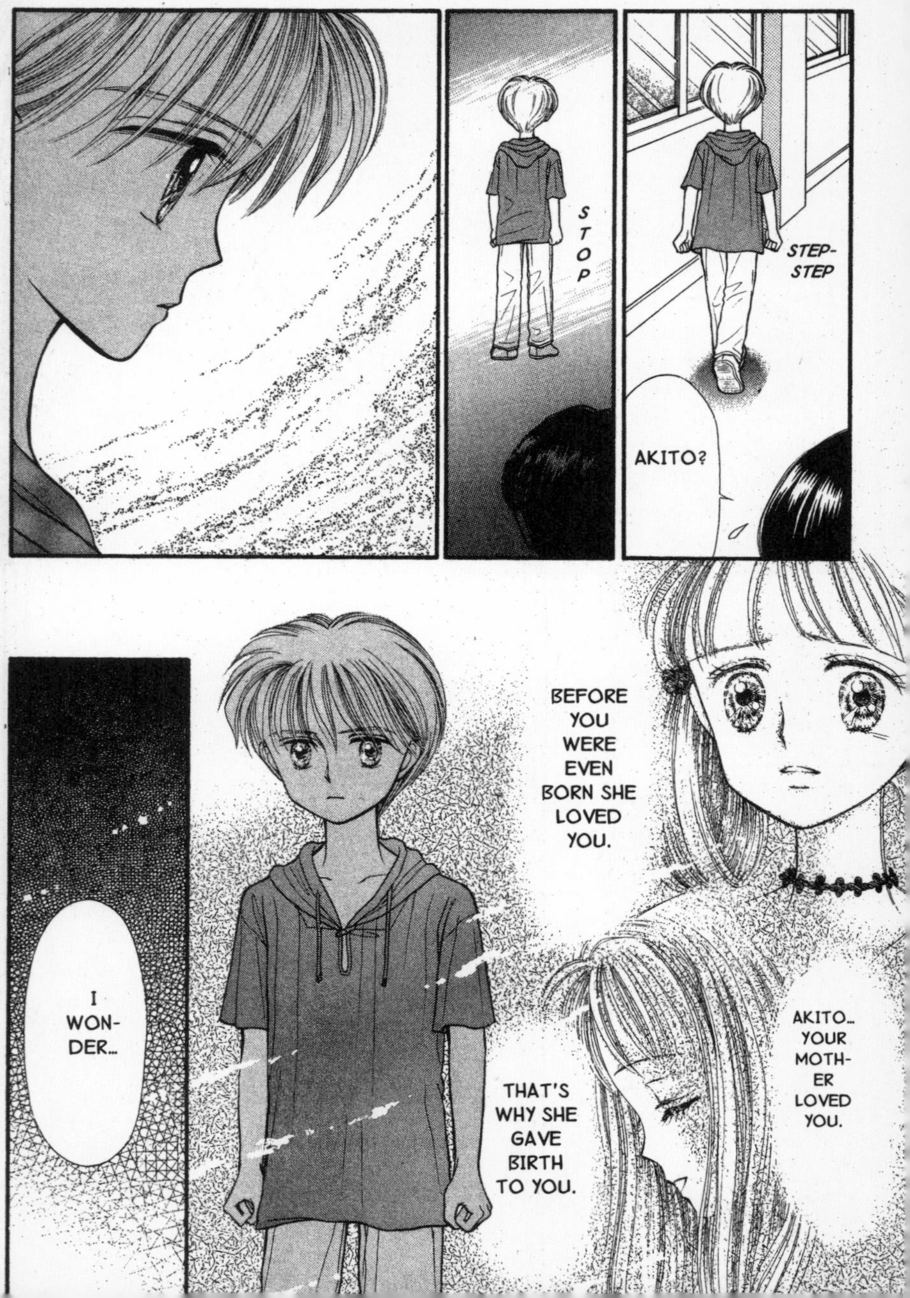
STEP-STEP
AKITO?
STOP
AKITO... YOUR MOTHER LOVED YOU.
BEFORE YOU WERE EVEN BORN SHE LOVED YOU.
THAT'S WHY SHE GAVE BIRTH TO YOU.
I WONDER...

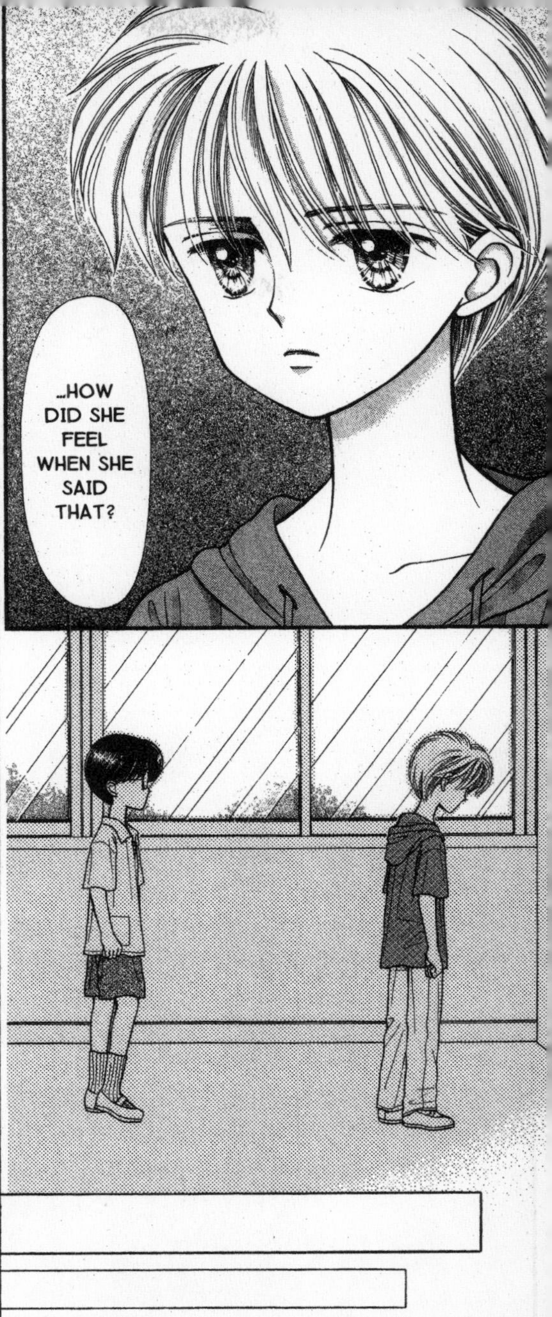

...HOW DID SHE FEEL WHEN SHE SAID THAT?

Thank you.

My last visit with you in this book! I have to confess, I now have no idea how long Kodocha is going to be. I usually get worried when I'm doing something with no definite end. But I guess I just gotta keep going. Each of these volumes consists of 5 episodes from Ribon magazine. When I first started the series, I had a bunch of different scenarios, from short to long (6-7 episodes, 20 episodes, and over 30). Obviously it's going to be long, so I've started adding new characters such as Naozumi. (I wouldn't have needed him if it had been one of the short simpler versions.) I keep trying to figure out a final count, but I'm always going wrong with it. Oh, boy. I hope it'll work out eventually. Ha, ha.

Alright, my final word: I really enjoy my work thanks to you guys. I wanna thank you for reading my comics. Please keep reading to find out what happens to Sana and Akito, and to see how they grow!

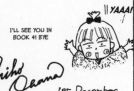

I'LL SEE YOU IN BOOK 4! BYE

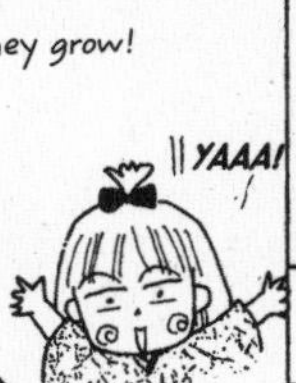

YAAA!

Miho Obana

'95 December

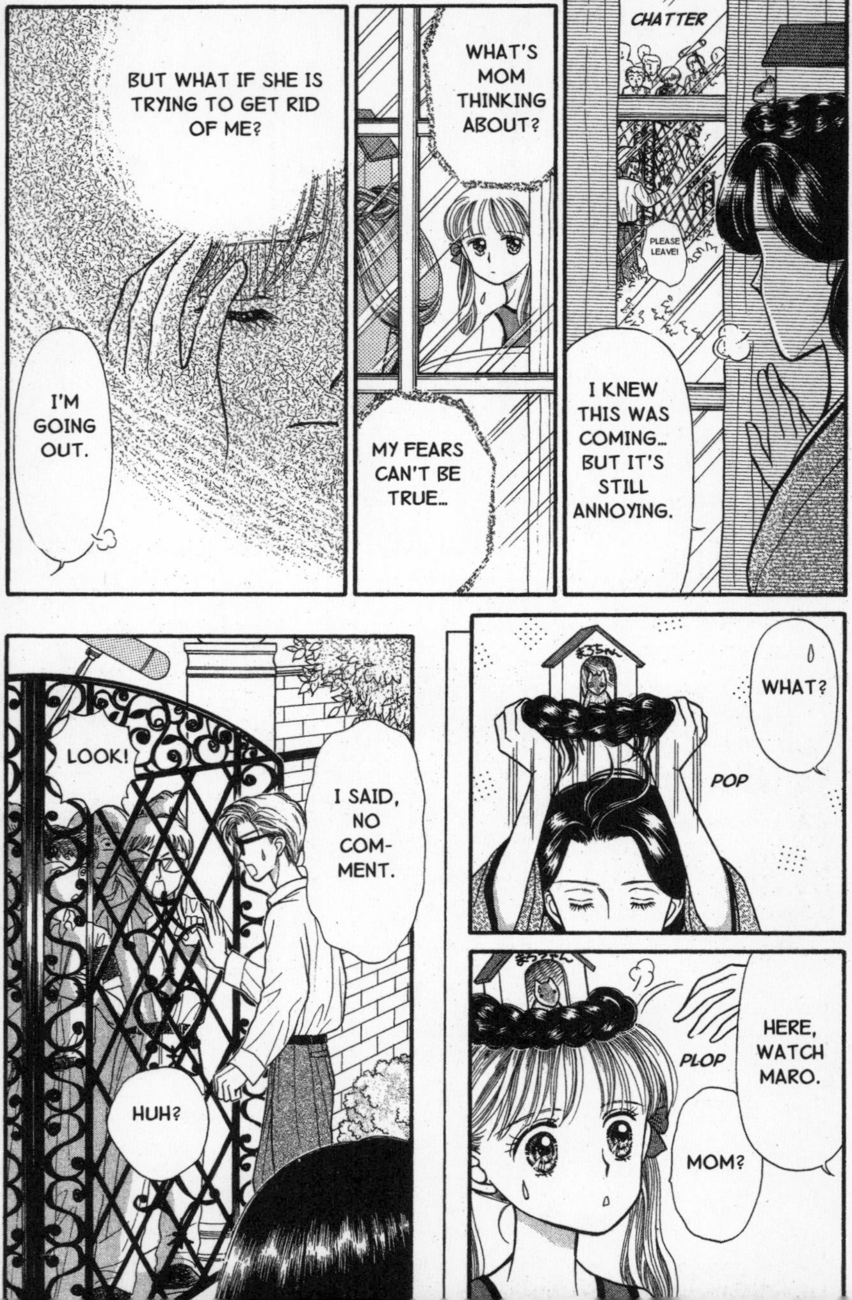
CHATTER
PLEASE LEAVE!
I KNEW THIS WAS COMING... BUT IT'S STILL ANNOYING.
WHAT'S MOM THINKING ABOUT?
MY FEARS CAN'T BE TRUE...
BUT WHAT IF SHE IS TRYING TO GET RID OF ME?
I'M GOING OUT.
WHAT?
POP
HERE, WATCH MARO.
PLOP
MOM?
I SAID, NO COM-MENT.
LOOK!
HUH?

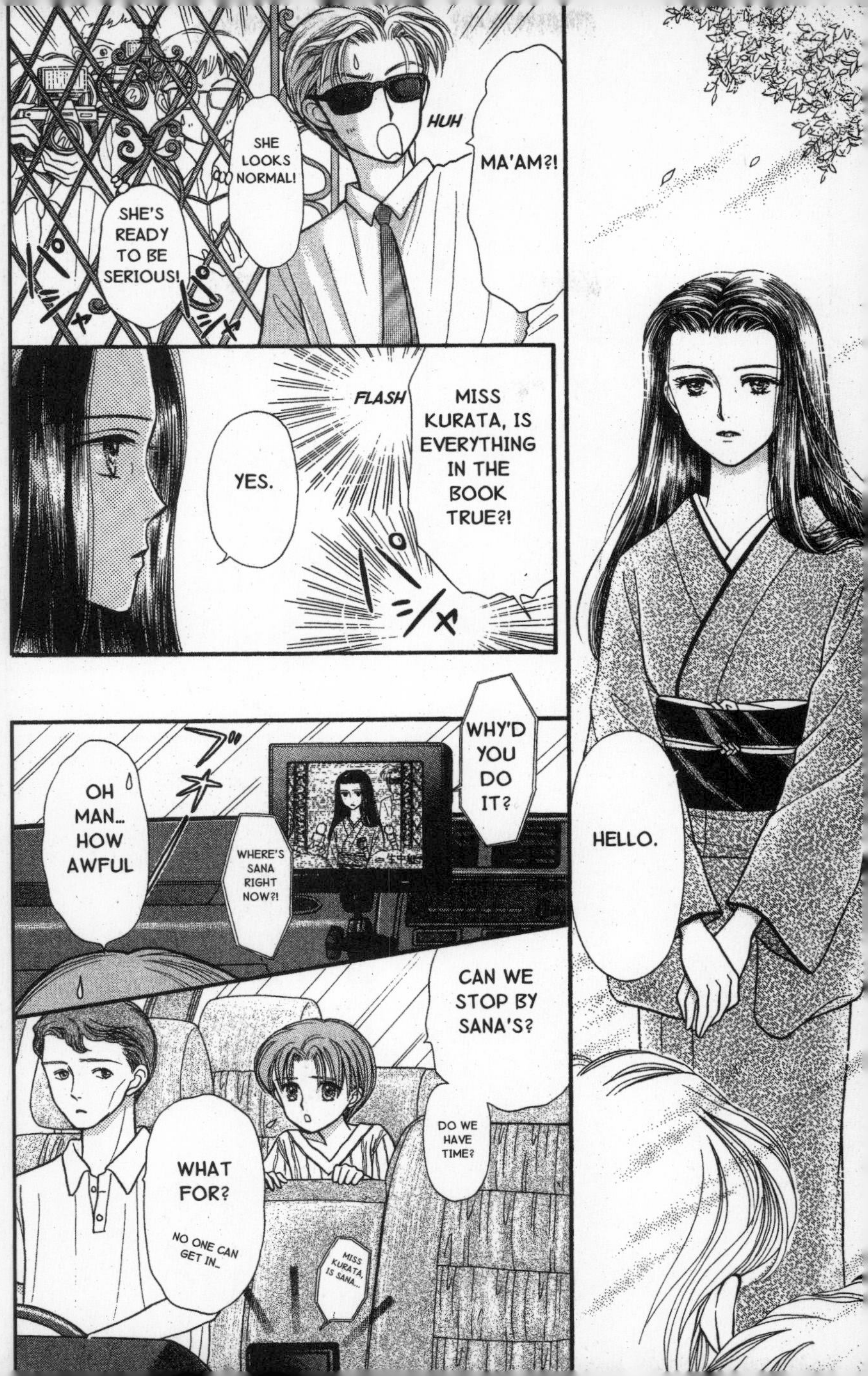
HELLO.
MA'AM?!
HUH
SHE LOOKS NORMAL!
SHE'S READY TO BE SERIOUS!
MISS KURATA, IS EVERYTHING IN THE BOOK TRUE?!
FLASH
YES.
WHY'D YOU DO IT?
WHERE'S SANA RIGHT NOW?!
OH MAN... HOW AWFUL
CAN WE STOP BY SANA'S?
DO WE HAVE TIME?
WHAT FOR?
MISS KURATA, IS SANA...
NO ONE CAN GET IN...

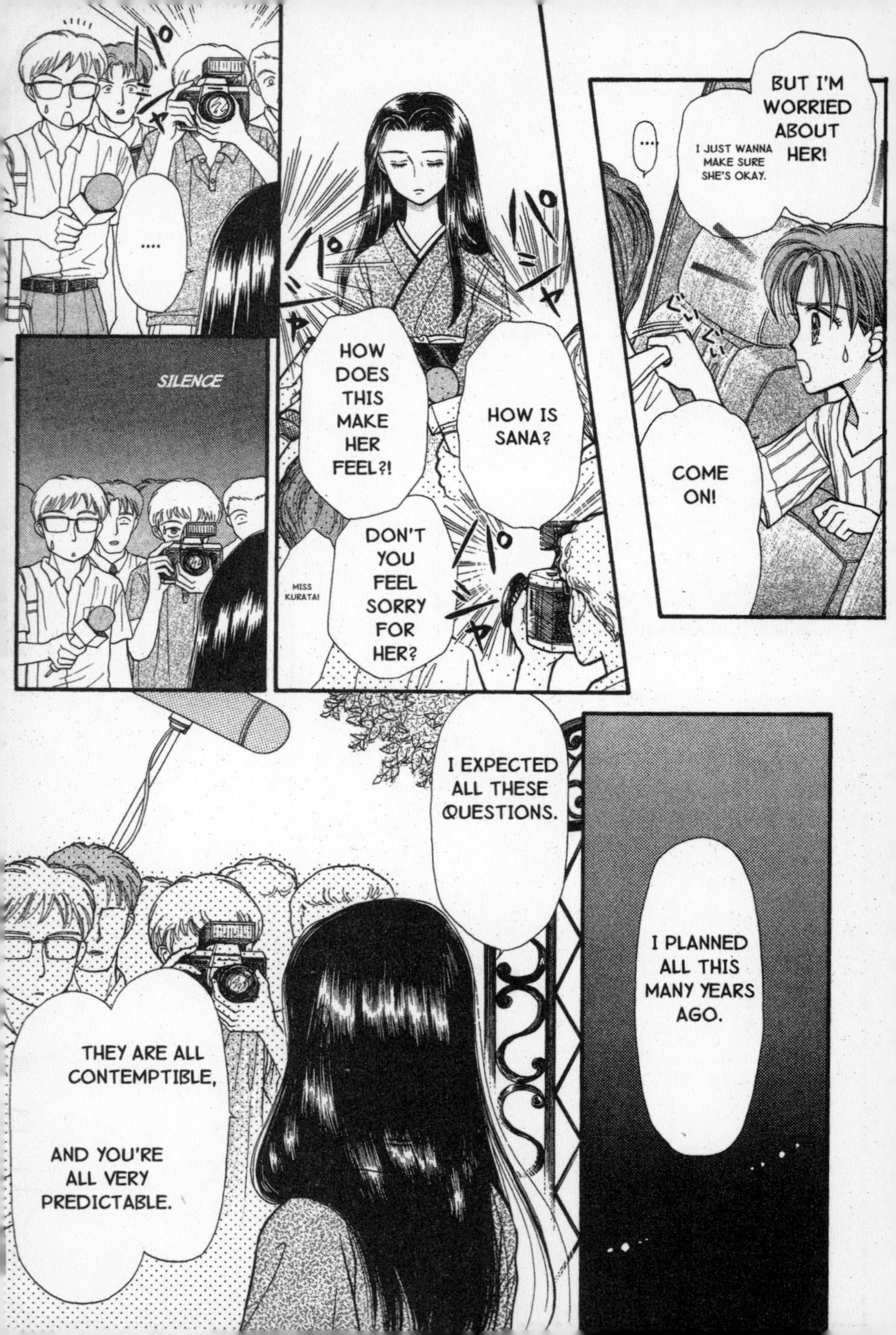

BUT I'M WORRIED ABOUT HER!
I JUST WANNA MAKE SURE SHE'S OKAY.
....
COME ON!
HOW IS SANA?
HOW DOES THIS MAKE HER FEEL?!
DON'T YOU FEEL SORRY FOR HER?
MISS KURATA!
....
SILENCE
I PLANNED ALL THIS MANY YEARS AGO.
I EXPECTED ALL THESE QUESTIONS.
THEY ARE ALL CONTEMPTIBLE,
AND YOU'RE ALL VERY PREDICTABLE.

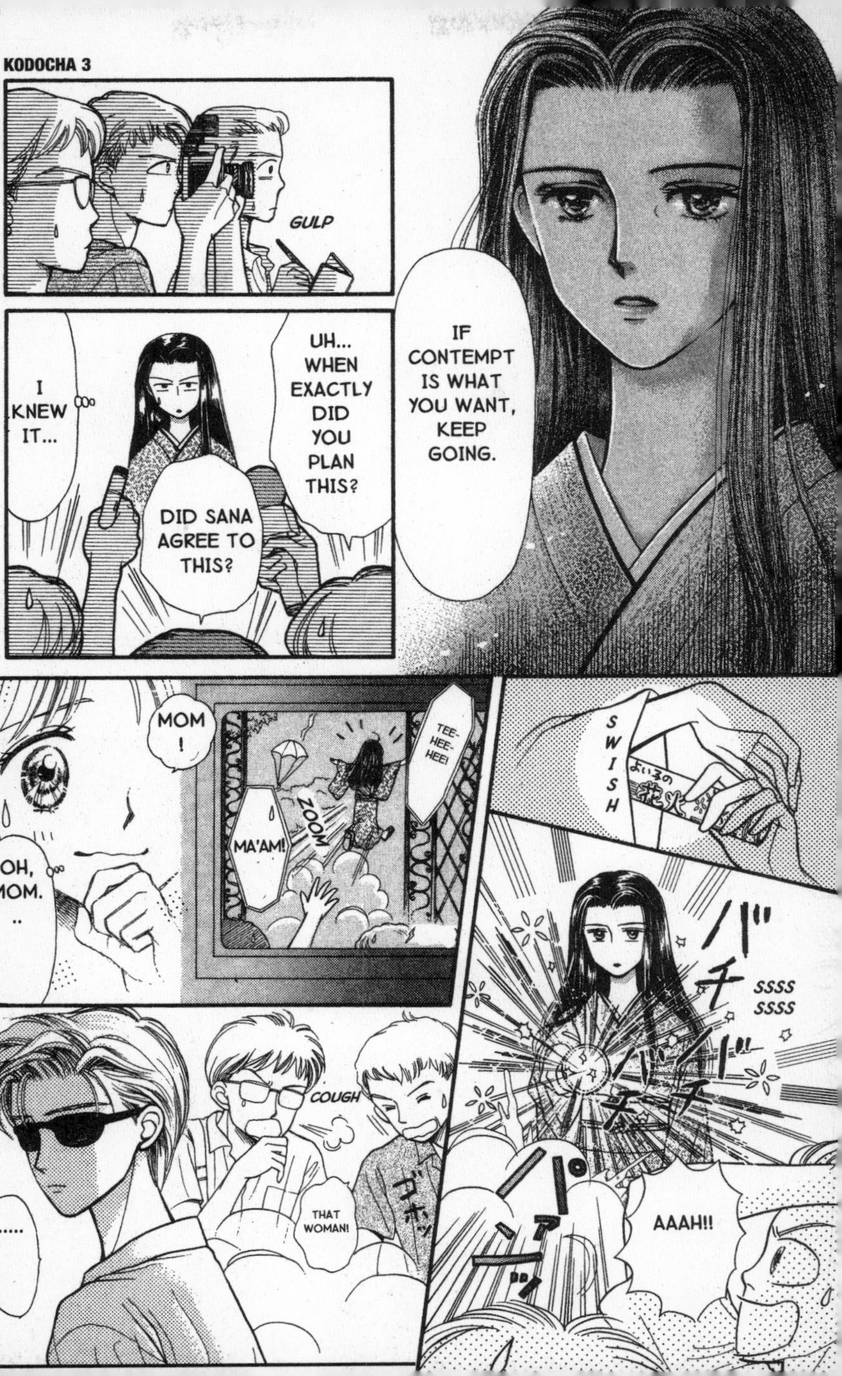
IF CONTEMPT IS WHAT YOU WANT, KEEP GOING.
GULP
UH... WHEN EXACTLY DID YOU PLAN THIS?
DID SANA AGREE TO THIS?
I KNEW IT...
SWISH
よい子の花火
バチバチ
SSSS SSSS
パーン
AAAH!!
TEE-HEE-HEE!
ZOOM
MA'AM!
MOM!
OH, MOM. ..
COUGH
ゴホッ
THAT WOMAN!
.....

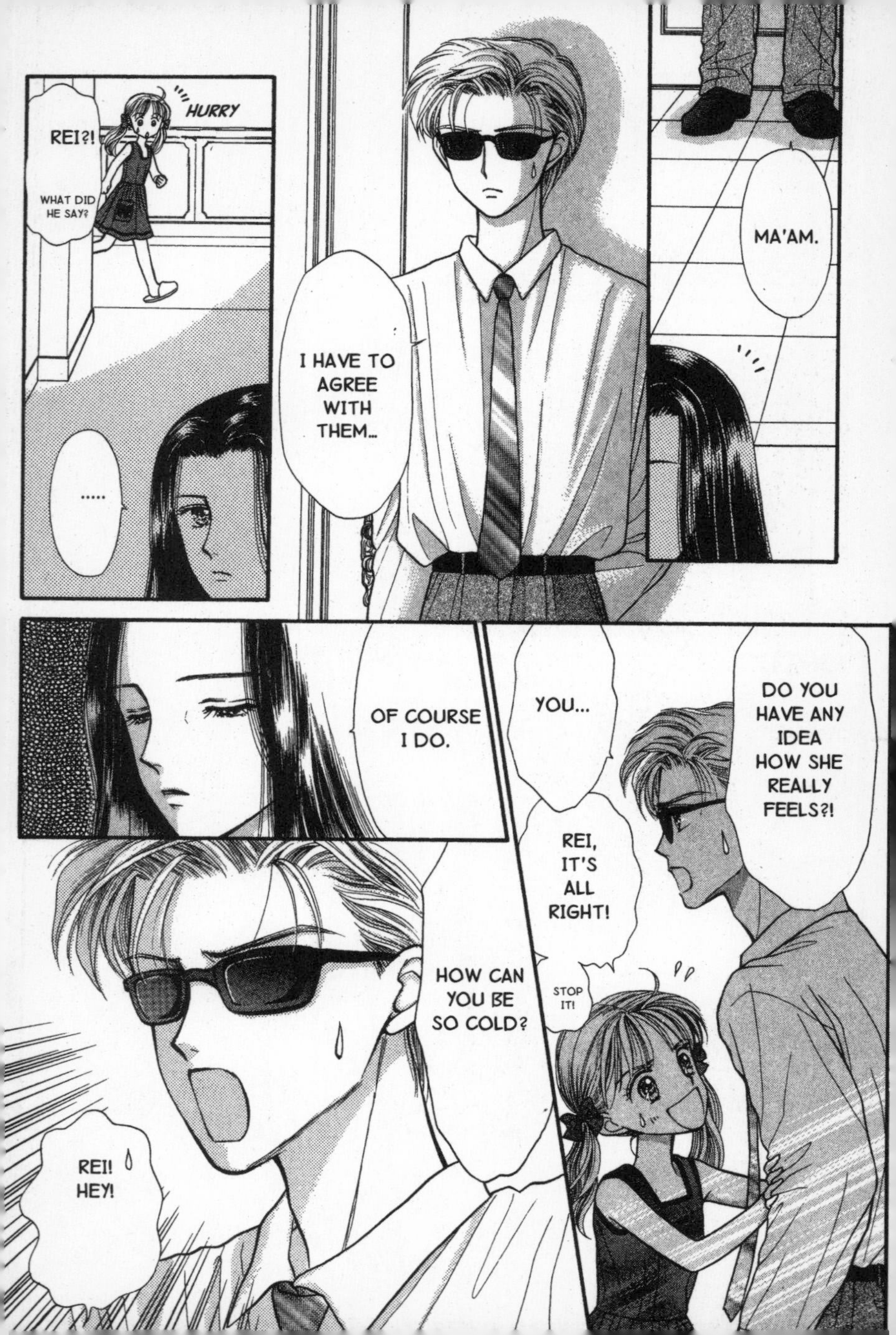
MA'AM.
I HAVE TO AGREE WITH THEM...
HURRY
REI?!
WHAT DID HE SAY?
......
DO YOU HAVE ANY IDEA HOW SHE REALLY FEELS?!
YOU...
REI, IT'S ALL RIGHT!
STOP IT!
OF COURSE I DO.
HOW CAN YOU BE SO COLD?
REI! HEY!

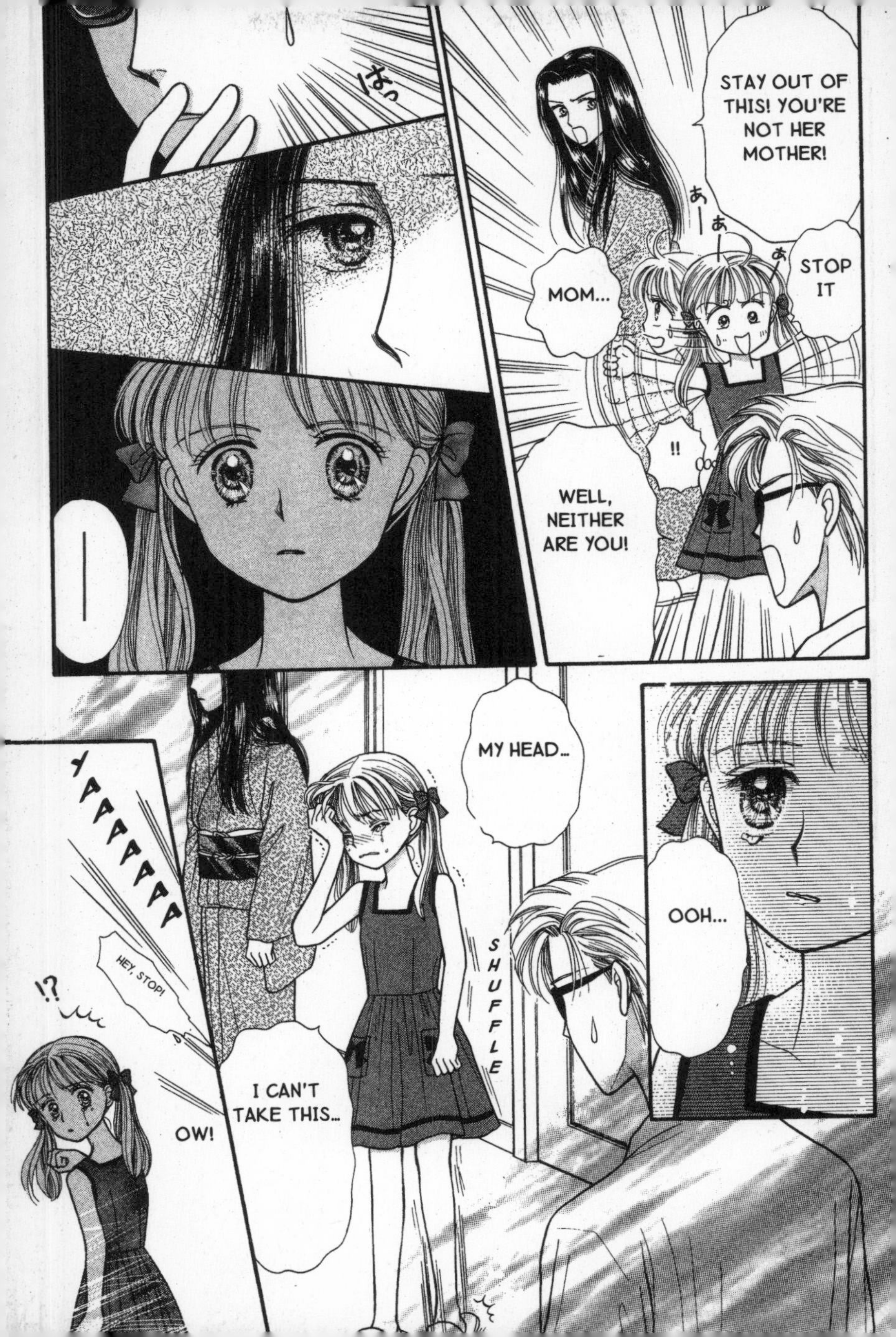
STAY OUT OF THIS! YOU'RE NOT HER MOTHER!
STOP IT
MOM...
!!
WELL, NEITHER ARE YOU!
ぱっ
OOH...
MY HEAD...
SHUFFLE
I CAN'T TAKE THIS...
HEY, STOP!
!?
OW!

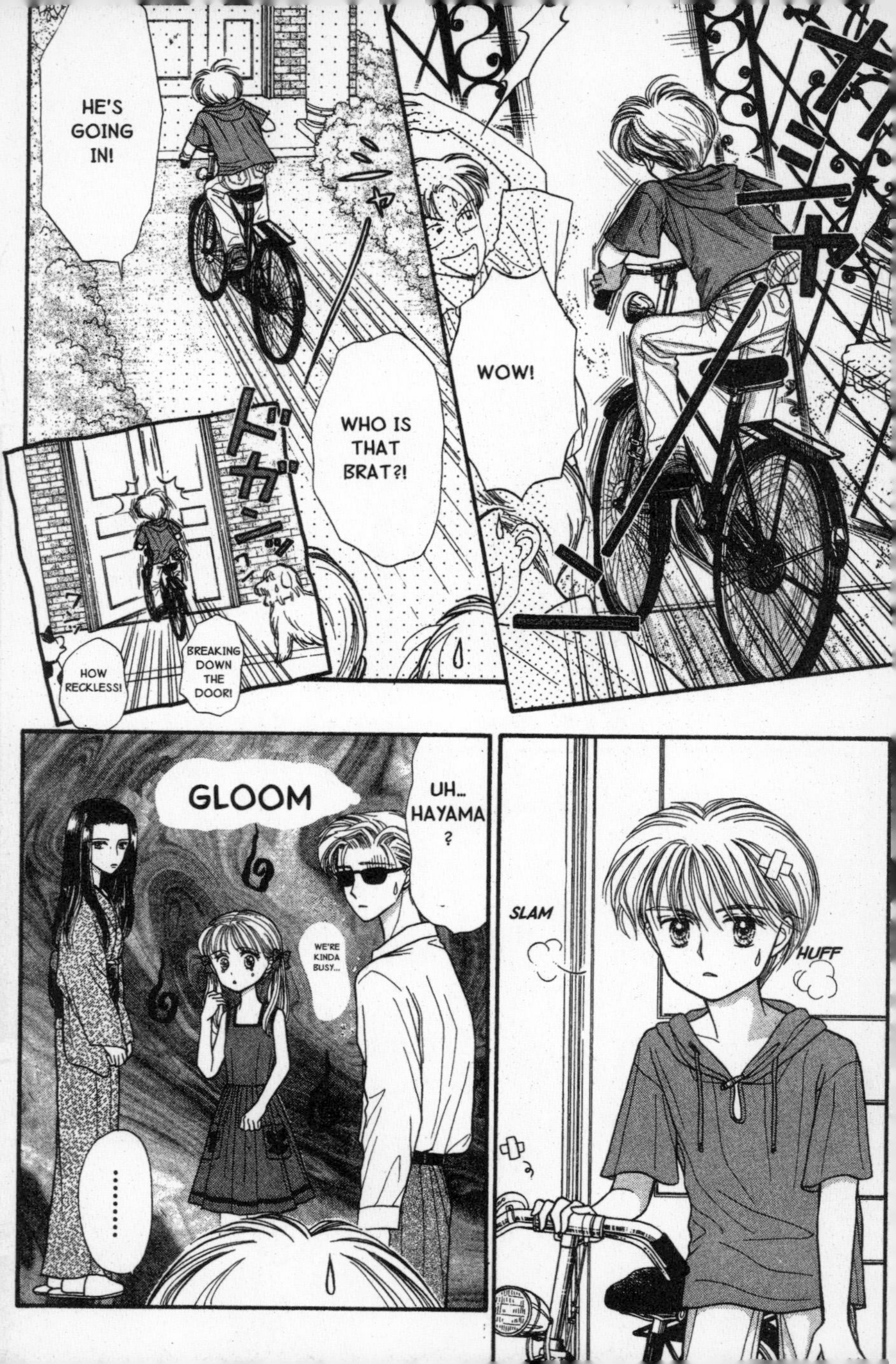
WOW!
WHO IS THAT BRAT?!
HE'S GOING IN!
BREAKING DOWN THE DOOR!
HOW RECKLESS!
SLAM
HUFF
UH... HAYAMA?
GLOOM
WE'RE KINDA BUSY...
....

AKITO...

......

HEY! WHA?!

HEY, STOP!

AKITO?!

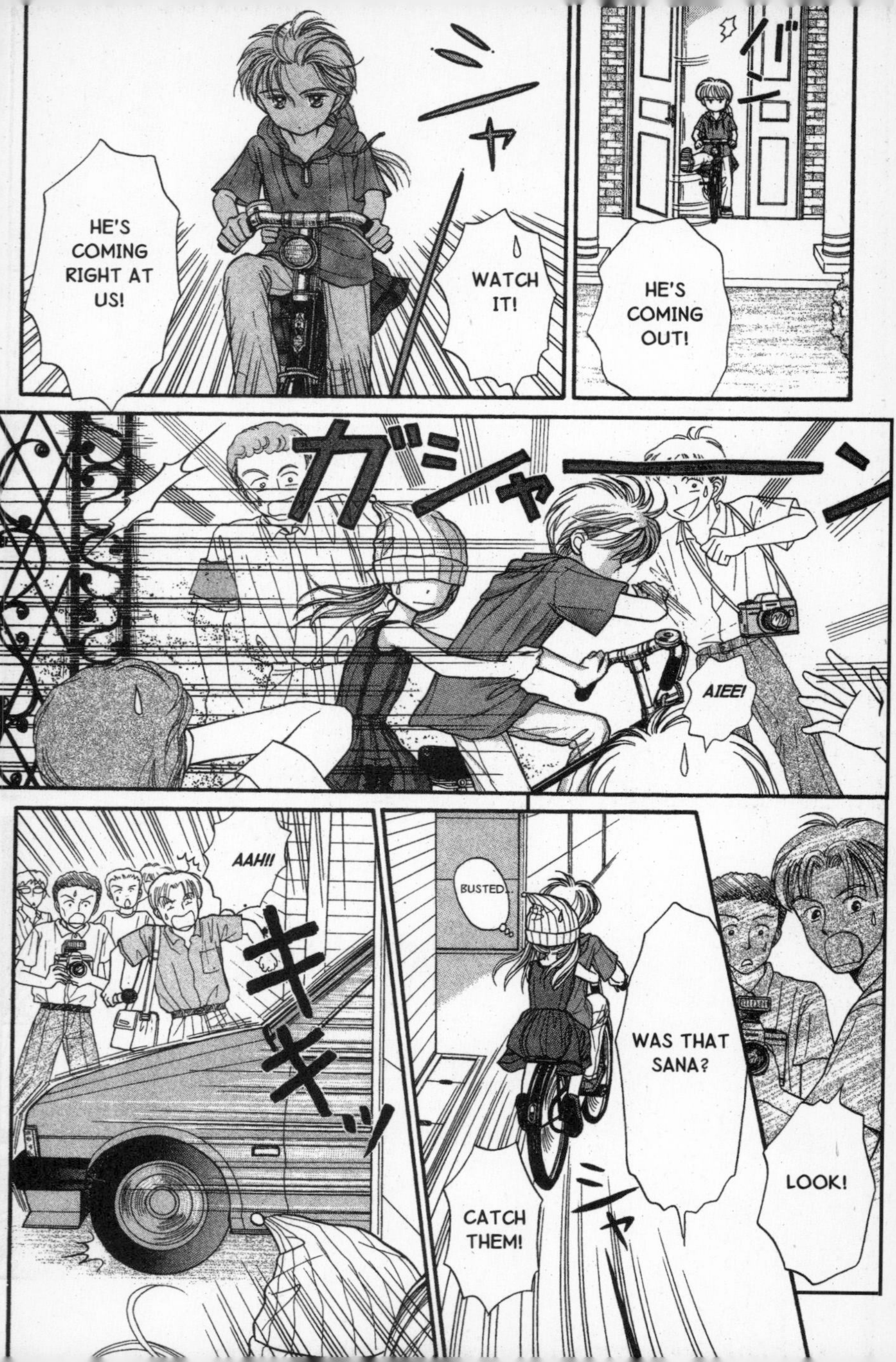
HE'S COMING OUT!
WATCH IT!
HE'S COMING RIGHT AT US!
AIEE!
LOOK!
WAS THAT SANA?
BUSTED...
CATCH THEM!
AAH!!

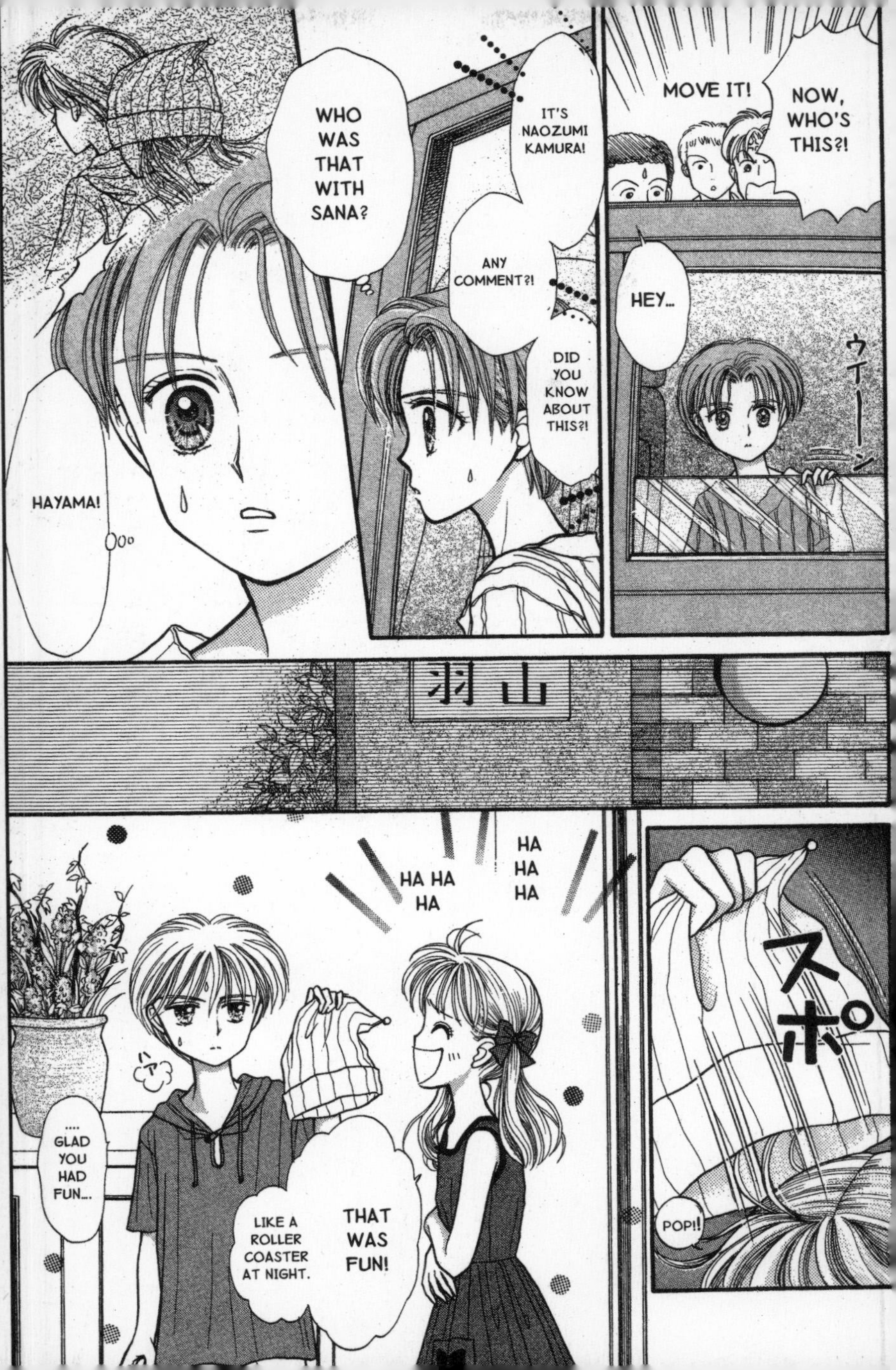
NOW, WHO'S THIS?!
MOVE IT!
HEY...
ウィーン
IT'S NAOZUMI KAMURA!
ANY COMMENT?!
DID YOU KNOW ABOUT THIS?!
WHO WAS THAT WITH SANA?
HAYAMA!
羽山
スポ
POP!!
HA HA HA
HA HA HA
THAT WAS FUN!
LIKE A ROLLER COASTER AT NIGHT.
.... GLAD YOU HAD FUN...

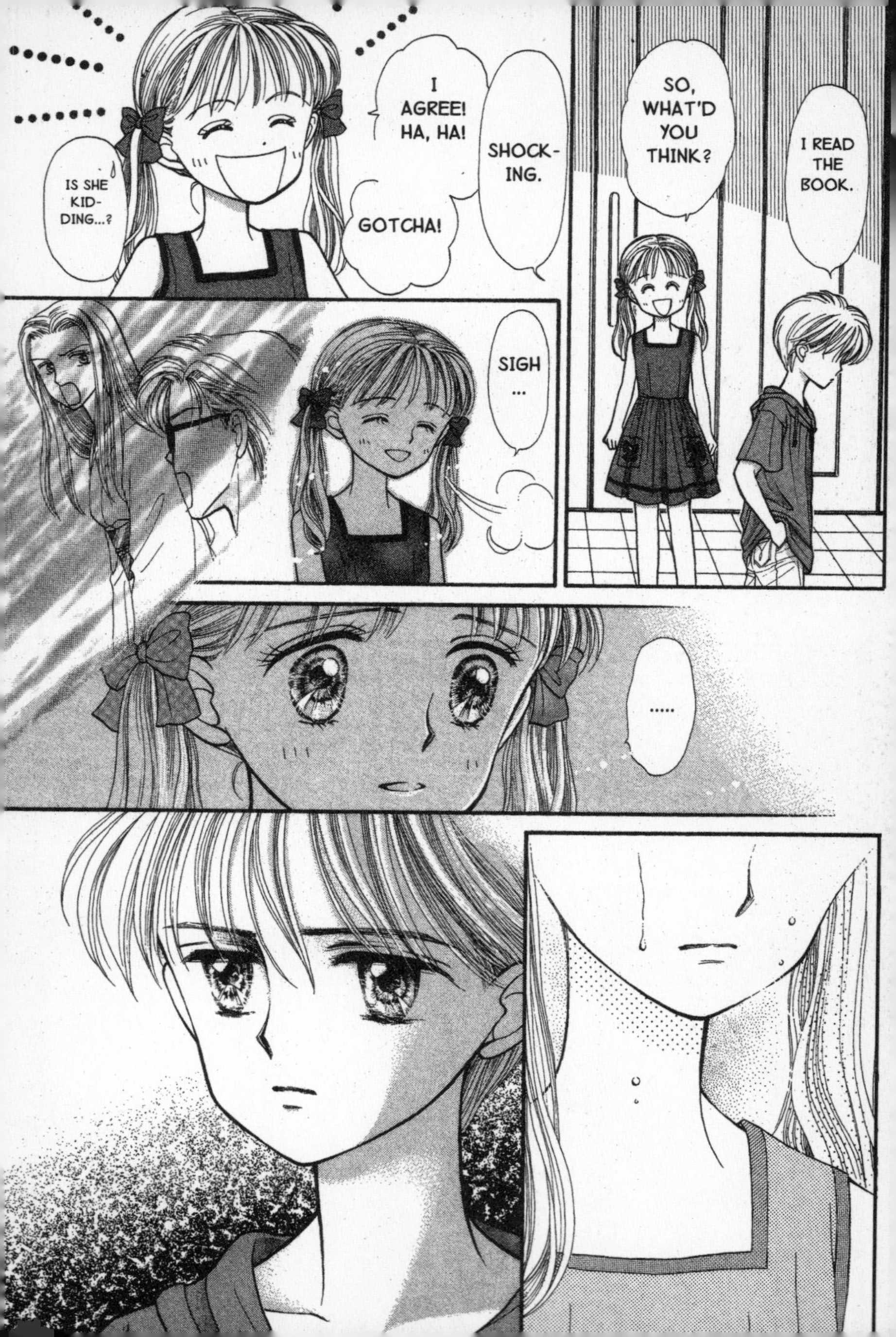
I READ THE BOOK.
SO, WHAT'D YOU THINK?
SHOCKING.
I AGREE! HA, HA!
GOTCHA!
IS SHE KIDDING...?
SIGH ...
.....

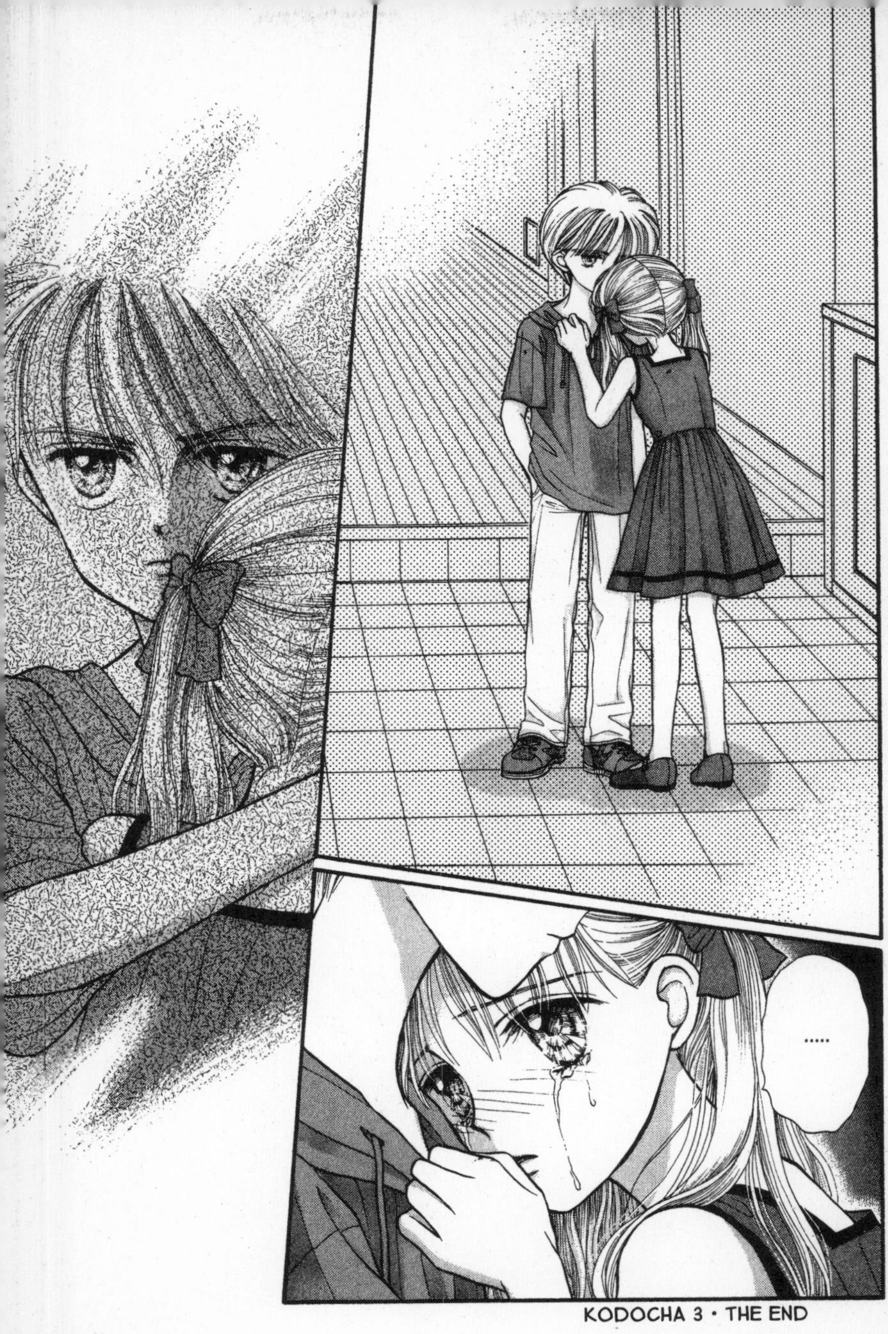
.....

KODOCHA 3 • THE END

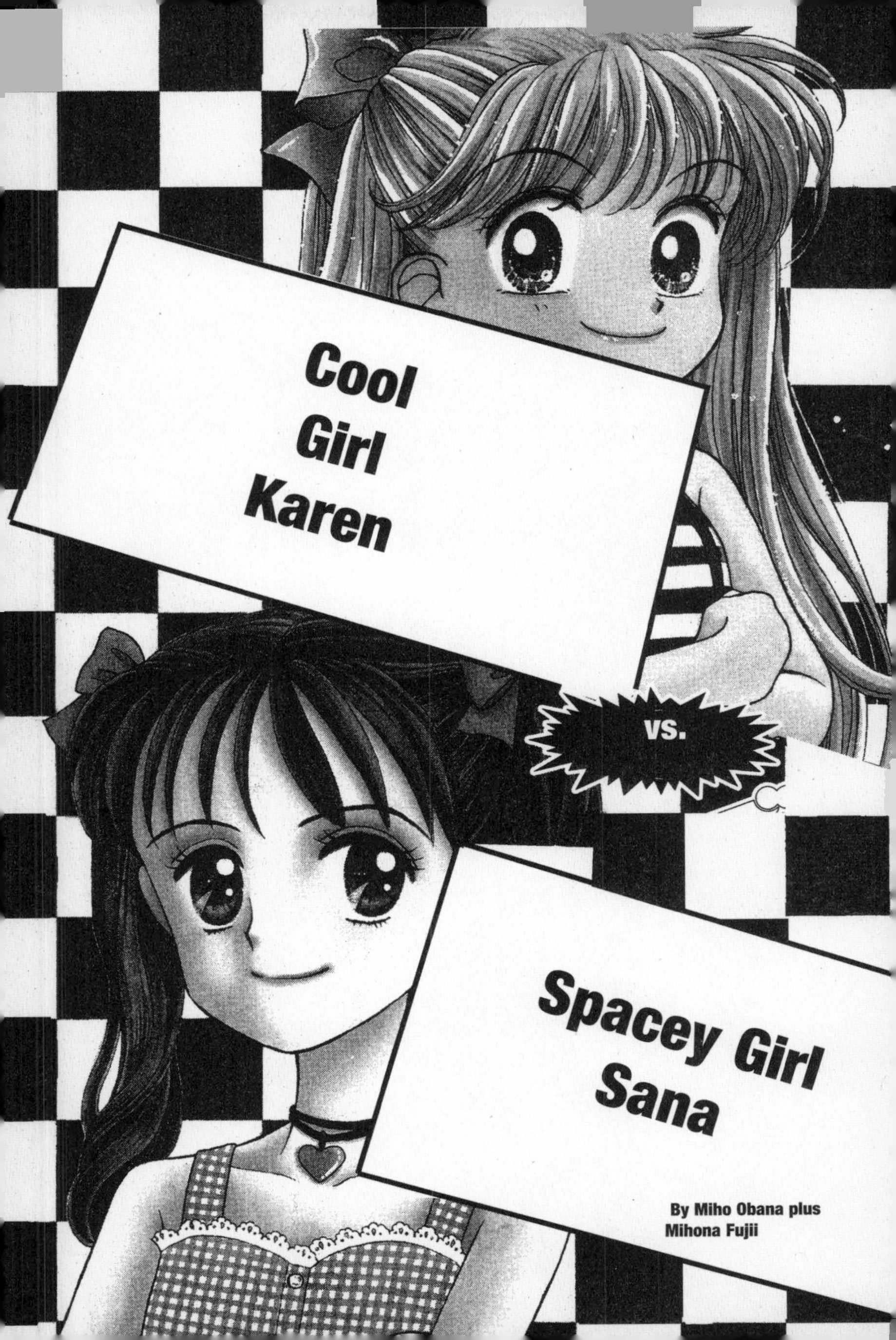
Cool Girl Karen
vs.
Spacey Girl Sana
By Miho Obana plus Mihona Fujii

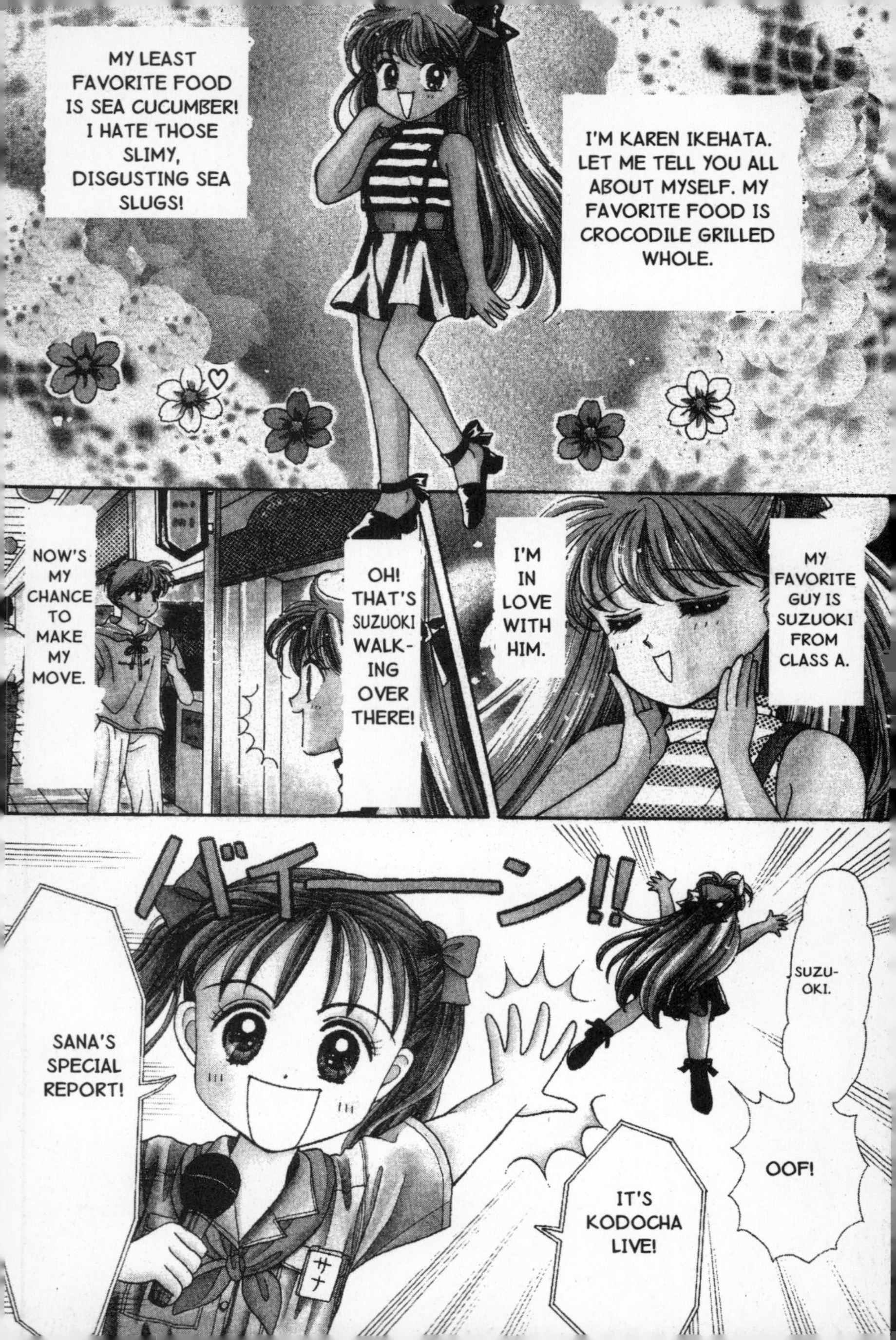
I'M KAREN IKEHATA. LET ME TELL YOU ALL ABOUT MYSELF. MY FAVORITE FOOD IS CROCODILE GRILLED WHOLE.
MY LEAST FAVORITE FOOD IS SEA CUCUMBER! I HATE THOSE SLIMY, DISGUSTING SEA SLUGS!
MY FAVORITE GUY IS SUZUOKI FROM CLASS A.
I'M IN LOVE WITH HIM.
OH! THAT'S SUZUOKI WALKING OVER THERE!
NOW'S MY CHANCE TO MAKE MY MOVE.
バイーン!!
SUZU-OKI.
OOF!
IT'S KODOCHA LIVE!
SANA'S SPECIAL REPORT!
サナ

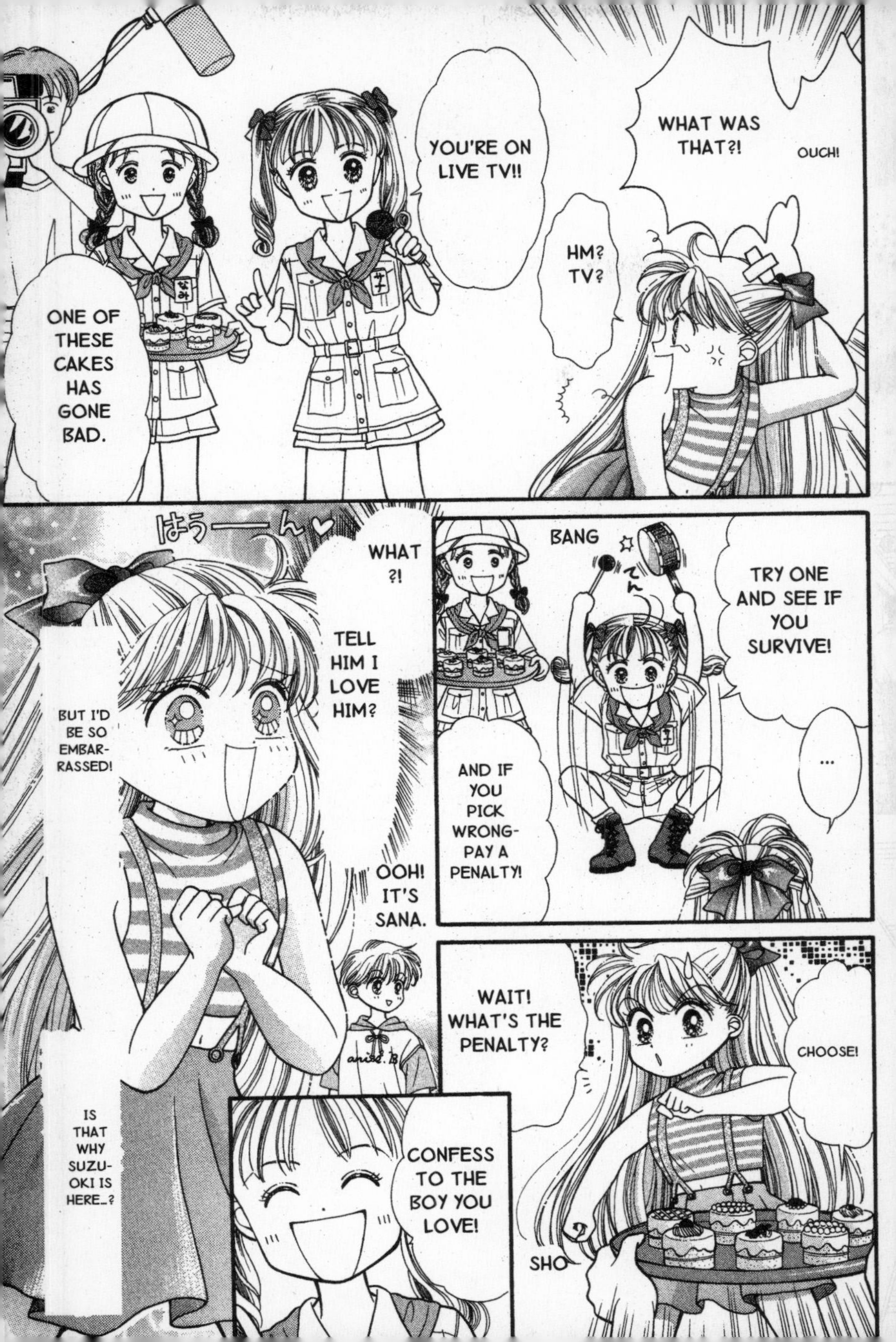
OUCH!
WHAT WAS THAT?!
HM? TV?
YOU'RE ON LIVE TV!!
ONE OF THESE CAKES HAS GONE BAD.
TRY ONE AND SEE IF YOU SURVIVE!
BANG
てん
...
AND IF YOU PICK WRONG- PAY A PENALTY!
CHOOSE!
WAIT! WHAT'S THE PENALTY?
SHO
CONFESS TO THE BOY YOU LOVE!
WHAT?!
TELL HIM I LOVE HIM?
はうーーん♥
BUT I'D BE SO EMBARRASSED!
OOH! IT'S SANA.
IS THAT WHY SUZUKI IS HERE...?

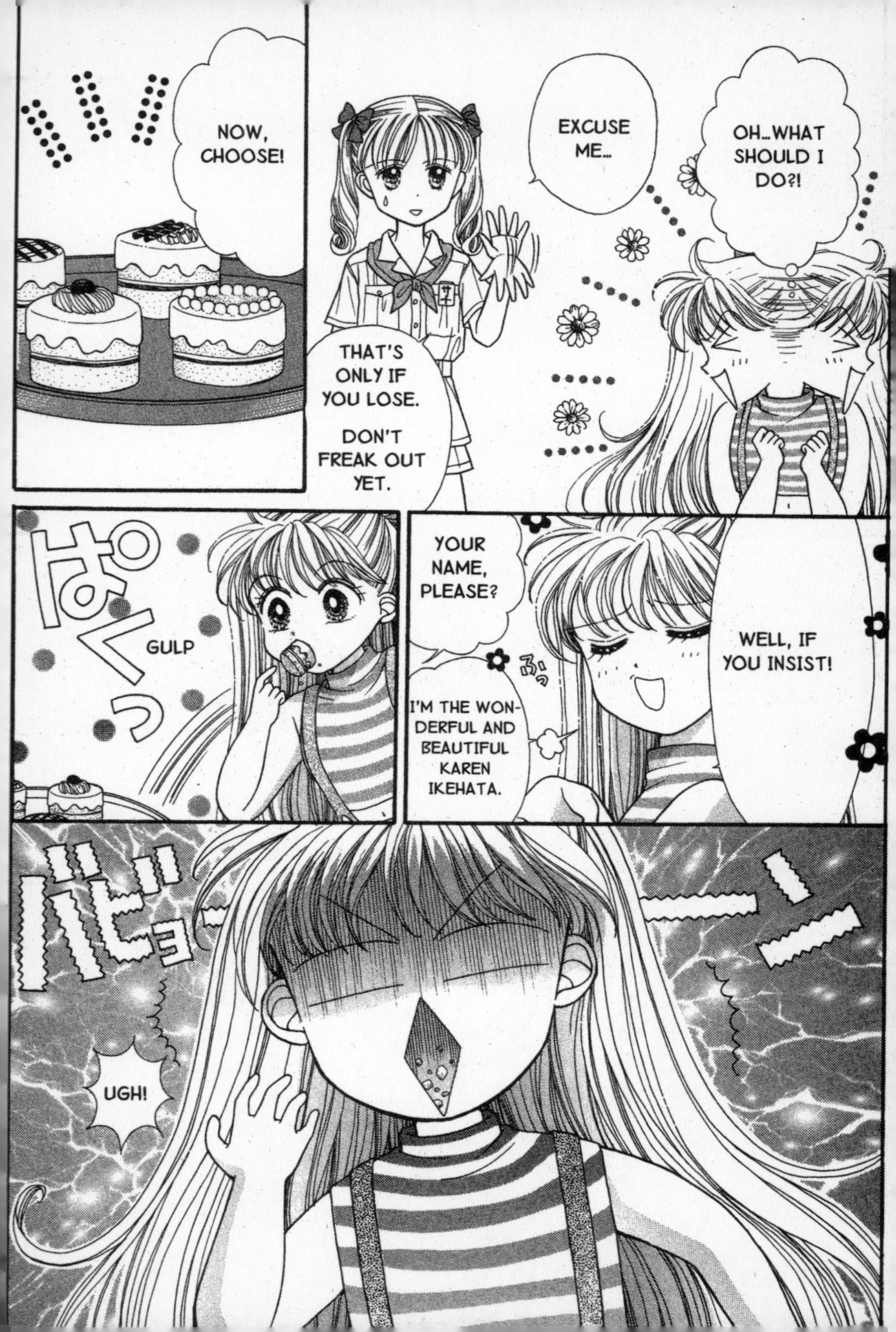
OH...WHAT SHOULD I DO?!
EXCUSE ME...
THAT'S ONLY IF YOU LOSE.
DON'T FREAK OUT YET.
NOW, CHOOSE!
YOUR NAME, PLEASE?
WELL, IF YOU INSIST!
ふっ
I'M THE WON-DERFUL AND BEAUTIFUL KAREN IKEHATA.
はぐっ
GULP
バビョーン
UGH!

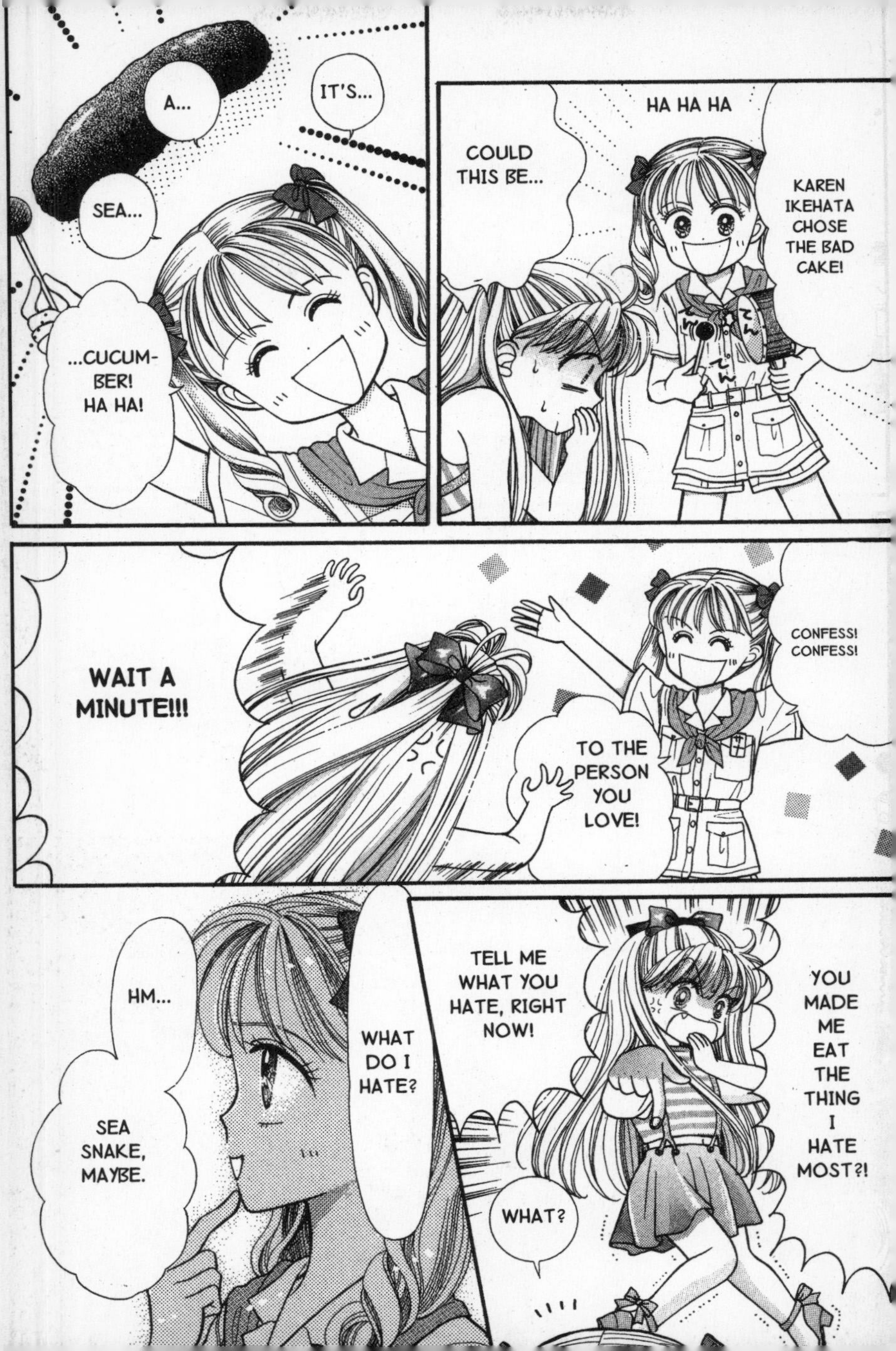
HA HA HA
KAREN IKEHATA CHOSE THE BAD CAKE!
COULD THIS BE...
IT'S...
A...
SEA...
...CUCUM-BER! HA HA!
CONFESS! CONFESS!
TO THE PERSON YOU LOVE!
WAIT A MINUTE!!!
YOU MADE ME EAT THE THING I HATE MOST?!
TELL ME WHAT YOU HATE, RIGHT NOW!
WHAT?
WHAT DO I HATE?
HM...
SEA SNAKE, MAYBE.

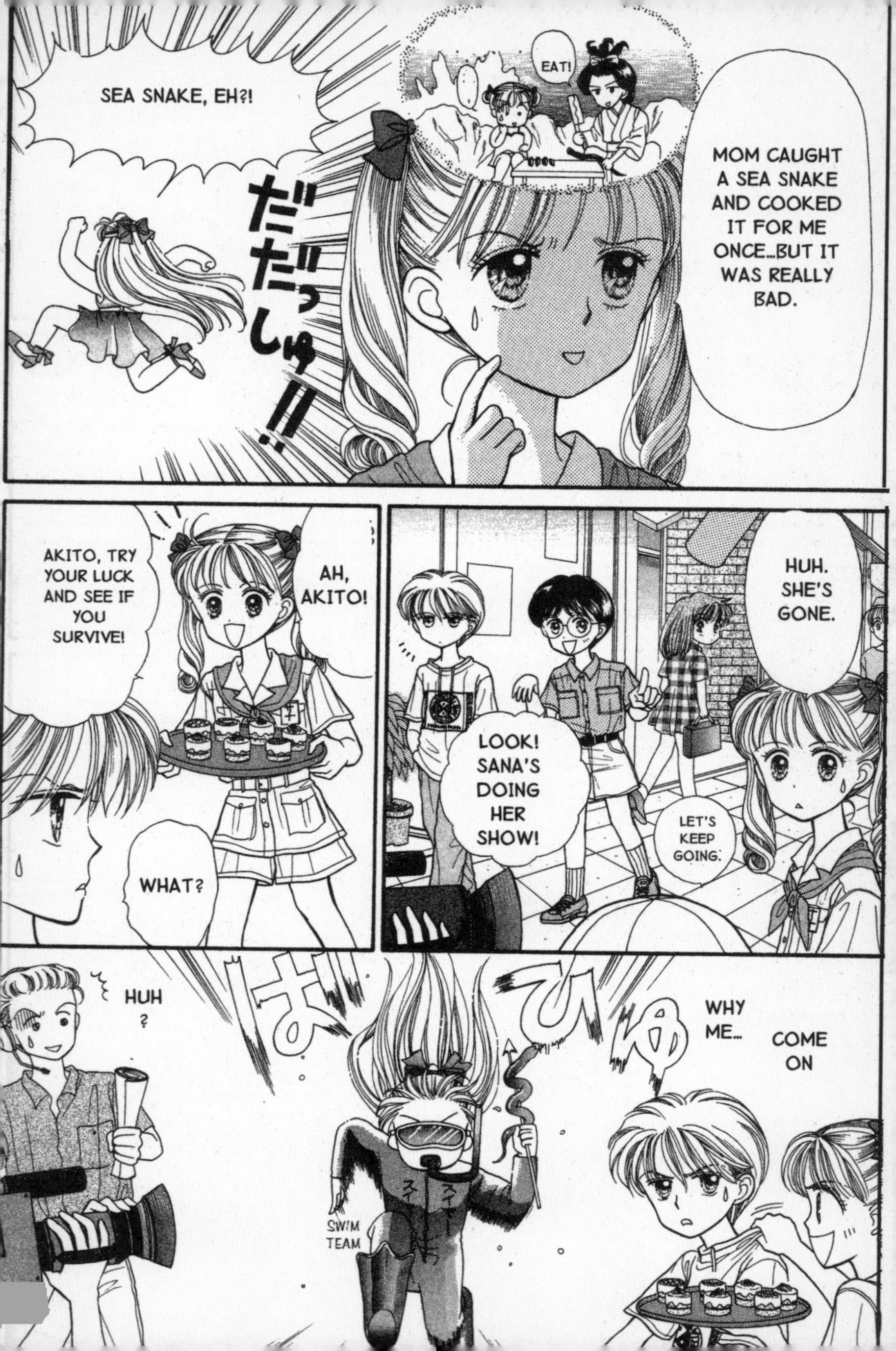
MOM CAUGHT A SEA SNAKE AND COOKED IT FOR ME ONCE...BUT IT WAS REALLY BAD.
EAT!
SEA SNAKE, EH?!
だだっしゅ!!
HUH. SHE'S GONE.
LET'S KEEP GOING.
LOOK! SANA'S DOING HER SHOW!
AH, AKITO!
AKITO, TRY YOUR LUCK AND SEE IF YOU SURVIVE!
WHAT?
COME ON
WHY ME...
SWIM TEAM
HUH?

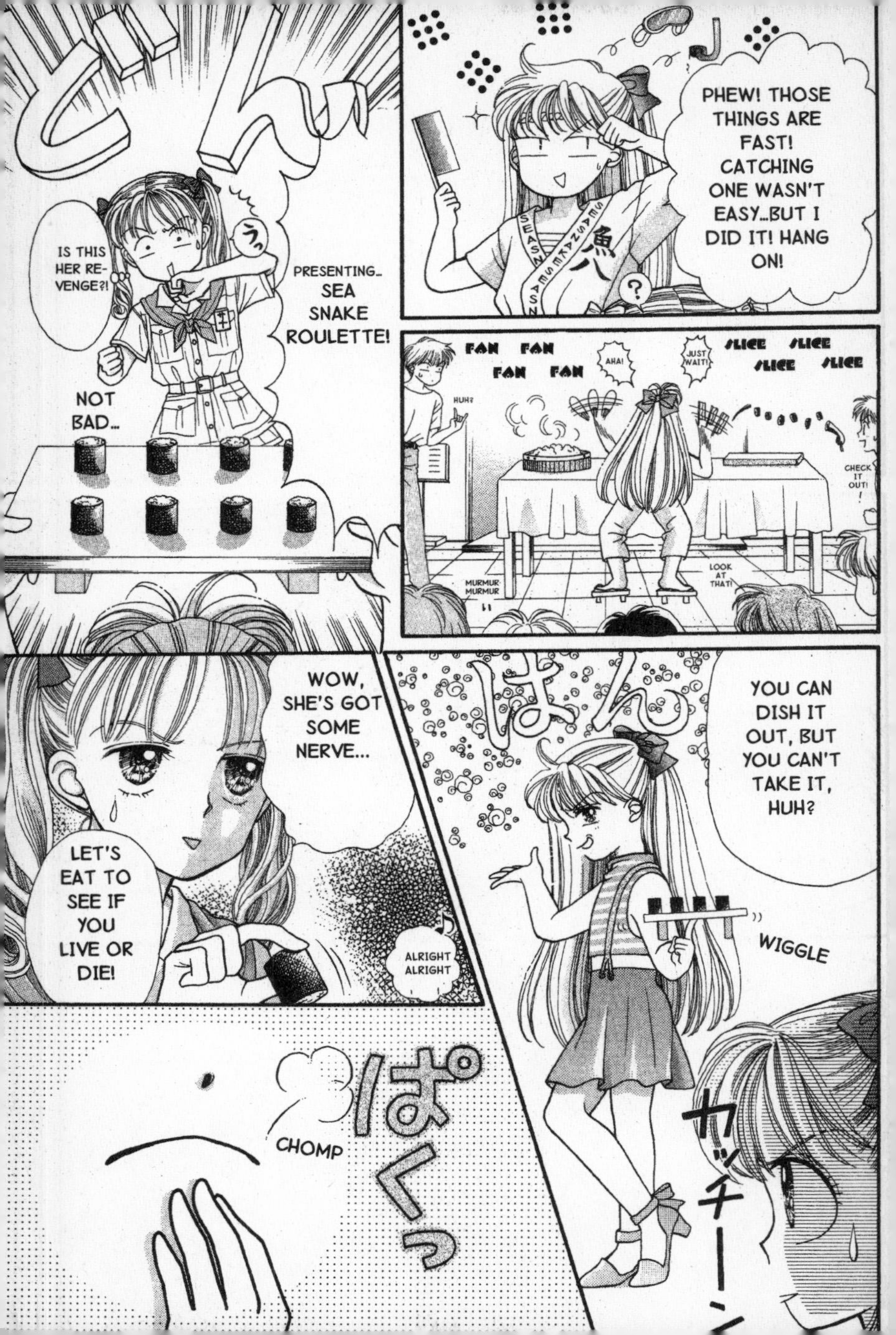
PHEW! THOSE THINGS ARE FAST! CATCHING ONE WASN'T EASY...BUT I DID IT! HANG ON!
?
SLICE SLICE SLICE SLICE
JUST WAIT!
AHA!
FAN FAN FAN FAN
HUH?
CHECK IT OUT!
LOOK AT THAT!
MURMUR MURMUR
PRESENTING... SEA SNAKE ROULETTE!
IS THIS HER RE-VENGE?!
NOT BAD...
ぽん
YOU CAN DISH IT OUT, BUT YOU CAN'T TAKE IT, HUH?
WIGGLE
WOW, SHE'S GOT SOME NERVE...
LET'S EAT TO SEE IF YOU LIVE OR DIE!
ALRIGHT ALRIGHT
ぱくっ
CHOMP

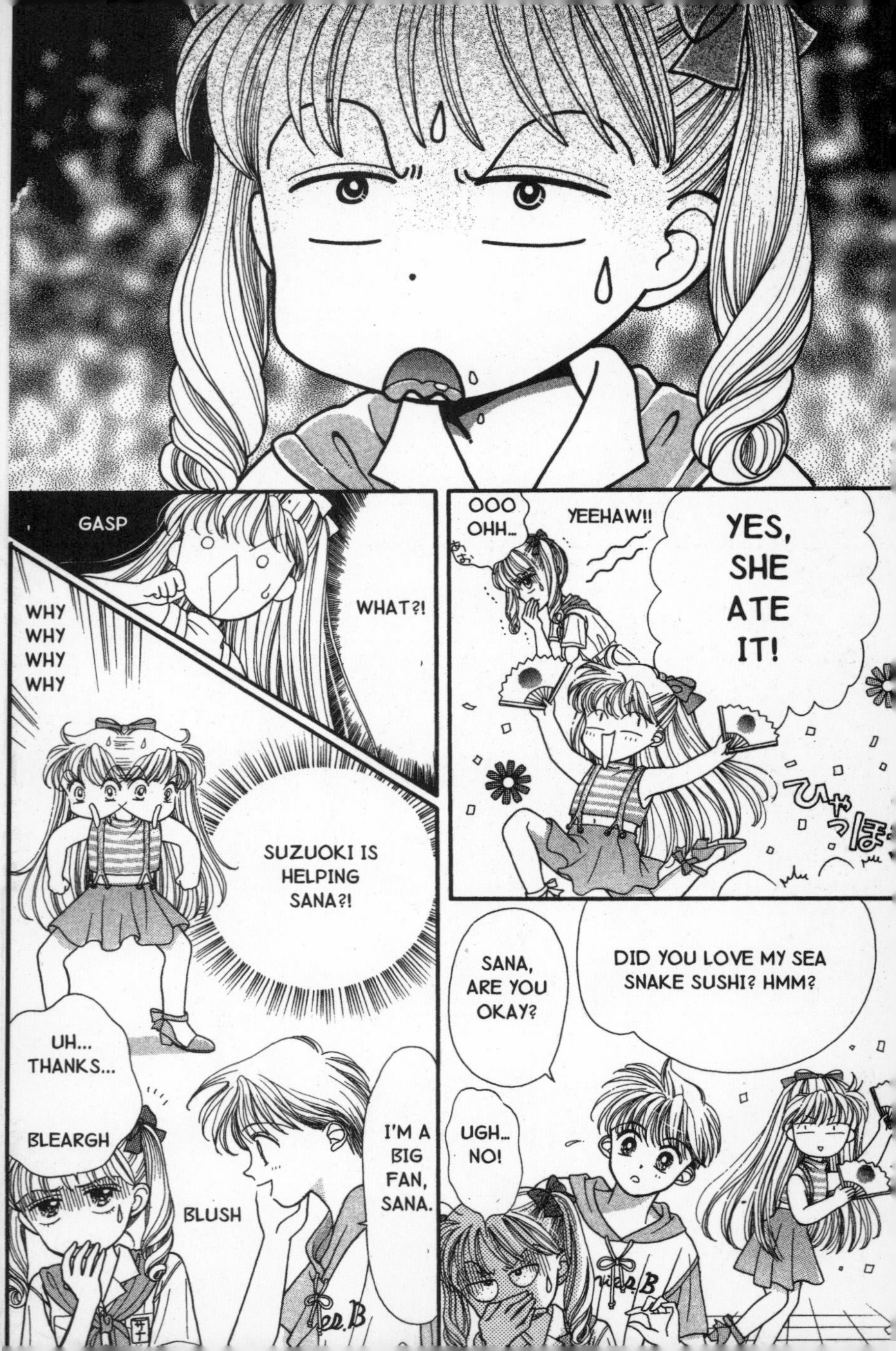

YES, SHE ATE IT!
YEEHAW!!
OOO OHH...
GASP
WHAT?!
WHY WHY WHY WHY
SUZUOKI IS HELPING SANA?!
DID YOU LOVE MY SEA SNAKE SUSHI? HMM?
SANA, ARE YOU OKAY?
UGH... NO!
I'M A BIG FAN, SANA.
UH... THANKS...
BLEARGH
BLUSH

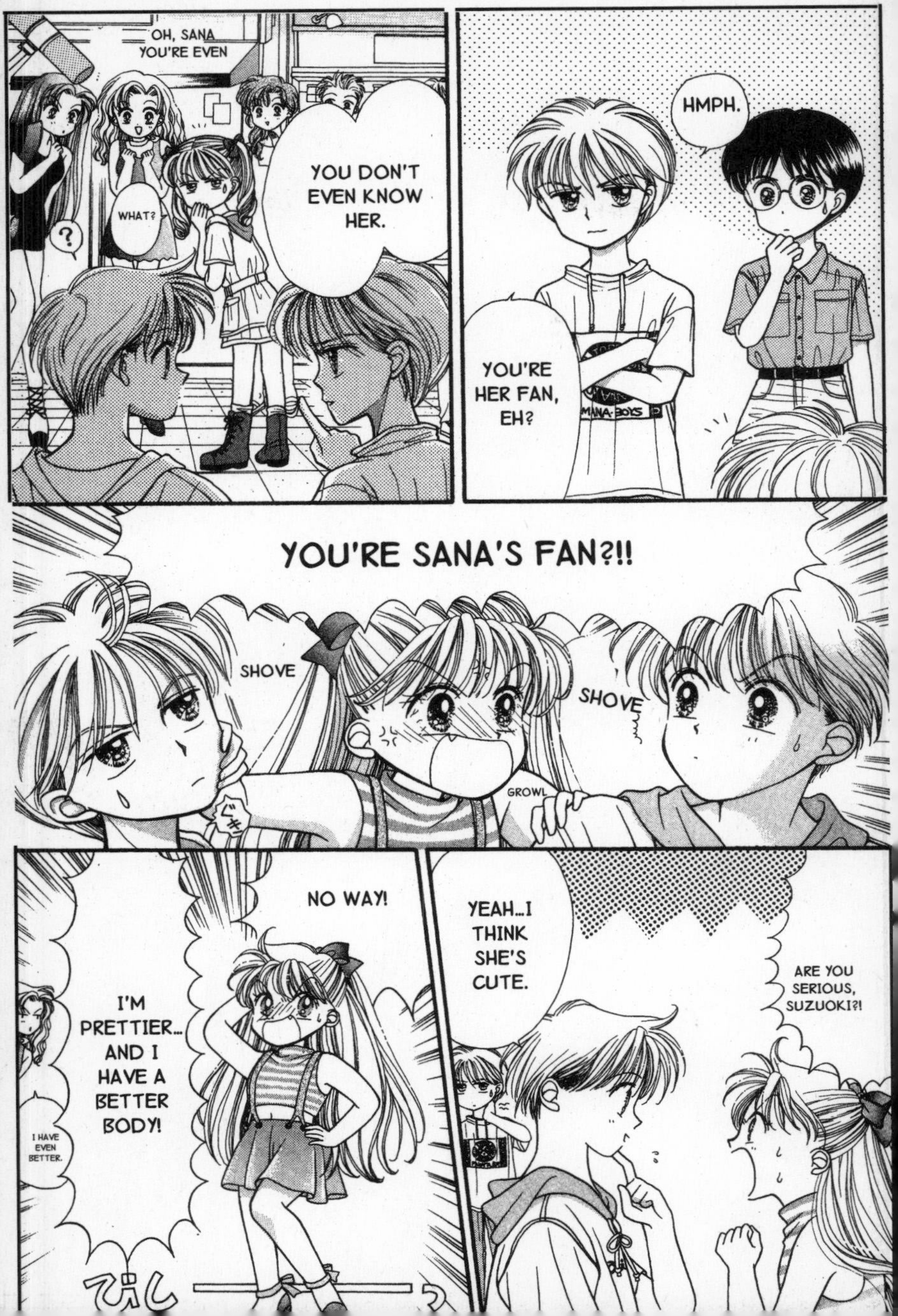
HMPH.
YOU'RE HER FAN, EH?
YOU DON'T EVEN KNOW HER.
OH, SANA YOU'RE EVEN
WHAT?
?
YOU'RE SANA'S FAN?!!
SHOVE
SHOVE
GROWL
YEAH...I THINK SHE'S CUTE.
ARE YOU SERIOUS, SUZUOKI?!
NO WAY!
I'M PRETTIER... AND I HAVE A BETTER BODY!
I HAVE EVEN BETTER.

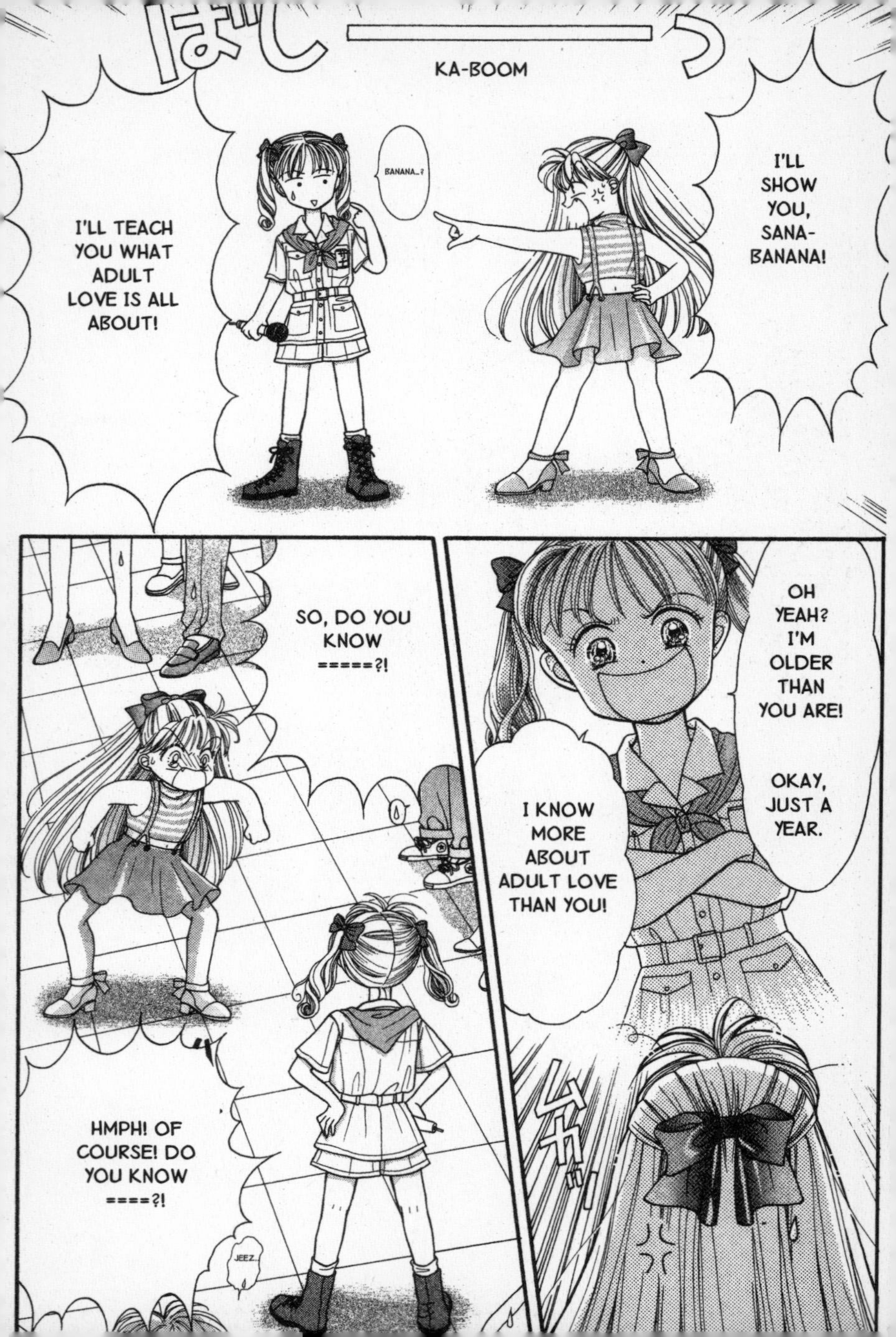
KA-BOOM
I'LL SHOW YOU, SANA-BANANA!
BANANA...?
I'LL TEACH YOU WHAT ADULT LOVE IS ALL ABOUT!
OH YEAH? I'M OLDER THAN YOU ARE!
OKAY, JUST A YEAR.
I KNOW MORE ABOUT ADULT LOVE THAN YOU!
SO, DO YOU KNOW =====?!
HMPH! OF COURSE! DO YOU KNOW ====?!
JEEZ..

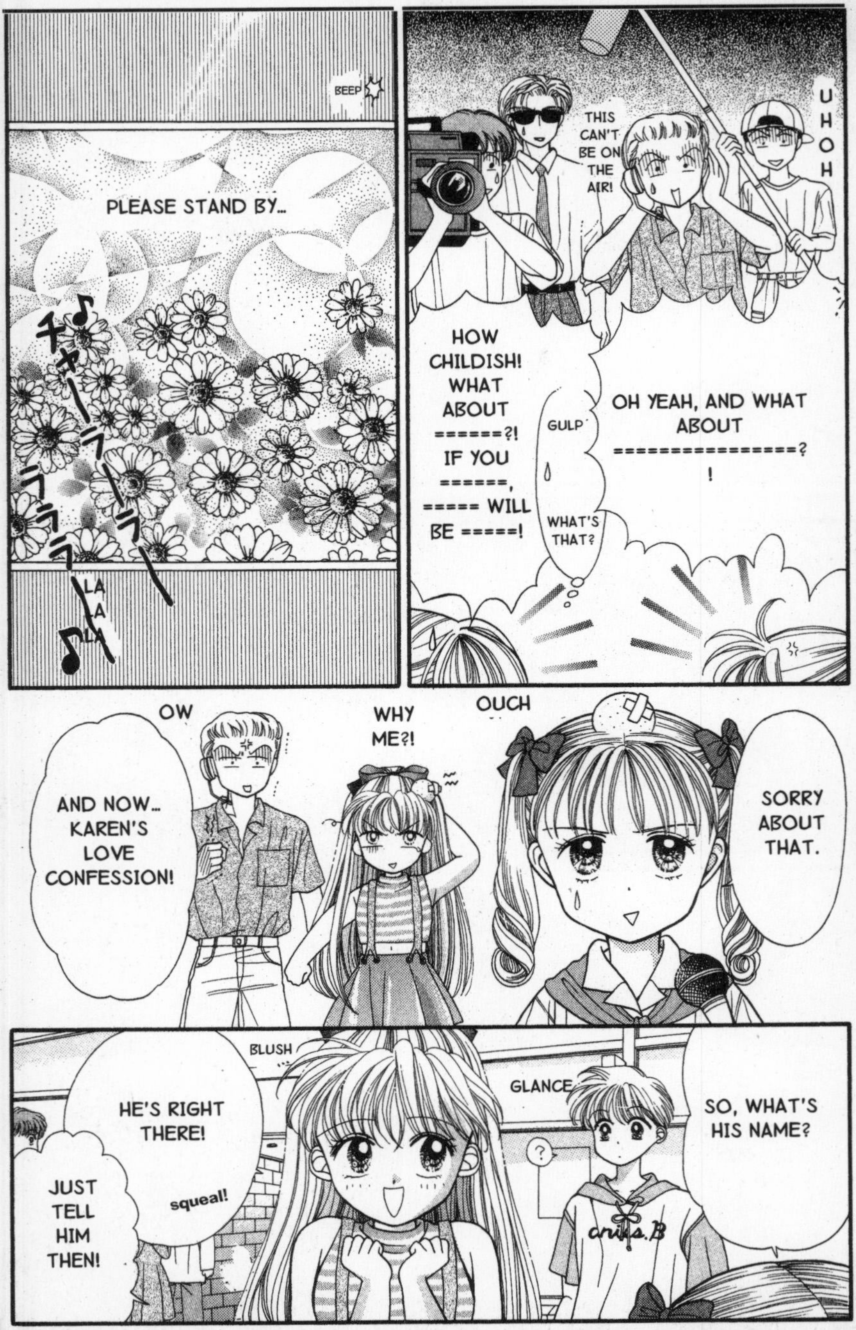
UH OH
THIS CAN'T BE ON THE AIR!
OH YEAH, AND WHAT ABOUT ================?!
GULP
WHAT'S THAT?
HOW CHILDISH! WHAT ABOUT ======?! IF YOU ======, ===== WILL BE =====!
BEEP
PLEASE STAND BY...
チャーラーラー
ラララー
LA LA LA
SORRY ABOUT THAT.
OUCH
WHY ME?!
OW
AND NOW... KAREN'S LOVE CONFESSION!
SO, WHAT'S HIS NAME?
GLANCE
BLUSH
HE'S RIGHT THERE!
squeal!
JUST TELL HIM THEN!

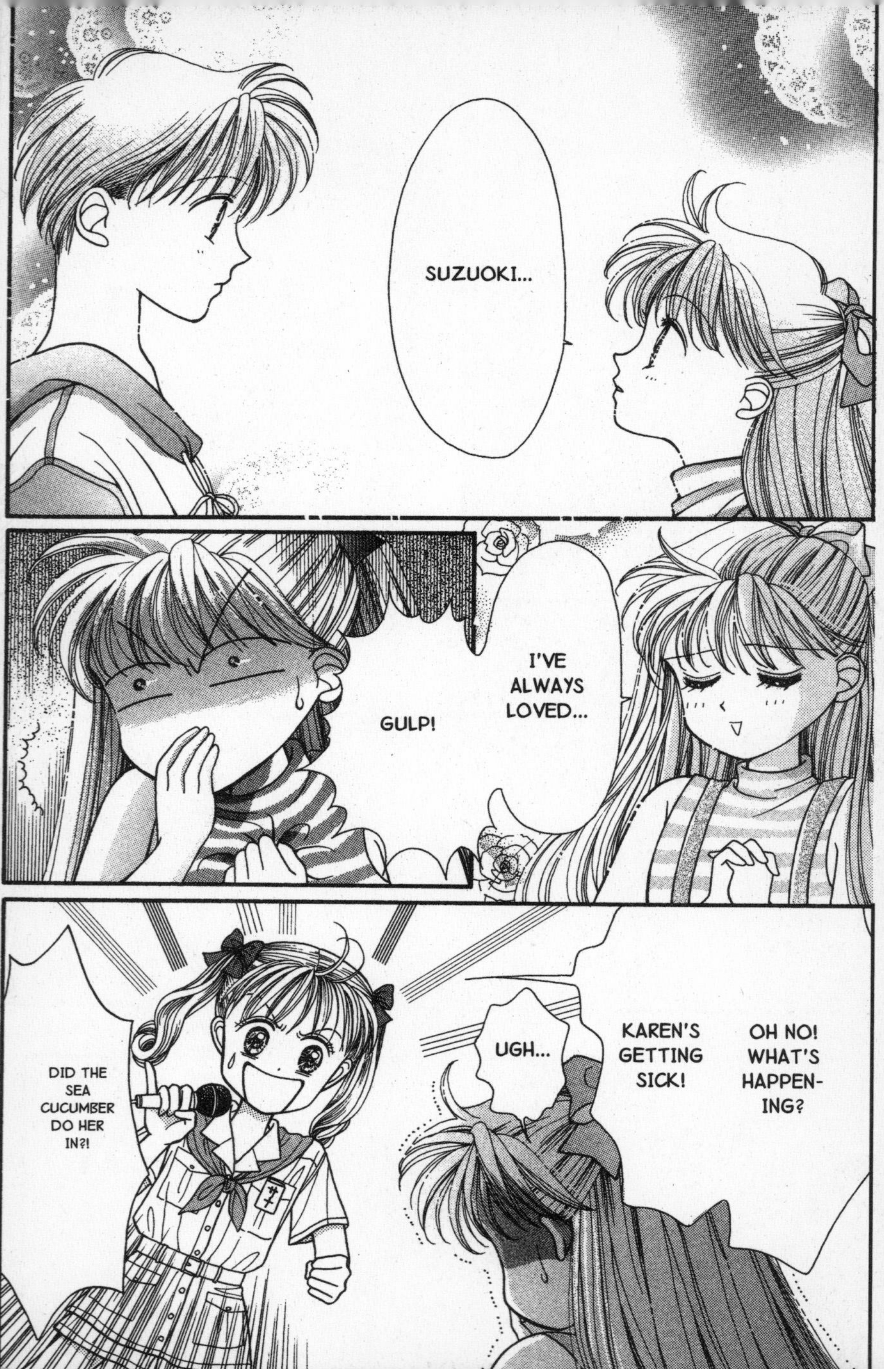
SUZUOKI...
I'VE ALWAYS LOVED...
GULP!
OH NO! WHAT'S HAPPEN-ING?
KAREN'S GETTING SICK!
UGH...
DID THE SEA CUCUMBER DO HER IN?!

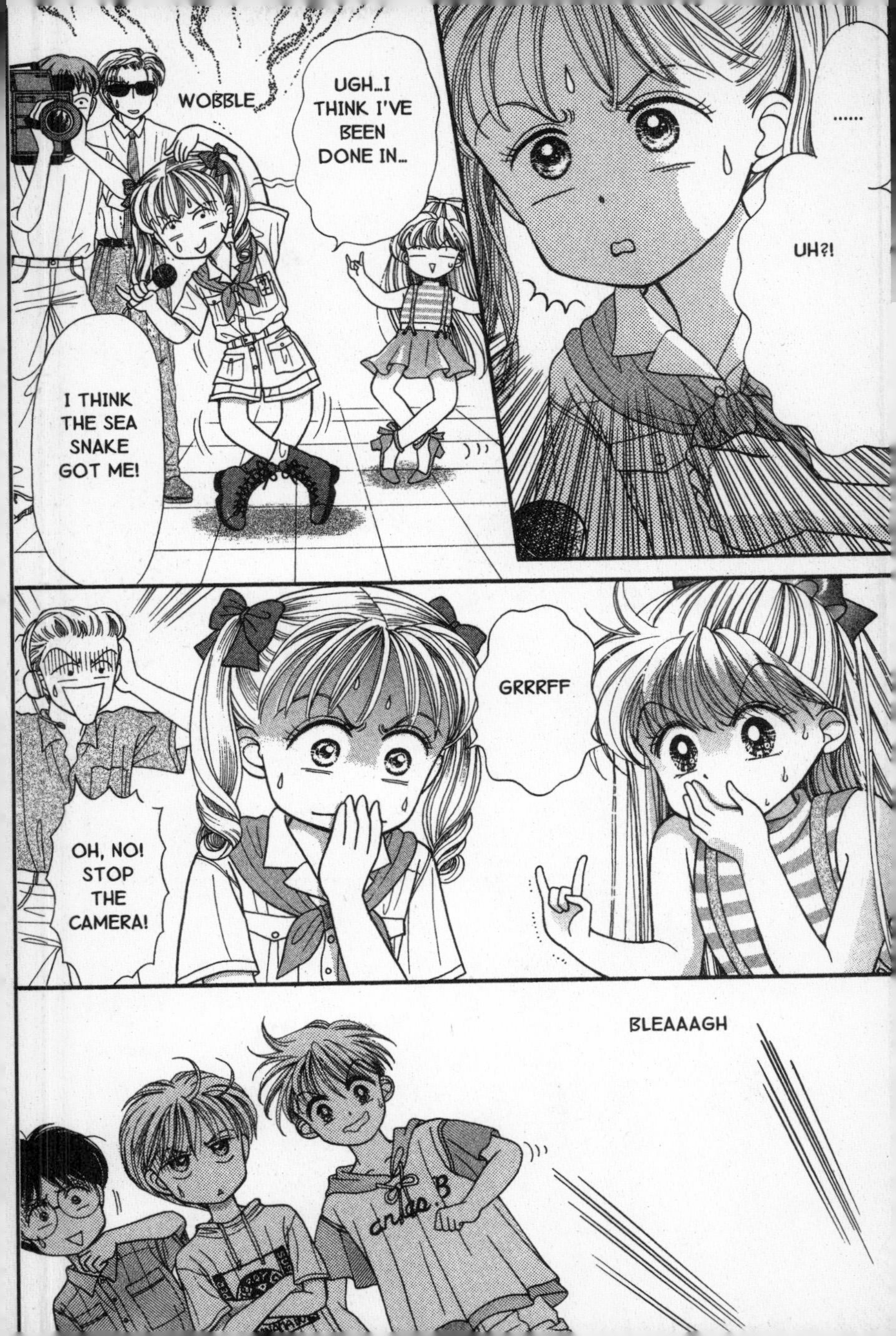
......
UH?!
UGH...I THINK I'VE BEEN DONE IN...
WOBBLE
I THINK THE SEA SNAKE GOT ME!
GRRRFF
OH, NO! STOP THE CAMERA!
BLEAAAGH

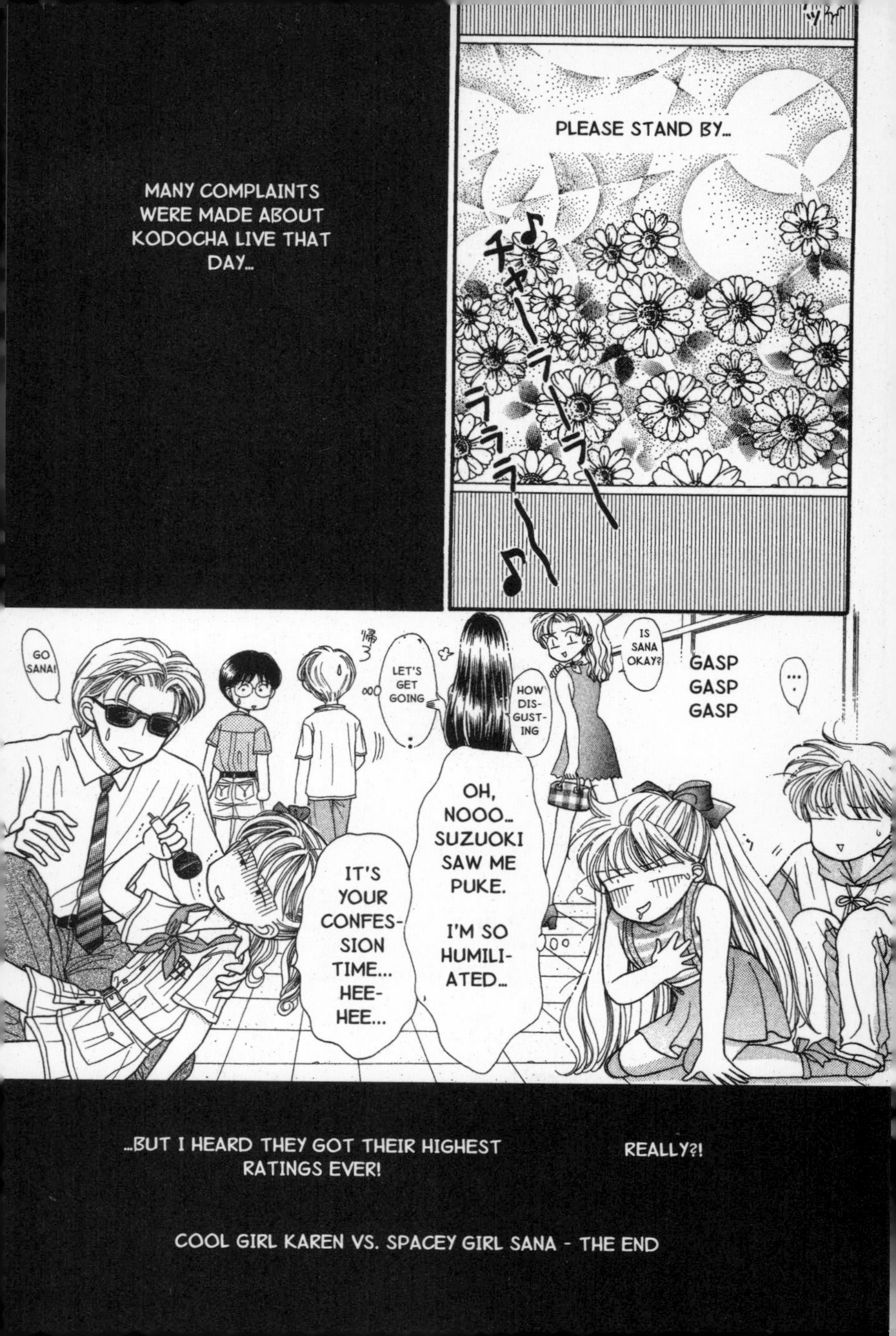
PLEASE STAND BY...
♪チャーラーラー ラララ〜〜♪
MANY COMPLAINTS WERE MADE ABOUT KODOCHA LIVE THAT DAY...
...
GASP GASP GASP
IS SANA OKAY?
HOW DIS-GUST-ING
OH, NOOO... SUZUOKI SAW ME PUKE.
I'M SO HUMILI-ATED...
LET'S GET GOING
帰る
IT'S YOUR CONFES-SION TIME... HEE-HEE...
GO SANA!
...BUT I HEARD THEY GOT THEIR HIGHEST RATINGS EVER!
REALLY?!
COOL GIRL KAREN VS. SPACEY GIRL SANA - THE END

Coming Next!

When Sana's mother releases her latest book, "My Daughter and I," a media frenzy ensues over who Sana's real mom actually is. As Sana searches for her roots, her life just keeps getting more and more confusing. Her former enemy, Akito, is sending her major mixed signals. Her manager, Rei, is pressuring her to star in a movie that she's not sure she wants to commit to. And when her new friend, Fuka, shares a shocking secret from her past, Sana begins to question everything she thought she knew about life—and love.

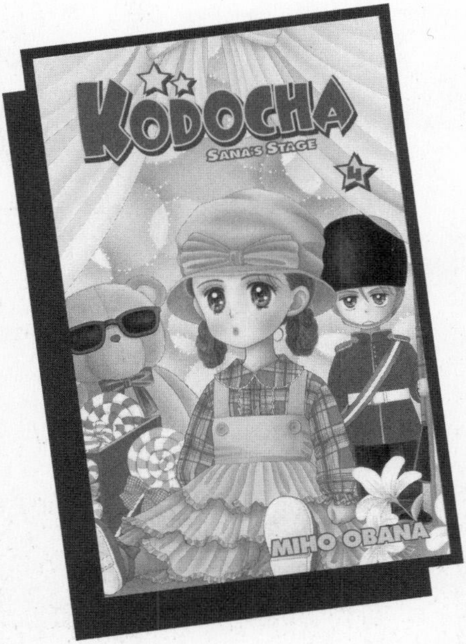
KODOCHA
SANA'S STAGE
4
MIHO OBANA

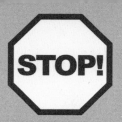

STOP!

This is the back of the book.
You wouldn't want to spoil a great ending!

This book is printed "manga-style," in the authentic Japanese right-to-left format. Since none of the artwork has been flipped or altered, readers get to experience the story just as the creator intended. You've been asking for it, so TOKYOPOP® delivered: authentic, hot-off-the-press, and far more fun!

1
I GOT THE STUFF, MOM.
WHAT'S THAT?
NOTHING
I STOPPED IN TO VISIT AKITO'S DAD.
THAT'S FINE.
2
A LITTLE MORE TO THE LEFT...
TSUYOSHI, WHERE'S DADDY?
WELL... HE'S...
3
TELL YOU WHAT, AONO, I'LL BE DAD FROM NOW ON.
SILLY, YOU CAN'T BE A DAD. YOU HAVE HAIR!
4
NOT ALL DADS ARE BALD, SHRIMP.
HEY, AKITO!
SHH, AKITO!
5
MOM, THE PHONE WON'T REACH THE OUTLET FROM HERE.
REALLY?
I'LL MOVE IT.

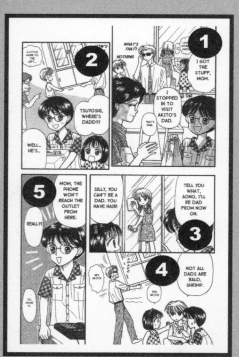

DIRECTIONS:

If this is your first time reading manga-style, here's a quick guide to help you understand how it works.

It's easy...just start in the top right panel and follow the numbers. Have fun, and look for more 100% authentic manga from TOKYOPOP®!